Mängelexemplar

Core Labour Standards and International Trade

Kofi Addo

Core Labour Standards and International Trade

Lessons from the Regional Context

Springer

Kofi Addo
International Baccalaureate
Geneva
Switzerland

ISBN 978-3-662-44618-8 ISBN 978-3-662-44619-5 (eBook)
DOI 10.1007/978-3-662-44619-5
Springer Heidelberg New York Dordrecht London

Library of Congress Control Number: 2014956663

Printed on acid-free paper

Springer is part of Springer Science+Business Media (www.springer.com)

I dedicate this book to the women in my life,
present and past:
my wife, Boatemaa, and daughters, Azariah,
Konadu, and Boateng
my mother, Doris Prempeh Owusu
my late grandmother, Mercy Gladys Anin

Short Description of Book and About Author

The history of the linkage between the core labour standards (CLS) and international trade dates back roughly 150 years and has recently become one of the most vexing issues facing policymakers. At the heart of the debate is the question whether or not trade sanctions should be imposed on countries that do not respect the CLS as embodied in multilateral conventions administered by the International Labour Organization (ILO). Concretely, this would entail inserting a social clause in the World Trade Organization (WTO) rules and would trigger the imposition of sanctions on those countries that do not adhere to the CLS.

This book examines the labour standard provisions in a number of regional and bilateral trade agreements and assesses the potential of using the relevant clauses in these trade agreements as a benchmark for a multilateral approach. Based on the lessons learned from the regional model, the book proposes a global labour and trade framework agreement (GLTFA) combined with a joint ILO/WTO enforcement mechanism to resolve the contentious issue of the link between the CLS and international trade.

Kofi Addo is a policy advisor with the Governance and Executive Support Department of the International Baccalaureate Organization. He holds a Ph.D. in law from the University of Bern, Switzerland.

Foreword

The status of labour and human capital in the process of production of products and of international trade ever since has been at the heart of economic theory and political debate. In domestic law, labour standards pertain to the core of law defining an economic system and the relationship of factors of production in a particular country. In international law, this is much less the case. While trade relations are legally defined in great detail in treaties and subject to law enforcement in the WTO, labour standards have been largely developed on the basis of soft law. The wide body of international agreements and conventions adopted by Members of the International Labour Organization (ILO) does not impose strict standards and leaves implementation to a process of reporting and monitoring. The resulting imbalance triggered a broad debate as to whether labour standards should be included in the multilateral framework of GATT and the WTO. Efforts so far failed to establish such linkages in explicit terms, while progress was made on the level of regional integration and preferential trade agreements.

The book looks into these regional and preferential efforts. In particular, it focuses on the NAFTA North American Agreement on Labour Cooperation (NAALC) and the new generation of preferential agreements concluded by the EU with ACP countries, especially the Cotonou Agreement and developments within the incoming Economic Partnership Agreements (EPAs). Upon exploring these and other preferential instruments, the work turns to the question to what extent these experiences offer the groundwork for a subsequent multilateralization of disciplines on labour relations in international law, combining ILO and WTO law. The author expounds the fruitful relation of trade liberalization, enhancing welfare, poverty reduction and enhanced labour relations. He takes issue with currently prevailing views in developing countries that binding labour standards reduce comparative advantages and lays the ground for a fresh look at what is a complex issue, both in terms of political economy and law.

The book is based upon a Ph.D. thesis in law written within the doctoral programme of the World Trade Institute and submitted to the Faculty of Law of the University of Bern, Switzerland, in 2010. It was a privilege to work with Kofi Addo, benefiting from his experience in the field and his dedication to the cause of improving labour conditions in the process of globalization in particular in developing countries. The present book makes an important contribution in laying the groundwork for the process of multilateralizing labour standards in the trading regime in coming years, and perhaps decades, to come.

Bern, Switzerland
July 2014

Thomas Cottier

Preface

Historically the issue of the correlation between core labour standards (CLS) and international trade, it has been one of the most vexing issues facing global trade policymakers—how to accommodate the growing consensus on the need to promote CLS within the framework of the multilateral trading system. The nature of the subject raises the issues of whether CLS need to be part of a global set of trade rules and whether doing so would be in the developmental interest of workers. The sensitive nature of the issue, and the fact that it has been recurring for a 150 years without any meaningful solution, makes the adoption of a novel approach very important as the solutions being offered at the multilateral level do not seem to satisfy both the supporters and critics of such a linkage.

Whilst developing countries oppose the inclusion of labour standards in the WTO Agreement, they are, however, entering into bilateral, free trade agreements or regional trade agreements, which include clauses on labour provisions among themselves and also with developed countries, notably the United States of America and the European Community.

Whilst there are some benefits to the inclusion of the core labour standards in these regional arrangements, there is the need for an international legal framework that would improve and strengthen the capacities of parties to these arrangements (especially the developing countries), as a means of ensuring that the dots between social, legal, and economic progress are connected, and also consolidate and sustain growth for employment creation. This is an issue that not only has economic consequences but also has legal, social, and political implications. And a discussion of the issue will show how these factors relate to the debate as a whole.

This book considers whether the labour standard provisions in some of the regional trade agreements could act as a stimulus for the multilateral system and whether the regional model that has acted as a laboratory for other areas in the multilateral trading system could again be relied upon to bridge the gap between the opposing views on the correlation between labour standards and trade. An assessment of the labour provisions in a number of RTAs is made to determine whether those provisions are an effective means of protecting labour standards in the specific countries that are party to those agreements. The most prominent of these agreements is the North American Free Trade Agreement (NAFTA) side agreement, the North American Agreement on Labor Cooperation (NAALC). Even though there are significant limitations that hinder its effectiveness as a tool of social change, its use since 1994 has enabled the rise of strong cross-border cooperation and also drawn the public attention to the respect for the core labour standards.

Regional trade agreements have become a testing ground for linking labour standards and international trade. The successes and failures of this model could hold the key in making trade work for development. This book proposes a legal framework based on the structure of recent international framework agreements (IFAs) that could act as a template to be adapted by signatories to these regional arrangements to ensure that the principles that have guided the ILO and to which the international community subscribe to are met. It is also a means to ensure that social objectives are taken into account in economic and trade policy decision-making—a simple but effective mechanism of resolving a contentious issue. The framework is structured on the ILO tripartite system (compared to agreements between governments), which has a greater potential to lead to constructive social dialogue and make a positive contribution to respect for the core labour standards.

In proposing a blueprint or international legal framework template based on the model in the regional trade agreements and also the IFAs, we are cognisant of the shortcomings. However, this approach appears to be the best tool available in reaching consensus on this vexing issue. The key is how the international community translates the lessons learned at the regional level onto the global scene and make the regional approach a force for good in promoting policy coherence at the multilateral level.

Such an agreement has a greater possibility of extending the protection accorded under the CLS beyond workers involved in production for export and workers who work for multinationals to also workers involved in domestic production. This in a way would help achieve the balance of equities both within the multilateral economic rule-making process[1] and through the incorporation of social concerns and also at the national and enterprise levels.

Geneva, Switzerland Kofi Addo

[1] Abbott, F. M. (2000). Distributed governance at the WTO–WIPO: A evolving model for open-architecture integrated governance. *Journal of International Economic Law, 3*, 65.

Acknowledgements

Foremost, I would like to express my sincere gratitude to my advisor Prof. Thomas Cottier for his patience, motivation, enthusiasm, and immense knowledge. His encouragement, dedicated involvement, and guidance helped me during the period of research and writing of this book. I cannot imagine having a better mentor for my doctoral research.

I would also like to thank Prof. Steve Charnovitz for his insightful comments on the earlier version of this book. His expert knowledge of the subject matter and the hard questions on the draft was instrumental in getting the book to its present state.

Special thanks to Anke Seyfried (Associate Editor, Law) for her kind assistance in getting the book to this stage. Thanks also to Julia Pelikan (Editorial Assistant, Law) for her wonderful editorial work and Dagmar Kern (Project Coordinator, Production). Thanks to all staff at Springer, who were involved in the publication process.

I thank Dr. Edwini Kwame Kessie for introducing me to the world of trade law. I am grateful to Donata Rugarabamu for reading the first draft of this book and for her comments. I also express my appreciation to Karen Curtis for the opportunity to work at the ILO, and also Dr. Konstantinos Papadakis for directing me to the international framework agreements. Working at the ILO gave me firsthand experience in understanding how international framework agreements could be adapted to the core labour standards and international trade issue.

To my mother, Doris Prempeh Owusu, who taught me the value of education, perseverance, and encouraged me to stay the course, thank you, as well as to my uncles, David Samson Effah and Felix Charles Kharsa, whose love of the law made me choose the legal path. To my wider family, in particular my sisters: Joyce and Linda, for their encouragement and support throughout the years.

I likewise thank my friend George "Billy" Addai for his encouragement during the years of writing, and for being a great and wonderful friend for more than three decades.

Finally, I wish to express my deepest gratitude and love to my children, Azariah, Konadu, and Boateng, and my wife, Boatemaa—deepest thanks for her loving support and for being the perfect partner for over a decade. My debt to her is immeasurable, as is my deepest love.

Table of Cases

1. International Court of Justice

Nicaragua Case, 1986 I.C.J. Rep. 14, 97.
Continental Shelf Case (Libya v. Malta), 1985 I.C.J. Rep. 13, 29.
Barcelona Traction, Light and Power Co. Ltd. (Belgium v. Spain) Second Phase, [1970] I.C.J. Rep. 4.
North Sea Continental Shelf Cases (F.R.G v. Den., F.R.G. v. Neth.), 1969 I.C.J. Rep. 3,
Asylum case (Colombia v. Peru), 1950 I.C.J. 276, at 277 (20 November).

2. WTO Panels and Appellate Body

Argentina – Footwear (EC) Appellate Body Report, *Argentina – Safeguard Measures on Imports of Footwear*, WT/DS121/AB/R, adopted 12 January 2000, DSR 2000:I, 515
Argentina – Footwear (EC) Panel Report, Argentina – *Safeguard Measures on Imports of Footwear*, WT/DS121/R, adopted 12 January 2000, as modified by Appellate Body Report WT/DS121/AB/R, DSR 2000:II, 575
Brazil – Retreaded Tyres Appellate Body Report, Brazil – *Measures Affecting Imports of Retreaded Tyres*, WT/DS332/AB/R, adopted 17 December 2007
Brazil – Retreaded Tyres Panel Report, Brazil – *Measures Affecting Imports of Retreaded Tyres*, WT/DS332/R, adopted 17 December 2007, as modified by Appellate Body Report WT/DS332/AB/R
Canada – Autos Appellate Body Report, *Canada – Certain Measures Affecting the Automotive Industry*, WT/DS/ 139/AB/R, WT/DS 142/AB/R, adopted 19 June 2000

Canada – Autos Panel Report, *Canada – Certain Measures Affecting the Automotive Industry*, WT/DS 139, WT/DS 142/R, adopted 19 June 2000, as modified by the Appellate Body Report WT/DS 139/AB/R, WT/DS 142/AB/R, DSR 2000

EC – Asbestos Appellate Body Report, *European Communities – Measures Affecting Asbestos and Asbestos-Containing Products*, WT/DS135/AB/R, adopted 5 April 2001, DSR 2001:VII, 3243

EC – Asbestos Panel Report, European Communities – *Measures Affecting Asbestos and Asbestos-Containing Products*, WT/DS135/R and Add.1, adopted 5 April 2001, as modified by Appellate Body Report WT/DS135/AB/R, DSR 2001:VIII, 3305

EC – Bananas III Appellate Body Report, *European Communities – Regime for the Importation, Sale and Distribution of Bananas*, WT/DS27/AB/R, adopted 25 September 1997, DSR 1997:II, 591

EC – Tariff Preferences Appellate Body Report, *European Communities – Conditions for the Granting of Tariff Preferences to Developing Countries*, WT/DS246/AB/R, adopted 20 April 2004, DSR 2004:III, 925

EC – Tariff Preferences Panel Report, *European Communities – Conditions for the Granting of Tariff Preferences to Developing Countries*, WT/DS246/R, adopted 20 April 2004, as modified by Appellate Body Report WT/DS/246/AB/R, DSR 2004:III, 1009

India – Quantitative Restrictions Appellate Body Report, *India – Quantitative Restrictions on Imports of Agricultural, Textile and Industrial Products*, WT/DS90/AB/R, adopted 22 September 1999, DSR 1999:IV, 1763

India – Quantitative Restrictions Panel Report, *India – Quantitative Restrictions on Imports of Agricultural, Textile and Industrial Products*, WT/DS90/R, adopted 22 September 1999, as upheld by Appellate Body Report WT/DS90/AB/R, DSR 1999:V, 1799

Japan – Alcoholic Beverages II Appellate Body Report, *Japan – Taxes on Alcoholic Beverages*, WT/DS8/AB/R,WT/DS10/AB/R,WT/DS11/AB/R, adopted 1 November 1996, DSR 1996:I, 97

Japan – Alcoholic Beverages II Panel Report, *Japan – Taxes on Alcoholic Beverages*, WT/DS8/R, WT/DS10/R, WT/DS11/R, adopted 1 November 1996, as modified by Appellate Body Report WT/DS8/AB/R,WT/DS10/AB/R,WT/DS11/AB/R, DSR 1996:I, 125

Turkey – Textiles Appellate Body Report, *Turkey – Restrictions on Imports of Textile and Clothing Products*, WT/DS34/AB/R, adopted 19 November 1999, DSR 1999:VI, 2345

Turkey – Textiles Panel Report, *Turkey – Restrictions on Imports of Textile and Clothing Products*, WT/DS34/R, adopted 19 November 1999, as modified by Appellate Body Report WT/DS34/AB/R, DSR 1999:VI, 2363

US – Gambling Appellate Body Report, *United States – Measures Affecting the Cross-Border Supply of Gambling and Betting Services*, WT/DS285/AB/R, adopted 20 April 2005, DSR 2005:XII, 5663 (Corr.1, DSR 2006:XII, 5475)

US – Gambling Panel Report, *United States – Measures Affecting the Cross-Border Supply of Gambling and Betting Services*, WT/DS285/R, adopted

20 April 2005, as modified by Appellate Body Report WT/DS285/AB/R, DSR 2005:XII, 5797

US – Gasoline Appellate Body Report, *United States – Standards for Reformulated and Conventional Gasoline*, WT/DS2/AB/R, adopted 20 May 1996, DSR 1996: I, 3

US – Gasoline Panel Report, *United States – Standards for Reformulated and Conventional Gasoline*, WT/DS2/R, adopted 20 May 1996, as modified by Appellate Body Report WT/DS2/AB/R, DSR 1996:I, 29

US – Section 211 Appropriations Act Appellate Body Report, *United States – Section 211 Omnibus Appropriations Act of 1998*, WT/DS176/AB/R, adopted 1 February 2002, DSR 2002:II, 589

US – Section 211 Appropriations Act Panel Report, *United States – Section 211 Omnibus Appropriations Act of 1998*, WT/DS176/R, adopted 1 February 2002, as modified by Appellate Body Report WT/DS176/AB/R, DSR 2002:II, 683

US – Shrimp Appellate Body Report, *United States – Import Prohibition of Certain Shrimp and Shrimp Products*, WT/DS58/AB/R, adopted 6 November 1998, DSR 1998:VII, 2755

US – Shrimp Panel Report, *United States – Import Prohibition of Certain Shrimp and Shrimp Products*, WT/DS58/R and Corr.1, adopted 6 November 1998, as modified by Appellate Body Report WT/DS58/AB/R, DSR 1998:VII, 2821

US – Shrimp (Article 21.5 –Malaysia) Appellate Body Report, *United States – Import Prohibition of Certain Shrimp and Shrimp Products – Recourse to Article 21.5 of the DSU by Malaysia*, WT/DS58/AB/RW, adopted 21 November 2001, DSR 2001:XIII, 6481

US – Shrimp (Article 21.5 –Malaysia) Panel Report, *United States – Import Prohibition of Certain Shrimp and Shrimp Products – Recourse to Article 21.5 of the DSU by Malaysia*, WT/DS58/RW, adopted 21 November 2001, as upheld by Appellate Body Report WT/DS58/AB/RW, DSR 2001:XIII, 6529

3. GATT

The reports are listed in order of the date of adoption or, if unadopted, the date of publication.

EBelgium – Family Allowances GATT Panel Report, *Belgian Family Allowances*, G/32, adopted 7 November 1952, BISD 1S/59 (1953)

EEC – Import Restrictions GATT Panel Report, *EEC – Quantitative Restrictions Against Imports of Certain Products from Hong Kong*, adopted 12 July 1983, L/5511, BISD 30S/129

EEC (Member States) – Bananas 1, *European Economic Community-Member States' Import Regimes for Bananas*, unadopted, Jun. 3, 1993, DS32/R.

Japan – Imported Wines and Alcoholic Beverages: *Japan – Customs Duties, Taxes and Labelling Practices on Imported Wines and Alcoholic Beverages*, adopted on 10 November 1987, BISD 34S/38 (1988)

Korea – Restrictions on Imports of Beef – Complaint by the United States, adopted 7 November 1989, L/6503, BISD 63S/268.

US – Tuna (Mexico) GATT Panel Report, *United States – Restrictions on Imports of Tuna*, DS21/R, DS21/R, 3 September 1991, unadopted, BISD 39S/155

US – Tuna (Mexico) GATT Panel Report, *United States – Restrictions on Imports of Tuna*, unadopted, 3 September 1991, DS21/R, BISD 39S/155

US – Tuna (EEC) GATT Panel Report, *United States – Restrictions on Imports of Tuna*, DS29/R, 16 June 1994, unadopted

US–Tuna I: *United States – Restrictions on Imports of Tuna*, not adopted, BISD, 39S/155 (1993).

US–Tuna II: *United States – Restrictions on Imports of Tuna*, not adopted, 33 I.L.M. (1994), pp. 839–903.

US – Tuna, GATT Panel Report, *United States – Restrictions on Imports of Tuna* (DS29/R), GATT Panel Report, circulated on 16 June 1994 (not adopted).

4. NAFTA/NAALC

(a) Canada

ITAPSA or Echlin Case, Canada NAO Submission No. 98-1 (April 6, 1998).

(b) Mexico

Sprint Case, Mexico NAO Submission No. 9501 (February 9, 1995).
Decoster Egg Case, Mexico NAO Submission No. 9803 (August 4, 1998).

(c) United States of America

U.S. NAO Submission No. 2005-03 (HIDALGO) (October 14, 2005).
U.S. NAO Submission No. 2003-01 (PUEBLA) (September 30, 2003).
Honeywell and General Electric Cases, U.S. NAO Submissions No. 940001 and 940002. (February 14, 1994).
Sony Case, U. S. NAO Submission No. 940003 (SONY) (August 16, 1994)

5. Domestic Courts

(a) United Kingdom

Jenkins v Kingsgate (Clothing Productions) Ltd [1981] Case 96/80 E.C.R. 911, ECJ.

Murphy v Bord Telecom Eirrean [1988] Case 157/86 ECR 673.

EC Commission v United Kingdom of Great Britain and Northern Ireland, [1982] ICR 578, [1982] IRLR 333, ECJ.

Sibson-v-United Kingdom (Case 4/1992/349/422) [1993] ECHR 18; 14327/88; [1993] ECHR 18.

(b) United States

State of Wisconsin ex rel v. Fitzgerald et al [2011, Case No: 11 CV 1244].

Doe, et al. v Unocal Corp. Case No. CV 96-6959 110 F. Supp. 2d 1294; 2000 US. Dist., March 25, 1997.

LFC, Inc. v. NLRB, 129 F.3d 1276 (D.C. Cir. 1997).

Sprogis v. United Air Lines, Federal Court of Appeals (Seventh Circuit), 16 June 1971.

Liggett Co. v. Lee 288 U.S. 517, 557-60 (1933)

Table of Abbreviations

AB	Appellate Body
ACP	Africa, Caribbean and Pacific countries
AFL-CIO	American Federation of Labor-Congress of Industrial Organizations
AGOA	Africa Growth and Opportunity Act
APEC	Asian-Pacific Economic Cooperation
CAFTA-DR	Central American Free Trade Agreement and Dominican Republic
CAP	Common Agricultural Policy (EU)
CARIFORUM	Caribbean Forum of Caribbean States
CAT	Centro de Apoyo al Trabajador
CAWN	Central America Women's Network
CBTPA	Caribbean Basin Trade Partnership Act
CEACR	Committee of Experts on the Application of Conventions and Recommendations
CEMAC	Economic Community of Central African States plus the Democratic Republic of Congo and São Tomé and Príncipe
CFA	Committee on Freedom of Association
CLS	Core Labour Standards
COLISIBA	Coordinadora Latinoamericana de Sindicatos Bananeros
CUSFTA	Canada–US Free Trade Agreement
CRTA	Committee on Regional Trade Agreement
CTM	Mexican Confederation of Labour
COMESA	Common Market for Eastern and Southern Africa
DSM	Dispute Settlement Mechanism
EAC	East African Community
EBA	Everything But Arms
EC	Economic Community
EEC	European Economic Community
ECE	Evaluation Committee of Experts

ECJ	European Court of Justice
ECOWAS	Economic Community of West African States and Mauritania
EPA	Economic Partnership Agreements
ECOSOC	Economic and Social Council (United Nations)
ELSA	Employment, Labour and Social Affairs Committee
ESA	Eastern and Southern Africa
EU	European Union
FOCAC	Forum on China-African Cooperation
FPE	Factor Price Equalization theorem
FDI	Foreign Direct Investment
FPRW	Fundamental principles and rights at work
FTA	Free Trade Agreement
FTAA	Free Trade Agreement of the Americas
FTVO-CROC	Federación de Trabajadores Vanguardia Obrera de la Confederación Revolucionaria de Obreros y Campesinos ("Workers Federation of the Revolutionary Confederation of Workers and Peasants")
GATT	General Agreement on Tariffs and Trade
GB	Governing Body
GC	General Council
GLTFA	Global Labour and Trade Framework Agreement
GSP	Generalized System of Preferences
IBT	International Brotherhood of Teamsters
ICFTU	International Confederation of Free Trade Unions
IFA	International Framework Agreement
ILC	International Labour Conference
ILO	International Labour Organization
IPR	Intellectual Property Rights
IMF	International Monetary Fund
ITO	International Trade Organization
IUF	International Union of Food, Agricultural, Hotel, Restaurant, Catering, Tobacco and Allied Workers' Associations
ITUC	International Trade Union Confederation
LDC	Least Developed Countries
LCM	Labor Cooperation Mechanism
MDGs	Millennium Development Goals
MFN	Most-Favoured Nation Principle
MMPA	Marine Mammal Protection Act
MNC	Multinational Corporation
MSN	Maquiladora Solidarity Network
MTS	Multilateral Trading System
NAALC	North American Agreement on Labor Cooperation
NAFTA	North American Free Trade Agreement
NAO	National Administrative Office

NBER	National Bureau of Economic Research
NLRB	National Labor Relations Board
OECD	Organisation for Economic Co-operation and Development
OPIC	Overseas Private Investment Corporation (USA)
OTAI	Office of Trade Agreement Implementation
OTLA	Office of Trade and Labor Affairs
PIF	Pacific Islands Forum
PPM	Process and Production Methods
RTA	Regional Trade Agreement
RLTFA	Regional Labour and Trade Framework Agreement
SADC	Southern Africa Development Cooperation
TPA	Trade Promotion Agreement
TRIPS	Trade-Related Intellectual Property Rights Agreement
UDHR	Universal Declaration of Human Rights
UE	United Electrical, Radio and Machine Workers of America
UNCTAD	United Nations Conference on Trade and Development
USAS	United Students Against Sweatshops
USTR	United States Trade Representative
VCLT	Vienna Convention on the Law of Treaties
WEF	World Economic Forum
WTO	World Trade Organization

Contents

List of Figures

List of Tables

List of Boxes

Chapter 1
Introduction

1.1 Thesis of the Book

Will compliance with the core labour standards (CLS) be universally achieved using the lessons learned from the regional approach in creating some international norms, such as a legal framework that would assist in bridging the gap between economic growth and social progress? What this, in effect, calls for are the measures that need to be put in place in this era of globalisation not only to ensure compliance with the CLS but also to improve social dialogue among government, employer, and worker organisations on how to address issues that lie at the intersection between the economic and social development of countries. The recent financial crisis with its attendant effects on job losses, the inability of many economies to sustain jobs, not to mention the creation of jobs, has shown how intertwined economic growth and social progress are.

The aim of this book is to examine the labour standard provisions in a number of regional and bilateral trade agreements and to determine whether the labour standard clauses in these trade agreements could be used as a benchmark in developing an enabling legal framework for the international community in resolving the contentious issue of the linkage between labour standards and international trade.

From the economic globalisation perspective, the linkages in the economies of the world have expanded through international trade. Whereas trade is not an end in itself, the emphasis on trade for development is what has in part contributed to improving the economic outlook of many countries.

Trade can provide potential developmental benefits. The development contribution that trade can make is significant. Through participation in international trade, countries can achieve development by promoting and rewarding the sectors of the economy where the countries enjoy comparative advantage, whether through

K. Addo, *Core Labour Standards and International Trade*,
DOI 10.1007/978-3-662-44619-5_1

labour efficiency or factor endowments. The countries are also able to take advantage of economies of scale.[1]

We argue in this book that since trade is good for development and development is good for compliance with the CLS, then trade, even if not directly impacting on CLS compliance, can have a positive effect on adherence to the CLS, which conversely meet the aspirations of workers in both developed and developing countries.

Whilst regional trade agreements (RTAs) have brought attention to the link between CLS and trade, the recent signing of international framework agreements (IFAs)[2] between representatives of management and workers in some multinational enterprises (which includes all the four CLS) could be the beginning of a combination of the efforts of governments, employers, and workers agreeing on a legal framework based on the ILO tripartite system in the development of a global legal framework agreement.

This book makes a case for the development of a global labour and trade framework agreement (GLTFA) to ensure worldwide compliance through international social dialogue, good practice, and the resolution of labour management disputes. This GLTFA could be adapted to suit regional trade agreements, in effect, the development of regional labour and trade framework agreement (RLTFA) as part of future RTAs.[3]

The IFAs to date are agreements with the aim of setting up a general framework as an enabling factor in creating a harmonious relationship between unions, both local and global, and the multinationals (which have signed) and their suppliers. Whilst in a sense the IFAs signed have not produced legally binding obligations with legal sanctions that can be relied on in national courts or lead to enforceable decisions and legal sanctions, there is reason to believe that the present and future IFAs could contribute to further development of sound industrial relations.[4]

The assessment of IFAs appears to indicate that they have a positive impact on industrial relations, especially for facilitating cross-border industrial relations in this age of globalisation.[5] What is recommended in this book based on the ILO tripartite system is how the proposed GLTFA based on the IFAs could assist in

[1] Todaro and Smith (2011), p. 581. See also, Jansen et al. (2011), p. 1.

[2] According to the ILO, "An international (or global) framework agreement (IFA) is an instrument negotiated between a multinational enterprise and a Global Union Federation (GUF) in order to establish an on-going relationship between the parties and ensure that the company respects the same standards in all the countries where it operates." See http://www.ilo.org/global/about-the-ilo/newsroom/news/WCMS_080723/lang--en/index.htm, accessed 10 December 2013. In this respect, IFAs come about as a result of social dialogue at the multinational level as a way of promoting and executing the core labour standards of the ILO.

[3] What is proposed here is a structure based on the ILO tripartism system. This is different from the norm, whereby trade agreements with labour provisions are only negotiated between governments. Future labour provisions in regional trade agreements should involve government, employers', and workers' organisations.

[4] Papadakis (2011a), p. 282.

[5] Papadakis (2011a), pp. 283 and 297.

achieving a high level of CLS compliance. This is in contrast to the government-to-government negotiations that lead to trade agreements and management and workers' organisations agreements in the case of IFAs. Such an agreement has a greater possibility to contribute to make the CLS legally binding obligations in contrast to the "best endeavour" or so-called voluntary standards that have no legal implications.

Further, such an agreement has a greater possibility of extending the protection accorded under the CLS beyond workers involved in production for export and workers who work for multinationals to also workers involved in domestic production. This in a way would help achieve the balance of equities both within the multilateral economic rule-making process,[6] and through the incorporation of social concerns, and at the national and enterprise levels.

1.2 Linkage Between the Core Labour Standards and International Trade

The issue of the correlation between labour standards and international trade has historically been one of the most vexing issues facing global trade policymakers[7]—how to accommodate the growing consensus on the need to promote CLS[8] within the framework of the multilateral trading system. The nature of the subject raises issues of whether CLS need to be part of a global set of trade rules and whether doing so would be in the developmental interest of workers.[9]

Even more compelling issues are the moral dimensions of the labour and trade debate and the absence of an international legal framework within which the economic integration of the global system can be reconciled with the principle of social equity.[10] In effect, how the international community can set the moral debate on globalisation within a legal framework to achieve sustainable development for all lies at the heart of this book.

The impact that trade has on people in every country and on their economic and social life and the reasons why the proponents of the CLS and international trade linkage are pushing for a legal approach can be found in the words of Julio Lacarte[11]:

---

[6] Abbott (2000), p. 65.

[7] See Charnovitz (1987), p. 565; Leary (1996a).

[8] The core labour standards are freedom of association and the effective recognition of the right to collective bargaining, the elimination of all forms of forced or compulsory labour, the effective abolition of child labour, and the elimination of discrimination in respect of employment and occupation.

[9] Langille B provides a good review analysis of the debates on the labour standards issue. See Langille (1997), p. 27.

[10] See Bronstein (2009), p. 91.

[11] Former Chairman of the WTO Appellate Body.

> Behind practically any WTO decision lie economic and social interests. A simple example: when a customs tariff is modified, consumers frequently gain or lose, producers in one place gain and those somewhere else lose. Jobs are gained and jobs are put in jeopardy.
>
> These consumers and producers are people, individuals who strive to lead a good life and be useful members of their community. Very often, they are unaware of WTO decisions that make them prosper or fail, have a gainful occupation, or join the ranks of the unemployed.
>
> Behind the terminology of the Preamble of the WTO Agreement and the many provisions ... there is the living reality that affects untold millions of people. This is a crucial facet of trade that is imperfectly conveyed and understood.[12]

The quotation above shows the importance of trade as an enabling factor in economic and social development and is the subject of much debate. In addition to generating wealth for nations, it has also helped spur employment growth.[13] It is no wonder then that trade negotiations have sometimes led to heated debates at the highest political levels.[14] As a result, trade negotiators work hard to ensure that their countries achieve the maximum gains from trade agreements that they sign onto.[15] It is also no wonder that proponents of a formal link between CLS and international trade, especially from the developed world, are very passionate about the issue.

At the heart of the debate surrounding this issue is whether or not trade sanctions should be imposed on countries that do not respect the core labour standards embodied in multilateral conventions administered by the ILO. This would entail the inserting of a social clause in the World Trade Organization (WTO) rules and would trigger the imposition of sanctions on countries that do not respect the CLS.[16] This raises a question that forms a major part of the debate: whether social policy aims can be grafted onto an institution designed to dismantle economic barriers.

In recent times, a new form of transnational social dialogue, termed international framework agreements (IFAs), has appeared, as an example of bipartite, corporation level social dialogue, mostly in the private sector. These agreements have been noted as breaking new ground, an innovative tool in the global debate on the

---

[12] Lacarte (2004), p. 686.

[13] Steve Charnovitz argues that whilst the WTO has strengthened "the world economy by promoting trade and investment in many parts of the world", he raises the question whether the WTO and trade negotiations led to increasing employment and income growth. He further argues that even if the WTO helps increase employment, the quality of such jobs is in doubt. He proposes that the WTO promote a robust employment dimension. See Charnovitz (2006), pp. 125–155.

[14] A case in point is the heated debates during the negotiations prior to the United States of America signing the North American Free Trade Agreement (NAFTA), the recent debates in both the United States and in Korea prior to the signing of their free trade agreement.

[15] Schefer Krista (2010), pp. 9 and 10.

[16] A social clause has been defined as a clause that aims at improving labour conditions in exporting countries by allowing sanctions to be taken against exporters who fail to observe minimum labour standards. A typical social clause in an international trade arrangement makes it possible to restrict or halt the importation or preferential importation of products originating in countries, industries, or firms where conditions are inferior to certain minimum labour standards (van Liemt 1989, p. 434).

importance of showing respect for the CLS.[17] These IFAs are a result of negotiations between multinational enterprises (MNEs) and global union federations (GUFs), as a way to promote minimum levels of labour standards and practices and also to organise common labour relation framework across the global operations of the MNEs, which sign onto these IFAs.

This book, in proposing a global trade and labour framework agreement (GTLFA), intends to use the IFAs as a benchmark. The IFAs signed to date are the direct result of negotiations between workers' and management representatives. The relevance of the IFAs' approach is that of the universality of the application of human rights and the CLS built into the agreements. Further to this are the joint monitoring mechanisms that are part of the IFAs signed to date.[18] Whilst the origin of IFAs is European, it is spreading to MNEs in other countries. In 2010, 12 of the 70 companies that had signed IFAs were non-European countries.[19] The number of IFAs by the middle of 2011 had increased to 80, covering nearly 6.3 million workers. The IFAs, together with the European framework agreements (EFAs), cover about eight million workers around the world.[20] The potential for the positive role of IFAs in ensuring compliance with the CLS whilst in their very initial stage can be instrumental when given global recognition.

Whilst the book focuses primarily on the legal aspects of the linkage between the CLS and international trade, it also refers to the political and economic aspects of the linkage. Though there are a number of free trade agreements (FTA) signed between the United States of America, the European Community (EC), Canada, and other developing countries, such as Chile, the analyses focuses mainly on the North American Free Trade Agreement (NAFTA) side agreement, the North American Agreement on Labor Cooperation (NAALC). This is the most prominent of these agreements. Even though there are significant limitations that hinder its effectiveness as a tool of social change, its use since 1994 has enabled the rise of strong cross-border cooperation and also drawn the public attention to the respect for the core labour standards.

Furthermore, the reason for this focus is that it is about the only FTA that has adjudicated labour disputes. The focus on the NAALC does not in any way indicate that the FTAs signed by the European Union (EU), Canada, and other countries are not relevant to the discussion of the linkage between the CLS and international in FTAs, but rather it indicates that all the agreements fit into the overall debate in finding a common ground for the resolution of this contentious issue.

The issue of the linkage affects both developed and developing countries, but in considerably different ways leading to serious differences in perspective as to the nature of the problem and possible solutions to it. In the case of child labour, for example, it does not only give countries that use child labour unfair advantage in

[17] Müller et al. (2008), p. 1.

[18] Papadakis (2011b), p. 2.

[19] Stevis (2010), p. 4.

[20] ILO (2012), p. 109.

international trade, but the children are likewise deprived of a better future as they are stopped from going to school. This is but one example of a social problem that is, to some extent, related to trade within the wider economic policy debate. A consideration of such social problems in economic policy could be instrumental in the labour standards and international trade linkage.

There appears to be wide differences in the views of the proponents of a formal link between trade and labour standards and the critics of such a link. Both tend to have valid arguments, making the issue very contentious and probably one that makes finding a common ground difficult to achieve. One of the principal arguments of the proponents of a formal link is that countries that do not adhere to the core labour standards administered by the ILO tend to gain competitive advantage in terms of lowering costs of production and may result in a "race to the bottom"[21] in labour standards worldwide.

The critics, on the other hand, argue that the linkage, if any, is tenuous and that protectionism is hidden behind the rhetoric. Whilst we embrace the goal of achieving a level playing field, we take the position that the solution to the problem lies in assisting developing countries to achieve economic growth and development that, in turn, would enhance labour standards. In our opinion, the imposition of sanctions on countries with weak labour standards would have negative ramifications.

Whilst the debate surrounding this issue is not new, it has recently been pushed to the top of the international trade agenda. This is because the ILO, as the custodian of the labour standards, appears to lack the enforcement powers necessary to achieve compliance, which is relevant to the debate as to whether labour standards should be left to the ILO or added to the WTO agenda since the WTO, through its dispute settlement mechanism, has more effective procedures for surveillance and for suspension of concessions. However, the majority of WTO Members are strongly opposed to the WTO getting involved in this controversial issue. During the Fourth World Trade Organization (WTO) Ministerial Conference in Doha, Trade Ministers reaffirmed their declaration made at the Singapore Ministerial Conference that the issue be left under the remit of the ILO.[22]

Whilst the majority of the community of nations (mostly developing) do not agree on linking trade and the CLS, a few countries and the International Confederation of Free Trade Unions (ICFTU)[23] are pushing for a linkage. This is reflected in some countries' unilateral and regional efforts in the area of trade agreements. The most prominent of such a country and regional grouping are the United States

[21] The memorable phrase was used by Justice Brandeis in *Liggett Co. v. Lee* 288 U.S. 517, 557–560 (1933) (Brandeis, J., dissenting in part), to describe the reducing of regulatory requirement in the competition between countries in order to attract business.

[22] WTO Members at the First Ministerial meeting held in Singapore in 1996 declared that "the International Labour Organization (ILO) is the competent body to set and deal with [internationally recognized core labour standards]".

[23] The ICFTU has, since the 1960s, been involved in the debate on linkage between trade and labour issues. The ICFTU argues that CLS are essential to achieve decent work, which in turn is essential to any serious strategy to achieve sustainable development.

of America and the European Union. In the case of the United States, since the 1980s it has become increasingly common to include international labour standard criteria in U.S. foreign economic legislation.

With the recent surge in free trade agreements or regional trade agreements (RTAs),[24] mostly between developed and developing countries, and the inclusion of labour standard clauses in these agreements, the argument by proponents of a labour/trade nexus is that RTAs will assist in the compliance of international labour standards, which, it is believed, could lead to higher wages, and that in their view is the fastest route to improving the lot of workers. The questions are whether a difference in labour standards between developed and developing countries creates economic and social issues that should be addressed in trade agreements[25] and, if so, whether the regional agreements or a multilateral agreement will best serve the interest of workers, mostly in developing countries.

The deal struck on 10 May 2007 between the United States Congress and the George W. Bush administration on a range of measures for all pending free trade agreements, notably a deal on the inclusion of labour standards, signalled the ever-growing desire to use RTAs to enforce internationally recognised labour standards in the absence of an agreement at the multilateral level. Dubbed "A New Trade Policy for America", the agreement is to have "legally enforceable" labour standards in all free trade agreements negotiated by the United States. Future trade deals will require signatories to "adopt, maintain and enforce" the five fundamental standards of the International Labour Organization (ILO). Whereas previous trade agreements have only included watery language about workers' rights, the new agreements are expected to contain tighter language on labour rights, including the possibility of imposing trade sanctions on countries that do not adhere to CLS.

In most developed countries, but more so in the United States of America, administrations particularly from the Clinton era have been under enormous pressure from labour groups and civil society to include labour provisions in trade agreements. In the 1997 NAFTA ratification debate, when public attention was particularly focused on the issues of labour standards and the environment, a *Business Week/Harris* poll found that 73 % of the respondents felt that free trade agreements "should seek to protect the environment" and "to lift labor standards in other countries".[26] The agreement of 10 May 2007 is a manifestation of this sentiment.

Almost two decades after the issue was raised at the multilateral level during the first WTO Ministerial Conference in 1996, the issue still remains unresolved. However, both the proponents and the critics have compelling arguments with respect to the linkage. Both agree, however, that adherence to core labour standards is required. Nevertheless, there remains a disagreement over the resolution of the

---

[24] Regional trade agreements and free trade agreements are used interchangeably.

[25] See Hornbeck (2003).

[26] *Business Week*, September 22, 1997, p. 34.

issue. Their disagreement lies in whether the core labour standards should be incorporated in the multilateral trade agreement.

The sensitive nature of the issue, and the fact that it has been recurring for a 150 years without any meaningful solution, makes the adoption of a novel approach very important as the solutions being offered at the multilateral level do not seem to satisfy both the supporters and critics of such a linkage.[27] The current approaches at the multilateral level through the International Labour Organization's (ILO) moral suasion to improving labour standards worldwide appear not to be working. On the other hand, there is resentment against making the observance of labour standards mandatory.

The debate surrounding the matter raises issues that go beyond the realm of economics to include the human rights dimension (workers' right). This raises questions on how to achieve equity in international trade relations, the moral principles involved in international trade, and the role of international organisations, notably the ILO, the WTO, the International Monetary Fund (IMF), and the World Bank, in addressing the concerns of the proponents and critics of the issue and their respective or joint roles in balancing the views of both parties.

During the latter part of the twentieth century, there was considerable discussion on the ethics of international trade, and one of the conspicuous features of the international economy during this period was the international division of labour whereby developing countries produced primary products for markets of the developed countries. From 1970s onwards, factors such as rising labour costs in developed countries, liberalisation of trade, decrease in transport costs, deregulation of markets with its attendant effects on the movement of capital, labour, and goods brought about changes in the volume and pattern of trade, with its associated changes in the international division of labour.

The volume of trade has increased in the last three decades, notably in the manufacturing sector. Developing countries have witnessed in this period a remarkable increase in the volume of their manufacturing goods, especially in the labour intensive sectors. International wage differentials and a pool of highly skilled labour force in some developing countries have encouraged the relocation of labour intensive production and the outsourcing of services from developed countries to the developing world. These developments, in spite of the theoretical and empirical evidence of minimal effects on the economies of the developed world, have led to fears of a "race to the bottom". This has led to a rise in public attention to the loss of unskilled jobs in developed countries to developing countries, what economists' term as the "comparative advantage" that the developing countries have, which in the discussion of the issue in the developed world has come to be seen as "unfair trade advantage". This has helped to rally support in developed countries for an

[27] The discussions to date may lead to the perception that the linkage between trade and labour standards is a new issue, but this linkage dates from the earliest concern about the conditions of workers during the Industrial Revolution in Europe.

international effort to address the "abusive" environment in which many of the imports coming into their countries are produced.[28]

Due to global consumption trends and the role of the media and nongovernmental organisations (NGOs), consumer interest has been generated in the conditions under which goods in developing countries are produced. This in turn has led to the development of private social standards (i.e., voluntary regulation developed to improve the performance of companies in relation to labour standards). However, in this thesis, the emphasis is on public standards, as is the case with the CLS administered by the ILO.

The issue of fair international labour standards in the context of trade policy dates back to the late nineteenth century. The first attempt at a major commitment in the twentieth century was made in the 1948 draft Havana Charter of the ill-fated International Trade Organization (ITO), which included an article on fair labour standards, as well as articles, *inter alia,* on restrictive business practices, commodity arrangements, and domestic employment practices. The argument for linking these issues with international trade was the conviction "that the failure of interwar attempts to secure international agreements liberalising trade was largely due to the practice of taking up trade questions in isolation instead of putting them in the more complex setting of economic policy as a whole".[29]

However, finding a midpoint that would be agreeable to both the supporters and critics of such a linkage has consistently eluded the international community. The arguments put forward by both parties indicate the extent to which the issue will continue to cause controversy at the international level.

Different approaches to resolving the issue have been put forward by both the proponents and critics of the linkage between labour standards and trade, but none seems to appeal to those on the opposite side of the spectrum. Both parties, however, agree that a solution needs to be found, given the increasing abuse of workers' rights, particularly those of child labourers. This makes it the more pressing, considering the controversy surrounding globalisation of the "world economy" and the view that it has not benefited most countries and that even within countries it has tended to disproportionately benefit the rich and marginalise the poor.

Since the proponents have not been able to include adherence of labour standards in the multilateral trading system, their response, particularly that of the United States, Canada, and the European Union, has changed strategy by inserting labour clauses in the regional and bilateral trade agreements (as shown by the deal of 10 May 2007 in the US)[30] stating that they are concluding with developing countries and also in their Generalized System of Preferences (GSP) schemes

[28] Kabeer (2004), p. 6.

[29] See Bidwell and Diebold (1949), at p. 214, quoted in Leary (1996b), at p. 198.

[30] Notable among such RTA's are North American Free Trade Agreement (NAFTA) side agreement (NAALC), US agreements with Chile, Jordan, Singapore, etc.

(evidenced by the EC "special incentive arrangements for the protection of labour rights"), which is viewed as a unilateral and autonomous approach.

But in the absence of the inclusion of a social clause in multilateral trade agreements, the ILO conventions on the rights of workers appear to be the best alternative as they seem to strike a careful balance between the various competing interests. Enforcement of these conventions, however, appears not to have had the desired effect, making the plight of workers a grave matter that needs to be addressed. Some policymakers and academics have argued that different approaches should be sought.

What model would be appropriate in an ever-changing world scene? Should policymakers continue to seek a resolution at the multilateral level even though no concrete results have emerged over the years? Or should they continue to rely on the ILO's moral suasion and diplomatic pressure, which has proven not to be very effective in achieving compliance? Compared to other international organisations, the WTO has a strong enforcement mechanism. In the event that labour standards are included in the WTO, it could be expected that the enforceability of the standards will be greatly improved. However, the WTO system can be compared to a two-edge sword. If it is not used for pro-labour-standards purposes, its free trade rationales will very possibly be used by free traders and undermine the efforts of labour advocates for labour rights protection.

It suffices to say that a model that is widely accepted could act as a bridge to achieving consensus in the multilateral system, thereby pushing the issue forward towards a resolution. Such a model needs to combine what both sides agree on, that trade liberalisation is needed to help resolve the issue, but then it needs to be linked with social protection. It appears, however, from the point of view of the critics that social protection is being sacrificed to achieve trade liberalisation. It is also this conflict between liberalisation and social protection and the perceived competitive advantage that developing countries tend to have in terms of lower standards, which makes the proponents advocate for a linkage by bringing the two relevant international organisations, the ILO and the WTO, together to work towards a resolution.

1.2.1 Regional Initiatives

The last decade has seen a rise in regional integration initiatives, which may accelerate as states have become frustrated with the slow pace of movement on a number of issues at the WTO, for example the lack of progress on the inclusion of a social clause in Article XX of the GATT/WTO Agreement. At the turn of the twenty-first century, nearly all members of the WTO are also parties to at least one RTA. This development has created both challenges and opportunities for the WTO: one such challenge is the issue of trade diversion.[31] An opportunity created

[31] Trade diversion occurs when the preferential treatment given to members of an RTA causes a member of such RTA to replace imports from the rest of the world with imports from a partner country.

may be the wider focus in the regional agreements on human rights, development and labour, the incentive for reform, and the flexibility that members of such agreements are given in the implementation of policies, which at the multilateral level may not for now be considered essential elements of trade negotiations. As such, RTAs could serve as a model and testing ground for future agreements.[32]

The apparent flexibility that states enjoy under regional agreements makes it an attractive model to use with respect to the labour/trade nexus in arriving at a resolution on this divisive issue. This model may, however, seem to be controversial due to the perceived limitations of RTAs. A number of legal and economic scholars have expressed dissatisfaction about the regional model; others, on the other hand, embrace the regional model as they see it as a force for good.[33]

With the inclusion of labour standard clauses in RTAs, the question has arisen whether it would not be advisable for developing countries to be negotiating the issue at the WTO where, as a group, they could negotiate a more favourable agreement that would ensure that labour measures are not used for protectionist purposes.

Labour groups and some politicians in developed countries such as the United States continue to press for the imposition of trade sanctions on countries that do not comply with internationally recognised labour standards. They want the recently signed free trade agreement between the United States and Jordan to become a model for future regional and multilateral trade agreements.[34] In addition to the controversy surrounding this issue are the implications of the recent WTO Appellate Body (AB) decision in the *European Communities—Conditions for the Granting of Tariff Preferences to Developing Countries.*[35] In that case (which is analysed in detail in Chap. 4), the AB stated that the EC's "special incentive arrangements for the protection of labour rights" (even though labour standards was not at issue in the case), in contrast to the drug arrangements, included detailed provisions setting out the procedure and substantive criteria that apply to a request by a country to become a beneficiary. The AB's statement appears to indicate that the special arrangements for labour rights under the *EC GSP* scheme are WTO compatible.

In light of the difficulty of harmonising the different legal systems (international labour standards and international trade law) and given the recurrence of this

[32] Serra and Kallab (1997), p. 8.

[33] See, for example, McCrudden and Davies (2000), p. 43. McCrudden and Davies make reference to four current ways of dealing with the labour standards and trade nexus. The four, according to them, are (i) a unilateral model, (ii) an NGO model, (iii) a regional model, and (iv) a multilateral model. They further proposed two alternative models should there be dissatisfaction with the four, namely (a) involuntary multilateralism and (b) voluntary multilateralism.

[34] The issue of trade sanctions raises the other issue of reciprocity. It is argued that a country should not invoke violations of workers' rights that it does not itself support, i.e., by ratification of relevant ILO conventions. The U.S. is frequently criticised for its own failure to ratify ILO conventions and thus contribute to a multilateral approach to the improvement of labour conditions. Leary (1996b), p. 182.

[35] WT/DS246/AB/R.

controversial issue, which has been dubbed "the issue that would not go away", this dissertation would also examine whether regional trade agreements could act as a stimulus for the multilateral system and whether the regional model that has acted as a laboratory for other areas in the multilateral trading system could again be relied upon to bridge the gap between the opposing views on the interface between labour standards and trade.

An assessment of the labour provisions in a number of RTAs would be made to determine whether those provisions are an effective means of protecting labour standards in the specific countries party to those agreements.

It is worthy to note that when a country ratifies an ILO Convention, it undertakes to discharge certain binding legal obligations and there is regular international supervision of implementation of these obligations by the country. Should labour standards be left to the ILO, added to the agenda of the WTO, or would a joint ILO–WTO effort be required to ensure compliance, leaving the principal role of judging compliance and providing technical advice and expertise to the ILO?

Under this arrangement, would the triggering of WTO-related sanctions only arise after the exhaustion of ILO procedures? If so, will the WTO dispute settlement mechanism be enough to dispel the fears of protectionism by developing countries and at the same time meet the concerns of developed countries? How effective will the compliance mechanisms put in place be? In the absence of a social clause in trade agreements, what mechanism should be put in place to promote core labour standards worldwide?

The limited success of adherence to minimum labour standards or CLS in some regional trade agreements would be very instrumental in the recommendations made in this dissertation in advocating that the experience of compliance with labour standards at the regional level be used as a benchmark. With the increasing fragmentation of the global economy into regional trading blocs or free trade areas, the question then is: to what extent can the lessons learned from the regional context be applied coherently at the multilateral level?

1.2.2 Legal Issues

A number of substantive legal issues arise with respect to a formal linkage of the core labour standards and international trade under international law, irrespective of whether the linkage occurs within a labour or trade forum. Within these different fora of international law, a linkage would encounter the problems of coherence and content of the different legal courses of adjudication. The issue is whether labour standard clauses should be made enforceable obligations under an international dispute settlement mechanism or be considered best endeavour goals.[36]

---

[36] See Charnovitz (1987), p. 565.

Whereas the core labour standards are the sole responsibility of the ILO, trade disputes fall under the ambit of the WTO. In the case of the ILO, the adoption of the conventions is of a voluntary nature falling within the ambit of private law as regulated by employment law practices pertaining to domestic enterprises. The WTO law, on the other hand, deals with public international law by restraining WTO Members from taking trade-restrictive measures and also by ensuring that a greater degree of equity in international economic relations is achieved. The different fora and the clear differences in approach would have major legal implications should there be attempts at linking the CLS and trade and, more so, at harmonising or integrating labour law and trade law in the adjudication of a labour-trade dispute and, most especially, in the enforcement of a decision.

Another major difference in approach is that the ILO relies on moral suasion, technical assistance programmes, and conduct educational programmes for Members. Further, the ILO conducts reviews of Member States and writes country reports; there is no private right of action for natural persons, nor is there any mechanism by which the Member States can bring any charges against one another.

In the case of the WTO, the Dispute Settlement Mechanism (DSM), whilst it does not provide for private action, allows Member States to bring an action in a dispute settlement.[37] The first stage is the consultation phase, whereby a WTO Member or Members makes a request to another in an "attempt to obtain a satisfactory adjustment of the matter".[38] Should the consultations succeed in resolving the matter, the parties to the dispute will have to notify the Dispute Settlement Body of their mutually agreed solution. However, should the consultations fail to resolve the matter after 60 days, the complaining party shall have the right to request the establishment of a panel.

The second stage in the dispute settlement proceeding is the panel stage, whereby a three-person panel, upon review of briefs and oral hearings, issues a decision within a period of 9 months from the establishment of the panel. The decision of the panel may be appealed to the WTO Appellate Body by either the plaintiff government or the defendant government. The Appellate Body, in its ruling, may uphold, modify, or reverse the legal findings and conclusions of the panel.[39] Under the rules of the WTO, the reports of the panel and the Appellate Body are automatically adopted by the WTO Dispute Settlement Body, which is different from the dispute settlement proceedings during the GATT era, whereby a WTO Member could block the adoption of the panel report.[40] Upon adoption of the report by the Dispute Settlement Body, the defendant Member is obliged to comply

---

[37] Understanding on Rules and Procedures Governing the Settlement of Disputes [hereinafter DSU], April 15, 1994, WTO Agreement, Annex 2, art. 3. THE LEGAL TEXTS: THE RESULTS OF THE URUGUAY ROUND AGREEMENTS INCLUDING THE AGREEMENT ESTABLISHING THE WORLD TRADE ORGANIZATION AS SIGNED ON APRIL 15, 1994 17 (World Trade Organization 1999), at 355.

[38] See Article 4 of the DSU.

[39] DSU, Arts. 6–18.

[40] DSU, Arts. 16.4, 17.14.

with the decision of either the panel or the Appellate Body. The WTO rules in order to prompt compliance provide for trade retaliation by the winning plaintiff Member against the noncomplying defendant Member.

The nature of the two disciplines raises other significant differences. The ILO conventions and standard setting are nonbinding, and as such the ILO cannot legally enforce them, in sharp contrast to the provisions of international trade law, which are legally enforceable. The ILO labour standards are more based on broader statements of principle on the worldwide improvement of labour conditions. Under the ILO tripartite structure (government, employers, and workers), any of these three parties can make a representation to the ILO with respect to violations of the conventions. The complaint is then examined by a Committee of Experts and reported by the ILO in their publications and also the International Labour Conference. Depending on the nature of the complaint, a Commission of Inquiry may be set up to investigate, and the ILO has the authority under Article 33 of the ILO Constitution to take further action. This article empowers the ILO to take broad remedial action against a country that persistently violates the ILO conventions.

The only time that Article 33 has been invoked was in 2000, against Myanmar, when the ILO requested that all multilateral agencies of the United Nations and the Breton Woods institutions withhold programme assistance to Myanmar. Myanmar had been criticised by the ILO for more than 30 years for gross violation of the Forced Labour Convention, 1930 (No. 29). This level of enforcement is what has prompted some commentators to label the ILO as having not enough "teeth" in ensuring that Member States comply with the international labour standards.

The WTO law, in contrast, deals with specific commitments undertaken by Members. In the event of noncompliance with the WTO Agreement alleged by a WTO Member against another Member, the dispute settlement system provides for resolution of the matter. Normally, a dispute arises when a WTO Member adopts a trade measure that another WTO Member considers to be inconsistent with the obligations of the WTO Agreement. The Agreement provides that Members should manage to reach a mutually agreed solution. Should this fail, the complainant is entitled to a rule-based procedure whereby the case is examined by an independent body (first, a panel and, should the complainant or respondent appeal, then the Appellate Body). If the complainant prevails, in that a measure by the respondent is found to be inconsistent with a covered agreement, the panel or the Appellate Body would recommend the Member concerned to bring the measure into conformity with the agreement. In this way, the dispute settlement system of the WTO provides a mechanism through which Members can ensure that their rights under the covered agreements can be enforced.

The international labour standards are obligations that governments owe to their nationals, and there are no provisions within the ILO whereby nationals can ensure that these obligations are enforced. Under international trade law, the provisions of the WTO Agreement are obligations that Members owe each other. Even though international trade is the flow of goods and services between Members, this trade is conducted by private economic operators, not the States that signed the WTO Agreements. These economic operators need stability and predictability in the application of the international trade rules. A central objective of the dispute settlement system is to give these private economic operators (traders and investors) a greater degree of security and predictability concerning the trade policy measures of all WTO Members. The different nature of enforcing obligations under the two systems raises a major issue of enforcement difficult to balance.

This publication draws heavily on ILO and GATT/WTO documents and focuses primarily on the legal aspects. Most of the literature on the subject has been written by economists or social scientists, who have been concerned primarily with the economic implications of the lack of adherence to CLS. Also, the economists, with respect to RTAs, have been concerned with the issue of trade diversion and trade creation and the impact of regional trade agreements on the multilateral trading system. This is an issue that not only has economic consequences but also has legal, social, and political implications. And a discussion of the issue will show how these factors relate to the debate as a whole.

1.3 Structure of the Book

This dissertation is divided into nine chapters. Chapter 2 discusses the issues in the global debate of the linkage between labour standards and international trade. This chapter also deals with the question of whether there is a case for international labour standards in trade agreements. It also examines the views and arguments of the proponents and critics of the linkage. This chapter also reviews the effect of the recent financial crisis on compliance with the CLS. The issue of the gap between economic progress and social development is raised and analysed.

Chapter 3 examines the history of the linkage between labour standards and trade and the early developments of the linkage. A definition and the criteria for the selection of core labour standards are provided. The chapter also discusses the ILO supervisory and enforcement mechanism and the universality of the CLS and whether they are universally applicable and whether there is any reason for *global* promotion and enforcement of labour standards.

In Chap. 4, we undertake legal analyses of the CLS within customary international law and the process and production method debate, in respect of their universally binding nature, whether CLS should be considered as *jus cogens* and whether CLS can be deemed workers' or human rights. This section also discusses CLS under the WTO Agreements and enforcement under the WTO legal system.

Chapter 5 discusses unilateral approaches, highlighting the social clauses in other international agreements. It also discusses the labour standard provisions in non-reciprocal preferential trading arrangements of United States and the European Union under the Generalised System of Preferences (GSP). The different forms of corporate social responsibility are briefly touched, and emphasis is placed on the international framework agreements, which are deemed to have the most potential in addressing the compliance of the CLS at the multilateral enterprise level across global supply chains.

Chapter 6 discusses the rise of regionalism and the legal basis for RTAs under the MTS. The chapter also reviews the relevant rules under GATT Article XXIV and the Enabling Clause and how the WTO *Turkey-Textiles* case has impacted on the linkage debate.

Chapter 7 reviews labour standard clauses in various regional trade agreements, specifically trade agreements signed by the United States, on one hand, and the European Union, on the other hand, with a number of developing countries. We also examine the labour standard clauses in RTAs signed between Canada and other countries, also the selection of other RTAs with labour provisions.

Chapter 8 considers whether regional trade agreements could act as a stimulus for the multilateral system and whether the regional model that has acted as a laboratory for other areas in the multilateral trade system could again be relied upon to bridge the gap between the CLS and international trade. We review the dispute resolution under the NAALC since it is about the only RTA that has reviewed labour cases that are trade related, as a model for the multilateral system. We also examine the impact of the Side Agreement from the view point of both the critics and supporters of the Agreement. The question discussed at the end of this section is whether free trade agreements advance workers' rights.

Chapter 9 summarises the salient points made and the lessons that could be learned from the regional approach. The point made is that the inclusion of labour clauses in RTAs is an indication of how the relationship between social issues and trade is being addressed. This provides a model for a multilateral approach. This section provides recommendations on how to address the linkage issue.

References

Abbott, F. M. (2000). Distributed governance at the WTO–WIPO: A evolving model for open-architecture integrated governance. *Journal of International Economic Law, 3*.

Bidwell, P. W., & Diebold, W. (1949). The United States and the international trade organisation. *International Conciliation, 27*.

Bronstein, A. (2009). *International and comparative labour law: Current challenges*. Geneva: ILO/Palgrave Macmillan.

Charnovitz, S. (1987). The influence of international labour standards on the world trading system: An historical overview. *International Labour Review, 126*(5).

Charnovitz, S. (2006). The (neglected) employment dimension of the World Trade Organization. In V. A. Leary & D. Warner (Eds.), *Social issues, globalisation and international institutions: Labour rights and the EU, ILO, OECD and WTO*. Leiden, Boston: Martinus Nijhoff.

Hornbeck, J. F. (2003). *The U.S.–Chile Free Trade Agreement: Economic and trade policy issues*. CRS Report for Congress, Updated 25 July 2003, CRS-14.

ILO. (2012). *Fundamental principles and rights at work: From commitment to action*. ILC, 101st Session, Geneva.

Jansen, M., Peters, R., & Salazar-Xirinachs, J. (Eds.). (2011). *Trade and employment: From myths to facts*. Geneva: International Labour Office.

Kabeer, N. (2004). Globalization, labor standards, and women's rights: Dilemmas of collective (in)action in an interdependent world. *Feminist Economics, 10*(1).

Lacarte, J. A. (2004). Transparency, public debate and participation by NGOs in the WTO: A WTO perspective. *Journal of International Economic Law, 7*(3).

Langille, B. (1997). Eight ways to think about international labour standards. *Journal of World Trade, 31*.

Leary, V. (1996a). Workers' rights and international trade: The social clause. In J. Bhagwati & R. E. Hudec (Eds.), *Fair trade and harmonization*. Cambridge, MA: The MIT Press.

Leary, V. (1996b). Workers' rights and international trade: The social clause (GATT, ILO, NAFTA, U.S. Laws). In J. Bhagwati & R. E. Hudec (Eds.), *Fair trade and harmonization, prerequisites for free trade*? (Vol. 2). Cambridge, MA: The MIT Press.

McCrudden, C., & Davies, A. (2000). A perspective on trade and labor rights. *Journal of International Economic Law, 3*(1).

Müller, T., Platzer, H. -W., & Rüb, S. (2008). *International framework agreements- opportunities and limitation of new tool of global trade union policy* (Briefing Papers No. 8). Friedrich-Ebert Foundation.

Papadakis, K. (2011a). Globalizing industrial relations: What role for international framework agreements? In S. Hayter (Ed.), *The role of collective bargaining in the global economy*. Cheltenham: Edward Elgar.

Papadakis, K. (2011b). *Shaping global industrial relations: The impact of international framework agreements*. Basingstoke: Palgrave Macmillan.

Schefer Krista, N. (2010). *Social regulation in the WTO: Trade policy and international legal development*. Cheltenham, UK/Northhampton, MA, USA: Edward Elgar.

Serra, J., & Kallab, V. (Eds.). (1997). *Reflections on regionalism: Report of the study group on international trade*. Washington: Carnegie Endowment.

Stevis, D. (2010). International framework agreements and global social dialogue: Parameters and prospects (*Employment Working Paper* No. 47). Geneva: ILO.

Todaro, M. P., & Smith, S. C. (2011). *Economic development* (11th ed.). Harlow, England: Pearson.

van Liemt, G. (1989). Minimum labour standards and international trade: Would a social clause work? *International Labour Review, 128*(4).

World Trade Organization. (1999). *Decision on the application and review of the understanding on rules and procedures governing the settlement of disputes, published in legal text. The legal texts: The results of the Uruguay Round of Multilateral Trade Negotiations*. Cambridge: Cambridge University Press.

Chapter 2
The Global Debate: The Linkage Between Labour Standards and International Trade

2.1 Introduction

What started in Seattle at the World Trade Organization (WTO) Ministerial meeting in December 1999 as a protest against globalisation brought international attention to the age-old issue of the correlation between labour standards and international trade and the plight of many workers in developing countries. What was brought to light were the obvious imbalances and asymmetries in the global trading system and the large divergence in power between developed and developing countries. In effect, a global debate was started as to whether or not there is a link between trade and labour standards and, if so, how best to resolve the issue to benefit the very workers for whom this whole debate was initiated.

The global debate on the linkage between CLS and international trade is one of the most vexing issues in international trade policy and international labour regulation. The continued debate raises questions of compliance under international law and also touches on disciplines outside the sphere of law. What is essential is how to find an appropriate solution that would satisfy both the critics and advocates of the linkage. Some major issues that arise are which of the core labour standards are trade related and whether the other non-trade-related labour standards should be included in the debate.

This chapter identifies the issues raised in the interface between standards and international trade under the banner of globalisation and the promotion of CLS and analyses the global debate on labour standards. Three rationales for the linkage between CLS and international trade have been advanced. First is the issue of unfair competition for workers and firms in developed countries with higher standards competing with firms and workers in developing countries that do not adhere fully to the CLS and, as a result, have lower costs of production. This, the proponents posit, could lead to the loss of market share and jobs on the part of the firms and workers in developed countries. Second, this form of unfair competition could lead to the so-called race to the bottom. Third, CLS should be considered as basic human

K. Addo, *Core Labour Standards and International Trade*,
DOI 10.1007/978-3-662-44619-5_2

rights as reflected in the United Nations Conventions.[1] Whilst this chapter explores in fuller detail on the first and second rationales, the third rationale is briefly considered here but is examined in detail in Chap. 4.

The public awareness in developed countries is high, which reflects an awareness of the impact of globalisation. The public also recognises that trade and foreign direct investment are meant to benefit the world population and support those that are involved in the production of goods and services and contribute to economic growth.[2] This growing awareness should be based on the recognition that fundamental rights and sustainable development go hand in hand with social development.

The existing international rules are skewed towards achieving economic development, giving the distorted view (at least from the viewpoint of many developing countries) that a country can develop economically without putting in place sound social policies, hence the view held by many that adherence to CLS is more an economic issue than a legal and social issue. It needs to be recognised, however, that economic and social policies are mutually reinforcing. But this can only be achieved by creating the legal basis on which to build a development strategy that addresses both the economic and social issues in a mutually satisfactory manner. It is generally believed that an equitable global economy should enhance social development and ensure fundamental workers' (human) rights and that the current global governance model does not sufficiently address these concerns.

The purpose of this debate is to identify the arguments of the linkage between labour standards and international trade, as well as the legal, social, political, economic, and development factors involved in the examination of this controversial issue in the global context. Quite often, the only issue considered is in terms of the economic implications for countries that make the effort to adhere to the CLS and those that do not. The other point that arises as a result of the economic implications is the legal implications of enforcing compliance. But the issue is

[1] Trebilcock (2011), pp. 172–173. Trebilcock argues that the first two rationales in the linkage debate pose some problems since the focus is on social welfare in the importing countries and not in the importing countries. He further argues that when objections are raised to this form of competition, there is the risk of depriving the developing countries of "one of their major sources of comparative advantage ..." He notes that although labour costs and labour productivity are closely correlated, note should be taken of the situations in the developing countries, which are a reflection of the absence or low quality of the factors of production. He buttresses his argument that international trade and FDI are not driven mostly by differences in labour costs and standards and that international trade and FDI are more a phenomena of the North–North relations rather than the North–South relationships. With respect to the third rationale, he states that since the focus is mainly on the social welfare situation in the exporting countries, it therefore "seems an entirely cogent basis for collective global action to ensure that core labour standards in all countries, conceived of as universal human rights ... are respected". See also, Charnovitz (1992) in Charnovitz (2002), pp. 59–82.

[2] Commission of the European Communities, Communication from the Commission to the Council, the European Parliament and the Economic and Social Committee, *Promoting Core Labour Standards and Improving Social Governance in the Context of Globalisation*, Brussels, 18.7.2001 COM(2001) 416 final, p. 3.

much more complicated as other factors tend to have a much greater influence in ensuring compliance than merely the legal and economic arguments often discussed.[3]

2.2 Overview of the Perspectives of the Proponents and Critics of the Labour and Trade Linkage

2.2.1 *A Brief View of the Proponents*

The proponents of a link between labour standards and international trade give two main reasons why they think such a link is warranted at the multilateral level. First, they argue that countries that do not comply with the CLS tend to gain competitive advantage over countries that adhere to the CLS, and that, in turn, could result in a "race to the bottom" in labour standards worldwide. What the proponents imply by this line of reasoning is that countries, by not observing the CLS, are able to reduce the cost of doing business, which may enhance their competitiveness. Second, other proponents tend to link the noncompliance of CLS to the rights of workers. These proponents contend that the fundamental principles of workers' rights should be adhered to by all countries engaged in international trade, and the inclusion of a social clause in trade agreements will ultimately benefit workers both in developed and developing countries. They further argue that the imposition of trade sanctions on countries that do not respect the CLS should not be seen negatively but should rather be viewed in a positive light as it could influence those countries to extend the fundamental rights of workers to their citizens.

2.2.2 *A Brief View of the Critics*

The critics of a formal link between labour standards and international trade, on the other hand, argue that the two issues are unrelated and should be kept separate. These critics argue that the true reason why some developed countries are pushing for a linkage between these two issues is the desire to protect their traditional ailing industries in sectors such as steel, textiles, and clothing, in which developing countries tend to have comparative advantage and are challenging the dominance of developed countries. In other words, developing countries see attempts to link trade and labour standards as nothing more than a protectionist measure to safeguard developed countries' declining industries and preserve jobs that otherwise might be lost, and the differences between labour standards in various countries

[3] See the further analysis in Bartels (2009).

should be seen as a source of comparative advantage in line with traditional economic thinking.

The critics point out that if developed countries really wanted to improve the living conditions for workers in the developing world, they should abolish all the barriers that they impose on developing countries' exports, especially on agricultural, textile, and clothing products, and that the rampant use of anti-dumping and safeguard measures should be restrained. They further argue that the solution to the problem lies not in restricting trade but in encouraging trade. The point is made that as developing countries derive more income from trade, they will improve the working conditions of their employees. They also point out that the proponents of a formal link between trade and labour standards have lost sight of the fact that it is poverty that gives rise to practices such as child labour and that poverty in developing countries could only be effectively tackled through a number of measures, including trade opportunities for developing countries.[4]

2.3 Is There a Case for International Labour Standards in Trade Agreements?

Having briefing consider the views of both the proponents and critics of the linkage between the CLS and international trade, the question that this poses is whether there is a case for these standards in international trade.

The words of President Bill Clinton in 1999 are instructive in making a case for the relevance of labour standards in trade agreements:

> [O]pen trade is not contrary to the interest of working people. Competition and integration lead to stronger growth, more and better jobs, more widely shared gains. Renewed protectionism in any of our nations would lead to a spiral of retaliation that would diminish the standard of living for working people everywhere.[5]

Globalisation of the world economy and the opening up of markets have, in the last decades, led to rapid economic growth and trade liberalisation. This has become possible as trade barriers have been dismantled and tariffs lowered with the signing of the Uruguay Round of trade negotiations, which led to the establishment of the WTO. As increased trade led to improved economic growth and development, the need was recognised by countries for a social pillar. This led to a process within the ILO for a set of fundamental principles and rights at work (FPRW).

This started with the development of proposals by the ILO within the context of the Uruguay Round that respect for a number of international labour standards should go hand in hand with participation in the developing multilateral trading system. For the ILO, this raised the question on how to ensure that the link between

---

[4] See, for example, Panagariya (2001).

[5] Clinton (1999).

economic growth and social progress is equitably achieved and also provide a framework for people to have an equitable share in the benefits of trade liberalisation. After much deliberation, the four categories of the fundamental principles and rights at work were agreed upon.[6]

During the 86th session of the International Labour Conference in 1998, the ILO provided insight into the choice of the eight fundamental conventions that form the FPRW. The ILO stressed in the preliminary work leading to the 1998 Declaration that "fundamental rights are not fundamental because the Declaration says so; the Declaration says that they are fundamental because they are".[7] From the ILO's point of view, the selection of the eight standards does not in any way mean that the other international labour standards should be disregarded; rather, the FPRW were chosen since they were deemed instrumental in promoting in general all the international labour standards and also in achieving the objectives of the organisation.[8]

It is relevant at this point to note that the eight international labour standards that form the FPRW are also considered as human rights in other sources of international law. For example, FPRW are enshrined in the Universal Declaration of Human Rights[9] and other United Nations human right treaties,[10,11] Furthermore, FPRW are enshrined in the International Covenant on Economic, Social and Cultural Rights.[12] FPRW are also considered in a number of regional conventions.[13]

---

[6] ILO (2012), p. 5.

[7] ILO (1998a).

[8] See, ILO (1998b), in ILO (2012), supra note 4, p. 6.

[9] In the Universal Declaration of Human Rights, 1948, Article 4 deals with the prohibition of slavery; Article 7 deals with the principle of non-discrimination; Article 20, with freedom of association; Article 23(2), the right to equal pay for equal work, without discrimination; Article 23 (4), the right to form and join unions; Article 25(2), special protection for children; and Article 26 deals with the right to education. These Articles, which were universally agreed upon, reinforce the international labour standards that form the FPRW.

[10] The ILO FPRW pre-dates the UN treaties and compliments them. As in the case of the Universal Declaration above, these treaties once again strengthen the universal appeal of the FPRW. These treaties are the International Convention on the Elimination of All Forms of Racial Discrimination, 1965; the Convention on the Elimination of All Forms of Discrimination against Women, 1979; the Convention on the Rights of the Child, 1989; the International Convention on the Protection of the Rights of All Migrant Workers and Members of their Families, 1990; and the Convention on the Rights of Persons with Disabilities, 2006.

[11] International Covenant on Civil and Political Rights, 1966; Article 8 deals with the prohibition of forced or compulsory labour; Article 22, on the recognition of the right to freedom of association, including the right to form and join trade unions; and Article 26, on the right of all persons to receive effective protection against discrimination.

[12] International Covenant on Economic, Social and Cultural Rights, 1966: Article 2 deals with the right to enjoy economic, social, and cultural rights without discrimination; Article 6, on the right to freely chosen and accepted work; Article 8, on the right to form trade unions, and this includes the right to strike, and Article 10 on the protection of children from economic and social exploitation.

[13] For instance, the European Convention on Human Rights, 1950; the European Social Charter, 1961, revised in 1996; the American Convention on Human Rights, 1969; and the African Charter on Human and Peoples' Rights, 1981.

The ILO considers the integration of the respect for FPRW into the policies and activities into the multilateral system as part of its overall work to promote policy coherence. According to the ILO:

> [t]he aim of policy coherence is to develop and strengthen mutually reinforcing economic and social policies that advance social justice through decent work, both within countries and globally.[14]

Furthermore, the ILO makes the case that FPRW have a major part to play in linking social progress and economic growth, and its decent work agenda is meant to forge a linkage and coherence between social and economic objectives.[15] Since trade has an impact on economic growth and that could lead to improved social progress, the coherence between the CLS and trade is closely intertwined.

2.3.1 Fundamental Principles and Rights at Work as Enabling Rights

For example, could the argument be made that forced labour is undoubtedly a good example of a trade-labour linkage? To start with, forced labour is seen as illegitimate, as evidenced by the universal condemnation of slavery as a fundamental norm of international law having the status of *jus cogen*.[16] In addition, forced labour lowers production costs since workers would be paid a lower wage, which affects the total cost of production. With regard to child labour, this definitely affects costs of production; however, there appears to be varying views in the way different cultures consider child labour and the various ways in which it is practiced.[17]

The elimination of forced labour, child labour, and discrimination is vital to ensure the dignity of people and also overcome the vicious cycle of poverty. Children who are made to work suffer from lack of education, with negative impacts on their health and overall development. These eventually create economic costs for countries that do not make the necessary effort to stamp out the violation of these rights.

Another core standard that could be considered trade related is that of union rights (freedom of association and the right to collective bargaining). The asymmetrical relationship between employers and employees, to some extent, affects production costs. The nature of the relationship is such that the employee cannot bargain on equal basis with the employer for wages, health and occupational hazard

[14] ILO (2011b). GB.312/HL/1, para. 6.

[15] ILO (2012), p. 98.

[16] See Chap. 4 for a discussion of CLS and *jus cogens*. It should be noted, however, that forced labour or even the FPRW has not, in the international community, reached the status of *jus cogens*.

[17] See Zaheer (2003–2004), p. 76.

conditions, and hours of employment. In addition to the economic arguments, the issue of core standards calls into question the moral and legal values of their enforcement.[18]

Freedom of association and the effective recognition of the right to collective bargaining are at the heart of the ILO's FPRW, and particular attention has, over the decades, been paid to these enabling rights. The ILO considers these rights as critical in enabling employers and workers to lay down the ground rules for a harmonious relationship and reconciling their differences. Freedom of association helps to secure the effectiveness of labour laws and leads to effective social dialogue. This could make a meaningful contribution to the development of economic and social policies in the areas of employment and social protection.

2.3.2 Why Intellectual Property and Not CLS

The proponents of the inclusion of labour standard provisions in trade agreements point to the introduction of new areas, including trade in services and protection of intellectual property rights, under the ambit of WTO as setting a precedent for the protection of labour standards in trade agreements. The argument is that intellectual property rights and worker rights are equally important and that both deserve to be protected.[19]

The proponents further contend that if the WTO is the appropriate venue for setting legally binding standards protecting intellectual property rights, then it and other trade agreements are the proper venues for similarly protecting labour rights. They see access to the dispute settlement processes typically included in trade agreements as a distinct advantage in ensuring that labour standards are enforced. According to Maskus (2000), the reason why the Trade-Related Intellectual Property Rights Agreement (TRIPS) became part of the WTO whilst other forms of business regulation did not is simply because intellectual property rights (IPRs) are integral to the trading system.[20]

During the Uruguay Round negotiations concerning the issue of whether intellectual property rights (IPRs) should be included in the WTO, Members, in agreeing to the inclusion, did not provide a criteria in their determination that IPRs are trade related. However, a set of criteria has been developed by Maskus, which he has applied to several standards, including intellectual property rights and labour. The criteria developed are the following: (a) determine how trade related the proposed standards are, (b) coordinate failures of countries to enforce collective interest through stronger standards, (c) determine the importance of international market or policy failures (i.e., an externality) the standards may address, and

[18] ILO (2012), p. 7.

[19] Maskus (1997).

[20] Maskus (2000), p. 4.

(d) consider the ability of the dispute settlement mechanism to deal with standards effectively.[21]

In relation to IPRs, Maskus' study found that IPRs (1) are strongly trade related; (2) by including IPRs in trade agreements, it will allow for stronger, more uniform standards, and (3) standards varying from country to country introduce the possibility of policy- or market-induced failure. The study established that both trade agreements and IPRs deal with similar commercial activities. In concluding, Maskus stated that the WTO dispute settlement process will be effective in dealing with intellectual property rights violations.[22]

On the other hand, the study stated that violations of core labour standards are not clearly trade related. The study further stated that the domestic sectors of the economy are the ones most likely to violate core labour standards and that the export sector is the sector that normally adheres to the core labour standards. In this respect, setting up standards that have the force of trade sanctions would, in most cases, penalise the most compliant sector. Moreover, if the most numerous violations are in the non-traded sectors, it is difficult to argue that trade-based labour standards are likely to develop stronger, more uniform standards to support the trading system.[23]

Furthermore, this study maintains that incorporation of labour standards in a trade agreement may actually cause a policy failure rather than correct existing market failures. For instance, as a result of trade sanctions, employment may fall in the impacted country's export sector and workers may be forced to seek employment in less-compliant sectors.[24]

Lastly, the study found that trade agreements are not well suited to deal with "moral" issues such as labour rights. Since trade agreements are typically structured to deal with quantifiable, commercial transactions, they may not be well equipped to deal with the judgments necessary in enforcing core labour standards. Furthermore, because the WTO takes decisions by consensus, resistance by developing countries to addressing core labour standards within the WTO could make it impossible to put core labour standards on the WTO agenda.[25]

Maskus' analyses touches on a point that makes it difficult to fully incorporate labour issues in the WTO agenda—how to accommodate social issues within a system created to deal with commercial damages. Whereas the argument could be made for IPRs, the same, in my view, cannot be made for an issue with social connotations.

The arguments advanced above goes to the very heart of the question that Charnovitz raises as to: "How broad should a treaty be?"[26] Charnovitz's question

---

[21] Maskus (2000), p. 14.

[22] Maskus (2000), pp. 17–18.

[23] Maskus (2000), p. 12.

[24] Maskus (2000), p. 12.

[25] Maskus (2000), p. 12.

[26] Charnovitz (1998) in Charnovitz (2002), p. 11.

is very pertinent to the discussion of the issue of whether labour standards should be put on the same level as IPRs in the debate. In a globalised work full of interlinkages and the impact of policies in one country and its attendant effects on others, the framework proposed by Charnovitz for evaluating policy linkage deserves great attention. The four reasons that he advances within his framework—(1) to enhance policy effectiveness, (2) to rebalance policies, (3) to build coalitions, and (4) to gain economies of scale—in my opinion help respond to the arguments that labour standards are not to be included in trade negotiations.[27]

2.3.3 *Views from Academia*

Rodrik (1997) also argues that importing items from a country with lower standards than those prevailing in the United States is a little different morally from producing the product in the United States with the same lower standards. He argues that the only difference between using child labour to produce footwear in a Honduran sweatshop versus producing the footwear with the same sweatshop process in the United States is that the production in the United States is against the law. He goes on to draw a distinction between a country having a comparative advantage in producing an item based on differences in resource endowments and a comparative advantage based on lower standards.[28]

Additionally, a group of 99 intellectuals and leaders of nongovernmental organisations, in an open letter, presented a developing country point of view. They asserted that arguments for including labour standards in trade agreements are made by one of two groups: politically powerful lobbying groups that are protectionist and morally driven human rights and other groups. They further contend that the morally driven groups are misguided because their actions may harm the developing country labourers they are trying to help by forcing them out of their jobs without providing a viable alternative.[29]

The authors concluded that the end result of trade-based labour standards, whether protectionist or morally motivated, is protecting developed country firms from developing country competition. Many economists agree and also point out that in addition to the possible adverse impact on developing country workers, consumers in developed countries may have a more limited choice of goods and face higher prices for the goods available.[30]

---

[27] Charnovitz (1998). Charnovitz also lists four arguments against linkage: '(1) there is no reason for linkage, (2) linkage would produce bad policy results, (3) linkage would slow down negotiations, and (4) linkage would drain an agency's resources and confound it mission'. See pp. 17–20.

[28] See Rodrik (1997).

[29] Bhagwati et al. (1994). See also Bhagwati (1994).

[30] Bhagwati et al. (1994).

Whilst the arguments of the "no-linkage" school of thought may hold in the short term, the linkage, if effectively achieved, has great benefits in the long term for the every worker in the developing countries and every consumer in the developed world they claim should be protected. Charnovitz's first reason why governments might want to link issues (see above) in broadening a treaty of international organisations, in this case the WTO and also the ILO, indicates how policy coordination enhances the effectiveness of policies, especially in the case of the labour standards–trade relationship.[31]

Charnovitz cites two quotations from the economist John Bell Condliffe, which are worth restating here. Condliffe stated that "It is inconceivable that international economic problems can be effectively handled unless various aspects – migration, labor, production, trade, finance, investment, and money – are considered in relation to one another".[32] Basing his further analysis on the quote above, Charnovitz examined the linkage between trade and IPR, competition policy and telecommunications, and further added that "[O]ther international organizations, besides the WTO, can seek to improve trade policy".[33] Whereas the link between trade and IPR is considered related in commercial terms and the WTO dispute mechanism can deal effectively with IPR issues, in the same way, labour as a factor of production, even if it is stated that labour is not a commodity,[34] is affected by trade relations and should also enjoy the benefits of cooperation at the international level.

In this respect, the mutual assistance provided by the WTO and ILO in achieving each organisation's agenda could provide one of the effective responses during economic crisis. From the angle of the WTO, better enforcement of the CLS is by fully integrating developing countries into the multilateral trading system. In the case of the ILO, its role is the creation of favourable conditions for the effective functioning of the tripartite system, in particular freedom of association, in addressing country-specific and global issues in a coherent manner to "enhance policy effectiveness". In this respect, their effective cooperation is essential in addressing the CLS issue.

The second quote from Condliffe responds well to the claim that the WTO is not well positioned to take on the so-called no trade issues, and given the cross-cutting nature of issues, Condliffe's statement is germane to the labour standards and trade issue. Condliffe further stated:

> This does not, indeed mean that a single institution can deal effectively with such a wide range of problems on the international, any more than on the national, plane, but it does imply the necessity of close liaison between such institutions as may be handling various aspects of a related problem.[35]

---

[31] Charnovitz (1998), p. 17.

[32] Condliffe (1940), p. 386, quoted in Charnovitz (1998), p. 17.

[33] Condliffe (1940).

[34] See ILO Declaration of Philadelphia, 1944.

[35] ILO Declaration of Philadelphia, 1944.

Charnovitz gives an example of how the IMF and the World Bank collaborate in policy interventions.[36] Writing in 1992, Charnovitz recommended that the GATT and the ILO work "to develop a voluntary code of fair labour practices for goods in international trade".[37] Also, "the GATT Council should develop procedures for soliciting the input of nongovernmental organisations (e.g., business, labour, environment etc.) on an on-going basis".[38] He pointed out that the very countries that criticise unilateral action on labour issues are the very ones that are blocking the establishment of a GATT group on the rights of workers. He rightly predicted that the naysayers will not have it both ways.

The events starting in 1994 with the inclusion of labour standards in the NAFTA side agreement on labour have vindicated Charnovitz's claim that unilateral action by the United States would continue in the absence of international rules on the labour standards and trade linkage. With the increasing interdependence of the world economy and the slowly growing realisation that employment policy has an international dimension,[39] the labour standards and trade interlinkages issue would not only be confined to the free trade agreements signed between the United States, Europe, and other developing countries, but it could have been foreseen that it would expand also to agreements entered into between developing countries (so-called South–South trade relations).[40]

2.4 Multidisciplinary of the Issue of Labour Rights and International Trade

The examination of whether a social clause should be inserted in the multilateral trade agreement is multifaceted. The approach to the issue can be appreciated from different viewpoints. Whereas the issue has most often been approached at from the *pro* and *contra* angles, this thesis seeks to examine it from the multidisciplinary perspective. The issue will be examined in light of developments and trends in a globalised world, with its impact on social and development policy of which the world of work is directly affected.

The issue raises legal, moral, and social implications; economic impacts; and political debates. Examples of how the views of the proponents and critics of the linkage face each other can be seen from the viewpoints of two quotations below. The first is the viewpoint of the International Confederation of Free Trade Unions (ICTFU), which favours the inclusion of a social clause in the following statement:

---

[36] ILO Declaration of Philadelphia, 1944.

[37] Charnovitz (1992), p. 80.

[38] Charnovitz (1992).

[39] See Charnovitz (1995) in Charnovitz (2002), pp. 301–324.

[40] See Chap. 7 for South–South RTAs with labour provisions.

> The moral case for workers' rights clause is unanswerable. Globalisation promises a great deal, but delivers insecurity and cruelty to millions. The world cannot tolerate an economic system that depends on repression for profit; that exploits children and young women; and that makes slavery a sound business option. A workers' rights clause would create a basis for really achieving workers' rights and economic development and growth on the basis of respect for human rights and improvement in living and working conditions for all world citizens.[41]

The other view held by Professor Jagdish Bhagwati is in opposition to the ICFTU's viewpoint above. Bhagwati, in his opposing argument, states:

> [T]he reality is that diversity of labour practice and standards is widespread in practice and reflects, not necessarily venality and wickedness, but rather, diversity of cultural values, economic conditions, and analytical beliefs and theories concerning the economic (and therefore moral) consequences of specific labour standards. The notion that labour standards can be universalized, like human rights such as liberty and habeas corpus, simply by calling the [sic] "labour rights" ignores the fact that this easy equation between culture-specific labour standards and universal human rights will have a difficult time surviving deeper scrutiny.[42]

The two views provide a glimpse into the contentious debate on the linkage between labour standards and international trade and the most effective approach that should be taken in the whole discussion. Whereas the ICFTU links workers' rights to human rights, Bhagwati, on the other hand, considers that the "diversity of labour practice" should be recognised and also a universal approach to labour standards is probably not feasible, given the difference between "culture-specific labour standards and universal human rights". What the two approaches indicate is the danger of entering a social debate through the legal door.

2.4.1 Legal Matters

The legal issues that these developments raise are a reflection of the situation in many countries. This, according to Friedman (1996), is because "[l]egal systems do not float in some cultural void, free of space and time and social context ..." Inherent in this legal debate is how workers' rights are defined under international human rights law. According to Leary (1996), "[w]orkers' rights are human rights ..."[43] And as can be inferred from Friedman's view above, in this age of globalisation, when the impact of trade appears to have a direct or indirect bearing on workers, it brings the issue of workers' rights to the trade bargaining and policy debates table. This makes the issue one that meets at the crossroads of trade law, human rights law, labour law, and public policy.

---

[41] International Confederation of Free Trade Unions (1998).

[42] Bhagwati (1997), pp. 487 and 498.

[43] See also Cleveland (2003), pp. 137–138.

The two views raised above also indicate the role that labour rights or labour standards as human rights should play.[44] However, it is from this perspective that jurists tend to enter the debate on the social dimension of globalisation. In a world in which globalisation has transformed and provided a new perspective of work, Supiot argues that the issue is not to carry out an analysis of the transformation of work in line with the existing legal categories but to conduct a legal analysis of the transformations of work. He further states that "[l]aw can only mirror what societies believe those relationships ought to be".[45] Supiot further explains the role of law as playing a central role in shaping the "concept of work".[46] The idea of work with the value and dignity that it is accorded today, and which is a major theme at the ILO with its decent work agenda, has legal underpinnings.

In this line of thought, the first Director General of the ILO writing in 1921 made an observation, which is relevant to the present debate. He stated:

> [j]urists have long ceased to confine themselves to studying the mechanical operation of institutions and laws. They seek to discover in each succeeding epoch the social reality which these embody.[47]

Thomas elaborated on this point by stating that very often when an institution is created with modest and limited jurisdiction, the requirements of the day could lead to an increase in its authority. How true the words of Thomas ring today. At a time when the confidence in the governance system, in particular governments and businesses, are at its lowest level due to the economic policies of the last three decades, in which a push for an increased gross domestic product (GDP) growth and the so-called trickle-down effect has not lived up to expectations, the preamble of the ILO Constitution rings true more today than at its inception.[48]

---

[44] Sykes, for example, has indicated that there appears to be a progressive relationship between a country's openness to trade and its tendency to show respect for human rights. This raises the question as to whether poor or developing countries should forgo respect for human rights in order to achieve economic growth. See Sykes (2003).

[45] Supiot (1996), pp. 604 and 606.

[46] Supiot (1996), p. 607.

[47] Thomas (1921).

[48] The preamble of the ILO Constitution states: "Whereas universal and lasting peace can be established only if it is based upon social justice; And whereas conditions of labour exist involving such injustice hardship and privation to large numbers of people as to produce unrest so great that the peace and harmony of the world are imperilled; and an improvement of those conditions is urgently required; as, for example, by the regulation of the hours of work including the establishment of a maximum working day and week, the regulation of the labour supply, the prevention of unemployment, the provision of an adequate living wage, the protection of the worker against sickness, disease and injury arising out of his employment, the protection of children, young persons and women, provision for old age and injury, protection of the interests of workers when employed in countries other than their own, recognition of the principle of equal remuneration for work of equal value, recognition of the principle of freedom of association, the organization of vocational and technical education and other measures;

Whereas also the failure of any nation to adopt humane conditions of labour is an obstacle in the way of other nations which desire to improve the conditions in their own countries."

The inability of countries to address the job crisis not only has led to social discontent in the countries most affected by the crisis but is also having a ripple effect on the global economy. Rather than improving the lot of many people, the policies of the last three decades have led to continued growth of inequality. In the midst of the recent financial and job losses, the history of the ILO has shown how its call for putting labour at the centre of development has stood the test of times, especially more now than when it was established in 1919.

During a period that witnessed phenomenal growth of many countries, the financial crisis that started in the United States of America in 2007 has affected the global economy. In the recent report of the ILO Director General to the International Labour Conference, it was stated:

> In this context, it is very clear that the Decent Work Agenda and a working ILO tripartism bring the possibility of better, more inclusive growth, of more peace, more equity and rights, less poverty and more stable development in economies, enterprises, workplaces and, ultimately, in society. ILO policies contribute to a world with fewer tensions, greater fairness and strengthened security. These are compelling contemporary echoes of the most striking passages of the ILO's founding constitutional texts. With our values and policies, we are on the right side of history.[49]

Why do the values and policies of the ILO make the organisation confident that it is on the right side of history? The status given to labour in the economic paradigm of the last decades has relegated labour to the position second to capital. The failure to consider labour as pivotal to the establishment of a just order[50] goes contrary to the very principles and ideals that led to the establishment of the ILO.

The call for a new model is very critical to establishing the universal and lasting peace during a period of crisis. But like the ideal of the founding fathers of the ILO, lasting peace can only be built on social justice.[51] The call by the ILO for a new era of social justice with its policy prescriptions provides a path to follow in meeting the aspirations of people in both the developed and developing worlds.

The whole idea is that there should be a new pattern of growth, a different paradigm that puts employment as a target of economic policies and not only macroeconomic stability. There is therefore the need for a more pro-employment macroeconomic framework, sectoral strategies, and industrial policies that help create jobs and high productivity.

---

[49] ILO (2011a), p. 3.

[50] Supiot (1996), p. 613.

[51] See the Preamble to the ILO Constitution.

2.4.2 *Social Perspective of Trade Regulation on Labour Rights*

Whilst trade regulation is mostly considered only from an economic perspective, there are actions taken by governments as Contracting Parties to the multilateral trade agreement and as signatories to bilateral trade agreements and also unilateral trade measures that have social connotations to the full exercise of rights at work.[52] Qureshi has elaborated on the concept of what he terms as 'non-trade' actions of trade regulation from different viewpoints:

> Considerations which are of non-trade character, may in international trade be defined as those state actions or omissions which impact or may impact the flow of trade, but which are 'external' to it. They are external in the sense that they comprise non-economic, non-trade state actions or omissions which may affect other trading partners (whether state or individual), or impact the flow of international trade. Whereas the distinction between trade and trade-related matters is a strained one, the distinction between them and non-trade measures is *prima facie* apparent. Non-trade considerations partake of political, moral, cultural, ideological, environmental and technical character. More specifically, examples of non-trade considerations include human rights[53] and national security.
>
> At a theoretical level, one must note that the clarity in distinguishing between trade and non-trade measures holds only at a superficial level as, ultimately, all economic activity is functional serving a particular end. The internal dynamics of economic processes are determined by the expectations that accompany them. Thus, the expectation of a certain degree of technical safety, health and environmental requirements may be rendered as integral to economic processes. Furthermore, some trade or trade-related measures or omissions may contain elements of both non-trade and trade characteristics. In such case, they may be found in either category. The element determining the characterization will depend on the persuasiveness of the case as well as the perceiver's standpoint.[54]

Qureshi's views indicate how WTO Members use trade regulation as a policy tool to achieve not only economic ends but also social factors as a means of changing the conditions governing the international economic order with respect to goods and services.

2.5 The Economic and Social Rights Divide in a Globalised World

The advent of the trade debate in the nineteenth century that eventually culminated in the establishment of the WTO was seen mostly as an economic issue. However, with globalisation and increase in trade among countries of different economic

---

[52] For full consideration of social trade regulation, see Schefer Krista (2010).

[53] This invariably includes labour rights.

[54] Qureshi Asif (1998), pp. 159 and 166.

levels, the debate has come to include, as mentioned above, a wide range of issues, notably social issues. This is attributed in part to the expanded scope of trade agreements since they are not only limited to reducing tariffs, finding ways of integrating developing and least developing countries into the multilateral trading system, but also include the rise in the importance of issues such as the environment and labour/human rights.

Whilst the multilateral system has tended to shy away from the inclusion of social policy considerations in the global system of trade, the inclusion of labour considerations in regional trade agreements has become a common feature, a trend that is certain to continue. The relevance of this development is the availability of evidence indicating that trade agreements can play a role by focusing attention on the inclusion of labour issues and social issues as a whole through the encouragement given to trading partners to enforce existing laws and further reform their laws to ensure that globalisation and respect for the core labour standards complement each other.

Research conducted by the World Bank indicates that countries that respect democratic rights (including freedom of association) encourages microeconomic reforms, and these are likely to lead to enhanced efficiency and economic growth.[55] The situation in some countries that have put in place adequate social institutions has been able to reap greater benefits from economic openness, and the evidence also points to their weathering storms such as financial crises.[56]

2.5.1 *Social Policy and Trade Policy*

Although the interaction between trade policy and social policy appears to be relatively new, the interlinkage is much deeper than initially thought. It is becoming widely acknowledged that globalisation, with its emphasis on economic growth and development, has social dimensions that need to be addressed. The activities of anti-globalisation movements (which are noted for demonstrating during the WTO Ministerial Conferences, the G8 meetings, and the annual meetings of the IMF and the World Bank) have raised public awareness of the social implications of the policies pursued by national governments and international organisations.

Globalisation of the world economy has also raised awareness that the chances available to people and the nature of the welfare states are formed in some ways by the policies formulated by international institutions, agencies, and forums. That these institutions and the social policies they advocate are important and have

[55] Aidt and Tzannatos (2002), p. 15.

[56] The case of South Korea during and after the Asian financial crisis is case in point. The South Korean case is an example of the positive impacts of globalisation and financial crisis on industrial relations. See Kim and Kim(2003).

generated widespread attention is the new field of enquiry that has sprung up—'global social policy'. The activities of NGOs and other social movements have brought the attention of the world community to the role these organisations play in shaping economic and social developments globally. Further to this is how a number of financial crises that have occurred in the last decade have highlighted the extent to which national economies and the global economy are so intertwined. These crises, and especially the recent financial crisis, have raised to greater levels the role of the policies of institutions such as the World Bank and the IMF and how these policies have contributed both to these crises and, subsequently, in easing their social impacts.

This explains the apparent strong link between the economic role that international economic organisations such as the WTO, for example, plays and the labour legislation role that the ILO plays. The world has changed; globalisation has brought changes and transformed the world economy. The issue of the link between labour legislation and the economic situation that was raised during the founding of the ILO, which had previously not been seriously considered, is now brought to the fore. The issue of core labour standards has helped catapult that. There is an increasing talk that flexibility is the key to economic development, and this has made many countries adopt policies on deregulation of the labour market.

2.5.2 Globalisation and Social Protection

The questions that this raises is, given the challenge of globalisation of the world markets and the liberalisation of domestic markets, can the same degree of social protection still be provided as before? Or must labour regulation be changed in order to stimulate competitiveness and create jobs? These questions raise the issue of the economic/social divide. The work of the WTO and that of the ILO seem to converge at the crossroads of economic development and social equity. The significance of international labour law institutions on the economic/social divide will no doubt be given attention anytime the issue of core labour standards is raised at the international level.

The many arguments put forward by the proponents of the inclusion of a social clause in Article XX of the GATT have so far based their arguments on the economic implications of lack of adherence to labour standards. With the possible exception of child labour, hardly do they comment on the social welfare implications of their arguments on the countries to be targeted. The failure to treat economic and social efficiency as equal partners is a major issue, and unless this subject is addressed, the issue of labour standards and trade cannot be adequately tackled.

The confusion stems more from trying to achieve economic efficiency in the absence of social efficiency. What many policymakers tend to forget is that the two are inseparable. There is much discussion about economic processes but little on social processes. Little can be achieved economically if the social ills of economic policies are not adequately addressed. The ILO, in its Declaration, has stated that even though economic growth is a prerequisite for social progress, economic growth alone is not in itself enough to guarantee social progress. To achieve social progress would entail laying down a number of social ground rules founded on common values. This would enable all those involved in generating the economic growth to have their fair share of the wealth. The aim of the Declaration captures the very essence of the economic-social rights debate: "[T]o reconcile the desire to stimulate national efforts to ensure that social progress goes hand in hand with economic progress and the need to respect the diversity of circumstances, possibilities and preferences of individual countries."[57]

Many developing countries recognise the need to comply with the ILO labour standards, especially with respect to child labour. However, the existence of child labour and other forms of labour exploitation is seen as the unavoidable side effect of underdevelopment and poverty and no need for government intervention. Even though it is evident that poverty results in children being sent out to work due to sheer economic necessity, the role of national governments in developing social protection measures alongside economic policies goes a long way in addressing the social implications of economic growth.

2.5.3 The Relevance of International Cooperation

This is one area where international cooperation and action could contribute to the efforts of national governments in bridging the economic and social development gap. The continued cooperation of the WTO, ILO, and other international organisations involved in shaping economic and social policies will help address this serious issue. The examples of many countries that have been able to raise the living standards of their citizens and, in the process, reduce poverty show that government spending and regulation could, when properly designed, provide the thrust for economic growth and that markets and a combination of economic and social regulations could help promote social justice. Based on this, it is no wonder that given the nature of the issue, it clearly reveals how the imposition of sanctions advocated by some proponents is bound to have the opposite of the desired effect.

The experience of Bangladesh in 1993 is a case in point. For example, the threat of U.S. sanctions under the 1992 Child Labour Deterrence Act led the terrified owners of garment factories in Dhaka to dismiss all children below the age of 16. Anecdotal evidence suggests that many of these children met a fate worse than in the factories: ending up in workshops and factories not producing for export or as prostitutes and street vendors.[58] The emphasis on sanctions should not only be in terms of trade and the after-effects considered as social and left to governments of

---

[57] http://www.ilo.org/dyn/declaris/DECLARATIONWEB.ABOUTDECLARATIONHOME?var_language=EN. Accessed 15 October 2013.

[58] Elliot and Freeman (2003), p. 112.

the targeted countries to deal with, but rather the so-called social effects should be considered in the light of whether sanctions are appropriate in correcting what may be regarded as a "social ill".

The Asian financial crisis has shown that economic efficiency and social efficiency are bedfellows. For 30 years, the region enjoyed economic prosperity but paid little attention to social efficiency. When the crisis started in Thailand in July 1997, the IMF failed to take into account the social implications of its structural adjustment policies, which led to social upheavals. The recent financial crisis has also drawn the attention of policymakers to the importance of linking economic development to social policy.

These crises illustrate the degree to which the economies of nations are interconnected through trade, finance, and the social consequences of the crises at the national level. The world learnt a lesson during the Asian financial crisis that "social needs are not the frosting on the cake, but rather the raison d'être of economic processes".[59] The recent crisis would hopefully continue the debate in which forces at the local, national, and global levels intersect in shaping a global social policy agenda and lead to greater engagement of all parties in finding ways of increasing the social welfare of everyone. One major way forward is the use of trade instruments in addressing the issue of compliance with the core labour standards. The example of the regional trade agreements could provide the stepping stone to reach an agreement at the multilateral level in recognising that labour standards, globalisation, and economic development are mutually reinforcing.

2.5.4 The Regional Model

The labour provisions in RTAs, in linking social development and economic development, have created a model that could be applied at the international level. Such a model is important, especially when we consider the point that was made by the ILO Director General in 1999 in the run-up to the WTO Seattle Ministerial Conference (USA). The Director General argued that to promote open trade, the world's poor should not be overlooked. The problem in his view was that economic and social developments have not been treated as equal partners. He further stated that "Economic efficiency and social efficiency are inseparable. Social development cannot be safely dispensed with until such time as economic development has been achieved."[60]

The approach in the RTAs adds credence to the view that whereas enhanced trade seeks to promote economic development, adherence of CLS seeks to enhance social development, and it is by striking a careful balance between the two, such that one is not put above the other, that it would be possible for workers to realise

[59] Nelson Julie (1998).

[60] Somavia (1999).

the benefits of any trade agreement. What this demonstrates is the need for a framework that includes the CLS as part of global governance and global development.[61]

2.6 Globalisation, Labour Standards, and International Trade Debate

The advent of globalisation in recent times has brought out the international dimension of labour standards and labour rights. Silbey, in her narratives of globalisation, provides a summary of this dimension:

> Each story of globalization, like all narratives, is structured through an opposition of forces representing good and evil, human agency and historic fate, desire and the law ... As narrative accounts of the triumph of a central character against its enemies, the stories of globalization convey moral lessons. The stories of globalization not only describe how social relations are organized globally; they also construct ethical claims about the way the world should be organized and how social relations should be governed. Each globalization narrative reveals a particular construction of justice and its possibilities.[62]

Whilst we have discussed the legal and social/moral dimensions above, the section below highlights the economic dimension.

2.6.1 The Concept of Globalisation

Globalisation is one of the most talked about concepts of our age. It has evoked emotions and debates across a wide spectrum of the world's populace, from those in power to the common person on the street. For some, it is a force for good; for others, it is to be blamed for everything that has gone wrong with the established order. For example, former President Jacques Chirac of France is reported to have stated that globalisation has not made life better for those most in need.[63] For many, globalisation has been pushed through without adequately considering the social dimension element. It appears rather to them that only the economic aspect of globalisation is on the minds of policymakers. But what exactly is globalisation?

Globalisation as a process appears to be surrounded by confusion as to what it really means. The literature provides a plethora of definitions, but the one definition that seems to expand on the other definitions is the one put forward by the former president of the Ford Foundation, Susan Berresford:

---

[61] Sengenberger (2005), p. 121.

[62] Silbey Susan (1997), p. 211.

[63] Stiglitz (2002), p. 5.

> The term [globalization] reflects a more comprehensive level of interaction than has occurred in the past, suggesting something different from the word 'international.' It implies a diminishing importance of national borders and the strengthening of identities that stretch beyond those rooted in a particular region or country.[64]

According to Mittelman, this definition captures key features of globalisation, cross-border flows, identities, and social relations, but it is ambiguous about the nature of social relations and silent about hierarchies of power.[65] Globalisation is not a new phenomenon; its origin lies many centuries back, when people from different parts of the world came into contact through conquests, trade, and migration; the world started becoming a global village. Today, the world is much smaller than it was at the onset of globalisation. The present form of globalisation has benefited many. It has promoted freer trade, opened societies, encouraged freer exchange of ideas and knowledge. It has made innovation, creativity, and entrepreneurship flourish. In some areas, for example in Southeast Asia, economic growth has benefited millions of people by lifting them out of poverty.

2.6.2 The Impact of Globalisation

The spread of information at a fast rate has made the plight of the world's disadvantaged known globally, as for example the plight of the tsunami victims in Southeast Asia. This has resulted in greater awareness of events in other parts of the world, which has resulted in enhancing social awareness; encouraged the development of social movements; and strengthened the fight for a democratic world. Satellite television coverage of the conditions of the world's poor and underprivileged has contributed to emergence of a global conscience, making people sensitive to the problems faced by people in other parts of the world. Fighting for the elimination of child labour, environmental degradation, and gender discrimination is unhindered by distance.[66]

Why then has globalisation that has created opportunities and benefited many become a topical issue? Foremost, it might appear as if there is something fundamentally wrong with globalisation. In spite of the tremendous growth in the last decade, there are still differing levels of development. The emphasis has been more on economic globalisation, which has progressed because of technological advancement and most especially through the policies of trade liberalisation. Trade liberalisation has contributed to the rapid economic development of economies such as South Korea, China, and India, just to mention a few. But what have

---

[64] Quoted in Mittelman (2000), p. 5.

[65] Mittelman (2000), p. 5.

[66] A Fair Globalisation: Creating opportunities for all, World Commission on the Social Dimension of Globalisation, 2004 ILO publications International Labour Office: Geneva, p. 3.

stayed local are the political and social institutions, which should go hand in hand with economic globalisation.

Globalisation of the economy suggests a global economic management, but existing international institutions were designed to coordinate a system of nation-states in which each state was meant to be sovereign over its own domestic economy.[67] What in effect has happened is that the global economy tends to be moving at a fast rate, with the flows of capital becoming increasingly globalised and mobile, and this has invariably impacted the other factor of production—labour, which has remained static. Capital and labour are the two main primary factors of production that fall within the linkage debate. In real terms, although labour is the most vulnerable in the globalised world, it is capital that is the most protected.

Ensuring global economic stability appears to have taken centre stage, as governments rush to stimulate growth through the use of trade, monetary, and fiscal policies. The International Monetary Fund (IMF), charged with preventing a global depression, wields great power over developing countries, formulating policies (especially urging developing countries in recession to reduce their deficits) for developing countries (which policies the developed worlds, the powers behind the IMF, would not prescribe for themselves),[68] policies that have been imposed with disastrous effects—high unemployment; poverty, invariably leading to child labour; and the very issues raised by the proponents of a linkage between labour standards and trade.

The ILO, on the other hand, established to ensure social justice for workers, has limited legal powers to enforce compliance with CLS. What in effect is happening is that one international institution imposes policies that sometimes lead to the problems associated with labour standards, and the other international organisation called upon to remedy the situation is given little or no power. We have argued above that in the globalisation process, the emphasis has been more on the economic aspect, making the other aspect—social—suffer as a result of it being subsumed under economic policy, which does not always favour labour policies. We now turn to the impact of globalisation on labour and the labour market.

2.6.3 Globalisation and the Labour Market

Globalisation, with its emphasis on the economic aspects, has many other dimensions—economic globalisation of the world economy, rapid growth in world trade, long-term direct foreign investment by multinationals, and cross-border financial

[67] Mittelman (2000), p. 44.

[68] Stiglitz states that at the urging of the United States of America, the IMF imposed policies on developing countries with grave consequences, but when it came to imposing the same policies on Europe and Japan—"whose growth had an enormous impact on our exports and thus on our growth—we weren't so convinced." Stiglitz (2003), p. 49.

flows, including short-term portfolio capital flows. It also involves the migration of people, both legal and illegal. But it is the effect of globalisation on labour, entailing the migration of jobs from developed to developing countries, wage inequality, and, most of all, a race to the bottom in labour standards worldwide, that we would analyse.

Globalisation of the world economy, with the ongoing debate on the implications of freer trade inasmuch as it has been welcomed as a panacea for the integration of the economies of the world, has also brought in its wake a significant level of apprehension over the implications of a globalised world on employment and wages, especially in developed countries. In developing countries today, globalisation is seen as a force for good, which will lift their economies from poverty. The World Economic Forum (WEF) carried out an extensive poll on global public opinion on globalisation with over 18,000 urban respondents in 19 countries. According to the poll, support for globalisation was especially high in developing countries, with 55 % stating that economic globalisation is positive for them and their family. The WEF presented its findings at its annual meeting in New York in 2002.[69]

Bhagwati (2004) calls this change in attitude towards globalisation an "ironic reversal".[70] He argues that in the 1950s and 1960s, whilst developed countries were busy liberalising their trade, investments, and capital flows, notable figures in the developing world were strongly opposed. Bhagwati cites, as example, Brazilian sociologist Osvaldo Sunkel, who used the phrase "integration into the international economy leads to disintegration of the national economy". What has caused the change towards globalisation is the economic success of countries in the Far East, which has become an example for other developing countries to turn more towards globalisation to take advantage of the opportunities offered by international cooperation.[71]

2.6.4 The Anxiety Over Globalisation

Globalisation has set in motion far-reaching transformation of the world economy. As with any other economic transformation, globalisation has generated both losses and gains. Why then is there widespread anxiety in developed countries over the impact of globalisation on the labour market? Lee (1996) states that the losses are clearly visible than the gains since the losses are concentrated among particular groups of workers. The gains, on the other hand, are less noticeable since they are widely diffused. With the continued uncertainty over the future effects of globalisation and the real effects of job losses in developed countries, for example in the

---

[69] http://www.environicsinternational.com/global/press_inside.html. Accessed 10 January 2014.

[70] Bhagwati (2004), p. 8.

[71] Bhagwati (2004), p. 9.

United States of America, it is understandable why the issue of the correlation between labour standards and international trade has taken centre stage in recent years.

But it is the perceived fear of labour groups, most notably the labour unions in the USA, that has compounded the fear posed by globalisation. A case in point is the complaint filed by the American Federation of Labor and Congress of Industrial Organisations (AFL-CIO), the largest US labour federation, with the U.S. Trade Representative on 16 March 2004, asking the Bush administration to impose economic sanctions on China.[72] The AFL-CIO's 301 trade petition was rejected by the Bush administration first in 2004 and again in 2006.

In the industrialised countries, the view that labour market regulations and the welfare state are key causes of the rise and persistence of unemployment has become increasingly influential. They are seen as reducing the incentives for workers to seek work and for employers to create jobs. This has led to policy change, deregulation of the labour market, and a cutback in the welfare state in search of more flexible labour markets. A clear example is the neoliberal views of the Thatcher/Major governments in the UK from 1979 to 1997, a period that saw the deregulation of the British labour market.

These views have also spread to many developing countries, for example, since the late 1970s in China, the mid-1980s in Latin America, and 1991 in India. There has been a remarkable shift towards market deregulation and economic policy liberalisation with its attendant effects on the labour market. This trend is also seen in structural adjustment programmes prescribed by the World Bank for developing and least developing countries.

---

[72] http://www.aflcio.org/issuespolitics/globaleconomy/ExecSummary301.cfm (accessed on 20 February 2014). The AFL-CIO filed a Section 301 petition charging that the Chinese government persistently and systematically denies workers' rights, hurting U.S. workers and communities, whilst also preventing Chinese workers from exercising their internationally recognised rights at the workplace. Under Section 301 of the U.S. Trade Act, this egregious repression of workers' rights is considered an unfair trade practice, and the President has the authority to impose trade sanctions or take other actions to induce the Chinese government to cease its violation of the rights of its own workers. Section 301 of the Trade Act of 1974 (as amended) authorises the President to impose trade sanctions and take any other action within his constitutional powers against countries that impose "burdens" on U.S. commerce by (a) violating trade agreements or (b) engaging in other "unreasonable trade practices". Section 301 explicitly identifies several "unreasonable trade practices". One "unreasonable trade practice" is a country's persistent failure to enforce any of the following "internationally recognized worker rights": (1) workers' freedom of association, (2) rights of organising and collective bargaining, (3) freedom from forced or compulsory labor, (4) freedom from child labor, and (5) standards of minimum wages, maximum hours, and occupational safety and health. Congress enacted the worker-rights provisions of Section 301 for the explicit purpose of ensuring that U.S. workers do not face unfair competition from workers overseas whose basic rights are violated, rectifying those violations and preventing U.S. corporations from moving jobs offshore to exploit those workers. Congress believed that economic development based on sweatshop production benefited overseas elites and global corporations but not the majority of people at home or abroad. The AFL-CIO's previous petition, filed 2 years ago, was the first to invoke the *worker-rights* provisions of Section 301.

2.7 Issues in the Labour Standards and International Trade Debate

Given the range of opinions on the pros and cons of international labour standards and the international trade linkage, we will now review some of the key questions raised.

Starting from the 1990s, globalisation brought developed country consumers cheap products, clothing, and electronics. Even as more manufacturing jobs were moved out of industrialised countries, especially America, the country created high-paying jobs, mostly in the service sector. The number of jobs created did offset the jobs lost in the manufacturing sector, which led to a fall in unemployment. A new era in the American economy had ushered in. Even though real wages did not increase, high growth and increasing productivity all led to increase in profit. With low interest rates and increase in profits, it meant a thriving stock market—in effect, the economy was booming.

Globalisation had brought prosperity to America and its multiplier effect on the world economy from the 1990s to the first quarter of the start of the millennium. Then a bust followed. First was the crash in technology stocks. The American economy, for the first time in a decade, went into recession from July 1990 till March 1991.[73] Within a year, the economy lost two million jobs. The unemployment rate jumped from 3.8 to 6.0 %, and some 1.3 million more Americans moved below the poverty level.[74] As the economy was forcing its way out of recession, the worst corporate scandals hit America and affected many major financial institutions, which also led to job losses. This downturn did not only affect the American economy but also affected much of the world. For many, the promised benefits of globalisation had not been realised. In such situations, the fear that globalisation will result in the loss of jobs leads to anxiety.[75]

And it is against this backdrop that this section will review four sources of anxiety about the effects of globalisation, most importantly the fact that it has a bearing on the ongoing debate of the linkage between labour standards and international trade. It should be borne in mind that the globalisation of the world economy has also led to anxieties on the part of developing countries (critics of the linkage between labour standards and international trade). The issues could be summarised as follows: that trade liberalisation could lead to job losses and rising wage inequality and the fear that globalisation could lead to a loss of their national autonomy and make their governments ineffective. The anxieties are namely

[73] The National Bureau of Economic Research (NBER) made a determination that the 8-month period between July 1990 and March 1991 was a recession. See http://www.nber.org/March91.html. Accessed on 3 March 2014.

[74] Stiglitz (2003), pp. 3–7.

[75] The impact of the recent financial crisis on the debate is discussed below.

- the apprehension in developed countries that globalisation will result in competition from developing countries, which will cause a rise in unemployment and a fall in relative wages among unskilled workers;
- the fear of jobs migrating from developed to developing countries;
- the fear that weak labour standards provide an illegitimate boost to competitiveness in favour of countries that do not adhere to the core labour standards;
- the apprehension in developed countries that the increasing flow of foreign direct investment to low-wage countries would mean the export of jobs from high-wage countries to low-wage countries and the anxiety that it would lead to a race to the bottom with respect to labour standards and wages.[76]

We will examine each of these views in turn. It should be noted that it is the perceived anxieties of the proponents that have rather fuelled the ongoing discussion. In the examination, we also build in the counterarguments of the critics of the linkage between labour standards and international trade.

2.7.1 Labour Standards and Wage Inequality in Developed Countries

There is the fear in the developed world that increased competition from developing countries in the form of imports from countries with a lower cost of production will lead to loss of manufacturing jobs, especially in labour-intensive sectors. The recent rise in unemployment in developed countries, for example in the Eurozone as a whole, has advanced the view that has developed from the factor price equalisation theorem (FPE), also known as Heckscher–Ohlin theorem. According to this theorem, when a developed country imports labour-intensive goods from a low-wage country, the relative price of labour-intensive goods and the relative wage of low-skilled workers would fall.

We could illustrate by comparing two nations A and B. Nation A is a low-wage country, which specialises in labour-intensive goods, and Nation B is a high-wage country specialising in capital-intensive goods. If Nation B imports more of the labour-intensive goods from Nation A, the relative price of the labour-intensive goods in Nation B falls, which, in turn, causes a fall in the demand for labour relative to the demand for capital. Workers in the labour-intensive sector in Nation B are forced to accept a downward adjustment in their wages; otherwise, there would be a rise in unemployment.[77]

The FPE theorem is based on assumptions that do not always hold in the real-world situation, but those assumptions are not analysed here. It is this fear among low-skilled workers that has caused labour unions in developed countries to

[76] Lee (1996), p. 486.

[77] Samuelson (1948), pp. 163–184.

generally favour trade restrictions. Even though the factor price equalisation theory states that international trade causes real wages and real income of labour to fall in capital-intensive countries such as the United States, would it not be in the interest of the U.S. to restrict trade? The answer is in the negative. This is because the loss that trade causes to labour is less that the gain received by owners of capital. So if there is an appropriate redistribution policy of taxes on owners of capital and subsidies to labour, both factors of production would benefit from international trade. The argument here is that it is not the perceived threat of "cheap" imports from low-wage countries that could cause the lowering of wages in developed countries.

The case for complying with internationally established labour standards also rests, in part, on the view that trade with low-wage countries has slowed the growth in, or even lowered, the wages of unskilled workers in industrialised countries over the past three decades. To the extent that low wages in developing countries are the result of poorly protected core labour rights, trade based on low wages is seen to be illegitimate. Bound and Johnson (1992) conducted studies to determine the source of the wage decline.[78] They decomposed the wage change for each skill category between technological efficiency, industry demand, factor supply, and allocation of employment across industries.

They argued whether the wage shifts attributed to technological change might not, in fact, be due to the influence of international factors. Others also argue that skill-biased technological change would drive up the demand for skill within each sector.[79] However, if the demand for skill is driven by international trade or defence spending, we should observe a shift in demand for skill between sectors of the economy. The evidence from the studies appears to support the view that technological change rather than international trade is the driving force behind the increased demand for non-production workers. In fact, the role of trade appears to be close to zero since most of the between sector shifts in employment were due to defence spending. Similar results were found for other countries other than the United States.[80]

The concern regarding the impact of trade on labour in industrialised countries seems to be theoretically supported by the Stolper–Samuelson theorem, which holds that when trade is conducted with an unskilled-labour-abundant country, the price of unskilled-labour-intensive goods will decline domestically. Factors of production leave the unskilled-labour-intensive sector and are re-employed in the skilled-labour-intensive sectors. As production of skilled-labour-intensive goods rises, an excess demand for skilled labour emerges. The labour market resolves the imbalance by raising the relative wage paid to skilled workers, as compared to unskilled workers. 'Firms' economy-wide response to the change in relative factor

[78] Bound and Johnson (1992). For a critical analysis of the studies, see also Brown (2000), pp. 14–15.

[79] Brown (2000).

[80] Brown (2000).

prices is by adopting a more unskilled-labour-intensive technique of production. Therefore, the tell-tale sign that trade with unskilled-labour-abundant countries is lowering domestic wages is that the ratio of skilled to unskilled workers should fall across all industries of the economy.[81]

Lawrence and Slaughter (1993)[82] found that just the opposite occurred in the U.S. economy throughout the 1980s. U.S. manufacturing firms consistently substituted toward skilled labour in spite of its rising cost. Such a pattern of behaviour by firms is only cost minimising if there has been a technological change rendering skilled labour relatively more productive. Similar patterns were witnessed in Japan and Germany. Furthermore, there does not appear to be any decline in the relative price of unskilled-labour-intensive production. Therefore, both links key to the connection between trade and factor prices appear to be missing. However, Brown (2000) argues that the growing wage inequality in developing countries is also instructive. Recent evidence finds increased wage dispersion in countries such as Chile, Columbia, Costa Rica, Mexico, and Uruguay. If Stolper-Samuelson type mechanics were at work, then we should have observed the opposite. Developing countries that export unskilled-labour-intensive goods should experience a convergence in the relative wage of skilled and unskilled workers rather than growing inequality. The fact that relative wages in developing countries follows trends in industrialised countries lends further evidence to the hypothesis that skill-biased technical change is the driving force behind changes in the relative wages rather than international trade.[83]

It is worthy to note here that the greater portion of manufacturing in developed countries is skill- and innovation-intensive industries (e.g., the development and manufacturing of heavy machinery) that are not under threat of relocation to low-wage countries. These industries in developed countries tend to have a competitive advantage for which factors as quality of the labour force, quality of the infrastructure, access to high technologies, manufacturing and services environment play to these countries' advantage. Irrespective of the trade with low-income countries that might affect the labour-intensive industries in developed countries, it would be incorrect to conclude that the same experience would befall the capital-intensive industries in the industrialised world.

Hepple argues that empirical evidence for these perceived threats to high-labour-standard countries is remarkably weak. The balance of evidence seems to suggest that trade and investment flows are only minor factors in the rise in unemployment and wage inequality in the industrialised countries and that the benefits from increased exports of skill-intensive goods and services outweigh the disadvantages of liberal trading regimes. Although developing countries have a comparative advantage as far as labour costs are concerned, high labour standards are conducive to high levels of labour productivity and hence long-term competitive advantage.

---

[81] Brown (2000).

[82] Brown (2000).

[83] Addo (2002), pp. 289–290.

Hepple further argues that the paradox is that free trade regimes tend to inhibit the ability of states to support selected industries or to pursue redistributive social policies at a time when, as a result of globalisation, there is a greater need than ever before to help displaced workers acquire new skills and to reduce inequality and exclusion.[84]

2.7.2 Trade and Employment and the Issue of Jobs Migration

One of the issues that are also a source of apprehension for the proponents of a social clause is that of job migration. The argument has been raised that the movement of jobs to developing countries does not alter the overall level of employment in developed countries, even though the pattern of employment changes.[85] With the recent loss of jobs in the service sector, the issue of jobs migration has taken on a different connotation on the political front. Workers in manufacturing had long known that they were exposed to foreign competition. But the new forces of competition have made strides in the service sector, which has caused the loss of jobs in developed countries. Why this has created concern is that the service sector in any advanced country constitutes a greater part of that country's economy. A case in point is that of the United States of America.

2.7.3 Outsourcing and the American Experience

It is a well-known fact that the purpose of economic activity is to increase the well-being of individuals, and the economic structures that are able to do so are more desirable. In recent years, the American economy has lost a number of jobs, and there is the call to halt this trend and put in place structures that would create jobs. So it is no wonder that the comments of N. Greg Mankiw, the former chief economic adviser of U.S. President George W. Bush, in his testimony to Congress in February 2004 sparked furore on both sides of the political aisle when he stated that America should seize the opportunity if a product or a service could be produced more cheaply overseas than in America, since it was to America's advantage to source cheap goods and services from overseas.[86]

What Greg Mankiw was in fact advocating was the theory of comparative advantage, first put forward by David Ricardo. The Democrats, joined by the then Republican Speaker of the U.S. House of Representatives, rebuked Mankiw for

---

[84] Hepple (1997), p. 356.

[85] See *The Economist* (2004), p. 11.

[86] *The Economist* (2004), 'Special report: Outsourcing', November 11. Mr Mankiw gave the example of radiologists in India analysing the x-rays sent via the internet.

giving the green light to American jobs going overseas. Mankiw's testimony came not too long in the heels of the signing of a bill by President Bush forbidding the outsourcing of federal contracts overseas.[87] It is also no wonder that Mankiw did not receive the full support of the Bush White House.

The issue of perceived job losses as a result of offshore outsourcing has been exaggerated since it is more of a political issue than an economic issue. The question that is raised here is whether the trend of outsourcing will lead to the loss of jobs and/or drive down real wages. The answer to this question is important since a response in the affirmative might cause public opinion in the USA to shift in the direction of the proponents of a linkage between labour standards and international trade. According to Drezner (2004), reviewers attempt to draw a link between offshore outsourcing and unemployment. In his opinion, the belief that offshore outsourcing leads to unemployment in the U.S. is the economic equivalent of believing that the sun rather revolves around the earth.[88]

The evidence indicates that the actual and prospective migration of jobs, especially in the service sector, is small, compared with the level of job creation. According to Drezner, although there was a loss of 70,000 computer programmer jobs between 1999 and 2003, more than 115,000 computer software engineers found higher paying job during the same period. Also, he stated that Delta Airlines outsourced 1,000 call centre jobs to India in 2003. Delta, as a result, saved $25 million, which it used in adding 1,200 reservation and sales positions in the United States. Drezner further argues that U.S. companies are able to save money, become more profitable, benefit shareholders, and increase investment on returns. The McKinsey Global Institute estimates that the US brings in between $1.12 and 1.14 for every dollar spent on outsourcing to India.[89] Although it cannot be denied that there has been a greater number of manufacturing jobs lost compared to the service sector, it has more to do with technological advancement rather than outsourcing.

A study of global manufacturing trends from 1995 to 2002 indicates that the U.S. saw an 11 % decrease in manufacturing jobs, which should have translated into increases in manufacturing jobs for its trading partners. However, the same study showed a 15 % decrease and also a 20 % decrease in manufacturing jobs in China and Brazil, respectively. The overall figure for loss of manufacturing jobs was equal to the U.S. figure of 11 %. This is in spite of the fact that global manufacturing output increased by 30 % for the period 1995 to 2002. This confirms the fact that it is technology and not trade that is the main cause of manufacturing job losses.[90]

In the field of technology, proximity of personnel to the customer is important, and this will continue to keep many service-sector jobs close to the customer. It is a

---

[87] This is the first federal law against outsourcing passed by the U.S. Senate barring doling out subcontracts to India and other countries by American companies to cut costs.

[88] Drezner (2004), p. 23.

[89] Drezner (2004), p. 30.

[90] Drezner (2004), p. 27.

fact that a lot of services are being supplied from overseas. For example, a firm in Ghana processes New York City traffic fines, and customers have had their calls for computer problems answered by technicians working in India. Bhagwati gives the example of old folks in a retirement home in New York who carry beepers on which they are reminded by someone in India to take their medicines: "Mrs. Stein, it is time for your Mevacor."[91] But it is not all kinds of services that can be supplied from abroad. There are some customers whose knowledge of computers is limited that the troubleshooter's efforts at helping them will not achieve much. A technician will have to be sent to help them out.

Drezner states that about 90 % of service jobs demand proximity and that the evidence does not support the view that jobs in the high-value-added sector are migrating. His view is supported by an analysis conducted by a United States firm on trends in IT services that service jobs outsourced are normally those requiring low skill and that "innovation and deep business expertise will continue to be delivered predominantly onshore".[92] And these are the jobs that bring in higher wages and huge profits for U.S. firms and help drive the economy. The evidence indicates that even though some jobs would be lost to outsourcing, others will be created onshore, which demand skills and are higher paid. The evidence also shows that trade protection will not save such jobs, which will be lost to automation if they do not go overseas'. Although it is generally believed that the U.S. imports large amounts of services from developing countries, the evidence again indicates otherwise; its surplus in services in 2002 was US$64.8 billion,[93] and in June 2009, the surplus was US$11.4 billion.[94]

2.7.4 Labour Standards and Developing Country Competitiveness

Brown opines that the flip side of the race-to-the-bottom argument is that imposing labour standards on the operations of foreign firms will not alter relative competitiveness either. Even if developed countries are successful in imposing labour standards internationally, foreign firms still can only afford to pay workers their marginal value product. Therefore, a rise in benefits must be matched by a fall in money wages. However, the worker, as a consequence, may be worse off because he is no longer receiving the benefits-money wage mix that is most desirable, but the costs of the firm remain.

For a similar reason, the concern of developing countries that the imposition of labour standards will erode their comparative advantage is somewhat off the mark.

[91] Bhagwati (2004), p. 21.

[92] Drezner (2004), p. 26.

[93] Drezner (2004), p. 30.

[94] See http://www.census.gov/indicator/www/ustrade.html. Accessed 15 March 2014.

It is commonly argued that developing countries' comparative advantage lies in low wages. Any demand that raises labour costs will deny developing countries their right to exploit their comparative advantage in international trade. Developing countries have low wages because of low productivity. The comparative advantage derives from a relative abundance of low-skilled labour. Brown concludes that imposing labour standards on developing countries will not necessarily raise the cost of labour. It will simply require labour in developing countries to divert some of their money and wage benefits, which may make workers worse off.

A recent study has tested the relationship between labour standards and competitiveness for a sample of developing countries. The study concluded that "core labour standards" do not play a significant role in shaping trade performance. The OECD paper (1996) concluded that "[t]he view which argues that low-standards countries will enjoy gains in export market shares to the detriment of high-standards countries appears to lack solid empirical support . . ." These findings also imply that any fear on the part of developing countries that core standards would negatively affect either their economic performance or their competitive position on world markets has no economic rationale. On the contrary, it is conceivable that the observance of core standards would strengthen the long-term economic performance of all countries.[95]

According to Maskus, international economists have long claimed that the linkages between varying international standards for labour protection and international trade policy, both in theoretical and empirical terms, are tenuous.[96] It seems, therefore, that the issue is being given more attention than it deserves. It also looks as if protectionism is hidden behind the apparent laudable motives. In that context, even if the economic case for a linkage between trade policies is weak, the political case may be overwhelming in the absence of alternative mechanisms for improving labour standards around the world.

2.7.5 *Labour Standards and Foreign Direct Investment Flows: Is There a 'Race to the Bottom'?*

The other area of apprehension is the effect that the increasing flows of foreign direct investment (FDI) to low-wage countries have on the workers in developed countries. There has been a steady increase in the flow of foreign direct investment in the last two decades to developing countries. The fear is that companies are attracted to economies with lower costs. The impact of this development is seen as being similar under the FPE theory whereby goods are increasingly imported from low-wage countries. What happens in this case is that low-skilled jobs are, as a

[95] OECD (1996) study on Trade, Employment and Labour Standards, p. 105.

[96] Maskus (1997), p. 1.

result, sent abroad to low-wage countries through the relocation of companies that, in turn, leads to a fall in demand for low-skilled workers in industrialised countries.

There is the fear that in the absence of international pressure to make countries enforce the core labour standards, it may lead to a "prisoner's dilemma" situation whereby if the other countries do not cooperate, it results in a competitive lowering of labour standards in all countries. Prisoners' dilemmas involve a strategic decision in circumstances where the reward to each party depends on the reward to others and the choice of each depends on the choice of others (Box 2.1). According to Lee (1997), the basic mechanism through which this is expected to happen is the pressure to cut costs of production in search of higher export shares and fight off import competition. This is reinforced by the competition for foreign investment, whereby the lowering of labour standards is believed to attract potential investors. So long as some trading nations resort to such behaviour, the remaining countries wishing to preserve higher labour standards are negatively affected. They are placed at a competitive disadvantage if they do not follow suit.[97]

Box 2.1: The Story of the Prisoners' Dilemma

Two prisoners are known to be guilty of a very serious crime, but there is not enough evidence to convict them. There is, however, sufficient evidence to convict them of a minor crime. The prosecutor separates the two and tells each that they will be given the option to confess if they wish to do so. If both of them confess, they will be convicted of the major crime on each other's evidence, but in view of the good behaviour shown in squealing, the District Attorney will ask for a penalty of 10 years each rather than the full penalty of 20 years. If neither confesses, each will be convicted only of the minor crime and get 2 years. If one confesses and the other does not, then the one who does not confess will go free and the other will go to prison for 20 years... What should the prisoners do? ... Each prisoner sees that it is definitely in his interest to confess no matter what the other does. If the other confesses, then by confessing himself this prisoner reduces his own sentence from 20 years to 10. If the other does not confess, then by confessing he himself goes free rather than getting a 2-year sentence. So each prisoner feels that no matter what the other does, it is always better for him to confess. So both of them confess guided by rational self-interest, and each goes to prison for 10 years. If, however, neither had confessed, both would have been in prison for only 2 years each. Rational choice would seem to cost each person 8 additional years in prison (Sen 1986).

The question that the FDI debate raises is whether due to competition among low-wage countries labour standards are intentionally lowered to attract foreign investment, thereby putting pressure on other governments to follow suit.

[97] Lee (1997), p. 181.

In response to the question raised above, two factors should be noted. First is to empirically determine the trend in government policy on labour standards as a whole. Second is the role that labour standards play in influencing FDI location. There are two lines of argument that tends to support the factors outlined above. With respect to the first factor, one could argue that foreign investors favour countries with weak labour standards. This being that weak labour standards means lower labour costs. This argument could hold on the ground that a government's refusal to grant basic freedom of association and collective bargaining rights could lead to lower labour costs. Concerning the second factor, it could also be argued that foreign investors prefer to locate their investment where labour costs are lower.[98] We will take these two factors in turn.

First, is there evidence that governments in low-labour-standard countries purposely lower their labour standards as a means of attracting FDI? Research conducted by the OECD on freedom of association rights in 75 countries, countries that together account for virtually all world trade and in inward and outward FDI, is useful in determining this factor. The data collected were valuable in identifying the relationship between labour standards and competition for FDI. The data did not reveal any significant drop in freedom of association rights in any of the 75 countries since the early 1980s (a period that saw heated competition to attract FDI). The research also revealed considerable progress in those rights in 17 countries.[99]

The other study conducted by Dani Rodrik suggests that there is no statistically significant relationship between a country's observance of core labour standards and its trade performance. Neither do weak labour standards encourage foreign direct investment by companies seeking to exploit workers.[100]

Second, the OECD study on the relationship between countries' level of enforcement of core labour standards and their trade competitiveness concluded that "empirical findings confirm ... that core labour standards do not play a significant role in shaping trade performance".[101] What the study revealed was that there is no empirical support for the view that countries with low standards will enjoy an increase in their export market share and thus attract FDI.

The OECD study also noted that the evidence did not support the view that a lowering of core labour standards would lead to a lowering of low unit costs. Kucera (2002b) argues that the evidence, on the other hand, indicates that higher core labour standards could lead to more rapid economic growth and that this is supported by several studies, with evidence that economic growth attracts FDI. It is interesting to note that from a survey conducted with several managers of transnational corporations and international experts on location criteria in order of importance out of 13 FDI location criteria, the two highest ranked criteria were growth of

---

[98] Kucera (2002a), p. 34.

[99] Oman (2000), pp. 97–99.

[100] Rodrik (1997). Quoted by Fischer (1999).

[101] OECD (1996) study on *Trade, Employment and Labour Standards*, quoted in Oman, p. 102.

market and size of the market. Cost of labour was ranked number nine.[102] What this implies is that the argument by the proponents of a linkage is, in this respect, not supported by empirical evidence since even if governments in low-wage countries artificially lower wages and standards in an attempt to attract FDI, they would rather deter FDI. This would not lead to the so-called race to the bottom.

Box 2.2: Links Between Trade and CLS: The Findings of Recent Empirical Studies

Recent empirical studies investigated the links between fundamental CLS and trade. An OECD survey revealed that low-standards countries do not enjoy better export performance than high standards countries. No evidence was found that freedom of association worsened in the countries that liberalized trade, or that these rights impeded subsequent trade liberalisation. The strongest result suggested that that there is "a positive association between successfully sustained trade reforms and improvements in core standards" and the observance of worker rights "may work as an incentive to raise productivity through investment in human and physical capital". On average, countries that improved rights of freedom of association experienced an increase in GDP from 3.8 per cent to 4.3 per cent, and manufacturing output growth from 2.4 per cent to 3.6 per cent within five years of implementing the change (OECD 1996). CLS reduce adverse effects during the transition to liberalized trade and may ease the adjustment arising from liberalisation. Countries where core labour standards are not respected continue to receive a very small share of global investment flows; they do not provide a haven for foreign firms. Investors increasingly seek locations with highly skilled labour. Some studies found a negative relationship between non-core standards and trade performance; fears about a "race to the bottom" are "probably exaggerated"; opinions continue to differ about the impact of trade on employment patterns and wage inequality. An econometric study of a sample of 100 countries in the period 1980 to 1999 found little support for any step in the following chain of reasoning: (1) countries refuse to ratify ILO Conventions so that (2) they can degrade labour conditions in order to (3) reduce labour costs in order to (4) raise exports and (5) attract FDI seeking cheap labour (Flanagan 2002). An ILO study on the impact of core CLS on labour costs and foreign direct investment in 127 countries found "no solid evidence in support of the conventional wisdom that foreign investors favour countries with lower labour standards, with all the evidence of statistical significance pointing in the opposite direction". The value of this study results from the use of newly constructed indicators of labour rights covering freedom of association and collective bargaining, child labour, forced labour and gender equality. Instead

(continued)

[102] Kucera (2002a), pp. 35–36.

Box 2.2 (continued)
of labour legislation the indicators focused on worker rights in practice. For example, in respect of freedom of association an index of the incidence and severity of violations of this right was used in the study (Kucera 2001, 2002b). In the mid-1990s, a survey of several hundred managers of transnational corporations and international experts around the world assessed the criteria for the destination of FDI according to their importance. The growth and size of the market in the host countries and profitability ranked top, closely followed by the political and social stability of the country, quality of labour supply, the legal and regulatory environment, quality of the physical infrastructure and of producer and commercial services. The search for lower labour costs was not among the most important motives. Ranking and scores of criteria used by investors for locating FDI:

Rank	Criterion	Source of importance
1	Growth of market	4.2
2	Size of market	4.1
3	Profit perspectives	4.0
4	Political and social stability	3.3
5	Quality of labour	3.0
6	Legal and regulatory environment	3.0
7	Quality of infrastructure	2.9
8	Manufacturing and services environment	2.9
9	Cost of labour	2.4
10	Access to technologies	2.3
11	Fear of protectionism	2.2
12	Access to financial resources	2.0
13	Access to raw materials	2.0

Source: Sengenberger (2005)

2.8 The Role of Trade

Trade can play an important role and is an engine of economic growth. Empirical evidence suggests that international trade can contribute to the generation of resources and development gains that can assist in the achievement of the Millennium Development Goals (MDGs). Trade is therefore inextricably linked with the MDGs. Trade, trade negotiations, and trade liberalisation can contribute to the MDGs by bringing about development gains.

These gains relate to export revenues and improved terms of trade; GDP growth and new investment; improvement of production and diversification, including through domestic value addition; job creation; increased incomes and their equitable distribution; poverty reduction; access to essential services like health and education; access to essential goods like cheap and affordable medicines to treat pandemics; increased food security; transfer of technology and skills development, and enhanced capacity of government to take measures to promote social economic development. The pursuit of the MDGs in turn creates the capacity to take advantage of trade opportunities.

Trade can provide potential developmental benefits. The development contribution that trade can make is enormous, but that depends on the capacity of especially developing countries to effectively participate in the global trading system. In addition, trade generates much needed investment and technology transfer in developing countries and stimulates increased productivity in their domestic industries. The impact would be felt more in the improvement of the viability commodity sector, which is a major factor in achieving the MDGs.

In the area of trade negotiations, the World Bank estimates that reducing the barriers in the agricultural sector would increase global income by as much as US$400 billion by 2015 and that a 50 % reduction in barriers to service trade would result in gains four times larger than gains from liberalisation of non-service trade.[103] A recent report by the Peterson Institute estimates that a 10 % reduction in service barriers by developed countries would increase global exports by at least US$56 billion a year and GDP by US$100 billion.[104] Stern, Deardoff, and Brown also estimate that reducing barriers to trade in agriculture, manufacturing, and services by a third could increase global income by US$686 billion, whilst doing away with all trade barriers could increase global income by as much as US$2.1 trillion dollars.[105] In a recent study by the International Food Policy Research Institute (IFPRI), the paper points out that failure to conclude the WTO Doha Development Round would prevent a US$336 billion increase in world trade that would have come from a reduction in tariffs and domestic support.[106]

Goal 8 of the MDGs includes a commitment to an open, equitable, predictable, and rule-based multilateral trading system as among the means to promoting development and eradicating poverty. To achieve this, there should be continued focus on the integration of development considerations into the principles and workings of the international trading system and, more significantly, into the multilateral negotiations under the WTO on trade rights and obligations. The particular needs of least developed countries (LDCs), landlocked and transit developing countries, Small Island Developing States, and countries lagging far behind

[103] World Bank (2002, 2004a). See also speech delivered by the former Director-General, Supachai Panitchpakdi, to the World Summit on Sustainable Development entitled "Trade and Sustainable Development: The Doha Development Agenda", in Johannesburg on 3 September 2002 quoting the World Bank report, at http://www.wto.org/english/news_e/spsp_e/spsp01_e.htm. Accessed 9 March 2014.

[104] Lamont (2009), p. 4.

[105] Multilateral, Regional, and Bilateral Trade-Policy Options for the US and Japan, 2002: http://www.fordschool.umich.edu/rsie/workingpapers/Papers476-500/r490.pdf. See further, Brown et al. (2002).

[106] Bouët and Laborde (2008).

in the achievement of the MDGs have to be given appropriate attention by the international community. The international measures need to be supported by national development strategies, policies, and plans that emphasise the role of trade in development. In this process, it is important to note that development is not a one-size-fits-all process and MDGs strategies have to be adapted to specific national and regional conditions and institutional settings. Trade liberalisation, for example, needs to be calibrated, paced, and sequenced in a manner by each country according to its trade, development, and financial needs and capacities.

As poverty appears to be the major factor in the non-adherence to core labour standards, the elimination of poverty could lead to an increase in the compliance with ILO Conventions. Instead of using the multilateral trading system that is supposed to dismantle economic barriers as a tool to impose sanctions, it would be reasonable to use that system to ensure greater participation of countries with low labour standards. Anderson (1996) states the example of the progress of social policy in the European Union (EU). He argues that the EU refrained from imposing sanctions on Members with low standards but rather adopted some minimum standards and mutual recognition. "Yet standards have risen rapidly with the acceleration of income growth in poorer EU countries." The EU, no doubt, realised the practical difficulties associated with enforcing its high standards on the acceding countries.[107] With increased trade, poorer Members have significantly improved their standards. In the same vein, elimination of trade barriers in developed countries could boost growth in developing countries.

It is in light of this that former President of the United States Bill Clinton, speaking at the World Economic Forum, Davos, Switzerland, in January 2000, stated: "We have to reaffirm unambiguously that open markets are the best engine we know of to lift living standards and build shared prosperity." The Clinton administration put these words into action when it sent a Trade Bill to the House of Representatives, which was decisively passed. The legislation grants more extensive trade privileges, including duty-free access to the American market for a significant number of products originating in African and other poorer countries.[108] Clearly, this is precisely what these poor countries need, if they will ever be able to comply with Conventions on core labour standards.

Dollar and Kraag have thrown more light on the effects of growth on the poor. They argue that policy-induced growth is as good for the poor as it is for the overall economy. That openness to foreign trade benefits the poor to the same extent that it benefits the whole economy. In fact, growth helps raise the incomes of the poor by as much as it raises the incomes of everybody else. They concluded that "... what we do learn is that growth generally does benefit the poor and that anyone who cares about the poor should favor the growth-enhancing policies of good rule of law, fiscal discipline, and openness to international trade".[109]

---

[107] Anderson (1996), p. 455.

[108] *New York Times*, May 5, 2000, p. A1.

[109] Dollar and Kraag (2000).

Bearing in mind that to sustain reductions in poverty would require continuous economic growth, the question is how an agreement as envisaged under the Doha Development Agenda (DDA) might improve trade, economic growth, and, conversely, adherence to core labour standards.

The WTO Doha Ministerial Declaration of November 2001 aims at ensuring that developing countries gain from the first development-oriented multilateral trade negotiation since the establishment of the WTO in 1995. The Doha Ministerial Declaration states:

> International trade can play a major role in the promotion of economic development and the alleviation of poverty. We recognize the need for all our peoples to benefit from the increased opportunities and welfare gains that the multilateral trading system generates. The majority of WTO Members are developing countries. We seek to place their needs and interests at the heart of the Work Programme adopted in this Declaration. Recalling the Preamble to the Marrakesh Agreement, we shall continue to make positive efforts designed to ensure that developing countries, and especially the least-developed among them, secure a share in the growth of world trade commensurate with the needs of their economic development. In this context, enhanced market access, balanced rules, and well-targeted, sustainably financed technical assistance and capacity-building programmes have important roles to play.
>
> We recognize the particular vulnerability of the least-developed countries and the special structural difficulties they face in the global economy. We are committed to addressing the marginalization of least-developed countries in international trade and to improving their effective participation in the multilateral trading system. We recall the commitments made by Ministers at our meetings in Marrakesh, Singapore and Geneva, and by the international community at the Third UN Conference on Least-Developed Countries in Brussels, to help least-developed countries secure beneficial and meaningful integration into the multilateral trading system and the global economy. We are determined that the WTO will play its part in building effectively on these commitments under the Work Programme we are establishing.[110]

Although progress on the Doha Development Agenda has been slow, the Doha Round of trade negotiations, as foreseen by the international community, is meant to integrate developing countries into the multilateral trading system and help them gain from increased trade. What the Doha Round intends to achieve was captured well by former U.S. President George W. Bush in a speech at the United Nations in 2004, when he stated: "The United States is ready to eliminate all tariffs, subsidies and other barriers to the free flow of goods and services as other nations do the same." Should the negotiations reach a successful conclusion, it holds the promise of raising the living standards of many people presently living in poor conditions, thereby considerably reducing poverty, addressing the inequity in the multilateral trade regime, and in so doing enhances international stability.[111]

The importance of the words of President Bush is seen from the assistance the developed and other developing countries give their farmers, which have negative

---

[110] Doha Ministerial Declaration of 2001. See http://www.wto.org/english/thewto_e/minist_e/min01_e/mindecl_e.htm. Accessed 10 April 2014.

[111] Hills (2005).

impact on the economies of many countries in Africa. For example, in 2005, the OECD country members spent about US$300 billion on agricultural subsidies. This is estimated to be about three times the total aid provided by developed to developing countries. This has led to some estimating the trade loss to African countries of about US$500 billion as a result of the subsidies given by developed countries to their farmers. The most noted example is the amount of money apparently spent by the European Union under its Common Agricultural Policy (CAP) on each cow within the Union—US$2.50 a day in subsidies. This is more that the amount of money that many poor people live on per day.

But it is not only the countries in the developed world that distort world trade. China is estimated to be providing US$1.5 billion annually to its cotton farmers, and Brazil, Egypt, India, Mexico, and Turkey together reportedly provided their cotton farmers between 2001 and 2002 approximately US$0.6 billion in each of that year.

The impact of these subsidies is felt by many countries, especially in Africa, where an increase in the living standards could move many people out of poverty and in so doing help achieve a high degree of compliance with the core labour standards. The case of the four West African cotton producing countries—Benin, Burkina Faso, Chad, and Mali is an example of such negative impact. These four countries are estimated to be losing about US$1 billion a year as a result of the cotton subsidies that are given to developed country cotton farmers. In the case of Mali, a third of its population depends on the income from cotton. Mali loses almost 2 % of its GDP and about 8 % of its export earnings.[112]

2.8.1 Trade and Poverty Reduction

In spite of the positive impacts of trade on poverty reduction, increased trade is not an end but rather a means to development. There appears not to be an automatic link between trade and poverty reduction, but as noted above, trade can contribute to poverty alleviation when the increased trading leading to increased incomes and increased government revenue is invested in social and productive activities that enhance the capabilities of people. Winters has noted: "Tracing the links between trade and poverty is going to be a detailed and frustrating task, for much of what one wishes to know is just unknown. It will also become obvious that most of the links are very case specific."[113]

Mandle (2003), also acknowledging the difficulty of assessing the direct relationship between globalisation and poverty reduction, states that the role of globalisation in reducing poverty could only be inferred by conducting a cross-sectional analysis by comparing the poverty levels in the more advanced countries with the levels in the developing countries. Having conducted his cross-sectional analysis,

[112] Moyo (2009), pp. 115–116.

[113] Winters (2000), p. 43.

Mandle concluded that "[t]o the extent that the cross section portrays what happens over time, it indicates that globalisation contributes to development and that, together, development and the integration of global markets have a substantial impact on poverty reduction".[114] However, making trade work positively for a country would entail making the trading regime serve broader development and social goals.

Considering the share of world trade, which represents about 23 % of global economic activity, begs the question if the successful conclusion of the Doha Development Round would have a far-reaching impact on poverty reduction. Also, considering the fact that many of the poor people in the world are not linked to their national economies, since they operate on a subsistence basis, let alone at the global level, makes it difficult to determine the impact of the Doha Round on their living standards. Hertel and Winters argue that "a poverty reduction of 100 million worldwide, even if it is just a fraction of global poverty, is very significant".[115]

Hertel and Winters further state that developing countries can only gain from a successful completion of the Doha Development Agenda when they pursue complementary domestic reforms. Reforms such as improving infrastructure, reform domestic market institutions, etc. will enable households to take advantage of the market opportunities that the Doha Round will make available.

The examples of the economic development of the East Asia countries (so-called Asian Tigers) China and India show how these countries were able to combine the trading opportunities offered by the multilateral system with domestic strategies in the areas of investment and institution building. These reforms helped in stimulating domestic entrepreneurship. These countries have been able to lift millions of their people out of poverty. In the case of Malaysia and Thailand, for example, the incidence of poverty was reduced from almost 50 % during the 1960s to below 20 % by the end of the twentieth century.[116]

However, achieving a development agenda would entail the need to shift from a multilateral system based solely on a market access perspective to one based on a development perspective. This shift would help create a more development-friendly multilateral trade environment, making countries use trade as a means for their development. This development mindset would ensure that the development of an MDG trading system is responsive to key human development issues by focusing on poverty alleviation, fighting pandemic diseases such as HIV/AIDS, ensuring the provision of basic social services essential to the poor and thereby propel issues such as the environment and labour standards to the fore.

Achieving an MDG-friendly multilateral trading system is much dependent on global trade politics. The nature of trade has shown how politically motivated the decisions of government are in influencing the commitments that they make at the

[114] Mandle (2003), pp. 21–23.
[115] Hertel Thomas and Winters Alan (2005), pp. 1069–1070.
[116] Stiglitz Joseph and Charlton (2005), p. 15.

negotiations. As the global financial crisis continues to loom, and unemployment continues to rise, and the room for more fiscal and monetary policymaking are exhausted, governments will come under increasing pressure to use trade barriers to address the economic problems. This is a clear indication of how difficult it is to conclude the Doha Round of trade negotiations. The politicised nature of trade relations has a great impact on labour standards and trade debate as a deal that will increase world trade is good for the global economy and achievement of social justice.

2.8.2 Changing Landscape of Trade Relations

World trade relations that were traditionally a North–South relationship have witnessed a change in the way trade is conducted. The winds of change have been blowing world trade since the last decade more in the direction of South–South trade. In 1995, South–South exports accounted for 11 % of world trade. By 2006, South–South export had increased to 17 % of world exports. Whereas there has been a tremendous increase in economic activity among South–South countries, it is the booming trade between Africa and Asia, in particular trade between Africa, China, and India, that has attracted a lot of attention. Asia is at the moment the main destination for Africa's South–South export.[117]

Since the 1990s, Africa's exports to Asia and its imports from Asia have shown a great increase compared to its imports and exports from other regions of the world. With the increasing trade between Africa and Asia, in particular with China vis-à-vis Africa's trade with Western countries, the influence of the Asian countries on policy in Africa will, in the near future, overtake that of Western countries. And this has implications for the labour standards and trade debate for the greater is the percentage of trade with a particular country or region, the greater is the influence on the setting of policy.

2.8.2.1 South–South Trade Relations

According to UNCTAD (2008),[118] exports from South–South trade have shown an increase at a much faster pace than exports from developed countries to the South. Between 1995 and 2005, exports from developed countries to the South increased by 140 %, whereas during the same period, exports from South to South increased by almost 200 %. From the period 1991 to 2001, South–South trade as a percentage of world trade increased from 6.5 to 10.7 %. In 2005, the figure increased to 18 %, and this represents an increase from US$222 billion in 1995 to US$562 billion in

[117] Ratna (2009).

[118] UNCTAD (2008).

2004. The UNCTAD report also indicates that Africa recorded the highest growth of exports to the South, a 277 % increase, whilst exports to the rest of the world increased by 179 %.

UNCTAD states that in 2011, South–South merchandise exports reached US$4 trillion. It further stated that between 2008 and 2009, the South exported more to other developing countries than to the North. Also, in 2011, South–South exports accounted for about 15 % of global exports compared to 13 % in 2001. What is even significant is that all developing countries have increased their exports in the past two decades.[119]

Whereas there has been a tremendous increase in economic activity among South–South countries, it is the booming trade between Africa and Asia, in particular trade between Africa, China, and India, that has attracted a lot of attention. Asia is at the moment the major destination for Africa's South–South export. Since the 1990s, Africa's exports to Asia and its imports from Asia have shown a great increase compared to its imports and exports from other regions of the world. Africa's exports between 1990 and 1995 grew annually by 15 %, and between 2000 and 2005 it grew by 20 %. Africa's imports from Asia grew by 13 % annually between 1990 and 1995 and by 18 % between 2000 and 2005. European Union (EU) exports to Africa during 2000 and 2005 fell by about half, putting Asia at par with the EU and the United States, the so-called traditional trading partners of Africa.

China's two-way trade with Africa from 2002 to 2003 doubled to US$18.5 billion and by 2007 had reached US$73 billion, becoming the second-largest trading partner of Africa after the United States (US$85 billion) and ahead of France and Britain. Africa's export to China has, between 2000 and 2005, increased at an annual rate of 48 %.[120] On the other hand, the two-way trade between Africa and India in 2007 was about US$25 billion. Africa's trade with both China and India shows about three times as fast as the rate of Africa's exports to the United States and about five times as fast as the rate of Africa's exports to the EU during the period 2000–2005. China and India as at 2008 bought 10 and 3 %, respectively, of all Africa's exports.

According to *the Economist* magazine, China as at the first quarter of 2013 was Africa's major business partner, with trade exceeding US$166 billion, with minerals accounting for about 80 % of Chinese imports from Africa. *The Economist* also reported that China's direct investment in Africa exceeded US$14.7 billion, an increase of 60 % from 2009, with another Chinese official stating that "China's investment in Africa of various kinds exceeds $40 billion".[121]

Although the figures tend to be small, it is the rate at which it is increasing that puts Africa's trade relations with both countries in the spotlight. As at 2012, India

[119] UNCTAD (2013).

[120] Hanson (2008).

[121] *The Economist* (2013b), p. 35.

firms' trade deals with African countries was about a third of that of Chinese firms but is estimated to rise to 50 %.[122]

Whilst China's and India's trade was initially concentrated in a few commodities, in particular oil, minerals, precious stones, metals, and alloys, there has been a change in recent years. With the increase in the middle class in China and India, the two countries are importing from Africa more than fuels, minerals, and metal products. Their imports at the moment include commodities like cotton, food products, and household consumer goods. Broadman (2007) argues that since the exports from China and India to Africa exceed their imports from Africa, the apparent imbalance exposes Africa to some trade risks. The goods from China and India tend to compete with African domestic goods. He further argues that given that China and India are beginning to import capital goods, the competitiveness of Africa's manufacturing sector is being bolstered.

Africa has, in the last decade, witnessed a rapid increase in foreign direct investment (FDI) from Asia, in particular from China. The flow of FDI from China to Africa in 2005, for example, was US$1.3 billion, whilst FDI inflow from India in 2004 was US$1.8 billion. During the period 2001–2006, China invested US$6.6 billion in Africa.[123] The two countries' investment was initially concentrated in a few countries and sectors, but investment has spread to other countries and many other sectors. The countries that received the highest FDI inflows were Nigeria, Sudan, and Zambia, mostly in the oil and extractive industries. However, FDI inflows have started to reach other industries, such as agro-processing, power generation, apparel, road construction, tourism, and telecommunications. The FDI has also spread to other countries such as Congo, Democratic Republic of Congo, Ethiopia, Kenya, South Africa, Senegal, Madagascar, Mauritius, United Republic of Tanzania, just to name a few. Investment in Africa is not only limited to China and India. Malaysia, South Korea, Taiwan, Singapore, and Pakistan are also among the Asian countries that are also investing in Africa. However, China and India are the two emerging leaders of foreign direct investment flows into Africa.

The interest shown by the Asian countries, notably China, India, and Japan, in Africa is evidenced by the initiation of the Forum on China–Africa Cooperation (the Forum) in 2000 and the Beijing summit of the Forum in November 2009. This was followed by a summit of African leaders in New Delhi in April 2008. In May 2008, Japan held its fourth Tokyo International Conference on African Development (TICAD), and in June 2013 it held its fifth conference.[124]

China has organised five Forums on China–African Cooperation with the recent one held in July 2012. The Forum on China–African Cooperation (FOCAC) started in 2000. The Beijing summits have been well attended by African heads of state and, since the first meeting, have marked a turning point in Sino–Africa relations.

---

[122] *The Economist* (2013a), p. 35.

[123] See www.ChinaView.cn. Accessed 22 March 2014.

[124] See http://www.ticad.net/. Accessed 18 June 2014.

During the third summit in 2006, the Chinese President announced eight measures designed to forge a new phase in China's strategic partnership and thereby strengthen its relations with Africa. The measures are meant to boost Africa's economic development. Among the measures are the provision of US$3 billion of preferential loans and US$2 billion of preferential buyers' credits to Africa between 2006 and 2009; the doubling of assistance by 2009; the setup of a China–Africa fund that is expected to reach US$5 billion to encourage Chinese companies to invest in Africa; the cancellation of debt in the form of all interest-free government loans; the further opening of the Chinese market to items of export interest to Africa from 190 to 440; the number of items receiving zero-tariff treatment; the training of about 15,000 African professionals; and the increase in the number of scholarships from 2,000 to 4,000 per year by 2009. During the second visit of the Chinese President to Africa after the 2006 summit, the President stated that China will "fully and punctually" implement the eight measures it announced in 2006.[125]

India, in what could be seen as a growing sign of its economic muscle during the first India–Africa summit attended by 14 African heads of state, promised to offer US$5 billion in credit and hundreds of millions of dollars in financial help to Africa. The Prime Minister further stated that India would provide US$500 million in grants for development in Africa. Even though trade between India and Africa is lower than the trade volume between Africa and China, the value of bilateral trade leaped from US$5.3 billion in 2001 to US$12 billion in 2005 and then to US$63 billion in 2011. The trade volume is expected to increase to US$176 billion by 2015.[126]

India's new-found interest in Africa is also evidenced by the duty-free access to most goods from least developed countries, of which 34 are in Africa. India has, over the past 5 years, extended concessionary credits to African countries to the tune of US$2.5 billion, and that is expected to increase to about US$5.4 billion by 2009. India is also planning a US$10 billion investment fund for Africa. In a growing sign of its partnership with Africa, India has also pledged to double the number of scholarships given to students from Africa from about 4,000 to 8,000 annually.[127]

Asia's interest in Africa could be summed up in the words of Japanese Prime Minister Fukuda, speaking at the TICAD summit in Tokyo in May 2008, who stated that "Africa is poised for a century of growth and could become a powerful engine driving the growth of the world". In an effort to boost its economic ties with Africa, the Japanese Prime Minister announced that Japan intends to double its official development assistance to Africa over the next 5 years. According to the Organisation for Economic Cooperation and Development (OECD), Japan gave out US$2.7 billion to sub-Saharan Africa in 2006. The Prime Minister further stated

---

[125] See www.ChinaView.cn. Accessed 22 March 2014.

[126] Confederation of Indian Industries (CII) and World Trade Organisation (WTO) (2013).

[127] *The Economist* (2008b), pp. 64–65 and http://un.org/ecosocdev/geninfo/afrec/vol22no2/222-japan-summit.html. Accessed 24 March 2014.

that part of the increase in Japan's aid over the next 5 years will be in the form of soft loans, totalling US$4 billion, for infrastructure development projects. As part of its assistance, Japan would double it grants and technical assistance, which will include the training of 100,000 African health workers over the next 5 years and the improvement of access to water.[128]

It is beyond doubt that trade with Asian countries, especially China, is having a profound impact on Africa. The rate of growth has increased with positive impact on poverty reduction. According to the World Bank, the percentage of Africans living on US$1.25 a day or less dropped from 59 to 51 % from 1996 to 2005 and has since further decreased.[129] As mentioned above, the flow of investment has been substantial and in large part was tied to development finance for Africa. What is happening in Africa is a sign of a global economy undergoing a radical change, a fundamental change in the global economic order, with China playing a central role, but for Africa this is highly significant.

In 2006, the OECD reported that foreign direct investment in Africa reached US$48 billion, and in 2008, the figure rose to US$88 billion. For the first time since 2006, foreign direct investment overtook foreign aid to the continent, and the gap between increased foreign direct investment and foreign aid tends to widen: a reflection of quadrupling of foreign direct investment since 2000. With the changing political and economic conditions in Africa, the International Monetary Fund (IMF) has put Africa's average annual growth rate for the period 2013–2014 at more than 5.5 %, an annual growth rate that appears to be better than the economic situations of any developed country economy.[130] This is in line with the prediction by the IMF that Africa will be in a position to weather the global recession and even grow at about 3.3 % in 2009.[131]

2.8.2.2 The Impact of South–South Trade Relations on the Linkage Issue

The presence of China in Africa should be seen within the context of China's central foreign policy. The guiding principle is officially termed as "non-interference in domestic affairs". Consequently, China's presence in Africa is based more on commercial considerations than on political considerations. China has always held the view that any attempt by other countries to link democracy and human rights to economic partnerships tends to violate the rights of sovereign states. African countries have, with open arms, accepted China's economic assistance and trade with no strings attached, as opposed to Western aid, which is tied to

---

[128] http://un.org/ecosocdev/geninfo/afrec/vol22no2/222-japan-summit.html. Accessed 24 March 2014.

[129] See *Time* (2009), p. 38.

[130] IMF (2013).

[131] *Time* (2009), p. 38.

good governance, human rights, and—for the purposes of this thesis—core labour standards. The Chinese approach of building a long-term relationship with Africa, whilst serving its own economic interest, has also opened up opportunities for a number of African countries that a decade ago was unthinkable.

China's sudden global reach, particularly in Africa (the so-called last frontier), even though has contributed to economic prosperity, is generating much anxiety in the Western world. Even some nongovernmental organisations are worried that Chinese companies in their quest to secure resources will ignore basic legal, environmental, and core labour standards. There is also the fear that since there is often no clear distinction between public and private ownership of Chinese companies, the Chinese government intervenes unfairly on behalf of its companies by offering aid to countries that welcome Chinese investment. This, is feared, could lead to Chinese companies being granted all the lucrative contracts, thereby denting the profits of big Western oil and mining companies and imperilling the access of the West to much-needed natural resources.

This has made many Western diplomats and pundits fear that the West is losing Africa and other developing countries. Inherent in this also is the fear that rather than following the Western view of economic liberalism and democracy, these countries would, to a certain extent, follow the "Beijing consensus" of state-led development and despotism.[132] In the view of the diplomats and pundits, China's sudden prominence will, to a great extent, reduce the clout of America and Europe in Africa. The fear is that countries such as China will through their economic ties and encourage ostracised regimes to defy the international community and international norms.

The situation in some African and other countries lend support to the fears of the diplomats and pundits. For example, the investment by China in Sudanese oil fields and support at the Security Council has empowered Sudan to defy the international community in the Darfur region. The massive investment of China in Angola made Angola in 2006 decide that it had no need of the IMF's assistance with all the tiresome requirements of transparency and sound economic management. Although these concerns are well founded, when analysed within the wider economic and social context, China's presence in Africa has both positive and negative effects.

Positive Impacts

The recipient countries of Chinese assistance, increased trade, and investments have witnessed economic growth rates in a continent once identified by its hardships. For instance, Africa registered a growth rate of 5.8 % in 2007, mainly because of Chinese investment. According to Hanson, experts acknowledge that the roads, dams, and bridges built by Chinese firms in Africa are at a lower cost of

[132] *The Economist* (2008a), p. 4.

good quality and are completed in a shorter period of time compared to the time needed by other companies.[133]

China, as a partner in Africa, provides a different model to Africa than the European and American models. China has, in the last decade, brought many of its people out of poverty than the population of sub-Saharan Africa. It is recommended here that Africa follow not the Chinese political model of no freedom of expression or democracy but the economic model of raising the living standards of its people. The investments being made by the Chinese in Africa has helped give African countries a voice: the ability to play strategic and economic diplomacy much better than in the past and improve their negotiating powers in their relations with Europe, America, and the multilateral agencies. This new-found model could be useful in relations with the West and in getting the best option—through increased Chinese investment, improved Western donor assistance, or, at best, a combination of both.

The increasing trade between Africa, China, and India tends to counter the 50 years of European and American trade and aid, which many argue has not helped Africa come out its woes. The approach of the Chinese and Indians could yield better results and lift Africa out of its economic woes and also help encourage other trading partners and donors to seek other efficient means of investing in Africa.

Negative Impacts

On the other hand, the non-interference policy could turn out to be bad for Africa should African countries turn away from undertaking the needed political and economic reforms. Furthermore, China in Africa could undermine efforts at the local level to improve good governance and also the efforts of the international community at bringing about macroeconomic reform.

To ensure that African leaders take advantage of India's and China's trade with Africa would be by pursuing bold reforms (both economic and social) that would serve Africa's self-interest. Should Africa and other developing countries successfully take advantage of their new-found investment and trade interests, by enacting reforms of their market institutions, investment regulations, infrastructure, and overhaul of their tariff structures, they could continue to reduce poverty, help move more people into the middle class, and thereby be in a position to adhere to the core labour standards. If, as the critics of the linkage between labour standards and trade posit, poverty is a major cause of lack of adherence, then Asia in Africa should be seen in a positive light for Asia's involvement with Africa has and could continue to offer a more promising future for the continent and its attendant effects on labour relations.

---

[133] Hanson (2008), p. 4.

2.9 The Financial Crisis and Labour Relations

The world economy during the latter part of 2008 and the first quarter of 2009 has witnessed a dramatic decline in investment, world trade, manufacturing output, consumption on a scale not seen since the Great Depression of 1930.[134] The economic crisis started as a mortgage crisis in the U.S. in the latter part of 2007 and had, by the beginning of 2008, taken on the form of a worldwide crisis unprecedented in recent economic history. The global economic crisis has led to unparalleled job losses and its attendant social effects across both the developed and developing worlds.

The ILO reports that in 2008, global unemployment increased by about 14 million, and in terms of the future, the organisation's prognosis points to a bleak outlook.[135] The OECD states that among its member countries, more than seven million persons became unemployed during the first quarters of 2008 and 2009.[136] In July 2009, the U.S. Labor Department reported an unemployment rate of 9.5 %, the highest level in the past 26 years.[137] The situation in countries such as Spain (loss of 766,000 jobs) and Republic of Korea (loss of 1.2 million jobs) and the rapid increase in job losses in Russia, Sweden, and Turkey indicate the toll that the global economic crisis is having on employment rates.[138]

The crisis that was initially thought to be a problem affecting only developed countries has touched every country in the world. For a period of time, there was the view that there was a decoupling—that since the crisis started in the United States, the economies of Europe and, especially, developing countries would be left intact. The situation in Europe and many developing countries indicates otherwise. Even countries in the developing world that had succeeded to some extent in managing their economies well by putting in place sound monetary policies and regulatory frameworks have fallen victim to the financial crisis.

South Africa (the biggest economy in Africa till 2013[139]), after enjoying on average a 5 % growth between 2003 and 2007, and having expanded its economy by about 3.1 % in 2008, is in 2009 expected to see a shrink in its economy by around 2 %.[140] Although total unemployment increased only marginally in the last quarter

---

[134] The Great Depression was the worldwide economic crisis that started in the United State and was marked by widespread unemployment, near halts in industrial production and construction, and an 89 % decline in stock prices. On 29 October 1929, what started as a stock market crash, the so-called Black Tuesday, led to the fall of the Dow Jones Industrial Average by almost 23 % and the loss of between $8 and $9 billion in value.

[135] www.ilo.org/trends.

[136] OECD (2009).

[137] New York Times (2009).

[138] For an overview of job losses, see ILO (2009a) (Hereinafter, ILO Global Trends 2009).

[139] On 6 April 2014, the BBC announced that Nigeria has overtaken South Africa as the biggest economy in Africa. See http://www.bbc.com/news/business-26913497. Accessed 17 June 2014.

[140] *The Economist* (2009b).

of 2008, 39,000 jobs were lost in the mining, manufacturing, and financial service sectors. During this period, the number of those unemployed was at 21.3 %, but even more disturbing is the number of discouraged people seeking employment, which stood at over one million, an increase of 9.1 %, by the last quarter of 2008.[141] In China, with an economy heavily dependent on exports, the fall in global aggregate demand has had a great impact leading to the loss of 20 million migrant jobs.[142] Across the developing world, countries have been affected in different ways. For example, countries that export labour such as India, Pakistan, the Philippines, Ecuador, El Salvador, and some East European countries have seen the return of thousands of migrant workers. The ILO reports that unemployment in Latin America moved up to 8.5 % in the first quarter of 2009 from an average of 7.5 % in 2008.[143]

2.9.1 Impact of the Crisis

The ILO states that in the worst case scenario, the crisis would lead to an increase in global unemployment and high poverty rates. It is expected that compared to 2007, in the last quarter of 2009 there would be an increase in global unemployment of more than 50 million and that about 200 million workers would move into extreme poverty.[144] The OECD estimates that the OECD area would experience a double-digit unemployment by the fourth quarter of 2010, about 10.1 %.[145]

Even more worrying for policymakers is that the world's economically active labour force of 3.3 billion in 2008 is increasing by about 45 million new entrants every year. Further to this are the millions of young people who leave school each year and will be entering a labour market that is not able to provide employment opportunities. This has far-reaching consequences as it might compromise the future employment prospects of the youth.

The financial crisis has also affected international trade flows, and it is even estimated that trade has contracted more in this crisis than it had at a comparable stage during the Great Depression.[146] According to the WTO, the collapse in global demand brought about by the crisis is certain to drive exports down by about 9 % in 2009. For developed countries, the contraction is expected to be severe with a fall in exports of roughly 10 %; for developing countries, more dependent on trade for growth, exports will shrink by about 2–3 %.[147]

---

[141] Statistics South Africa, 2009, Quarterly Labour Force Survey, at www.statssa.gov.za.

[142] LaFraniere (2009).

[143] ILO, Global Trends 2009.

[144] ILO, Global Trends 2009.

[145] OECD: Economic outlook, *Interim report*, March 2009.

[146] Eichengreen and Irwin (2009).

[147] http://www.wto.org/english/news_e/pres09_e/pr554_e.htm. Accessed 30 December 2013.

The World Bank analyses of data from 45 countries show an average fall in exports of 37 % compared to 2008, with 37 countries seeing declines in exports by more than 15 %. The data show a drop in exports across the world. For example, exports from Argentina in January 2009 were 36 % lower than in 2008, Canada 35 % lower, Chile 41 %, and Japan 35 %. This is due to the shortfall in global trade finance of US$100 billion, which accounts for about 90 % of world trade finance.[148]

The fall in global demand and world trade, which is the engine of economic growth, indicates the extent to which the crisis would impact on employment generation and, in turn, countries' compliance with the core labour standards. The fall in global demand is a reflection of the way the global supply chain is organised today, in contrast to the theory of comparative advantage posited by David Ricardo that countries specialise in products. Today, countries specialise in steps in the production process, in what economists term "vertical specialisation".[149] Whilst vertical specialisation has led to much faster growth in world trade and in turn spurred on economic growth, the decline in demand, the "oil which lubricated" this growth, is the same mechanism that has caused a slump in global trade flows.

In the wake of this slump is the fall in global output, which slowed to 1.7 % compared to 3.5 % in 2007. The WTO estimates that it is expected to fall by between 1 and 2 % in 2009, the first such decline in total world production since 1930, with its impact on world trade. The globalisation of the world economy has shown that even countries with dynamic economies such as China has not been able to insulate themselves from the global downturn. In the case of China, most of the countries it exports to are in recession and as such have weakened import demand for Chinese-produced goods (this, for example, accounts for the loss of the 20 million jobs mentioned above). With the continued weakened demand for some time, the prospects of those unemployed finding employment within this period look grim.

Coupled with this is the fall in world economic growth or GDP. For example, world economic growth in 2008 has been the slowest since 2001, below the 10-year average rate of 2.9 %. Trade in services, on the other hand, rose in spite of the crisis increasing by 11 % in 2008, amounting to US$3.7 trillion, and could be considered as resilient in comparison with trade in goods. Comparison of data between trade in goods and trade in services lends support to this view. For instance, in April 2009, America's imports of goods were 34 % lower than the same period in 2008 and exports were 27 % lower. But its imports and exports of services were down by only 10 %. America's imports of business, professional, and technical services were 4 % higher in the first quarter of 2009, more than that of the first quarter of 2008. The increase in trade in services appears to be worldwide with Africa's commercial services growing by 13 % in 2008 to US$88 billion and imports at 15 %, increasing to US$121 billion. In spite of the service sector being less affected as compared to

---

[148] World Bank data quoted in *The Economist* (2009a).

[149] Example of vertical specialisation is, for instance, the production of cars—the steel for the car may be sourced from India and stamped and pressed in Japan before the car is exported.

trade in goods, the sector alone cannot create enough jobs to accommodate the shortfall in jobs needed to provide employment for those who have lost their jobs and generate enough for the new entrants.

2.9.1.1 Remittances

Another consequence of the financial crisis is decrease in international transfers by migrant workers, also known as remittances. The monies sent are an important source of income, both at the family level and also at the national level. The World Bank estimates that remittances in 2008 totalled US$397 billion, of which US$305 went to developing countries. But the remittances in reality are larger since many migrants frequently send money through informal channels. The remittances are estimated to be from about 190 million migrants or 3 % of the world population. According to the World Bank, the flows of remittances have been on the rise for the past 5 years, rising at about 15–30 % per year. Due to the crisis, it is expected that there will be a decline in the total amount sent in 2009 of about 5 to even 8 % reduction.

However, the World Bank has reported that after a modest decline in 2009, there has been a steady increase in remittances. The figures for 2011 was US$351 billion, 2012 was US$377 billion, 2013 was US$404 billion, and the estimate for 2014 is US$436 billion and expected to rise to US$516 billion in 2016.[150]

The number one remittance-receiving country is India, which is estimated to have received about US$45 billion in 2008, followed by China and Mexico in third position with US$26 billion in transfers. Due to the high unemployment among migrants, it is predicted that remittances from the United States to Central and South America would fall by 7 %. This would mean that about a million households will not receive money in 2009 and about four million households will receive 10 % less. Even a 7 % decline in remittances to the region represents a loss of US$4.5 billion.[151]

The recent increase in remittances was important for the economies of many developing countries as other private financial flows into the developing world declined considerably. It is estimated that the net inflows of private capital to developing countries fell by nearly two-fifths, i.e. from US$1.6 trillion in 2007 to US$707 billion. The reduction in private investment, in addition to the decline in remittances, is a major setback for the economies of developing countries in terms of both economic growth and improving of living and labour conditions.

---

[150] World Bank (2004b).

[151] See World Bank figures, http://remittanceprices.worldbank.org/. Accessed 15 May 2014.

2.9.2 The Impact of the Crisis on Core Labour Standards Compliance

Failure to address the financial crisis, which appears will get worse before it gets better, will have a negative impact on achieving the MDGs, addressing the food security concerns, and could lead to social tensions and political unrests. The implications of the financial crisis takes on wider ramifications when analysed in light of the testimony of the United States Director of Intelligence, when he stated before a Senate Committee that "[t]he primary near-term security concern of the United States is the global economic crisis and its geopolitical implications. . . . the global financial crises have exacerbated what was already a growing set of political and economic uncertainties."[152] The grim assessment by the intelligence director indicates the impact that a prolonged financial crisis could have leading to much wider economic, social, and political crisis.

The history of labour relations indicates to a great extent that as economies grow, so too does respect for the rights of workers. In fact, the link between growth-enhancing policies and improved labour conditions also point to the link between globalisation and labour conditions. The extent to which a country opens its economy to freer trade and takes advantage of a globalised world economy enhances its growth rate and accordingly alters the labour conditions. In light of this, what is of grave concern is the impact of the crisis on efforts by governments to ensure that worker rights and the core labour standards are not lowered in the process of addressing the challenges.

We have argued earlier that the view by some countries that their lower level of labour standards compliance is an advantage is off the mark. This argument is further strengthened here that instead of viewing the financial crisis in isolation to the issue of adherence to the core labour standards, rather the observance of the core labour standards must be made part of the solution. Countries, by respecting the fundamental principles and rights at work, which is conducive to maintaining social justice and peace, would be placed in a much better position in addressing social tensions and political unrests.

Policymakers' willingness to maintain labour standards is a boost in stimulating the economy. Furthermore, the measures taken would help create an equitable environment, thus enabling vulnerable workers to deal with labour market risks and provide support for stimulus packages. Sometimes it's a crisis that forces change. The change that the crisis could usher in is that whereas a global stimulus package or a global effort is needed to address the world economy, the decision-making powers is at the national level. This is due to the fact that each country weighs the benefits to its own economy.

The globalised nature of the world economy, on the other hand, requires a coordinated approach. The world that emerges out of this crisis won't be the

[152] Blair Dennis (2009).

same for globalisation has created a web of interlinkages that a national approach based on the most benefit to a country and focusing only on national stimulus spending is not enough since there would be no spillovers for the benefit of other countries. Only an approach that has global impact would bring about the most benefit for all.[153]

In as much as the present financial crisis has created woes in terms of economic and social developments, it has also created an opportunity to address the disparity between the economic and social divide. It is an opportunity to put in place social protection mechanisms to ensure that each member of society enjoys a basic level of social security in terms of income and better conditions of living. The examples of the efforts by policymakers in creating the conditions for social dialogue, tripartism, and participation by all in the Republic of Korea (as discussed above) and Singapore (Box 2.3) in the aftermath of the Asian financial crisis point the way forward in meeting the challenges of the present financial crisis and in curving a way forward to address future crisis. The examples of these two countries indicate how significant social dialogue is as a key to developing strategies to redressing the financial crisis and securing the continued commitment of governments, employers, workers, and unions in buying into the strategies formulated and ensuring their successful implementation.[154]

Box 2.3: Labour Relations in Singapore (1997–1998)
Singapore: To counter the 1997–1998 financial crises, the government introduced new labour policies. In particular, as a result of a tripartite agreement, employers received financial incentives if they avoided layoffs. Tripartite institutions as well as ad hoc tripartite agreements were very effective in articulating conflicting interests between the three parties, resulting in more effective formulation and implementation of social and economic policies (ILO 2009b).

References

Addo, K. (2002). The correlation between labour standards and international trade – Which way forward? *Journal of World Trade, 36*(2).

Aidt, T., & Tzannatos, Z. (2002). *Unions and collective bargaining: Economic effects in a global environment*. Washington, DC: World Bank.

Anderson, K. (1996). The intrusion of environmental and labor standards into trade policy. In W. Martin & L. Winters (Eds.), *The Uruguay round and the developing countries*. New York: University of Cambridge.

Bartels, L. (2009). Social issues: Labour, environment and human rights. In S. Lester & B. Mercurio (Eds.), *Bilateral and regional trade agreements: Commentary and analysis*. Cambridge: Cambridge University Press.

[153] Stiglitz (2009).

[154] ILO (2009b), pp. 52–53.

Bhagwati, J. (1994). A view from Academia. In G. Schoepfle & K. Swinnerton (Eds.), *International Labor Standards and global integration: Proceedings of a symposium*. Washington, DC: US Department of Labor, Bureau of International Labor Affairs.

Bhagwati, J. (1997). Trade liberalisation and 'Fair Trade' demands: Addressing the environmental and labour standards issues. In J. Bhagwati & V. N. Balasubramanyan (Eds.), *Writings on international economics*. Delhi: Oxford University Press.

Bhagwati, J. (2004). *In defense of globalisation*. Oxford: Oxford University Press.

Bhagwati, J., et al. (1994). *Third world intellectuals and NGOs statement against linkage*. http://www.Columbia.edu/~jb38/. Accessed 10 Feb 2014.

Blair Dennis, C. (2009). *Testimony to the Senate Select Committee on Intelligence*, 12 February, http://www.dni.gov/testimonies/20090212_testimony.pdf. Accessed 15 Jan 2014.

Bouët, A., & Laborde, D. (2008, December). *The potential cost of a failed Doha Round* (IFPRI Issue Brief 56). http://www.ifpri.org/pubs/ib/ib56.pdf. Accessed 4 Apr 2014.

Bound, J., & Johnson, G. (1992). Changes in the structure of wages in the 1980's: An evaluation of alternative explanations. *American Economic Review, 82*(3).

Broadman, H. (2007). *Africa's Silk Road: China and India's new economic frontier*. Washington, DC: The World Bank.

Brown, D. (2000). *International trade and core labour standards: A survey of the recent literature* (OECD Labour Market and Social Policy Occasional Papers, No. 43). OECD Publishing.

Brown, D. K., Deardoff, A. V., & Stern, R. M. (2002). *Computational analysis of multilateral trade liberalisation in the Uruguay round and the Doha development round* (Discussion Paper 489).

Charnovitz, S. (1992). Environmental and labour standards in trade. *The World Economy, 15*.

Charnovitz, S. (1995). *Intereconomics, 30*.

Charnovitz, S. (1998). Linking topics in treaties. *University of Pennsylvania Journal of International Economic Law, 19*.

Charnovitz, S. (2002). *Trade law and global governance*. London: Cameron May.

Cleveland, S. (2003). Why International Labor Standards? In R. J. Flanagan & W. B. Gould (Eds.), *International Labour Standards: Globalization, trade and public policy*. Palo Alto: Stanford University Press.

Clinton, W. J. (1999). Remarks by the President to the International Labour Organisation Conference, June 16, Geneva. http://clinton2.nara.gov/WH/New/Europe-9906/html/Speeches/990616.html. Accessed 20 Dec 2013.

Condliffe, J. B. (1940). *The reconstruction of world trade* (p. 386).

Confederation of Indian Industries (CII) and World Trade Organisation (WTO). (2013). India–Africa: South–south trade and investment for development, Geneva. http://www.wto.org/english/tratop_e/devel_e/a4t_e/global_review13prog_e/india_africa_report.pdf. Accessed 23 Mar 2014.

Dollar, D., & Kraag, A. (2000). *Growth is good for the poor*. Washington, DC: The World Bank Development Research Group.

Drezner, D. (2004). The outsourcing Bogeyman. *Foreign Affairs, 83*(3).

Eichengreen, B., & Irwin, D. (2009, July). *The slide to protectionism in the great depression: Who succumbed and why?* (NBER Working Paper No. 15142).

Elliot, K. A., & Freeman, R. B. (2003). *Can labor standards improve under globalisation?* Washington, DC: Institute for International Economics.

Fischer, S. (1999). *Global markets and the global village in the 21st century: Are international organizations prepared for the challenge?* Speech delivered to the German Society for Foreign Affairs, November 19.

Flanagan, R. J. (2002). Labour standards and international competitive advantage. In R. J. Flanagan & W. B. Gould (Eds.), *International Labour Standards: Globalization, trade and public policy*. Palo Alto: Stanford University Press.

Friedman, L. M. (1996). Borders: On the emerging sociology of transnational law. *Stanford Journal of International Law, 32*.

Hanson, S. (2008). *China, Africa and Oil*. Council on Foreign Relations, 6 June 2008. http://www.cfr.org/publication/9557/. Accessed 29 Dec 2013.
Hepple, B. (1997). New approaches to International Labour Regulation. *Industrial Law Journal, 26*(4) (Special Issue).
Hertel Thomas, W., & Winters Alan, L. (2005). Estimating the poverty impacts of a prospective Doha development agenda. *The World Economy, 28*(8).
Hills, C. A. (2005). The stakes of Doha. *Foreign Affairs* (WTO Special Edition), December.
ILO. (1998a). *Consideration of a possible Declaration of principles of the International Labour Organization concerning fundamental rights and its appropriate follow-up mechanism*. Report VII, ILC, 86th Session, Geneva, 1998, section II.
ILO. (1998b). *ILO Declaration on Social Justice for a Fair Globalization*. ILC, 97th Session, Geneva, 10 June 1998.
ILO. (2009a). Global Employment Trends 2009. http://www.ilo.org/wcmsp5/groups/public/---dgreports/---dcomm/documents/publication/wcms_101461.pdf. Accessed 15 Mar 2014.
ILO. (2009b). *The financial and economic crisis: A decent work response*. Geneva: International Institute for Labour Studies.
ILO. (2011a). *New era of social justice*. Report of the Director-General to the International Labour Conference, 100th Session (Report I(A), paragraph 13.
ILO. (2011b). *Policy coherence in the multilateral system*. Governing Body, 312th Session, Geneva, November 2011.
ILO. (2012). *Fundamental principles and rights at work: From commitment to action*. ILC, 101st Session, Geneva.
IMF. (2013). Regional economic outlook: Sub-Saharan Africa, Building Momentum in a Multi-Speed World, May. https://www.imf.org/external/pubs/ft/reo/2013/afr/eng/sreo0513.htm. Accessed 17 June 2014.
International Confederation of Free Trade Unions. (1998). *Fighting for workers' human rights in the global economy*. http://www.icftu.org/displaydocument.asp?Index=990916201&Language=EN. Accessed 7 Nov 2013.
Kim, D.-O., & Kim, S. (2003). Globalization, financial crisis and industrial relations: The case of South Korea. *Industrial Relations, 42*(3).
Kucera, D. (2001), *The effects of core worker rights on labour costs and Foreign Direct Investment: Evaluating the conventional economic wisdom* (Discussion Paper No. 130/2001). Geneva: International Institute for Labour Studies.
Kucera, D. (2002a). Core labour standards and foreign direct investment. *International Labour Review, 141*(1–2).
Kucera, D. (2002b). Effects of labor standards on labour costs and FDI flows. In J. Bhagwati and Corbet (Eds.), *Labor standards in an integrating world economy*.
LaFraniere, S. (2009). 20 million migrants have lost jobs, China says. *International Herald Tribune*, 2 February.
Lamont, J. (2009). Doha deal 'close to conclusion'. *Financial Times*, 3 September.
Lawrence, R. Z., & Slaughter, M. J. (1993). Trade and US Wages: Great sucking sound or small hiccup? *Brookings Papers on Economic Activity, 2*, 161–226.
Leary, V. (1996). Workers' rights and international trade: The social clause (GATT, ILO, NAFTA, U.S. Laws). In: J. Bhagwati & R. E. Hudec (Eds). Fair trade and harmonization, prerequisites for free trade*?* (Vol. 2). Cambridge: The MIT Press.
Lee, E. (1996). Globalization and employment: Is anxiety justified. *International Labour Review, 135*(5).
Lee, E. (1997). Globalisation and labour standards: A review of issues. *International Labour Review, 136*(2).
Mandle, J. R. (2003). *Globalisation and the poor*. Cambridge: Cambridge University Press.
Maskus, K. E. (1997, August). *Should core labour standards be imposed through International Trade Policy?* (Policy Research Working Paper 1817). The World Bank Development Research Group.

Maskus, K. E. (2000, January). *Regulatory standards in the WTO: Comparing intellectual property rights with competition policy, environmental protection, and core labor standards* (WP 00-1). Washington, DC: Institute for International Economic.
Mittelman, J. H. (2000). *The globalisation syndrome transformation and resistance*. Princeton: Princeton University Press.
Moyo, D. (2009). *Dead aid: Why aid is not working and how there is another way for Africa*. London: Allen Lane.
Nelson Julie, A. (1998). Labour, gender and the economic/social divide. *International Labour Review, 137*(1).
New York Times. (2009, July 2). *Joblessness hits 9.5%, deflating recovery hopes.*
OECD. (1996). *Regional integration and its place in the multilateral trading system*. Paris: OECD.
OECD. (2009). *The job crisis. What are the implications for employment and social policy?* DELSA/ELSA/WP5. Accessed on 7 Feb 2014.
Oman, C. (2000). *Policy competition for Foreign Direct Investment – A study of competition among governments to attract FDI*. Development Centre of the Organisation for Economic Co-operation and Development.
Panagariya, A. (2001). *Labor standards and trade sanctions: Right end wrong means*. http://www.columbia.edu/~ap2231/Policy%20Papers/Hawaii3-AP.pdf. Accessed 20 Dec 2013.
Qureshi Asif, H. (1998). International Trade and Human Rights from the perspective of the WTO. In F. Weiss, E. Denter, & P. de Waart (Eds.), *International Economic Law with a human face*. The Hague: Kluwer Law International.
Ratna, R. S. (2009, February). *Promoting south–south trade: Recent developments and options* (ARTNet Policy Brief, Brief No. 17, UNESCAP). http://artnet.unescap.org/pub/polbrief17.pdf. Accessed 10 Mar 2014.
Rodrik, D. (1997). *Has globalisation gone too far?* Washington, DC: Institute for International Economics.
Samuelson, P. A. (1948). International trade and the equalisation of factor prices. *Economic Journal, 58*.
Schefer Krista, N. (2010). *Social regulation in the WTO: Trade policy and International Legal Development*. Cheltenham, UK/Northampton, MA, USA: Edward Elgar.
Sen, A. (1986). Behaviour and the concept of preference. In J. Elster (Ed.), *Rational choices*. New York: New York University Press.
Sengenberger, W. (2005). *Globalization and social progress: The role and impact of International Labour Standards*. A Report Prepared for the Friedrich-Ebert Stiftung, 2nd revised and extended revision, Bonn, September 2005.
Silbey Susan, S. (1997). Let them eat cake: Globalization, postmodern colonialism, and the possibilities of justice. *Law & Society Review, 31*(2).
Somavia, J. (1999). If you want to promote open trade don't overlook the world's people. *International Herald Tribune*, 1 December.
Stiglitz, J. (2002). *Globalisation and its discontents*. New York: W.W. Norton & Company.
Stiglitz, J. E. (2003). *The roaring nineties: A new history of the world's most prosperous decade*. New York: W.W. Norton & Company.
Stiglitz, J. (2009). The global crisis, social protection and jobs. *International Labour Review, 148* (1–2).
Stiglitz Joseph, E., & Charlton, A. (2005). *Fair trade for all: How trade can promote development*. Oxford: Oxford University Press.
Supiot, A. (1996). Perspectives on work: Introduction. *International Labour Review, 135*(6).
Sykes, A. O. (2003, May). *International Trade and Human Rights: An economic perspective* (Olin Working Paper No. 188). University of Chicago Law and Economics.
The Economist. (2004). February 21st–27th.
The Economist. (2008a). March 15th–21st, Special report: China's quest for resources.
The Economist. (2008b). April 12–18.
The Economist. (2009a). March 24th–29th.

The Economist. (2009b). August 21st–September 1st.
The Economist. (2013a). March 23rd–29th.
The Economist. (2013b). More than minerals. March 23rd–29th.
Thomas, A. (1921). The International Labour Organisation. Its origins, development and future. *International Labour Review, 1*(1) [reprinted in *International Labour Review, 135*(3–4), 262–263].
Time. (2009). March 13.
Trebilcock, M. J. (2011). *Understanding trade law*. Cheltenham, UK/Northampton, USA: Edward Elgar.
UNCTAD. (2008). *Handbook of statistics*. New York and Geneva: UNCTAD.
UNCTAD. (2013, July). *South–south trade monitor* (No. 2). http://unctad.org/en/PublicationsLibrary/webditctab2013d1_en.pdf. Accessed 27 Feb 2014.
Winters, L. A. (2000). Trade and poverty: Is there a connection? In D. Ben David, H. Nordstrom, & L. A. Winters (Eds.), *Trade, income disparity and poverty* (Special Study No. 5). Geneva: World Trade Organisation.
World Bank. (2002). *Global economic prospects and developing countries: Making trade work for the poor*. Washington: World Bank.
World Bank. (2004a). *Global economic perspectives 2004: Realizing the development promise of the Doha agenda*. Washington: World Bank.
World Bank. (2004b, April). *Migration and development brief*. http://siteresources.worldbank.org/INTPROSPECTS/Resources/334934-1288990760745/MigrationandDevelopmentBrief22.pdf. Accessed 15 May 2014.
Zaheer, D. A. (2003–2004). Breaking the deadlock: Why and how developing countries should accept labor standards in the WTO. *Stanford Journal of Business and Finance, 9*.

Chapter 3
The History of Core Labour Standards

3.1 The History of the Linking of Labour Standards and Trade

The issue of whether or not a formal link could be established between trade and labour standards (core labour standards) is an issue that has a long history. Current events have demonstrated that it has not only managed to crawl its way back onto the multilateral trade agenda, but it has also created divisions between the developed and developing nations, the so-called North/South conflict. The discussions to date may lead to the perception that the linkage between trade and labour standards is a new issue, but this linkage is a century and a half old, dating from the earliest concern about the conditions of workers during the Industrial Revolution in Europe in the early 1900s. During that period, harmonisation of national labour laws was perceived as necessary in order to improve the condition of workers in every European country.[1] As old as the issue is, it still needs to be taken seriously. The current dimensions of the issue and the wedge it has created between proponents of a formal link and its critics, both having valid arguments, make the issue one of the most difficult ever faced by policymakers as the twentieth century drew to an end and the world looked forward to the new millennium.

Why has the issue become so prominent in recent times? Lee (1997, p. 174) argues that the shift towards neoliberal views in economic and social policies since the 1970s has led to a questioning of the value of labour standards in general. These views have emphasised a smaller role for the State, including the regulation of market activity. Regulation is seen as essentially distortionary, impeding the efficient functioning of markets and causing inferior outcomes in terms of growth, employment, and even income distribution. Labour market regulation, in Lee's view, has not escaped this neoliberal scrutiny.

[1] Leary (1996a), p. 183.

K. Addo, *Core Labour Standards and International Trade*,
DOI 10.1007/978-3-662-44619-5_3

In the industrialised countries, the view that labour market regulations and the welfare state are key causes of the rise and persistence of unemployment has become increasingly influential. They are seen as reducing the incentives for workers to seek work and for employers to create jobs. This has led to policy change, deregulation of the labour market, and a cutback in the welfare state in search of more flexible labour markets. A clear example is the neoliberal views of the Thatcher/Major governments in the UK from 1979 to 1997, a period that saw the deregulation of the labour market, a policy that the British Labour Government under Tony Blair and Gordon Brown followed and that the coalition government since 2010 also seems to be following. These views have also spread to many developing countries. This is seen in structural adjustment programmes prescribed by the International Monetary Fund (IMF) and the World Bank.[2]

Apart from the neoliberal argument, two other developments contributed to labour standards gaining prominence. First is the increasing globalisation of the world economy. A common view is that globalisation increases the pressures to cut costs (including labour costs) and to achieve greater flexibility in the production system. In addition, the growing mobility of capital is also believed to be increasing the bargaining power of employers vis-à-vis both governments and workers. Governments keen to retain and attract foreign direct investment have to make concessions, whilst workers are in a weakened bargaining position in the face of the threat of relocation.[3] The other reason is that in spite of significant progress in improving labour conditions across the world over the past decades, there are still significant pockets of poor and morally unacceptable labour conditions in low-income countries.

Problems of child labour in inhuman conditions, of bonded labour, of physically taxing work processes, of discrimination in access to employment in the workplace, and of inadequate returns to work still prevail. As Anderson argues, the issue is gradually becoming more prominent, not just because of the declining trade and investment barriers that have meant cost-raising standards are more important determinants of international competitiveness.[4] Enhanced communication networks have also meant that citizens of high-standard countries have more access to information on labour standards in other countries. That, together with the growing sense of a 'global village', allows concern for human rights to spread beyond national boundaries, a tendency that can be expected to continue indefinitely as global economic growth and integration proceed. He argues further that around that upward trend in concern will be fluctuations in the opposite direction to the business cycle: the worse the labour market is performing in high-wage

---

[2] Rodrik (2001). Mr. Rodrik states that senior officials of the WTO, IMF, and other international agencies advice developing country governments that "open trade and investment policies are the surest ways to achieve economic growth and poverty alleviation" and that instead of a development strategy global integration has become the substitute.

[3] Lee (1997), p. 175.

[4] Anderson (1996), p. 450.

countries, the more likely it is that imports from low-wage countries will be blamed, notwithstanding clear evidence that such imports are at most only a minor contributor.[5]

The global communications revolution and the tremendous growth of 'Dot.com' companies have brought to fore public awareness of appalling labour conditions, such as the exploitation of child labour and harsh labour processes for women workers in export processing zones. At the same time, the new wave of democratisation and the proliferation of nongovernmental organisations with social concerns across the world have brought about more active advocacy of action for dealing with morally unacceptable labour practices, reinforcing the traditional role of trade unions. In the industrialised countries, this has resulted in movements such as consumer boycotts of goods produced with child or forced labour. Product labelling and demands for multinational enterprises to avoid dealings with exploitative producers have been among the principal means of action.[6] In order to understand why the issue has been with us for so long and is still on the world agenda, we turn our attention to its early development and the reasons behind the founding of the ILO.

3.2 Early Developments of the Linkage Between Trade and Labour Standards

The issue of the correlation between international trade and the rights of workers was first raised in Europe in the middle of the nineteenth century. At that time, the working conditions were appallingly bad in the industrialised countries of Europe. Concerns regarding child labour and working hours were raised. The response to this was the call for the adoption of treaties establishing common labour standards that, it was hoped, would be ratified by all European industrialised countries, as well as the establishment of an international organisation to supervise the treaties.[7]

The Industrial Revolution, which began in England in the 1800s, brought to fore the worst horrors of the new system, and the English took steps to curb that. An Act passed in 1802 limited to 12 h a day the employment of children in the textile factories. These child labourers were generally sent to the factories from the workhouses for the poor and were housed in such miserable conditions that the law also stipulated they should not sleep more than two to a bed in factory dormitories.[8] This Act was the first law to introduce the principle of factory inspection, although the prevailing opinion at that time was in favour of economic

---

[5] Anderson (1996), pp. 450 and 451.

[6] Lee (1997), pp. 175 and 176.

[7] Follows (1951), p. 57.

[8] ILO (1995), p. 11.

laissez-faire or free-for-all economic development. Whilst some deplored its consequences, people generally felt it to be natural and inescapable.

The earlier medieval system of guilds and corporation, in which crafts workers had associated to regulate their profession and trade, was then widely believed to hamper technical progress and restrain economic growth. Although the new expansion of industry and trade was disorderly and costly in human suffering, it clearly produced greater wealth than ever before, and many people were firmly convinced that governments should do nothing to hinder or interfere with the seemingly natural process of competition in which the weak went to the wall and only the strong survived. Hence, the first efforts of workers to associate were condemned as a return to the system of guilds and corporations and a threat to free enterprise.[9]

Whereas the nineteenth century concern for the plight of workers appears to be genuine, the present-day concern lends itself to suspicions that the proponents of a linkage have a different agenda. Labour organisations and human rights activists in the United States and the Organisation for Economic Cooperation and Development (OECD) countries are concerned about the impact of globalisation on employment and income distribution.

As stated above, there is the fear that globalisation and free trade among nations may lead to a lowering of standards to the level of countries with inadequate labour standards and practices. This is because the growing proportion of world trade is between countries with different levels of labour rights and labour costs. It is felt that could lead to 'social dumping', i.e., the export of products that owe their competitiveness to low labour standards. This may also encourage a so-called race to the bottom. However, the present-day concern lends itself to suspicions that protectionism is hidden behind the rhetoric.

Irrespective of the arguments of both the proponents and critics of the labour/international trade linkage, the reference to labour standards in the UDHR UN Charter and its implicit reference in the WTO Agreement show how important the issue is to the overall debate. The linkage between labour standards and international trade reflects basic or universal human rights. An examination of the legal texts of both the ILO and the WTO indicates how explicitly and implicitly the linkage between core labour standards, better standards of living, and the right to decent work is entirely consistent with the objectives enumerated under the liberal trading regime.

Article II of the Marrakesh Agreement states that "[t]he WTO shall provide the common institutional framework for the conduct of trade relations among its Members in matters related to the agreements and associated legal instruments included in the Annexes to this Agreement".[10] The 'common institutional framework' cannot be achieved when the workers' rights are not put on the same level as international human rights generally.

---

[9] ILO (1995), p. 12.

[10] URUGUAY ROUND AGREEMENT, Marrakesh Agreement Establishing the World Trade Organization, at http://www.wto.org/english/docs_e/legal_e/04-wto_e.htm. Accessed on 30 March 2014.

3.3 The Pioneers of the Interface Between Trade and Labour Standards

There were few thoughtful individuals in the first half of the nineteenth century; among them were some employers who shared the rising aspirations for justice of those at the bottom of the social heap. For various humanitarian, economic, and political reasons, they promoted such pioneering social legislation as the abolition of child labour and worked towards the adoption in England of the Factory Act of 1833, which created a corps of four inspectors to supervise factory conditions. Further, a Swiss banker, Jacques Necker (1732–1804), who served as Minister of Finance in France both before and after the French Revolution was the first proponent of international agreements for worker protection. But the proposal received little support.

The owner of a Scottish cotton mill, Robert Owen, the so-called grandfather of British trade unionism, was the chief inspirational force and lobbyist behind a Bill passed by the British Parliament in 1819 to limit working hours in the mills. Owen had set an example at his own factory, where he improved working conditions and provided housing and educational and leisure facilities for the workers and their children. Other employers protested at such measures, which they thought would make their goods too costly to meet the competition in world markets from goods made more cheaply in countries that had no social legislation.

Robert Owen, referred to as a pioneer in international labour legislation, is credited as writing two memorials in 1818. These memorials were presented to the representatives of the major European powers of the day—Austria, France, Prussia, Russia, and the United Kingdom, then meeting at the Congress of Aix-la-Chapelle (Aachen), to suggest that the Congress set up a Labour Committee to discuss social and economic questions. But the Statesmen ignored Owens's proposal, just as they had rejected Necker's.[11]

However, according to Follows, the honour should rather go to Charles Frederick Hindley, a member of the British Parliament from 1835 to 1857.[12] Hindley in 1833 is said to have proposed a foreign treaty on labour legislation. Hindley is referred as the founder of the idea of international labour legislation and described as having "a clear insight into the interdependence between nations that was created by foreign trade and international competition".[13] The working conditions that were raised in Hindley's proposal dealt with hours of work.

In 1838, a French liberal economist, Jérome Blanqui, wrote to advance the trade argument for international labour legislation. He wrote of the need for European countries to harmonise their labour legislation:

[11] ILO (1995), pp. 11 and 13.

[12] Follows (1951), p. 10.

[13] Hansson (1983), p. 12.

> There is only one way of accomplishing it [the reform] while avoiding its disastrous consequences: this would be to get it adopted simultaneously by all industrial nations which compete in the foreign market.[14]

Another pioneer, the French manufacturer Daniel Le Grand, made insistent appeals to British, French, German, and Swiss politicians and civil servants for international labour laws covering working hours, a day of rest, night work, unhealthy or dangerous occupations, and child employment, after he had been told by the French Government that it could not promulgate workers' welfare legislation because of international competition.[15]

Le Grand warned that if governments did not co-operate to make such reforms, they would face a growing tide of popular unrest. Based on concrete studies of the actual conditions of work and the existing labour legislation in various industrial countries, Le Grand's proposals were a precursor of the work of the ILO. His ideas found other advocates through private initiatives, such as the International Benevolent Congresses (held in 1856 and 1857). They proposed international legislation for the regulation of industrial labour and worker's protection.[16]

In the latter half of the nineteenth century, a series of European congresses, promoted by different organisations of labour leaders, socialists, reformers, professors, and economists, took up the issue of labour law reforms, with many pointing out that labour reform was not solely a national issue.[17] The main concerns of these congresses related to child labour, hours of work, weekly rest for children and adult female workers, and, eventually, what we would refer to today as occupational safety and health—referred to then as "hygiene in the workplace".

Concern over international competitiveness was a recurrent preoccupation. The long-awaited conference on international labour law, which had first been proposed by the Swiss Federal Council, was eventually held in Berlin in March 1890 and was attended by representatives of a dozen European governments. During the 2 weeks of discussions, a series of detailed recommendations were produced. Among them were suggestions that children under 12 should not be permitted to work at all and that women and children under 14 should not be allowed to work in the mines or to work anywhere for more than 6 h at a stretch. All workers were to be given weekly day of rest. Questions of workers' health and safety in the workplace and accident insurance were also discussed.

The recommendations were sent to the governments, but they had no immediate practical effect. What was important was that the Berlin international factory and mine conference marked the first occasion on which governments met to study the

[14] Blanqui Jerome A Cours D'Economie Industrielle. 1838–1839 (1839), quoted in Hansson (1983), at p. 12.

[15] Jacques Necker (mentioned above), used international competition as an argument against abolishing Sunday work in France.

[16] ILO (1995), pp. 11, 13 and 14.

[17] Hansson (1983), p. 12.

social consequences of the Industrial Revolution and to envisage drafting international legislation to improve labour standards.[18]

The seeds for the eventual adoption of international labour conventions and international labour organisation were immediately laid in 1897. Delegates representing workers in 14 countries met at an International Congress on Labour Protection in Zurich in 1897 and urged the Swiss government to invite other governments to set up a labour office. Also, in 1897, a conference of professors, economists, and politicians from Belgium, France, England, etc. met in Brussels to discuss various issues relating to labour legislation in the European countries and set up a committee to establish an international association for labour protection, aiming, *inter alia*, at the adoption of international labour legislation. Statutes of the International Association for Labour Legislation were adopted in Paris in 1900 and an International Labour Office was opened in Basel in 1901. For instance, Hansson[19] points out that in the pre-World War I period, a number of bilateral agreements were also negotiated dealing with common conditions of work.

A Franco-Italian treaty of 1904 required Italy to regulate working conditions in line with conditions in France and gave Italian workers in France the same treatment as domestic workers regarding compensation for industrial accidents and pensions. By 1914, European countries had negotiated 28 bilateral agreements, relating mainly to the treatment of migrant workers.[20]

In 1913, at a conference in Berne, delegates adopted two new conventions: one related to hours of work for minors and women and the other on prohibition of night work for minors. These developments were overtaken with the advent of the First World War. As a result, the diplomatic conference at which the conventions were to be signed never took place. However, the post-war developments led to a new era in the development of harmonisation of labour law with the founding of the International Labour Organization.[21]

3.4 The ILO and the Link Between Labour Standards and International Trade

The founding of the International Labour Organization (ILO) by Part XIII of the Treaty of Versailles in 1919 and the subsequent adoption of multiple international labour conventions by the Organization are turning points in the history of the relationship between workers' rights and trade. The establishment of the ILO could be seen as a logical development from the century-old concern about the relationship between international trade and labour standards. The setting up documents of

[18] ILO (1995), p. 17.

[19] See Hansson (1983), at p. 185.

[20] Leary (1996a), at p. 185.

[21] Leary (1996a), at p. 185.

the ILO made explicit reference to the link. The 189 ILO Labour Conventions serve today as reference for the meaning of "internationally recognised core labour standards".[22] It might appear surprising that a treaty that was focussed on issues of peace after a major war also led to the creation of a labour charter and the ILO. But then the situation in post-war Europe made the perception of a link between peace and labour understandable.

Whilst in the intervening years, the link between achieving peace and workers' rights had not been invoked, there are many references to the link between democratic values and achievement of peace. However, the social upheavals in Greece in 2013 and the negative social impact of the financial crisis that started in 2008 tend to bring up memories of the events that led to the founding of the ILO. In a period that has seen the rise of economic policies that have "overvalued the capacities of markets to self-regulate, undervalued the role of the State, public policy and regulations . . ., the dignity of work and the social service and welfare functions in society"[23] and also policymakers having profoundly underestimated the long-term effects of globalisation that have led to challenges with regard to jobs, incomes, and poverty, the importance of the ideals of the ILO needs to be reignited, in what the Director General calls as a new era of social justice that he believes should be inspired by a vision of sustainable development.[24]

The link between international competitiveness and labour conditions was at the forefront of the founding of the ILO. The objective behind the establishment of the ILO was to undertake joint international action to improve labour conditions worldwide. The Preamble of the ILO Constitution expressly refers to the link between conditions of workers and harmonisation of labour conditions.[25] It relevantly states:

Whereas universal and lasting peace can be established only if it is based upon social justice; and whereas conditions of labour exist involving such injustice, hardship and privation to large numbers of people as to produce unrest so great that the peace and harmony of the world are imperilled. Whereas also the failure of any nation to adopt humane conditions of labour is an obstacle in the way of other nations which desire to improve the conditions in their own countries . . .[26]

According to Lee (1997), there were several interrelated motives reflected in the Preamble. The first motive was social justice and humanitarian concern over the existence of conditions of labour that cause hardship and deprivation to large numbers of people. The second motive was prudential: to stave off unrest that would imperil the peace and harmony of the world. The Russian Bolshevik Revolution, with its emphasis on the rights of workers, was very much on the minds of Western European diplomats. The third motive rested on the notion of the need to

---

[22] http://www.ilo.org/dyn/normlex/en/f?p=1000:12000:0::NO. Accessed on 29 December 2013.

[23] ILO (2011a), p. 3.

[24] ILO (2011a), p. 3.

[25] Leary (1996a), at p. 186.

[26] ILO Constitution, see http://www.ilo.org/ilolex/english/constq.htm.

eliminate the negative cross-border externalities generated by countries, which failed to observe humane conditions of labour.

The method chosen by the ILO to establish a certain degree of harmonisation of conditions of labour is the adoption of international labour conventions by the annual International Labour Conference to be accepted by states through ratification. Nonbinding recommendations are adopted containing more detailed standards. These Conventions have the force of international law on ratifying countries backed up by supervisory machinery. The rate of ratification varies from country to country. The system has weathered the challenges of the Great Depression, the rise of fascism and the Second World War, the decolonisation of the developing world, and, more recently, the collapse of communism.[27]

Although conceived in the colonial era, it has evolved into a system with universal coverage, reflected in the ILO's present 185-member governance structure by virtue of the tripartism that is enshrined in the ILO's Constitution. There has in fact been, for some time, a functioning global system of international labour standards.[28] The ILO tripartism nature helps bring together representatives of employers' groups and governments, as well as workers' groups. The ILO is the only international body where workers can make their voices heard officially and can negotiate on an equal footing with employers and governments about matters that affect their economic and social well-being.

At the time of the founding of the ILO, the focus was on the industrialised countries of Europe, which were then at a relatively equal state of economic development, few countries (United States, Britain, France, Germany, etc.) were independent at that time or active participants in the international community. Early ILO Conventions made exceptions for states then at a different state of economic development, in particular India and Japan. Later, ILO Conventions contained "flexibility clauses" that took account of the varying economic development of countries.[29]

In the drafting of detailed technical labour conventions, the ILO has been conscious of the need to take account of differences in economic development. At the same time, it has emphasised that differences in economic development should not excuse violation of the fundamental human rights embodied in such conventions as those relating to freedom of association and collective bargaining, forced labour, discrimination in employment, and child labour.

[27] Lee (1997), 1997/Summer, p. 174.

[28] Lee (1997), p. 174.

[29] Leary (1996a), at p. 187.

3.5 The ILO Supervisory and Enforcement Mechanism

The ILO has developed a supervisory system to support its labour standards. The purpose of this system, which is unique internationally, is to ensure that the ILO Members implement the conventions they have ratified. The ILO, through this system, regularly examines how countries are applying the standards and points out to countries the areas where the application would be more effective. Where the ILO finds that countries are facing problems in their application of the standards, it provides assistance through social dialogue and provision of technical assistance.[30]

The main supervisory bodies are the Committee of Experts on the Application of Conventions and Recommendations (Committee of Experts) and the Conference Committee on the Application of Standards (Conference Committee). There are also other bodies involved in the supervisory process: the Governing Body, the International Labour Office, and the International Labour Conference. The Governing Body is built on a tripartite system (comprising of representatives of government, employers' associations, and workers' organisations) and oversees the work of the International Labour Office, the ILO Secretariat, and the International Labour Conference.

The ILO's system of supervision is diversified, and there are two kinds of the supervisory mechanism: (1) regular system of supervision and (2) special procedures. In this section, we will analyse the two supervisory mechanisms and the enforcement systems the ILO uses.

3.5.1 *Regular System of Supervision*

When an ILO Member ratifies a convention, it has the obligation to report on a regular basis the measures it has taken to implement the convention. In respect of the application of the eight fundamental and four priority conventions, governments are required to submit reports every 2 years outlining the measures they have taken in law and practice in their application. With respect to other conventions, the reports must be submitted every 5 years.

The ILO constitutional basis for Members to report on ratified conventions is Article 22 of the ILO Constitution:

> Each of the Members agrees to make an annual report to the International Labour Office on the measures which it has taken to give effect to the provisions of Conventions to which it is a party. These reports shall be made in such form and shall contain such particulars as the Governing Body may request.

[30] See http://www.ilo.org/global/standards/applying-and-promoting-international-labour-standards/lang--en/index.htm. Accessed 3 June 2014.

The ILO Constitution also obliges Members to report on non-ratified conventions. This is governed by Article 19 (5e) of the ILO Constitution:

> If the Member does not obtain the consent of the authority or authorities within whose competence the matter lies, no further obligation shall rest upon the Member except that it shall report to the Director-General of the International Labour Office, at appropriate intervals as requested by the Governing Body, the position of its law and practice in regard to the matters dealt with in the Convention, showing the extent to which effect has been given, or is proposed to be given, to any of the provisions of the Convention by legislation, administrative action, collective agreement or otherwise and stating the difficulties which prevent or delay the ratification of such Convention.

Members are similarly obliged to report on Recommendations. This is governed by ILO Constitution, Article 19 (6d):

> Apart from bringing the Recommendation before the said competent authority or authorities, no further obligation shall rest upon the Members, except that they shall report to the Director-General of the International Labour Office, at appropriate intervals as requested by the Governing Body, the position of the law and practice in their country in regard to the matters dealt with in the Recommendation, showing the extent to which effect has been given or is proposed to be given, to the provisions of the Recommendation and such modifications of these provisions as it has been found or may be found necessary to make in adopting or applying them.

At the same time, governments are required by Article 23 of the Constitution to provide copies of their reports to employers' and workers' organisations, who may, if they so wish, comment on the reports and can also send their comments concerning the application of the conventions directly to the ILO. Article 23 refers to the communication of reports on ratified and non-ratified instruments:

> 1. The Director-General shall lay before the next meeting of the Conference a summary of the information and reports communicated to him by Members in pursuance of articles 19 and 22.
> 2. Each Member shall communicate to the representative organizations [. . .] copies of the information and reports communicated to the Director-General in pursuance of articles 19 and 22.

3.5.1.1 Committee of Experts on the Application of Conventions and Recommendations

A major pillar of the ILO regular supervisory system is the Committee of Experts on the Application of Conventions and Recommendations (CEACR) (the Committee). This body is not referred to in the ILO Constitution but was set up in 1926 by the Governing Body of the ILO to examine government reports on the application of Conventions and other obligations relating to international labour standards set out in the ILO Constitution. The Committee was also established to examine reports from governments on conventions that Members have ratified, pursuant to Articles 19, 22, and 35. This was in response to the growing number of reports that governments provided to the ILO, their complexity, and the technical nature of the reports. The same resolution that created the Committee of Experts also created the Conference Committee.[31]

The Committee has evolved since its first meeting in 1927, composed of eight members to its present composition of 20 members (eminent jurists: judges of supreme courts, professors of law, legal experts, etc.), from all parts of the world acting independently of the ILO. The Committee members are appointed by the Governing Body to serve for a period of 3 years. The Committee's role is to review the reports and provide an independent or impartial and technical assessment of the state of application of the ratified labour standards.[32] The Committee meets annually in private sessions, and its deliberations are confidential.

In its examination of the application of the labour standards, the Committee of Experts makes two types of comments: (1) observations and (2) direct requests. The observations contain the Committee's comments on essential questions as a result of the state of application of a convention in a Member state. The Committee of Experts publishes its observations in its annual report. The Committee's direct request concerns technical questions or requests for governments to provide further information. These requests are communicated directly to the governments in question and are not published.[33]

The Committee of Experts has, over the more than 80 years of its existence, had an impact on all fields covering all the Conventions adopted by the ILO. But it is the Committee's impact on the eight fundamental Conventions covering the core labour standards that this study is confined.

Based on its examination of the reports provided by governments to the Committee, and in line with its operating procedure, the Committee refers in its comments to cases by expressing either its satisfaction or interest at the level of progress achieved in a country's application of the respective Conventions. The identification of cases of progress started in 1964, when the Committee submitted its report to the 48th Session of the International Labour Conference, and has since then been following the same general criteria.

The Committee expresses satisfaction in cases in which governments, in response to the Committee's comments on a specific issue, have made changes, either through the adoption of an amendment to the country's legislation or the making of a significant change in its national policy or practice in order to fully comply with its obligations under ratified Conventions.

The Committee has stated that the reasons for identifying cases of satisfaction are twofold: "to place on record the Committee's appreciation of the positive action taken by governments in response to its comments, and to provide an example to other governments and social partners which have to address similar issues".[34] The

[31] ILO (2011b), p. 11.

[32] ILO (2009a), p. 80.

[33] ILO (2009a), p. 80.

[34] ILO (2009b), paragraph 52, p. 18.

Committee, through the expression of its satisfaction, indicates that the specific matter in its view has been resolved.

In 1979, the Committee formalised within the cases of progress the distinction between the cases of satisfaction and the cases of interest. On the whole, the cases of interest relate to measures taken by a government that are adequately advanced in order to justify the expectation that further advancement would be made in the future. The Committee has, for example, listed some of such measures: draft legislation before parliament or even proposed legislative changes not communicated to the Committee; consultations within the government and with social partners; new policies; activities developed and implemented within the framework of technical assistance programmes; judicial decisions, depending on the level of the court; etc.[35] In the view of the Committee, what is of great importance is that the measures taken by the government would make an impact in achieving the aims of a particular Convention.

Since the Committee started listing cases of progress in its report in 1964, the Committee has expressed satisfaction at the progress achieved in a total of 2,669 cases. From the period 2001–2005, the Committee noted 208 cases of progress, with most of the cases concerned with fundamental rights at work, which in most instances involved major changes.[36] For the 2001–2005 period, the Committee noted with satisfaction 107 cases of progress with respect to fundamental rights at work, which accounted for approximately 52 % of the total number of cases of progress. Between 2007 and 2009, the Committee noted 145 cases of progress and 335 cases of interest. The cases of progress on the fundamental rights at work for this period accounted for almost 37 % of the total number of cases of progress registered. These cases covered

- freedom of association and effective recognition of the right to collective bargaining,
- the elimination of all forms of forced or compulsory labour,
- the effective abolition of child labour and a prohibition on the worst forms of child labour, and
- the elimination of discrimination in respect of employment and occupation.

It is interesting to note that a greater number of the countries that have signed FTA agreements with the United States are included in the 2007–2009 cases of progress. In addition to these countries are the countries within the Africa, Caribbean and Pacific (ACP) group of countries, which are in the process of negotiating economic partnership agreements with the European Union. For example, in the 2009 Committee of Experts report, four countries that have signed FTAs with the United States (plus Colombia—its FTA with the U.S. is pending before the U.S. Congress) were listed among the 40 cases of progress, and also 10 ACP countries were listed. Among the 103 cases of interest, 12 countries that have

[35] ILO (2009b), paragraph 56, p. 19.

[36] See Boivin and Odero (2006), p. 210.

signed FTAs with the United States were listed (as were Colombia and Korea—yet to be approved by the U.S. Congress). In the case of the ACP group of countries, 28 were listed.

In spite of the number of cases of progress noted by the Committee, the complaints before the Committee on Freedom of Association indicates that much more progress need to be made under the freedom of association and effective recognition of the right to collective bargaining Conventions (Conventions 87 and 98).

The number of cases of satisfaction and interest listed by the Committee of Experts indicates that the ILO supervisory system is working towards the global promotion for the core labour standards. The Committee, through its work of analysing the legislation of Member States, sends direct requests to governments seeking clarification; the dialogue it establishes with governments and also the measures that governments take in response to the comments of the Committee so the failure of the Member State is not discussed in public all go to show the relevance of the Committee's work. However, the cooperation mechanisms and monitoring systems that have been built into FTAs to ensure compliance with the core labour standards show the important role these FTA mechanisms and inclusion of labour clauses in other bilateral agreements are playing in promoting adherence to the ILO principles.

3.5.1.2 The Conference Committee on the Application of Standards

The Conference Committee is a political body and standing committee of the Conference. It is a tripartite committee made up of government, employer, and worker delegates. Its terms of reference are set out in article 7 of the Standing Orders of the Conference, which reads:

> 1. The Conference shall, as soon as possible, appoint a Committee to consider:
>
> (a) the measures taken by Members to give effect to the provisions of Conventions to which they are parties and the information furnished by Members concerning the results of inspections;
>
> (b) the information and reports concerning Conventions and Recommendations communicated by Members in accordance with article 19 of the Constitution, except for information requested under paragraph 5 (e) of that article where the Governing Body has decided upon a different procedure for its consideration;
>
> (c) the measures taken by Members in accordance with article 35 of the Constitution.
>
> 2. The Committee shall submit a report to the Conference.[37]

The report of the Committee of Experts produced annually is submitted to the International Labour Conference for it to be examined by the Conference Committee on the Application of Standards. In its examination of the Committee of Experts report, this Committee selects some of the observations for further discussion. The governments that are the subject of the discussion are requested to appear before the

[37] Standing Orders of the International Labour Conference, Part I, General Standing Orders, Article 7 "Committee on the Application of Conventions and Recommendations".

Committee and respond to queries and also provide information on the situation being discussed. The Committee's sessions are open to the public, and it publishes its discussions and conclusions in its report.[38]

3.5.2 The Special Procedures

The ILO Constitution has provisions for Members to make a representation or a complaint. Below we discuss the three procedures for such submissions.

3.5.2.1 Procedure for Representation in Applying Ratified Conventions

This representation procedure is governed by Articles 24 and 25 of the ILO Constitution. Article 24 states:

> In the event of any representation being made to the International Labour Office by an industrial association of employers or of workers that any of the Members has failed to secure in any respect the effective observance within its jurisdiction of any Convention to which it is a party, the Governing Body may communicate this representation to the government against which it is made, and may invite that government to make such statement and may invite that government to make such statement on the subject as it may think fit.

Article 24 grants employers' or workers' associations the right to make a representation or submit allegations to the ILO of the failure of an ILO Member State to adopt satisfactory measures within that Member's legal system for the application of a Convention that it has ratified. Upon receipt of such a representation, the Governing Body may set up a three-member tripartite committee to examine both the representation of the organisation and the government's response to the allegations. This ad hoc Committee submits a report to the Governing Body stating the legal and practical facets of the case and the steps taken in its examination of the information received and provides recommendations.

Article 25 of the ILO Constitution states that where a government fails to respond within a reasonable period of time or where its response is not deemed to be satisfactory, the Governing body has the right to publish the representation and the response.[39] Should a representation be made with respect to ILO Convention Nos. 87 and 98, these are referred to the Committee on Freedom of Association, discussed below.

---

[38] ILO (2009a), p. 81.

[39] See http://www.ilo.org/global/standards/applying-and-promoting-international-labour-standards/representations/lang--en/index.htm. Accessed 5 March 2014.

3.5.2.2 Procedure for Complaints Concerning Ratified Conventions

The complaints procedure is regulated by Articles 26–34 of the ILO Constitution. Under this procedure, a Member State is allowed to file a complaint against another Member State when, in its opinion, the other Member State has not adopted the necessary measures needed to give proper effect to a Convention it has ratified. When the Governing Body receives such a complaint, it may form a Commission of Inquiry, made up of three independent members. The Commission is then tasked with carrying out a complete investigation of the complaint. The Commission gathers all the facts of the case through the information received not only from the complaining party but also from third parties and organisations.[40]

3.5.2.3 Procedure for Complaints with Respect to Freedom of Association

Given the importance of freedom of association and collective bargaining as among the core conventions of the ILO, the ILO realised that the principle of freedom of association required further supervisory procedure to ensure compliance in countries that had not ratified the relevant conventions.[41] At the initiative of the Governing Body, the Committee on Freedom of Association (CFA) was established in 1951 as a tripartite body of the Governing Body.

The CFA is composed of independent chairperson and three representatives each of governments, employers, and workers. The purpose of the CFA is to examine allegations of non-compliance of freedom of association, irrespective of whether or not the country in question has ratified Conventions 87 and 98.[42] Employers' and workers' organisations can bring a complaint against a Member state. Should the CFA decide to receive a case, it first establishes the fact in dialogue with the government concerned. Should it find that the government has violated the standards and principles of the Convention on freedom of association, the CFA issues a report through the Governing Body. The CFA also provides recommendations as to how to remedy the situation. The concerned government is then required to provide a report on how it is implementing the recommendations. In a case where the country concerned has ratified the conventions, the legislative aspects of the case may, if the CFA so wishes, refer to the Committee of Experts.[43] The CFA also has the option of using the "direct contacts" approach. Though this is not a supervisory procedure, its purpose is to facilitate a representative of the Director General of the ILO to directly contact the government concerned to examine ways on how to address the issues raised, together with the social partners in the country.

---

[40] Leary (1992), p. 610.

[41] ILO (2009a), p. 88.

[42] Gravel et al. (2001), p. 10.

[43] ILO (2009a), p. 88.

3.6 Evaluation of the ILO Supervisory Mechanism

Is the ILO supervisory and enforcement mechanism the most effective? Certainly not. It could be argued that no international system for protecting the rights of people is yet good enough.[44] However, the ILO supervisory and enforcement mechanism can, by international comparisons, be said to be effective.[45] The ILO's supervisory roles, also compared to other international organisations, are more highly developed for two reasons. First is its tripartite nature—comprising of representatives from government, employers', and workers' organisations. The second is due to the independence and expertise of the members of the supervisory bodies. These experts are, as pointed out above, appointed not by governments but by the Governing Body of the ILO, upon recommendation of the ILO Director General.[46]

The ILO system has the two-tier system of the regular reporting system that is used by UN organisations and the special procedures system akin to a quasi-judicial structure. When a country refuses to comply with the recommendations of a Commission of Enquiry, the ILO Constitution authorises the use of sanctions in accordance with Article 33, which states:

> In the event of any Member failing to carry out within the time specified the recommendations, if any, contained in the report of the Commission of Enquiry, or in the decision of the International Court of Justice, as the case may be, the Governing Body may recommend to the Conference such action as it may deem wise and expedient to secure compliance therewith.

It is interesting to note that in the 1919 ILO Constitution at Article 419, governments in cases of substantiated complaints were allowed to impose economic sanctions against the defaulting nation. Article 419 states:

> In the event of any Member failing to carry out within the time specified the recommendations [. . .] any other Member may take against that Member the measures of an economic character indicated [. . .] as appropriate to the case.[47]

Any Member, by virtue of Article 419, could impose economic sanctions for the defaulting Member's failure to follow the recommendations of the Commission of Enquiry or of the Permanent Court of International Justice. Between 1919 and 1946 (when the Constitution was amended), the ILO never exercised this right to recommend the imposition of sanctions under Article 419.

A revision of the Constitution in 1946 removed the "measures of an economic character" language and substituted the language now in Article 33.[48] This language appears to be ambiguous and has since removed trade sanctions from the ILO

[44] Leary (1996b), p. 42.

[45] Swepston (2003), p. 75.

[46] Valticos (1998), p. 143.

[47] 1919 ILO Constitution, Article 419.

[48] 1946 ILO Constitution, Article 33.

mandate. This change in the ILO's mandate has created a situation whereby any WTO Member, should it impose sanctions as a result of a request from the ILO, might be made to defend its actions before the WTO dispute settlement mechanism (i.e., if that Member is also a WTO Member). The defending Member could itself face trade penalties should the sanctions be found to be in violation of WTO rules.

This has left the ILO enforcement mechanism with the only option of moral suasion and drawing the international community's attention to the practices in Member states, as a means of shaming them to change.

In the history of the ILO, Article 33 has only once been invoked, when the ILO Governing Body requested the International Labour Conference to investigate the allegations of forced labour practices in Myanmar (formerly known as Burma). This case was initiated by 25 workers' delegates from a cross section of developed and developing countries to the 83rd Session of the International Labour Conference in June 1996. The Governing Body established a Commission of Inquiry, which submitted its recommendations on 2 July 1998.[49] In 2000, the ILO adopted a resolution that invoked the organisation's constitution compliance clause. The ILO resolution requested Member states, governments, and other international organisations to evaluate their relations with Myanmar and also to assist in the implementation of the recommendations of the ILO Commission.[50]

The ILO investigation led to international outcry against Myanmar and generated calls for economic sanctions. The Government of Myanmar agreed to site visits from ILO officials and also agreed to a permanent ILO presence in the country. The Government also made efforts in developing specific domestic labour reforms.[51] More notably is the imposition of economic sanctions by ILO Member states. For example, the United States Congress passed the Burmese Freedom and Democracy Act of 2003,[52] which specifically made reference to the ILO resolution as a reason for imposing a general ban on imports from Myanmar[53] until after consultations between the President and the ILO Director General, and it is determined that the Government of Myanmar "no longer systematically violates workers' rights, including the use of forced and child labor, and conscription of child-soldiers".[54]

---

[49] See "Report of the Commission of Inquiry Appointed under Article 26 of the Constitution of the International Labour Organization to Examine the Observance by Myanmar of the Forced Labour Convention" (1998) 80 ILO Official Bulletin, 2 July 1998.

[50] International Labour Organization, Resolution Concerning the Measures Recommended by the Governing Body Under Article 33 of the ILO Constitution on the Subject of Myanmar, ILO Conf. 88th Sess. (June 14, 2000), available at http://www.ilo.org/public/english/standards/relm/ilc/ilc88/resolutions.htm#I. Accessed 23 January 2014.

[51] Maupain (2005), pp. 85 and 91.

[52] Burmese Freedom and Democracy Act of 2003, 50 U.S.C. § 1701, Pub. L. 108–61, §§ 1 to 9 (2006).

[53] Burmese Freedom and Democracy Act of 2003, 50 U.S.C. § 1701, Pub. L. 108–61, § 2(10). See also, Helfer (2006), pp. 712 and 713.

[54] Burmese Freedom and Democracy Act of 2003, 50 U.S.C. § 1701, Pub. L. 108–61, § 38a)(3)(A). The European Commission suspended GSP trade privileges, and Australia conducted a review of its trade relations with Myanmar. See ILO, GB.280/6, para. 16.

In spite of the ILO's and other countries' efforts to bring about change in Myanmar, the Government of Myanmar continued to violate the Convention on Forced Labour. The ILO Governing Body in 2005 reiterated its 2000 measures. In 2007, the military government concluded a Supplementary Understanding with the ILO to implement on a trial basis the agreed upon mechanism for addressing complaints over forced labour.[55]

The Myanmar case illustrates both the effectiveness and the limited tools available to the ILO under its enforcement mechanism. Whilst the ILO was able to achieve some success in bringing about change, it also showed the dependence of the ILO on the political will of Member states to enforce its rules. At the same time, the Myanmar case also revealed the willingness of Member states to use the tools, even if limited, to ensure compliance with the ILO's fundamental principles.

Even more significant is the impetus that was generated for linking adherence to a core labour standard with a strong trade regime. Even though it is not clear the impact that the trade sanctions had on Myanmar, it showed that should there be a need, ILO Members can and might be willing to use trade sanctions on other Members to make them comply with the CLS.[56]

The case of Myanmar is both an example of the effectiveness and the shortcomings of the ILO implementation system. It demonstrates how the various enforcement techniques work and what they are able to achieve. The case is noteworthy because it is the first case in which the ILO recommended measures under Article 33 of its Constitution.

It is important to note that the ILC, at its meeting in June 2013, voted in a historic move to lift all the remaining restrictions on Myanmar after it lifted some of the restrictions at its 2012 ILC meeting. The ILC 2013 resolution to lift the remaining restrictions recognised that Myanmar had made progress in its compliance with Convention No. 29 on Forced Labour. The ILC called on the ILO Member states to provide financial assistance to Myanmar in its efforts in eliminating forced labour. ILC also requested the Governing Body to examine the situation in Myanmar on all ILO related activities.

The resolution demanded that the ILO and the Government of Myanmar carry on the commitment made in applying the terms of the 2007 Supplementary Understanding, the 2012 Memorandum of Understanding, and the actions that had been drawn in the effort to eliminate all forms of forced labour by 2015. Finally, the ILC requested the ILO Director General to submit a report every March at the Governing Body sessions until such time that Myanmar eliminates all forced labour in the country.[57]

---

[55] See Supplementary Understanding (26 February 2007) at http://www.ilo.org/public/English/region/asro/yangon/docs/supplementary_understanding.pdf. Accessed 2 July 2014.

[56] Thomas (2009), pp. 259 and 260.

[57] See http://www.ilo.org/ilc/ILCSessions/102/media-centre/news/WCMS_216355/lang--en/index.htm. Accessed 4 March 2014.

The work of the supervisory system of the ILO has had some impact. The ILO states that since 1964, as a result of the work of its Committee of Experts, over 2,300 cases of progress have been noted.[58] In the area of freedom of association, the ILO states that "more than 60 countries on five continents have acted on its recommendations and have informed it of positive developments on freedom of association during the past 25 years".[59]

The reports by the Committees under the regular system of supervision and special procedures provide proof of the level of compliance or of non-compliance with the CLS. These reports, as the Myanmar case has shown, could enhance the role of the ILO and more importantly play a vital role in pushing for increased adherence to the CLS. Furthermore, the increase in RTAs with reference to the CLS, in particular, could over time lead to a high degree of compliance and improve the effectiveness of the CLS at the national and regional levels and possibly lead to an international framework for compliance.

As the ILO CLS take on more importance in RTAs, the regulatory and supervisory mechanism of the ILO could be strengthened and advances in labour matters improved. As discussed below in Chap. 7, a number of trade agreements envisage the possibility of involving the ILO's advice and support in dispute resolution. This has the potential of moving the CLS beyond the question of ethics to becoming a major consideration in economic competition.

3.7 Labour Standards at the International Level: The Definition and Selection of Core Labour Standards

Labour standards are the regulatory framework that governs the relationship between employers and employees. Core labour standards that fall under labour standards as a whole are the standards that are deemed to be fundamental to the employer–employee relationship. These standards are related to fundamental human rights and go beyond the regulation of the material conditions of employment to protect fundamental values of freedom and equality and to ensure the material well-being, as well as the personal dignity, of workers.[60]

The Core Conventions or core labour standards deal with (a) freedom of association, (b) effective recognition of the right to collective bargaining, (c) the elimination of all forms of forced or compulsory labour, (d) the effective abolition

[58] The ILO has also provided information on at least six cases in countries that have implemented its recommendations and the changes that have resulted. See http://www.ilo.org/global/standards/applying-and-promoting-international-labour-standards/the-impact-of-the-regular-supervisory-system/lang--en/index.htm. Accessed 4 March 2014.

[59] See http://www.ilo.org/global/standards/applying-and-promoting-international-labour-standards/committee-on-freedom-of-association/lang--en/index.htm. Accessed 4 March 2014.

[60] Hensman (2000), p. 1248.

of child labour, and (e) the elimination of discrimination in respect of employment and occupation. According to Brown, the five standards have been selected based on two criteria. First, they are regarded as a fundamental component of basic human rights. Second, the above standards play a role in supporting the efficient function of labour markets by granting labour certain freedoms.[61] The CLS are the Forced Labour Convention, Convention No. 29 (1930); the right to organise and bargain collectively dealt under ILO Convention No. 87; the Freedom of Association and Protection of the Right to Organise Convention (1948) and Convention No. 98; and the Right to Organise and Collective Bargaining Convention (1949) and Convention No. 105, the Abolition of Forced Labour Convention, 1957, which deal with the elimination of forced labour.

3.7.1 The Core Labour Standards

ILO Convention No. 87 states that the right to organise will be granted to all workers and employers; only the armed forces and police may be exempted. Workers and employers are guaranteed the right to establish and join the organisation of their choice. The state cannot interfere with these organisations or suspend or dissolve them. These organisations have the right to establish and join federations and confederations, which have the same rights. All of these have the right to affiliate with international organisations of workers or employers. The significance of this ILO Convention in securing the rights of individuals to join or not to join a union is illustrated by a case decided by the European Court of Human Rights (ECHR), where the dismissal of three railway workers because of a closed shop was held by a majority of 18–3 justices to be contrary to Article 11 of European Convention on Human Rights, which contains the right to free association and to join a trade union.[62] The Court also held that it was a breach of the Convention to exert pressure of this kind to compel individuals to join an association contrary to their convictions.[63]

ILO Convention No. 98 states that workers will be protected from anti-union discrimination and victimisation. For example, employers should not make employment conditional on not belonging to a union, nor should they dismiss or victimise workers in any way for joining a union or participating in its activities. Employers should not interfere with workers' organisations, for example, by setting up employer-dominated unions or trying to control unions in any way. Moreover,

---

[61] Brown (2000), p. 4.

[62] *Young, James and Webster v United Kingdom* [1981] IRLR 408. The ECHR distinguished the Young case from that of *Sibson v United Kingdom* [1993] 17 EHRR 193 and stated that Mr. Sibson was not subjected to a form of treatment striking at the very substance of the freedom of association guaranteed by Article 11.

[63] Smith and Thomas (1996), p. 516.

the State is under an obligation to promote voluntary collective bargaining between employers and workers' organisations with a view to arriving at collective agreements regulating terms and conditions of employment.

These Conventions protect the more general fundamental right to freedom of association, but in the context of work and employment. The ILO considers them the most basic of the principles underlying its work. Therefore, ILO Members agreed in 1950 that even states, which have not ratified these Conventions, should be subjected to a special system of supervision, to make sure that they respect organisational and collective bargaining rights. In 1951, a tripartite Committee on Freedom of Association was established to examine complaints from workers' organisations, employers' organisations, and governments that member states are not respecting the basic principles of freedom of association. The Committee meets three times a year and can examine complaints even against countries that have not ratified the ILO Conventions.

Evidently, such explains why the ILO considers these Conventions to be fundamental: if workers are free to organise themselves and bargain collectively, they can win many other rights. If these conventions are implemented worldwide, especially in developing countries, they would abolish the non-bargainable category in the organised, sector as well as rule out the systematic victimisation of workers who try to form or join unions in the unorganised sector.

ILO Convention No. 29 bans the use of forced or compulsory labour in all its forms, except when it is decreed by the state in an emergency or for military or public service. In such cases, the workers must be granted normal wages, working hours, and weekly days offs; compensation for sickness or accidents; and support for their families if they are disabled or die. It cannot be for more than 60 days in a year. It is estimated that about 12 million people worldwide are victims of forced labour, with about ten million of them working in the private sector. According to the ILO, the profits from the forced labour of people trafficked were about USD 32 billion in 2007.[64]

In a recent case, the plaintiffs alleged that the defendants, who had entered into a joint venture with the Myanmar Government, were liable for international human rights violations perpetrated by the Burmese military. The claim failed on the grounds that even though the defendants knew about the use of forced labour they sought not to employ forced or slave labour.[65]

ILO Convention No. 105 refers to the abolition of debt bondage, where workers are advanced money by the employer and then forced to continue working for the same employer with the excuse that they have not paid back the debt. In some countries, for example, India, such bondage is sometimes even passed on to the workers' children.[66] This Convention states that wages should be paid regularly. It

---

[64] ILO (2007), p. 10.

[65] *Doe, et al. v Unocal Corp.* Case No. CV 96-6959 decided on 31 August 2000. The point stressed here is that the Court recognised that the ILO is primarily responsible for all matters relating to the rights of workers.

[66] Hensman (2000), p. 1248.

rules out methods of payment, which deprive the worker of a genuine possibility of ending or changing employment. Forcing someone to work against his will is obviously a violation of that person's human rights. What may be less obvious is that such practices tend generally to undermine workers' rights. If some people can be forced to work against their will, often for below-minimum wages, or even no wages at all, this reduces the demand for labour and exerts a downward pressure on everyone's wages and conditions.

ILO Convention No. 138, the Minimum Age Convention, 1973, and Convention No. 182, Worst Forms of Child Labour Convention, 1999, cover the abolition of child labour. This calls for a national policy to ensure the effective abolition of child labour. It specifies that for most member states, the minimum age for employment should not be less than 15 years, but less developed countries may initially specify a minimum age of 14 years. If the work is a risk to the health, safety, and morals of a young person, the minimum age should be 18. But it may be lowered to 16, provided the health, safety, or morals of these young workers are fully protected and they receive proper vocational training. Of all the core labour standards, the one that has raised much controversy is the abolition of child labour, with some people arguing that it is caused by poverty and can only be abolished if poverty is eliminated.

That child labour is a grave economic, social, and human rights issue is because of the widespread nature of number of children employed around the world. The ILO estimates that more than 200 million children are working throughout the world, with many of them working full time. These children do not have access to education and are deprived of good health and the basic freedoms. Out of the estimated 200 million working children, about 126 million are engaged in hazardous forms of child labour. This is a danger to their mental, physical, and moral well-being.[67]

ILO Convention No. 100 calls for equal pay for men and women for work of equal value. This applies to basic wages or salaries and all other payments, both direct and indirect. Deciding whether work is of equal value would require objective evaluation of jobs on the basis of the work to be performed, without any discrimination based on sex. The European Court of Justice (ECJ) (influenced by Convention 100 above and ILO Recommendation No. 90) ruled in EC Commission v United Kingdom of Great Britain and Northern Ireland[68] that the existing equal pay laws did not comply with the requirement of the Equal Pay Directive that a woman should be able to claim equal pay for work of equal value. The ECJ has held, on a number of occasions, that Article 119 of the Treaty of Rome (which deals with the principle of equal pay for equal work) incorporates the principle of equal value.[69]

---

[67] ILO (2007), p. 11.

[68] [1982] ICR 578, [1982] IRLR 333, ECJ.

[69] Case 69/80 *Worringham v Lloyd's Bank Ltd* [1981] IRLR 178; Case 96/80 *Jenkins v Kingsgate (Clothing Productions) Ltd* [1981] E.C.R. 911, ECJ; Case 157/86 *Murphy v Board Telecom Eirrean* [1988] ECR 673.

ILO Convention No. 111 calls for a national policy to eliminate discrimination in access to employment, training, and working conditions on grounds of race, colour, sex, religion, political opinion, national extraction, social origin, or anything else and to promote equality of opportunity and treatment in employment or occupation. Governments are required to pass laws and organise educational programmes to promote acceptance of equality of opportunity and treatment and to set up a national authority to implement the policy. A case decided in a United States Federal Court sheds light on the application of this Convention. An airline made it a condition for hiring or retaining stewardesses that they be unmarried; there was no analogous rule for male cabin staff. The Equal Employment Opportunity Commission held that this constituted discrimination on the grounds of sex, in violation of the Civil Rights Act, 1964. The Court upheld the determination of the Commission.[70]

3.7.2 The Emergence of CLS

It is important in order to determine the relevance of labour standard to recognise the atypical nature of the labour market and labour market regulation. In the field of economics, it is generally accepted that labour be treated like any other commercial good, and the same principles and laws of demand and supply should be applied to the labour market, just as is the case for other markets. The unorthodox view, on the other hand, portrays a different perspective. The 1944 ILO Declaration of Philadelphia provides clear evidence of this. The 1944 Declaration stated simply: "labour is not a commodity." The message of the framers was that labour is a peculiar market. The labour market functions differently from other markets such as for corn, automobile, and iron ore Table 3.1.

Over the years, the rationale for setting of international labour standards as they have evolved since the founding of the ILO has been based on several elements:

i. The human rights element is one of the major components. This rationale shows the recognition that is attached to basic human rights as constituting an essential element in the improvement of workers' conditions of work. Notable examples are the Conventions and Recommendations on Freedom of Association, Freedom from Forced Labour and Freedom from Discrimination. The aim is to positively contribute to the self-identity, personal development and fulfilment of workers, to recent development of the decent work agenda of the ILO.
ii. The issue of achieving an equitable balance of power at the work place, in the economy and in society as a whole is also central to the dignity of workers. Due to the asymmetrical nature of the employer – employee relationship, the employee is at a disadvantage. Should there be no social protection in the relationship, the employee is in a weak position, because he has no alternative way to make ends meets than to accept employment and sell his labour services under the conditions imposed by the employer. In

[70] *Sprogis v. United Air Lines*, Federal Court of Appeals (Seventh Circuit), 16 June 1971. *Fair Employment Practice Cases* (Washington), Vol. 77 p. 621.

Table 3.1 Core ILO Conventions and number of ratifications

Convention No.	Title and aim of convention	Ratifications (at September 2013)
No. 29	**Forced Labour Convention (1930)** Requires the suppression of forced or compulsory labour in all its forms; certain exceptions are permitted, such as military service, convict labour properly supervised, and emergencies such as wars, fires, and earthquakes	177
No. 87	**Freedom of Association and Protection of the Right to Organise Convention (1948)** Establishes the right of all workers and employers to form and join organisations of their own choosing without prior authorisation and lays down a series of guarantees for the free functioning of organisations without interference by public authorities	152
No. 98	**Right to Organise and Collective Bargaining Convention (1949)** Provides for protection against anti-union discrimination, for protection of workers' and employers' organisations against acts of interference by each other, and for measures to promote bargaining	163
No. 100	**Equal Remuneration Convention (1951)** Calls for equal pay and benefits for men and women for work of equal value	167
No. 105	**Abolition of Force Labour Convention (1957)** Prohibits the use of any form of forced or compulsory labour as a means of political coercion or education, punishment for the expression of political or ideological views, workforce mobilisation, labour discipline, punishment for participation in strikes, or discrimination	174
No. 111	**Discrimination (Employment and Occupation) Convention (1958)** Calls for a national policy to eliminate discrimination in access to employment, training, and working conditions on grounds of race, colour, sex, religion, political opinion, natural extraction, or social origin and to promote equality of opportunity and treatment	172
No. 138	**Minimum Age Convention (1973)** Aims at the abolition of child labour, stipulating that minimum age for admission to employment shall not be less than the age of completion of compulsory schooling	166
No. 182	**Worst Forms of Child Labour Convention (1999)** Calls for immediate and effective measures to prohibit and eliminate the worst forms of child labour, including all forms of slavery, the use of child labour for prostitution, pornography, illicit activities, and work harmful to the health, safety, and morals of children	177

Source: ILOLEX. www.ilo.org/ilolex/english/docs/declworld.htm. Accessed on 3 December 2013

contrast, the employer is in a much better position, since he controls the capital and has alternatives when it comes to employment. The employer can replace an employee with another, he can install labour saving machinery to reduce the number of workers, and he can subcontract the job to another firm, or even put his capital to other uses. Conventions on Right to Organise and Collective Bargaining and rights of association are very important in addressing such imbalances.

In addition to the asymmetrical nature of the working relationship, there are also particular groups of workers who are also vulnerable, such as women, youth, the disabled, and migrants. Members of this group without protection of a special nature are at a great disadvantage or will even be kept out of the labour market. It is for such group of workers that Core Labour Conventions such as Force Labour, Abolition of Forced Labour, Discrimination, Minimum Age, and Worst Forms of Child Labour were created.

3.7.3 Benefits of CLS

Further to the rationale for the creation of the international labour standards are the benefits of such standards in an ever-globalising world. The ILO lists four such benefits, namely[71]

a. Realising decent work: Since work is part of every human being's daily life and is essential to his dignity, well-being and development, creating working conditions in which people are able to utilise their full potential and thereby improve their lives, makes it necessary to create standards to ensure that worker's aspirations are fulfilled.
b. Securing a fair globalised world based on an international legal framework: The goal of decent work is not possible without efforts at the international level. As the world economy evolves, legal instruments are being created to ensure that balance is achieved in the areas of finance, trade, environment, labour and human rights. The contribution of the ILO is the creation of a legal framework on the promotion of international labour standards aimed at "making sure that economic growth and development go along with the creation of decent work." Due to the tripartite nature of the ILO standards setting, the international labour standards created is a reflection of standards agreed upon by all players in the world economy.
c. Levelling the playing field: The establishment of an international legal framework on labour standards prevents the so-called "race to the bottom". This prevents countries from lowering their standards in the belief that they will gain competitive advantage in the global economy. When standards are lowered all countries suffer in the sense that, it encourages the spread of low wages, low skills, and eventually prevents a country from developing skilled human capital and also prevents other countries from developing their economies. The application of labour standards world-wide ensures that the efforts of countries are not undermined.
d. Contributing to economic efficiency: Adhering to labour standards could sometimes be perceived as raising the cost of production, and thereby making firms and even countries

[71] See http://www.ilo.org/global/standards/introduction-to-international-labour-standards/the-benefits-of-international-labour-standards/lang--en/index.htm. Accessed 4 March 2014.

> not competitive. Evidence on the ground, however, indicates otherwise. The economic development of countries where there is high incidence of compliance point to high levels of economic efficiency, in which case, managers are forced to compete through improvement in productivity and quality with great benefits for their firms. Compliance also leads to regulatory efficiency with lower levels of industrial accidents and reduction of health care costs, dropping the costs for the firm. In firms where employees feel safe, they are motivated to take risks and the firm benefits through increased employee innovations, lower staff turnover. By ensuring equal opportunities, equal treatment, creating an enabling environment through freedom of association and collective bargaining not only avoids social conflict, but also leads to higher economic growth and help alleviate poverty. The effect is that, the country as a whole gains in terms of management, unions and workers working together to solve problems and effective resolution of issues.

Furthermore, putting a system in place that guarantees income security leads to the elimination of forced labour, and child labour not only is a moral imperative but also has huge advantages in strengthening the efficiency and stability of the employers', unions', and workers' relationship. This stable industrial relations environment makes the country become attractive to foreign investors, which in the long run contributes to economic efficiency and human capital formation. In an analysis of the criterion for investors' choice of countries to invest in, investors in terms of ranking consider, for example, political and social stability and the quality of the workforce over that of cost of labour. This shows that compliance with the labour standards pays off than attempts to reduce the cost of production.

3.7.4 *Freedom of Association and Development*

A recent publication by the ILO has shed more light on the importance of core labour standards on development.[72] The publication highlights the importance of freedom of association as a cornerstone of ILO's approach to development through the decent work agenda.[73] Respect for freedom of association is considered as a fundamental right and an essential part of the ILO structural characteristic, i.e., the tripartism nature of the organisation. According to the ILO, freedom of association is the key element in ensuring respect for other fundamental rights at work, without which, the advancement of the common welfare and the principle of tripartism could be impaired and thus harm the chances for greater social justice.[74]

The publication acknowledges that economic growth is essential to the development process and also states that inclusive growth and governance are needed to ensure that economic development contributes to the well-being of the greatest number of people, especially the most vulnerable.[75] However, this is achievable

[72] ILO (2011c).

[73] ILO (2011c), p. 1.

[74] ILO (2011c), p. 2.

[75] ILO (2011c).

when there are strong and independent trade unions and employer organisations. These organisations can help promote development through getting their members involved in contributing to economic and social policy issues, which facilitate consultation with a broad cross section of different interest groups and spur employment rich growth. In situations where the government reaches agreement with the employers' and workers' organisations, this can help provide broad-based support for policy and legal reforms across a variety of social and economic areas.[76]

In spite of the positive role that respect for freedom of association can bring to development outcomes, there are still challenges in that this right is not universally recognised or uniformly implemented in all countries. According to Freeman (2011), there are two competing views in the world of economics on the impact of trade union and related labour organisation with which freedom of association is explicably linked.

The first view holds that unions impede the operation of otherwise perfect markets and could lead to the strengthening of the welfare state at the expense of economic growth. The proponents of this view also hold that strong labour rights lead to increased labour cost and adversely affect trade competitiveness. The implication of this for policymaking is that freedom of association and the activities of trade unions should be restricted or curtailed in countries that want to promote economic development. In line with this thinking, for example, Australia in 2005 through the Works Choices legislation sought to discourage collective contracts. Also in 2011, whilst a number of United States of America state governments were seeking to remove the rights of state and local employees to collective bargaining, the state of Wisconsin passed legislation that eliminates most collective bargaining rights for public workers and also requires them to contribute more towards pension and health coverage.[77]

The second view supporting the role of unions holds that unions help workers to negotiate in an imperfect labour market and also balance the bargaining power of employers and are able to influence government policy to distribute the benefits of growth more equitably. The implication of this view is that government should guarantee the rights of workers to form unions and negotiation with employers.

In light of the two views above, the question this raises is which view presents an accurate picture of the impact of labour organisations to development outcomes. Freeman (2011) concludes that in spite of the fact that the impact of trade unions on the overall economic efficiency is difficult to determine, nevertheless the evidence that unions and other labour organisations produce more egalitarian economic outcomes in wages and benefits is incontestable. Freeman links his conclusion to Coase's theorem, that when two parties bargain, they bargain efficiently so that they "leave no money on the table". He supports this strand of reasoning with the following argument:

---

[76] ILO (2011c), p. 3.

[77] http://www.nbcnews.com/id/41996994/ns/politics-more_politics/t/wis-governor-officially-cuts-collective-bargaining/. Accessed 5 March 2014.

> With efficient bargaining labor organizations and management negotiate to produce the same allocation of resources and output as a perfectly competitive market but distribute more of the revenues from production to workers. The evidence on whether collective bargaining is efficient in this sense is equivocal.[78]

Furthermore, if it is acknowledged that economic development has social objectives, then the role of trade unions is essential to achieving that goal. In addition, the ILO publication on "Freedom of Association and Development" has highlighted the essential role of freedom of association in fostering and maintaining sustainable development, encompassing social, environmental, and economic dimensions. The publication outlines how respect for freedom of association can contribute to development outcomes in at least four key areas, namely fostering inclusive economic growth and poverty reduction, creating a positive business environment, cooperating in times of crisis, and contributing to strengthening democracy and improving governance.[79]

What respect for freedom of association, and in effect the other CLS, fosters is the development of a spirit of partnership and cooperation, which are significant in overcoming the challenges to economic development.[80]

3.8 The ILO Declaration on Fundamental Principles and Rights at Work, 1998

On June 18, 1998, the International Labour Conference adopted the 'ILO Declaration on Fundamental Principles and Rights at Work and its Follow-up' (the Declaration). This Declaration aims to ensure that social progress goes hand in hand with economic progress and development. The Declaration makes it clear that these rights are universal and that they apply to all people in all States—regardless of the level of economic development. It particularly highlights groups with special needs, including the unemployed and migrant workers. It recognises that economic growth alone is not enough to ensure equity and social progress and to eradicate poverty.[81] It declares that all Member states have an obligation to implement the Core Conventions even if they have not ratified them.

All ILO Members are required to respect, promote, and realise, in accordance with the Constitution, the principles pertaining to fundamental rights that are subject to the conventions in the following categories:

- freedom of association and the effective recognition of the right to collective bargaining,

---

[78] Freeman (2011), p. 6 (The paper was submitted as a draft for discussion only).

[79] ILO (2011c), p. 3.

[80] ILO (2011c), pp. 69–75.

[81] http://www.ilo.org/dyn/declaris/DECLARATIONWEB.ABOUTDECLARATIONHOME?var_language=EN. Accessed 28 March 2014.

- the elimination of forced or compulsory labour,
- the abolition of child labour, and
- the elimination of discrimination in respect of employment and occupation.

The ILO Conventions mentioned above are considered not only in terms of the social implications for workers but also in this era of globalisation; as the world economy merges into one, there is much talk about the economic implications not only for the country where these Conventions are not adhered to but also for the world economy as a whole.[82] It is this argument that has motivated some governments and individuals to call for the inclusion of a social clause in Article XX of the GATT Agreement to be adhered to by all countries. President Clinton reiterated this during the Third WTO Ministerial Conference in Seattle, that member states that violate these Core Conventions should be penalised by trade sanctions.

Developing countries are opposed to this inclusion; to them, protectionism is hidden behind the rhetoric, making the issue a complex one. Do developed countries have valid reasons for placing labour standards on the global agenda, thereby calling for the imposition of sanctions on countries that do not adhere to the ILO Conventions on the core labour standards? This calls for a determination of which labour standards affect international trade.

Box 3.1: ILO Declaration on Fundamental Principles and Rights at Work

Whereas the ILO was founded in the conviction that social justice is essential to universal and lasting peace;

Whereas economic growth is essential but not sufficient to ensure equity, social progress and the eradication of poverty, confirming the need for the ILO to promote strong social policies, justice and democratic institutions;

Whereas the ILO should, now more than ever, draw upon all its standard-setting, technical cooperation and research resources in all its areas of competence, in particular employment, vocational training and working conditions, to ensure that, in the context of a global strategy for economic and social development, economic and social policies are mutually reinforcing components in order to create broad-based sustainable development;

Whereas the ILO should give special attention to the problems of persons with special social needs, particularly the unemployed and migrant workers, and mobilize and encourage international, regional and national efforts aimed at resolving their problems, and promote effective policies aimed at job creation;

Whereas, in seeking to maintain the link between social progress and economic growth, the guarantee of fundamental principles and rights at

(continued)

[82] Reich (1994).

Box 3.1 (continued)
work is of particular significance in that it enables the persons concerned, to claim freely and on the basis of equality of opportunity, their fair share of the wealth which they have helped to generate, and to achieve fully their human potential;

Whereas the ILO is the constitutionally mandated international organization and the competent body to set and deal with international labour standards, and enjoys universal support and acknowledgement in promoting Fundamental Rights at Work as the expression of its constitutional principles;

Whereas it is urgent, in a situation of growing economic interdependence, to reaffirm the immutable nature of the fundamental principles and rights embodied in the Constitution of the Organization and to promote their universal application;

THE INTERNATIONAL LABOUR CONFERENCE

1. Recalls:
   (a) that in freely joining the ILO, all Members have endorsed the principles and rights set out in its Constitution and in the Declaration of Philadelphia, and have undertaken to work towards attaining the overall objectives of the Organization to the best of their resources and fully in line with their specific circumstances;
   (b) that these principles and rights have been expressed and developed in the form of specific rights and obligations in Conventions recognized as fundamental both inside and outside the Organization.
2. Declares that all Members, even if they have not ratified the Conventions in question, have an obligation arising from the very fact of membership in the Organization to respect, to promote and to realize, in good faith and in accordance with the Constitution, the principles concerning the fundamental rights which are the subject of those Conventions, namely:
   (a) freedom of association and the effective recognition of the right to collective bargaining;
   (b) the elimination of all forms of forced or compulsory labour;
   (c) the effective abolition of child labour; and
   (d) the elimination of discrimination in respect of employment and occupation.
3. Recognizes the obligation on the Organization to assist its Members, in response to their established and expressed needs, in order to attain these objectives by making full use of its constitutional, operational and budgetary resources, including, by the mobilization of external resources and support, as well as by encouraging other international organizations with

(continued)

Box 3.1 (continued)

which the ILO has established relations, pursuant to article 12 of its Constitution, to support these efforts:

(a) by offering technical cooperation and advisory services to promote the ratification and implementation of the fundamental Conventions;
(b) by assisting those Members not yet in a position to ratify some or all of these Conventions in their efforts to respect, to promote and to realize the principles concerning fundamental rights which are the subject of these Conventions; and
(c) by helping the Members in their efforts to create a climate for economic and social development.

4. Decides that, to give full effect to this Declaration, a promotional follow-up, which is meaningful and effective, shall be implemented in accordance with the measures specified in the annex hereto, which shall be considered as an integral part of this Declaration.
5. Stresses that labour standards should not be used for protectionist trade purposes, and that nothing in this Declaration and its follow-up shall be invoked or otherwise used for such purposes; in addition, the comparative advantage of any country should in no way be called into question by this Declaration and its follow-up.

Adopted by the International Labour Conference at its 86th Session, Geneva, 18 June 1998 (Annex revised 15 June 2010).

The ILO 1998 Declaration has captured the underlying issue of the link between labour standards and international trade by calling for the bridging of the economic and social divide. This divide as a major part of the growing inequality in the world with its attendant problems has, although not gained the needed attention, nevertheless also been captured in a number of RTAs.[83] Whilst it might appear for now as mere rhetoric, the recognition by the parties in their trade arrangements that economic and social policies are mutually reinforcing components of sustainable development is a good sign and an example for a multilateral blueprint or as part of an international framework.

[83] The RTAs signed by the EU and Canada recognises the link between economic and social developments. See Chap. 7 under the trade agreements signed by EU and Canada.

3.9 Labour Standards as Universal Standards

Should global standards be made universal? In 1995, world leaders at the Copenhagen World Summit for Social Development recognising the link between economic development, social development, and environmental protection stated:

Safeguarding and promoting respect for basic workers' rights, including the prohibition of forced labour and child labour, freedom of association and the right to organise and bargain collectively, equal remuneration for men and women for work of equal value, and non-discrimination in employment, fully implementing the conventions of the International Labour Organization (ILO) in the case of States parties to those conventions, and taking into account the principles embodied in those conventions in the case of those countries that are not States parties to thus achieve truly sustained economic growth and sustainable development.[84]

The Copenhagen Summit defined a set of fundamental workers' rights that were based on ILO Conventions. The declaration and programme of action of the World Summit made special reference to ILO Conventions pertaining to prohibition of forced and child labour, the freedom of association, the right to organise and bargain collectively, and the principle of non-discrimination. In response to this, the ILO launched a campaign for universal ratification of the labour standards that was referred to in the declaration and programme of action during the World Summit for the adoption of its Declaration on Fundamental Principles and Rights at Work and its follow-up.

The ILO considered the adoption of the Declaration as the third step after, first, the adoption of the Declaration and Programme of Action in Copenhagen in 1995 and, second, the declaration by WTO Members at the 1996 Singapore Ministerial Conference. In the view of the ILO, adopting the CLS as universally applicable was simply to take up the challenge that the international community presented it both in 1995 and 1996, that is, to "safeguard and promote respect for basic workers' rights" and that the ILO is the competent body to deal with that.

The way international labour standards are set shows the universality of the standards. The standards are set as a result of discussions among governments, employers, and workers after consultations with experts from around the world. The officials involved in setting the standards are a representation of the international consensus to tackling labour problems at the global level and a reflection of the knowledge and experience that they bring from all parts of the world.

The tripartite nature of adopting conventions and recommendations testifies to the universality of the CLS that are at issue. Governments', employers', and workers' representatives draw up the conventions and recommendations, which are then adopted at the ILO International Labour Conference held annually.

---

[84] Report of the World Summit for Social Development, (Copenhagen, 6–12 March 1995), A/CONF.166/9, Annex II, Programme of Action of the World Summit for Social Development, Paragraph 54(b).

Member states are required under the ILO Constitution after the adoption of a convention or recommendation to submit it to their competent authority, in most cases to parliament, for consideration. However, in the case of conventions, the consideration would lead to ratification. Once the convention has been ratified, it would come into force in that country a year after the date of the ratification. A country that ratifies a convention commits itself to apply the convention nationally and to report on its application to the ILO at regular intervals.

The legal nature of the conventions or standards calls for their application in the legal system of the country that has ratified them. This also forms part of the body of international law, which all ILO Members adhere to. According to Sengenberger (2005), a fundamental attribute of ILO Conventions is that they lay down minimum standards and are not meant to prescribe economically unworkable levels of provision.

Caire (1977) has identified three possible roles of international standards, which, although he applied specifically to freedom of association, could also be applied to the other standards, in particular to the CLS. The three roles are as follows: how to gauge the influence of the standards in the legal field, how to assess their educational role, and finally how to advance their roles through ILO technical assistance, especially in developing countries. Even though the educational role can have a positive influence on public opinion and government practice, and technical assistance is important for the promotion and protection of the CLS, it's the legal role that we will confine ourselves to. Caire states that the nature of the international Conventions lends support to the view that their effectiveness as legal instruments has been considerable:

> As a legal standard, an international Convention must fulfil certain conditions if it is to ensure the promotion of a universal set of values: the right to be protected must reflect a widely shared set of expectations among significant actors, governmental and non-governmental, although these expectations need not be identical; it must be general in nature so as to be capable of triggering activity and demands in social and economic fields close to, but not identical with, the original area of concern; the right to be protected must nevertheless be specific enough to permit the investigation and rational evaluation of charges of violations; it must be important enough to be valued by its constituency apart from and beyond the particular political context of the time and place; and it must be protected by a minimum international machinery. Freedom of association fulfils all these conditions. It is a right which broadly reflects the expectations of the social actors since the two relevant Conventions were adopted by very large majorities (127 votes to 0, with 11 abstentions, in the case of Convention No. 87; 115 votes to 10, with 25 abstentions, in the case of Convention No. 98) and are currently those that have been most widely ratified. The right is sufficiently general to apply to all kinds of economic and social contexts, as is apparent from the ratification of the relevant Conventions by countries at such diverse stages of economic development as France and Upper Volta,[85] with such diverse political regimes as the USSR and Belgium, and with such different legal traditions as Nigeria and Senegal. The right is nevertheless specific enough to have given rise to a whole body of case law. It is important enough to have been embodied in the constitution of a number of

[85] Upper Volta is now named as Burkina Faso.

countries. In addition, as has been seen, it is protected by special legal machinery which is both original and effective.[86]

A major concern that rises from standards setting is how in a world of great diversity and considering the different levels of economic development, the institutional and cultural make up of each and every country, these standards could have universal appeal.[87] The ILO, from the very beginning of its establishment, has been conscious of the different economic and social conditions of its membership. It is in this respect that Article 19(3) of the ILO Constitution states:

> In framing any Convention or Recommendation of general application, the conference shall have due regard to those countries in which climatic conditions, the imperfect development of industrial organization, or other special circumstances make the industrial conditions substantially different and shall suggest modifications, if any, which it considers may be required to meet the case of such countries.

The ILO, in the course of its existence, has made special provisions for countries to implement the conventions and recommendations. In a case in point is that of the Hours of Work Convention, 1919. The ILO allowed Japan and former British India (now India) a slower implementation of the above-mentioned Convention. The ILO also allowed that the above Convention not apply to China, Persia, and Siam. In these countries, they were allowed to reconsider the limitations on the hours of work and to apply them at a later time.

However, the ILO, whilst not overlooking the diversity of its membership, recognises that there is a limit to allowing member states to deviate from the norm across countries. The ILO has not permitted the setting of different standards for each country and has also not permitted the setting of regional standards. The ILO has, on the other hand, permitted countries to not immediately apply a standard. For example, it tolerates the ratification of parts of Conventions. It also allows flexibility in the implementation of standards, taking into consideration the socioeconomic and cultural peculiarities of nation-states.[88]

Sengenberger (2005) gives the example of how the ILO permits national authorities to choose methods that are appropriate to the national conditions and practice in that country. The example refers to Convention No. 111, 1958, which requires ratifying countries to state and follow a national policy for the elimination of discrimination in access to employment, training, and working conditions on grounds of race, colour, sex, religion, political opinion, national extraction, social origin, or anything else, which has the effect of nullifying or impairing equality of opportunity or treatment in employment or occupation.[89]

In sum, the aim of reaching universality of the standards is through equivalence and not uniformity. The import of the equivalence is the coordination of

---

[86] Caire (1977), at p. 135.

[87] See Sengenberger (2005), for an in-depth analysis of the universality of standards in respect of how effective standards are in the informal economy and cultural relativism, pp. 51–56.

[88] Sengenberger (2005), p. 50.

[89] Sengenberger (2005), p. 50.

international policymaking. For example, the provisions on minimum wages and social security are not to institute the same minimum wages worldwide, but rather it states that Members should introduce a minimum wage commensurate with their level of development. Given the level of development, for example in Norway and Ghana, it cannot be expected that the minimum wage level would be the same. This rather calls for the establishment of a global-wide method of calculating the minimum wages for each country. As such, the universality of the standard rests in the process of arriving at the standard and how to implement it—the goals connected with the standards rather than the means for attaining the results.

Box 3.2: International Labour Standards
Throughout the ILO, a system of international labour standards and labour Conventions was developed during the last century. Workers' rights include both core labour standards around which there is widespread international agreement and other basic rights. The core rights, encompassed in international Conventions, include freedom of association and the right to collective bargaining; elimination of all forms of forced or compulsory labour; elimination of discrimination in respect of employment and occupation; and the effective abolition of child labour. The longstanding commitment of the ILO to protecting the core rights of all workers irrespective of where they work was reinforced in 1998 when the International Labour Conference unanimously adopted a Declaration on Fundamental Principles and Rights at Work that applies to all those who work, regardless of their employment relationship. Most recently, the ILO has explicitly incorporated the informal economy in its policy framework called "Decent Work". Most ILO standards apply to all workers or, if targeted at workers in the formal economy, have explicit provisions for extension to other categories of workers. One ILO Convention—the Home Work Convention, 1996 (No. 177)—focuses on a specific category of worker in the informal economy: home workers or industrial outworkers who work from their homes. And two ILO Conventions—one on rural workers, the other on indigenous and tribal peoples—focuses on groups who are often in the informal economy.

Source: ILO: Decent work and the informal economy: Abstracts of working papers (Geneva, 2002).

References

Anderson, K. (1996). The intrusion of environmental and labor standards into trade policy. In W. Martin & L. A. Winters (Eds.), *The Uruguay round and the developing countries*. New York: University of Cambridge.

Boivin, I., & Odero, A. (2006). The committee of experts on the application of conventions and recommendations: Progress achieved in national labour legislation. *International Labour Review, 145*(3).

Brown, D. (2000). *International trade and core labor standards: A survey of the recent literature* (Discussion Paper 2000–2005). Department of Economics, Tufts University.

Caire, G. (1977). *Freedom of association and economic development*. Geneva: ILO.

Follows, J. W. (1951). *Antecedents of the International Labour Organization*. Oxford: Clarendon.

Freeman, R. B. (2011). *What do labor organisations do to equitable and inclusive growth*? Paper presented at the United States Department of Labor Seminar on Labor Organizations, Collective Bargaining, and Dispute Resolution, 11 March 2011.

Gravel, E., Duplessis, I., & Gernigon, B. (2001). *The committee on freedom of association: Its impact over 50 years*. Geneva.

Hansson, G. (1983). *Social clauses and international trade*. New York: St. Martin's Press.

Helfer, L. R. (2006). Understanding change in international organizations: Globalization and innovation in the ILO. *Vanderbilt Law Review, 59*(3).

Hensman, R. (2000). World trade and workers' rights, to link or not to link? *Economic and Political Weekly*, 8 April.

ILO. (1995). *The ILO in the service of social progress, a workers' education manual (2nd rev ed.)*. Geneva: International Labour Office.

ILO. (2007). *The ILO at a glance*. Geneva: ILO.

ILO. (2009a). *Rules of the game: A brief introduction to International Labour Standards* (2nd rev ed.). Geneva.

ILO. (2009b). *Report of the Committee of Experts on the Application of Conventions and Recommendations*. Report III (Part 1 A).

ILO. (2011a). *Report of the Director General; a new era of social justice, international labour conference*. 100th Session, 2011, Report I (A).

ILO. (2011b). *The committee on the application of standards of the international labour conference: A dynamic and impact built on decades of dialogue and persuasion*. Geneva.

ILO. (2011c). *Freedom of association and development*. Geneva.

Leary, V. A. (1992). Lessons from the experience of the International Labour Organization. In P. Alston (Ed.), *The United Nations and human rights, a critical appraisal*. Oxford: Clarendon.

Leary, V. (1996a). Workers' rights and international trade: The social clause (GATT, ILO, NAFTA, U.S. Laws). In J. Bhagwati & R. E. Hudec (Eds.), *Fair trade and harmonization, prerequisites for free trade?* (Vol. 2). Cambridge, MA: The MIT Press.

Leary, V. (1996b). The paradox of workers' rights as human rights. In L. Compa & S. F. Diamond (Eds.), *Human rights, labor rights, and international trade*. Philadelphia: University of Pennsylvania Press.

Lee, E. (1997). Globalisation and labour standards: A review of issues. *International Labour Review, 136*(2).

Maupain, F. (2005). Is the ILO effective in upholding workers' rights? Reflections on the Myanmar experience. In P. Alston (Ed.), *Labour rights as human rights*. Oxford: Oxford University Press.

Reich, R. (1994). *Keynote address*. International Labor Standards and Global Economic Integration: Proceedings of a symposium. Bureau of International Labor Affairs, U.S. Department of Labor, July

Rodrik, D. (2001). *The developing countries' hazardous obsession with global integration*, January 8. http://bev.berkeley.edu/ipe/readings/RodrickLDCsobsession.PDF. Accessed 30 Mar 2014.

Sengenberger, W. (2005). *Globalization and social progress: The role and impact of International Labour Standards, A report prepared for the Friedrich-Ebert Stiftung* (2nd revised and extended revision). Bonn, September 2005.

Smith, I. T., & Thomas, G. H. (1996). *Industrial law* (6th ed.). London: Butterworth.

Swepston, L. (2003). Closing the gap between international law and U.S. labor law. In J. A. Gross (Ed.), *Workers' rights as human rights*. Ithaca: Cornell University Press.

Thomas, C. (2009). The WTO and labor rights: Strategies of linkage. In S. Joseph, D. Kinley, & J. Waincymer (Eds.), *The World Trade Organization and human rights: Interdisciplinary perspectives*. Cheltenham: Edward Elgar.

Valticos, N. (1998). International labour standards and human rights: Approaching the year 2000. *International Labour Review, 137*(2).

Chapter 4
Legal Analysis: CLS, International Law, and the Process and Production Method Argument

4.1 Introduction

This chapter analyses the legal issues that the CLS and trade debate raises. We will consider the link between CLS and customary international law, the Vienna Convention on the Law of Treaties (VCLT). Further, this chapter will consider the issues as to whether CLS could be considered as *jus cogens* and whether CLS fall within the human rights discussion. The chapter will also review labour standards within the WTO and the process and production method (PPM).

International law embodies legal rules that apply between sovereign states and such other entities that have been given international personality by sovereign states. Further, international law, as used in the United States Restatement of Foreign Relations Law, "consists of rules and principles of general application dealing with the conduct of states and of international organizations and with their relations inter se, as well as with some of their relations with persons, whether natural or juridical".[1] As such, the ILO Conventions, in particular the CLS, as discussed above having general application could be classified as international labour law forming part of public international law.

Under international law, the status of a legal rule is the determination of its source as law. At the basic level, international law is derived from four sources, as enumerated in Article 38(1) of the Statute of the International Court of Justice: (1) treaties, (2) customary international law, (3) general principles of law, and (4) 'judicial decisions and the teachings of the most highly qualified publicists of the various nations, as a subsidiary means for the determination of rules of law'. Out of these four sources, the most relevant for our purposes are the first two (treaties and customary international law).

---

[1] American Law Institute's Restatement of Foreign Relations Law, 1987 Revision, Restatement Section 101 (hereinafter referred to as Restatement).

K. Addo, *Core Labour Standards and International Trade*,
DOI 10.1007/978-3-662-44619-5_4

Considering the two sources of international law for our consideration, treaty law is based on the consent of states and customary international law is binding on states. According to the Restatement, "customary international law results from a general and consistent practice of states followed by them from a sense of legal obligation."[2] In this respect, customary international law is binding on all states without exception and even if they have not consented.[3]

4.2 Customary Law

The ILO Declaration (discussed above) contains the CLS, which obliges Members to implement even if they have not ratified them. However, the ILO Declaration is not a legally binding mechanism, which makes it fall under the soft law concept. Whereas the CLS fall under the second source of international law, namely custom, nevertheless the debate as to which labour standards can be considered as part of customary international law is an ongoing debate.[4]

Given the universality of the CLS and given the fact that the Declaration has created legal obligations for all ILO Members, can the CLS be considered as part of customary international law binding all States irrespective of their ILO Membership and as to whether they have ratified the ILO Conventions that form the basis for the CLS?

4.2.1 CLS and Customary International Law

In order to determine whether the CLS have achieved the status of customary international law, an analysis of the customary nature of labour standards in general is warranted.

The International Court of Justice (ICJ) in the *Asylum* case laid down the two requirements of customary international law:

> [t]he party which relies on custom ... must prove that this custom is established in such a manner that it has become binding on the other party ... that the rule invoked ... is in accordance with a constant and uniform usage, practiced by the States in question, and that this usage is the expression of a right appertaining to the State granting asylum and a duty incumbent on the territorial State.[5]

The two requirements deduced from the *Asylum* case are, first, a state practice that is established, widespread, and consistent and, second, *opinion juris sive*

---

[2] Restatement, Section 102.

[3] Howse and Mutua (2000), p. 59.

[4] Kaufmann (2008), p. 5.

[5] *Asylum case* (Colombia v. Peru), 1950 I.C.J. 276, p. 277 (20 November).

necessitates (opinion as to law or necessity).[6] Also, in the 1985 *Continental Shelf Case (Libya v. Malta)*, the ICJ stated that the substance of customary international law must be "looked for primarily in the actual practice and *opinio juris* of States".[7]

4.2.2 State Practice as Customary Law

State practice is also referred to as the objective or material element. State practice includes physical acts such as diplomatic acts, public instructions and governmental acts, and official statements. Silence or inaction could mean either tacit agreement or that the state lacks interest in the issue, and this may constitute state practice.[8] For an action to constitute state practice, it must be of a comparatively short duration, and in which case it must be general and consistent. The practice can be general even though it might not be universally followed. There is no means of determining how widespread this practice is, but in any case, there should be widespread recognition in states that are involved in this activity. However, a principle of customary law is that it is not binding on a state that has indicated its opposition from the principle in the course of its development.[9]

When the ILO Declaration was adopted, 19 Member states abstained, but they have since been cooperating in the implementation of the Declaration by conforming to ILO reporting procedures. This could be considered as state practice for these 19 countries in line with those ILO Members that voted for the Declaration. This could be seen as a consensus in the universal recognition of the CLS.[10]

4.2.3 Opinion Juris

Opinion juris is also referred to as subjective or psychological element. A state practice can become part of customary international law when it appears that the states that follow the practice or rule do so out of a sense of legal obligation.[11] There should be evidence of a general practice, a determination of a Court or other international tribunals.[12] In this case, the treaties, resolutions, and the acts of

---

[6] Hereinafter *opinion juris*.

[7] *Continental Shelf Case* (Libya v. Malta), 1985 I.C.J. Rep. 13, 29, para. 27. The ICJ also stated in the *Nicaragua Case*, 1986 I.C.J. Rep. 14, 97, para. 183, that the Court had to "direct its attention to the practice and opinio juris of States".

[8] Carter et al. (2003), p. 125.

[9] Carter et al. (2003).

[10] See Kaufmann (2008), p. 6.

[11] Carter et al. (2003), p. 125.

[12] Vandaele (2005), p. 240.

international organisations and also in national constitutions are evidence of state practice and also of *opinion juris*.[13] States must show their willingness to follow a practice due to their belief rather than the demands of courtesy, reciprocity, comity, morality, or simple political expediency.[14]

The ICJ has laid down a rigorous approach when it stated in the *Continental Shelf case*:

> [n]ot only must the acts concerned [constituting state practice] amount to a settled practice, but they must also be such, or be carried out in such a way, as to be evidence of a belief that this practice is rendered obligatory by the existence of a rule of law requiring it. The need for such a belief, i.e., the existence of a subjective element, is implicit in the very notion of the *opinio juris sive necessitatis*. The States concerned must therefore feel that they are conforming to what amounts to a legal obligation.[15]

Following our examination of the two element theory under customary international law, the CLS and the ILO Declaration, as shown under the analyses of state practice and *opinion juris*, appear to indicate that there is widespread recognition of the CLS by ILO Members and in the international community as a whole. Further, ILO Member states appear to follow the practice of applying the CLS and conforming to the reporting mechanism out of a sense of legal obligation. Whilst it might appear that the CLS and the Declaration are part of customary international law, the debate about whether all of the CLS or only some of the CLS can be considered as customary law need further analyses.

4.3 Vienna Convention on the Law of Treaties (VCLT)

With the establishment of the WTO as an international organisation, and the recognition of the Agreement as a treaty, it becomes subject to the rules of interpretation under customary international law. In this respect, the Appellate Body has stated:

> The WTO Agreement is a treaty – the international equivalent of a contract. It is self-evident that in an exercise of their sovereignty, and in pursuit of their own respective national interests, the Members of the WTO have made a bargain. In exchange for the benefits they expect to derive as Members of the WTO, they have agreed to exercise their sovereignty according to the commitments they have made in the WTO Agreement.[16]

---

[13] Vandaele (2005).

[14] See Lepard Brian (1993).

[15] North Sea Continental Shelf Cases (F.R.G v. Den., F.R.G. v. Neth.), 1969 I.C.J. Rep. 3, 44, para. 77.

[16] See *Japan – Taxes on Alcoholic Beverages* – Report of the Appellate Body, WT/DS11/AB/R, 4 October 1996. Adopted by the Dispute Settlement Body on 1 November 1996.

The Appellate Body stated that under Article 3.2 of the Dispute Settlement Understanding,[17] it is directed to clarify the provisions of GATT 1994 and other "covered agreements" of the WTO in accordance with customary rules of interpretation of public international law. The Appellate Body further stated:

> Following this, in *United States – Standards for Reformulated and Conventional Gasoline,*[18] we stressed the need to achieve such clarification by reference to the fundamental rule of treaty interpretation set out in Article 31(1) of the *Vienna Convention.*[19] We stressed there that this general rule of interpretation "has attained the status of a rule of customary or general international law".[20] There can be no doubt that Article 32 of the *Vienna Convention*, dealing with the role of supplementary means of interpretation, has also attained the same status.

With this, the Appellate Body has confirmed that Article 31 of the VCLT provides the words that form the foundation for interpreting the WTO Agreement. Mathis, however, states that the question of application of VCLT Articles to all WTO provisions and in relation to other treaties is not settled. He further argues that it might appear that only VCLT Articles 26–38 titled "Observance, application and interpretation of treaties" would be applicable to the WTO.[21] In this respect, Mathis further argues that this view recognises the fact that not all WTO Members are signatories to the VCLT and the reference to the customary rules of public international law that is stated in the Dispute Settlement Understanding (DSU) is only restricted by it terms to interpretations of provisions within disputes.[22]

Article 3 of the DSU provides that "[T]o clarify the existing provisions of those agreements in accordance with customary rules of interpretation of public international law". It appears to some legal scholars that Article 3 refers not only to the principles of international law with respect to interpretation only but also to the principles of international law in general.[23] For the purposes of the regional trade agreements, we will consider VCLT Articles 30 and 41.

---

[17] Article 3.2 of the DSU states in pertinent part states:

> ...The Members recognize that [the dispute settlement system] serves to preserve the rights and obligations of Members under the covered agreements, and to clarify the existing provisions of those agreements in accordance with customary rules of interpretation of public international law.

[18] *United States – Standards for Reformulated and Conventional Gasoline*, WT/DS2/AB/R, adopted 20 May 1996, DSR 1996:I, 3.

[19] Vienna Convention on the Law of Treaties (VCLT), concluded at Vienna 23 May 1969, entry into force, 27 January 1980, UN Doc A/Conf 39/28, UKTS 58 (1980), 8 ILM 679.

[20] *United States – Standards for Reformulated and Conventional Gasoline*, WT/DS2/AB/R, adopted 20 May 1996, DSR 1996:I, 3–28.

[21] Mathis (2002), p. 272.

[22] Mathis (2002).

[23] See McRae (2000), pp. 27–41.

4.3.1 VCLT Article 30

Article 30 is entitled *Application of successive treaties relating to the same subject matter*. The relevance of Article 30 is due to the fragmented nature of public international law. This has the probability of leading to contradictions and thus the need for a sequence of rules to resolve such conflict. When there are rules that are aimed at resolving conflicts between treaties, this not only enhances legal certainty and provides clarity, but it also helps contribute to the states observing the treaties and, in so doing, observing public international law.[24]

Article 30 does refer to all kinds of treaties, irrespective of their content, their nature, and the number of Parties to the agreement, in which case the WTO Agreement is included. Paragraph 1 exemplifies the hierarchical principle, in which case, a treaty when of a higher legal rank prevails over all treaties of a lower legal rank.

The pertinent rules in Article 30 are in paragraphs 3 and 4. In a case none of the colliding treaties include a conflict clause, the rules stated in paragraphs 3 and 4 apply. Paragraph 3 refers to situations whereby the States that are Parties to both treaties are identical. In which case, where the Parties to conflicting treaties are identical, the later treaty prevails but "applies only to the extent that its provisions are compatible with those of the later treaty".

Paragraph 4 refers to the rule to be observed in situations where the rules are not identical. Under the provisions in this paragraph, two situations are considered: (i) in cases where States are Parties to both treaties (4(a)) and (ii) the relationship between a State that is party to both treaties and a State that is party to only one of the two treaties (4(b)). In the latter case, paragraph 4(b) states that "the treaty to which both States are parties governs their mutual rights and obligations".

The rules in both paragraphs 3 and 4 are based on the *lex posterior* principle that the provisions of the later treaty prevails. Further, the provisions of Article 30 embody the principles of *pacta sunt servanda* and *pacta tertiis*.[25]

Paragraph 5 lists all the situations that otherwise remain unaffected by the rules governing the conflict between treaties. The first situation that is not affected has to do with agreements to modify multilateral treaties between certain of the parties only, the rule as stated in Article 41.

4.3.2 Article 41: Modification to Treaties

The prevailing situation in international relations is beset with conflicting interests that require amendments to multilateral treaties and agreements. In such situations, amending a treaty with a large number of parties is a challenging and burdensome

[24] See Dörr and Schmalenbach (2012), p. 507.

[25] Dörr and Schmalenbach (2012), p. 517.

process. But in some cases, it might be that only some of the Parties to the treaty wish to modify the treaty as between themselves alone.[26] In which case, the Parties that modify the treaty between themselves might do so because these have common interests or to strengthen their relationship. It could also be that they want to ensure that they achieve higher standards of treaty obligations and lead the way in this regard. The signing of RTAs has seen the inclusion of the so-called WTO-plus obligations and, for our purposes, the inclusion of labour standards in RTAs.[27]

During the Vienna Conference, the issue of the modification of multilateral treaties was considered not a common practice. Although there are examples of clauses in treaties that provide for the possibility of modifications as far back as the nineteenth century, there appeared not to be any common rules and also no jurisprudence on the issue.[28]

The VCLT provides in Article 41, entitled *Agreements to modify multilateral treaties between certain of the parties only*:

1. Two or more of the parties to a multilateral treaty may conclude an agreement to modify the treaty as between themselves alone if:
   (a) the possibility of such a modification is provided for by the treaty; or
   (b) the modification in question is not prohibited by the treaty and:
      (i) does not affect the enjoyment by the other parties of their rights under the treaty or the performance of their obligation;
      (ii) does not relate to a provision, derogation from which is incompatible with the effective execution of the object and purpose of the treaty as a whole.
2. Unless in a case falling under paragraph 1(a) the treaty otherwise provides, the parties in question shall notify the other parties of their intention to conclude the agreement and of the modification to the treaty for which is provides.

The term *inter se* was coined by the International Law Commission, and according to Mathis the drafters of Article 41 thought that an *inter se* agreement was very likely to disrupt the object and aims of a multilateral treaty as compared to a treaty amendment that all Parties participated. This, in his view, made the conditions under which Parties to the multilateral treaty could modify as between themselves only more narrowly prescribed.[29]

Article 41 provides for two possibilities: first, where the treaty permits a "contracting out" by Parties signatory to it, the possibility for such a modification expressly stated in the treaty. However, should the treaty only allow for certain kinds of modifications only, then all other modifications shall be prohibited under subparagraph 1(a). It has been argued that the term "or" at the end of subparagraph

---

[26] We consider in Chap. 7 below some of the reasons for such a modification: could be for political or economic reasons or even for both reasons.

[27] Dörr and Schmalenbach (2012), p. 719.

[28] Dörr and Schmalenbach (2012), pp. 721–722.

[29] See Mathis (2002), pp. 274 and 275.

1(a) and the introductory words of subparagraph 1(b) indicate that a modification falls either under subparagraph 1(a) or under 1(b).[30]

The second possibility is where the treaty does not prohibit modifications. Article 41 in subparagraph 1(b) provides the additional requirement or first conditions that the enjoyment of the rights of other parties are not affected and does not add to their obligations. The second condition is that any modification will not cause derogation from a provision that is incompatible with the effective execution of the object and purpose of the treaty in its entirety. In which case, if the object and purpose of the treaty can no longer be effectively executed, then the modification is not permitted.

4.3.3 *Modification Under GATT Article XXIV*

The question is whether GATT 1994 permits a modification in line with Article 41 that two or more parties to a treaty can modify as between themselves alone. GATT Article XXIV:5 states:

> Accordingly, the provisions of this Agreement shall not prevent, as between the territories of contracting parties, the formation of a customs union or of a free-trade area or the adoption of an interim agreement necessary for the formation of a customs union or of a free-trade area; Provided that:...

It appears from the wording of Article XXIV:5 that Parties to the GATT/WTO Agreement are permitted to make modifications when they form free-trade areas and custom unions after having met some conditions. The Appellate Body, in its ruling in *Turkey-Textiles*,[31] stated that the right to modify the GATT/WTO Agreement is subject to showing that the conditions in paragraphs 8 and 5 are met. In meeting the conditions in paragraph 5 for modification of the agreement, the subset of Parties are required to notify the Contracting Parties. In this respect, Article XXIV:7 requires the submission of the plan and schedule, as stated in paragraph 5. What is apparent from this in light of GATT 1994 is that Article 41 1(a) VCLT provides that "the possibility of such a modification is provided for by the treaty".[32]

---

[30] Dörr and Schmalenbach(2012), p. 724.

[31] The ruling of the Panel and Appellate Body in the *Turkey-Textiles* case is reviewed in detail in Chap. 6 below.

[32] For an in-depth analysis of GATT Article XXIV as a modification provision; see Mathis (2002), pp. 277–285.

4.4 Core Labour Standards as *Jus Cogens*?

The question of interest to labour standards advocates is whether the CLS could be considered peremptory norms recognised by the international community. The vast majority of states that recognise the CLS are evidence of their universality and also their widespread support among nations. Nevertheless, as our examination of the CLS under customary international law above has shown, it has to be apparent that the CLS would fall under customary international law, which would thus pave the way for the CLS to reach the status of *jus cogens*.[33] This section will review the concept of *jus cogens* and consider its impact on the CLS.

4.4.1 Brief Overview of Jus Cogens

Are there rules of international law that, by consent, individual subjects of international law cannot modify? International *jus cogens* convey the idea of rule of international law that may not be changed by consent between individual subjects of international law.

Article 53 of the Vienna Convention on the Law of Treaties (VCLT) states:

> A treaty is void, if, at the time of its conclusion, it conflicts with a peremptory norm of general international law. For the purposes of the present Convention, a peremptory norm of general international law is a norm accepted and recognised by the international community of States as a whole as a norm from which no derogation is permitted and which can be modified only by a subsequent norm of general international law having the same character.[34]

In Article 64 of the Vienna Convention, the International Law Commission envisaged the emergence of new rules of *jus cogens* at a future time. This shows the Commission's view that the concept of *jus cogens* is still evolving. Article 64 states: "If a new peremptory norm of general international law emerges, any existing treaty which is in conflict with that norm becomes void and terminates." The VCLT negotiations did not produce any list of rules that constitute *jus cogens*.

However, violations of human rights, slave trade or slavery, and genocide have come to be regarded universally as peremptory norms of international law or, in other words, *jus cogens*. It is important to note that from the enforcement point of view, *jus cogens* apply *erga omnes* (i.e., to everyone). This implies that non-compliance of the rules under *jus cogens* may be reprimanded by any legal body under international law. The International Court of Justice made this point clear in the *Barcelona Traction, Light and Power Company Ltd* case. In that case, the Court's opinion reads in part:

---

[33] See Vandaele (2005), p. 295.

[34] Vienna Convention on the Law of Treaties, 23 May 1969, Article 53.

> [A]n essential distinction should be made between the obligations of a State towards the international community as a whole, and those arising vis-a-vis another state in the field of diplomatic protection. By their very nature the former concern all States. In view of the importance of the rights involved, all States can be held to have a legal interest in their protection; they are obligations *erga omnes*. Such obligations derive, for example, in contemporary international law, from the outlawing of acts of aggression, and of genocide, as also from the principles and rules concerning the basic rights of the human person, including protection from slavery and racial discrimination. Some of the corresponding rights have entered into the body of general international law...; others are conferred by international instruments of a universal or quasi-universal character.[35]

Concerning the consequences of identifying an international violation as *jus cogens*, Bassiouni (1997) raises the threshold question of whether such a status places *obligations ergo omnes* upon states or merely gives them certain rights to proceed against perpetrators of such crimes. Bassiouni further states that the threshold question carries with it the full implications of the Latin word obligatio or that it is denatured international law to signify only the existence of a right rather than a binding legal obligation.[36]

4.4.2 Jus Cogens *and Core Labour Standards*

Has the CLS acquired the status of peremptory norms to qualify as *jus cogens*? Vandaele (2005) provides a two-test approach. First, the CLS should be recognised by the whole international community of States. In respect of this, the CLS, as stated in the ILO Declaration, have to a great extent been recognised by all ILO Members and WTO Members that are also Members of the ILO.

The second test is whether the CLS are norms that are non-derogable. The non-derogative character of a right brings to fore the definition of *jus cogens* given by the Mexican delegate to the United Nations Conference on the Law of Treaties, when he stated:

> The rules of *jus cogens* [are] those rules which derive from principles that the legal conscience of mankind deem[s] absolutely essential to coexistence in the international community.[37]

This definition was further echoed in the opinion of the German Federal Constitutional Court, when the Court stated:

> The quality of such peremptory norms [*jus cogens*] may be attributed only to such legal rules as are firmly rooted in the legal conviction of the community of nations and are indispensable to the existence of the law of nations as an international legal order and the observance of which can be required by all members of the international community.[38]

---

[35] *Barcelona Traction, Light and Power Co. Ltd.* (Belgium v. Spain), [1970] I.C.J. Rep. 4, para 33–34.

[36] Bassiouni (1997), p. 65.

[37] Quoted in Parker and Neylon (1989), p. 415.

[38] Judgment of April 7, 1965, Bundesverfassungsgericht, BVerfGE, West Germany, quoted in Parker and Neylon (1989).

The questions that the definition and opinion above raise for the CLS debate are whether a derogation from the CLS norms affects the conscience of the international community so as to require all countries to seek the observance thereof. If we are to go by the argument that considering the number of countries that have accepted the CLS as international norms and have incorporated them into their national laws, given the fact that 185 Member States have accepted the 'ILO Declaration on Fundamental Principles and Rights at Work and its Follow-up' by virtue of their membership in the ILO, all Members have an obligation to promote those rights listed above even if they have not ratified the individual conventions. Then the CLS could possibly be considered as peremptory norms to be protected as *jus cogens*.

Further to this is the argument that the CLS are part of the large body of human rights and have acquired an obligatory character in international law. The acceptance of CLS in principle as part of human rights by many States has elevated the CLS as legal obligations in international law.

Does this, however, indicate that the CLS have reached the level of international acceptance that they should be considered as jus cogens? In spite of the reasoning above, it cannot be concluded that CLS have reached the level of *jus cogens*. In addition, it is not clear as to whether the international community is prepared to promote the CLS irrespective of their universal acceptance by virtue of the ILO Membership under the 1998 Declaration to the level of peremptory norms that should qualify as *jus cogens*.

4.5 Core Labour Standards as Workers (Human) Rights

Workers' rights (just as human rights) have sometimes been regarded as inalienable rights that, irrespective of nationality, are a right by virtue of being human. In the global economy, workers' rights meet at the point where human rights law, trade law, labour law, and public policy intersect. This has important developments for the field of international labour or workers' rights for trade lawyers and trade policy analysts. It raises the question of the extent to which workers' rights, such as trade union rights, should be treated as economic rights, which should be regulated by governments in a free market environment. On the other hand, it raises the question of how workers' rights could be regarded as human rights and protected by international standards, equal to the market place and economic regulation.[39]

The fundamental question is whether workers' rights are human rights. Leary (1996a) argues that workers' rights are human rights but further states that the international human rights movement has, over the decades, devoted very little attention to worker's rights. On the other hand, the international trade union movement and labour leaders have also rarely sought the support of human rights organisations—what Leary terms as "regrettable paradox"—since the two groups

[39] Compa and Diamond (1996), p. 3.

seem to run on parallel tracks and hardly do their views converge.[40] Furthermore, Leary states that the bellwether for the status of human rights, in general, at the national level starts with the status of workers' rights.[41] And this, Leary states, starts with the violation of freedom of association—one of the most fundamental rights of workers. Whilst human rights were originally conceived as individual rights, together with labour standards they are collective in nature, both have collective dimensions. For example, rights that on face value might seem to be individual rights, such as working hours or social security, carry weight when exercised in a collective manner.[42]

4.5.1 Human Rights and Workers' Rights: Individual and Collective Labour Standards

An issue prominent in human rights law is the clash between individual and collective rights. At the heart of this issue is whether the human rights laws built principally on the recognition of individual rights can also facilitate collective rights. In our view, the answer is yes. Whilst the international human rights framework might appear to advocate only individual rights, it also envisages collective rights.

In recent times, a number of proposals appear to push the collective rights agenda, such as the right to development, the rights of peoples, and the rights of mankind. Whilst such rights have gained acceptance on a wider scale, it has faced opposition from a number of legal experts steeped in the traditionalist line of thinking.[43]

The international labour standards, in particular the CLS, are examples of how the ILO, whilst advocating for collective rights, also allow for individuals to enjoy rights at the individual level. This raises the issue of whether the individual as part of a group can enjoy his individual right without achievement at the collective level.

For example, ILO Convention 111 on Discrimination (Employment and Occupation) requires the enactment of legislation for the elimination of discrimination in access to employment, training, and working conditions, on grounds of race, colour, sex, religion, political opinion, natural extraction, or social origin, and to promote equality of opportunity and treatment. This Convention has both individual and collective rights embedded in it. In a country where there is a policy of discrimination against a certain group, the right of the individual to employment and occupation is inextricably linked to the respect for the collective rights of his group. Failure to recognise the collective right of the group will definitely affect

---

[40] Leary (1996a), p. 22.

[41] Leary (1996a).

[42] See Valticos (1998), p. 135.

[43] Valticos (1998), p. 137.

the right of an individual belonging to this group. In effect, the right of an individual cannot be looked at in isolation.

4.5.2 Workers' Rights at the International Level

Cleveland (2003) also argues that at the basic level, the international human rights standards and the international labour standards are the same. She argues that the theory underpinning the international human rights movement is that all persons are entitled to certain minimum standards.[44] It is important to note that the attempt to abolish slavery was a labour rights movement.[45] In addition, incorporated in the 1919 Treaty of Versailles was the call for domestic protection of freedom of association, reasonable wages, eight-hour-work per day, forty-eight-hour work week, equal rights for migrant workers, prohibition of child labour, and equal pay for men and women. The CLS have, over the years, been viewed as falling under international human rights as envisaged under the Universal Declaration of Human Rights (UDHR), 1948.[46] Under the Universal Declaration, a "common standard of achievement for all peoples and all nations"[47] includes under its umbrella a general prohibition against discrimination, the rights to freedom of association and to form and be able to join unions, the prohibition against slavery, and the rights to work, to free choice of employment, to equal pay for equal work, etc.

The linkage between the CLS and human rights is clearly seen in respect for human rights, better standards of living, full employment, and social and economic progress, which after the Second World War were perceived as important factors in keeping the peace. For instance, Article 55 of the UN Charter states:

With a view to the creation of conditions of stability and well-being which are necessary for peaceful and friendly relations among nations based on respect for the principle of equal rights and self-determination of peoples, the United Nations shall promote:

a. higher standards of living, full employment, and conditions of economic and social progress and development;
b. solutions of international economic, social, health, and related problems; and international cultural and educational cooperation; and
c. universal respect for, and observance of, human rights and fundament al freedoms for all without distinction as to race, sex, language, or religion.

[44] Cleveland (2003), p. 137.

[45] Cleveland (2003).

[46] See Article 23 of the Universal Declaration of Human Rights.

[47] Preamble to the Universal Declaration.

These objectives are also expressed in the International Covenant on Civil and Political Rights and the International Covenant on Economic, Social and Cultural Rights. The existence of more than 100 multilateral and bilateral treaties on the protection of human rights, which almost all WTO Members have ratified, obliges members to accept and respect workers' rights both under international law and under their respective domestic laws. Even though human rights are not explicitly mentioned in the WTO Agreement, the acceptance of all 160 Members[48] of the Agreement is recognition of the importance of human rights in the trade agreement. The Preamble of the Marrakesh Agreement Establishing the World Trade Organisation states:

> Recognizing that their (Contracting Parties/Members) relations in the field of trade and economic endeavour should be conducted with a view to raising standards of living, ensuring full employment and a large and steadily growing volume of real income and effective demand, and expanding the production of and trade in goods and services, while allowing for the optimal use of the world's resources in accordance with the objective of sustainable development, seeking both to protect and preserve the environment and to enhance the means for doing so in a manner consistent with their respective needs and concerns at different levels of economic development.

The International Court of Justice (ICJ) has also ruled that all United Nations (UN) member states have legal obligations to respect human rights under the UN Charter and under general international law.[49]

Since World War II, international law has changed human rights law in significant ways. It is now generally acknowledged that the treatment by the state of its citizens is not only a matter under that particular state's jurisdiction but also a matter of international concern. The advent of globalisation and the rising dominance of global capitalism, with its influence in the political and economic spheres, have in many ways weakened the authority of the sovereign state. Nowhere is this clearly seen than in the debates in the linkages between core labour standards and international trade.

The labour standards were internationally acclaimed about a quarter of a century before the inclusion of human rights in the Universal Declaration and also in the UN Charter. In fact, René Cassin, the principal author of the Universal Declaration writing in 1950 stated that the ILO Constitution, which was a central part of the peace treaty at Versailles in 1919, represented the first instance of a contractual foundation for "international law regarding fundamental individual freedoms".[50]

---

[48] As at June 2014.

[49] Petersmann (2003), pp. 243 and 245 [referred to ICJ cases of *Barcelona Traction* (ICJ reports 1970, 32) and the *Nicaragua* judgment (ICJ Reports 1986, 114)].

[50] Valticos (1998), p. 135.

4.6 Labour Standards and the WTO

A number of questions have been raised as to the legality of trade measures under WTO law in addressing the labour standards and international trade. The main question is whether the inclusion of a social clause in the WTO Agreement, which when violated, would entitle a country to impose trade sanctions. As discussed above, the characterisation of core labour standards are considered as basic human rights by many proponents and falls within the realm of human rights, which could be dealt with under the WTO legal system.

This raises the question whether the WTO legal system supports a Member's use of its trade regulation to pursue a social goal. Whilst generally international law does not eliminate a state's right to use economic sanctions and trade regulations to achieve a social good, it to some extent limits this right. Further, legal protections for human rights and international humanitarian law do not prohibit the use of trade measures, as long as countries take safeguard measures as to the proportion and welfare of civilians. However, a number of issues are taken into consideration, such as the nature of the social goal in question, the kind of trade measure, the countries that would be affected by the measure, and the history of the country's compliance with that very goal.[51]

The law governing the WTO, however, does not lend itself to the flexibility of permitting Members to use the trade retaliation measures to pursue social objectives. In effect, the WTO is the only competent body to deal with the regulation of international trade. Since the period of the GATT and now the WTO, the Members have not allowed the organisation to intervene in national and international social goal policies or to mix social goals with economic objectives or to set social standards. The prevailing view is that agencies that specialise in social issues are better qualified to deal with those issues.

Does this mean that policymakers in a WTO Member country cannot use a trade instrument to pursue a social goal? Or put differently, how can these policymakers within the confines of WTO law legitimately determine whether a trade instrument is an appropriate measure to use to achieve a social goal? In this case, does the production process under which goods are produced have a bearing on the lives of those involved in the manufacture of the product, and, if so, how can that be distinguished from the production process of other physically similar products?

This subsection considers whether the WTO system, particularly its dispute settlement mechanism, can appropriately deal with the trade and social goals nexus. Before considering the rules under the WTO/GATT, first a brief history of the World Trading System and why the proponents of the labour–trade link argue that the WTO may be a better option than the ILO in tackling the issue.

---

[51] Schefer Krista (2010), p. 267.

4.6.1 A Brief History of the Multilateral Trading System

The World Trade Organization's (WTO) creation in January 1995 was a milestone in the history of international trade relations as it is the first formal institution to be created to oversee world trade and provide a forum for further trade negotiations and the resolution of trade disputes. Its establishment capped almost 50 years of unsuccessful attempts to establish such an organisation following the demise of the Havana Charter, which would have established the International Trade Organization (ITO). The WTO is responsible for overseeing the multilateral trading system that has gradually evolved over the last 50 years.

The WTO also provides a forum for continuing negotiations to liberalise the trade in goods and services through the removal of barriers and to develop rules in new trade-related subject areas. These trade-related subjects are the environment, investment, and intellectual property. This raises the issue of whether labour standards are not trade-related and why it is not included in the WTO agenda. The exclusion of labour standards is quite conspicuous and has led proponents of a formal link between trade and labour standards to demand the insertion of a clause on labour standards similar to the clause in the Havana Charter.

The 1948 draft Havana Charter of the ill-fated International Trade Organization (ITO) included an article on fair labour standards, as well as articles, *inter alia,* on restrictive business practices, commodity arrangements, and domestic employment practices. The argument for linking these issues with international trade was the conviction *that the failure of interwar attempts to secure international agreements liberalising trade was largely due to the practice of taking up trade questions in isolation instead of putting them in the more complex setting of economic policy as a whole*[52] [italics mine].

The General Agreement on Tariffs and Trade (GATT) would have been subsumed under the Havana Charter, but, whilst the ITO never entered into force, the GATT has been provisionally applied since 1948. The GATT was limited to traditional commercial aspects of trade in goods and did not include an article on fair labour standards or on most of the other trade-related issues included in the Havana Charter. Following the decision of the then American administration not to submit the Havana Charter to the United States Congress, the ITO was effectively dead. The GATT survived as a separate agreement, but not as an organisation, and in the form of a provisionally applicable agreement, which continued for almost 50 years.

The new World Trade Organisation (WTO), established at Marrakech in April 1994, incorporates the updated (to 1994) General Agreement on Tariffs and Trade, as well as the Uruguay Round agreements on agriculture, services, intellectual property, and investment, and it includes more substantial dispute settlement provisions than existed in the GATT.

---

[52] Bidwell and Diebold (1949), p. 214, quoted in Leary (1996b), p. 198.

The provision on fair labour standards in the 1948 draft Havana Charter (Ch.II, Art. 7) reads:

> 1. The Members recognize ... that all countries have a common interest in the achievement and maintenance of fair labour standards related to productivity, and thus in the improvement of wages and working conditions as productivity may permit. The Members recognize that unfair labour conditions, particularly in production for export, create difficulties in international trade and, accordingly, each Member shall take whatever action may be appropriate and feasible to eliminate such conditions within its territory.
> 2. Members which are also members of the International Labour Organisation shall co-operate with that organization in giving effect to this undertaking.
> 3. In all matters relating to labour standards that may be referred to the Organisation ... [under dispute settlement provisions or the Charter] ... it shall consult and co-operate with the International Labour Organisation.[53]

No similar provision was included in the GATT, and with the demise of the proposed ITO the linkage of trade and workers' rights was no longer explicit in an international instrument. As noted earlier, the demand for the inclusion of a provision on labour standards in the GATT has been raised repeatedly since it entered into force in 1948, and also during the intervening years, and resurfaced during the concluding negotiations of the Uruguay Round. A concerted effort was made by some contracting parties of the GATT to include labour standards in the agenda of the Uruguay Round.[54]

4.6.2 *WTO Legal System: Trade Measures and Core Labour Standards*

The GATT imposed obligations on Members under the different type of agreements and depending on the form of the agreement. The use of any of such agreements in enforcing adherence to the CLS could potentially lead to violation of a number of GATT obligations, and the dispute settlement system does not consider the objective of the measure in its rulings.[55]

[53] *Havana Charter for an International Trade Organization*, Dep't of State Pub. No. 3117, Commercial Policy Series 113 (1948), quoted in Leary (1996b), p. 198.

[54] Addo (2002), p. 293.

[55] The Panel on *Quantitative Restrictions against Imports of Certain Products from Hong Kong*, adopted on 12 July 1983, L/5511, BISD 30S/129, para. 27, in respect of Articles XI and XIII, '[t]he Panel considered the arguments put forward by the European Community regarding the social and economic conditions which prevailed in the various product categories under examination. The European Community did not claim any corresponding GATT provision in justification for these arguments. The Panel was of the opinion that such matters did not come within the purview of Articles XI and XIII of the GATT, and in this instance concluded that they lay outside its consideration.'

A major characteristic of the multilateral trading system is that it is a rule-based non-discriminatory system, so any difference in the treatment among Members is certain to violate Article I—the most-favoured-nation principle. Furthermore, the suspension of any bound concessions could also lead to a Member being in breach of its obligations under Article II under the Schedule of Concessions. Any difference in the treatment between domestic products and like imported products could also be an infringement of Article III—National Treatment. The most notable exception to these obligations is Article XXIV on rules relating to Regional Trade Agreements.[56] The relevant provisions in the WTO agreement are discussed below.

4.6.2.1 GATT Article I: Most-Favoured Nation (MFN) Principle

Article I of GATT states the non-discrimination principle that has come to be generally known in international trade law as the unconditional most-favoured-nation (MFN) treatment. By virtue of this Article, the use of trade measures in enforcing compliance with the CLS could infringe the MFN principle in Article I of GATT. This principle states:

> With respect to customs duties and charges of any kind imposed on or in connection with importation or exportation or imposed on the international transfer of payments for imports or exports, and with respect to the method of levying such duties and charges, and with respect to all rules and formalities in connection with importation and exportation, and with respect to all matters referred to in paragraphs 2 and 4 of Article III, any advantage, favour, privilege or immunity granted by any contracting party to any product originating in or destined for any other country shall be accorded immediately and unconditionally to the like product originating in or destined for the territories of all other contracting parties.

This principle applies to the trade relations among Members of the WTO, in relation not only to border measures but also to internal measures. Article I categorically states that all WTO/GATT Members should be treated equally in respect of like products. The Article also states that the treatment should be granted without any conditions. Under this principle, should any Member use the lack of adherence to CLS as a measure to restrict trade with another Member, it would be in violation of WTO rules.[57]

---

[56] Article XXIV is analysed in detail in Chap. 6 below.

[57] See *Belgian Family Allowances* case, adopted on 7 November 1952. In this case, the Panel examined the complaint submitted by two other WTO Members regarding the application of the Belgian law on the levy of a charge on foreign goods purchased by public bodies when the goods originate in a country whose system of family allowances does not meet specific requirements. Belgium had granted exemptions from the levy for goods originating from some countries and charged levy on goods from other countries. The only exception to the principle was if the Members granted the exemption were Members of a regional arrangement. In this particular case, the complaining parties were part of a regional agreement of which Belgium was a Member and as such were discriminated against. The Belgian legislation was found to be inconsistent with Article I of GATT.

4.6.2.2 GATT Article II: Schedule of Concessions

Article II obliges WTO Members not to increase duties above the level bound in their respective Schedule of Concessions.[58] This obligation is subject to conditions stated in that Schedule. In respect of duties, the Schedule of concessions can be taken as establishing a ceiling for applying the MFN principle in Article I. It is important to note that the normal practice is that countries bound their tariffs at a certain rate but apply a different rate, which is lower than the bound rate. The relevant section of Article II states:

> *(a)* Each contracting party shall accord to the commerce of the other contracting parties treatment no less favourable than that provided for in the appropriate Part of the appropriate Schedule annexed to this Agreement.
>
> *(b)* The products described in Part I of the Schedule relating to any contracting party, which are the products of territories of other contracting parties, shall, on their importation into the territory to which the Schedule relates, and subject to the terms, conditions or qualifications set forth in that Schedule, be exempt from ordinary customs duties in excess of those set forth and provided therein. Such products shall also be exempt from all other duties or charges of any kind imposed on or in connection with the importation in excess of those imposed on the date of this Agreement or those directly and mandatorily required to be imposed thereafter by legislation in force in the importing territory on that date.

In cases where there is the suspension of concessions under agreements that provide for trade preferences, the concessions do not violate the bound rate set out in the Schedule. However, under Article II:1, any attempt to use a trade measure for CLS reasons would most likely be a violation of GATT obligations.

4.6.2.3 GATT Article III: National Treatment

On a general note, GATT permits the government of an importing country to impose measures on imported products, as long as the imported products are not treated less favourably than similar domestic products. Under Article III, discrimination between domestically produced goods and like imported goods is prohibited. The Article also prohibits discrimination between domestic and imported like products by means of any other internal regulations. The two paragraphs relevant for our purposes are paragraphs 2 and 4 of Article III, which state:

---

[58] It is important to note that the concessions granted are not restricted only to tariffs. See *Korea – Restrictions on Imports of Beef – Complaint by the United States*, adopted on 7 November 1989, L/6503, BISD 63S/268. In this case, the US argued that the quotas, import bans, state trading monopoly, and other restrictions on the importation of beef by the Government of Korea were inconsistent with Articles II, X, XI, and XIII and that the restriction impaired and nullified benefits accruing to the U.S. within the meaning of Article XXIII of GATT. The Panel found the measures by Korea to be inconsistent with its obligations under GATT.

2. The products of the territory of any contracting party imported into the territory of any other contracting party shall not be subject, directly or indirectly, to internal taxes or other internal charges of any kind in excess of those applied, directly or indirectly, to like domestic products. Moreover, no contracting party shall otherwise apply internal taxes or other internal charges to imported or domestic products in a manner contrary to the principles set forth in paragraph 1.
4. The products of the territory of any contracting party imported into the territory of any other contracting party shall be accorded treatment no less favourable than that accorded to like products of national origin in respect of all laws, regulations and requirements affecting their internal sale, offering for sale, purchase, transportation, distribution or use. The provisions of this paragraph shall not prevent the application of differential internal transportation charges which are based exclusively on the economic operation of the means of transport and not on the nationality of the product.

The national treatment obligation states that WTO Members are to treat equally like domestic and foreign products. Under this principle, once foreign products enter the domestic market of a WTO Member from another WTO Member country, the products should not be subject to treatment less favourable than that accorded the like domestic products.

4.6.2.4 GATT Article XI:1: Quantitative Restrictions

The principle of quantitative restrictions is important to the labour standards and trade debate since WTO Members are prohibited from banning the importation or exportation of goods or from subjecting them to quotas. The principle states:

1. No prohibitions or restrictions other than duties, taxes or other charges, whether made effective through quotas, import or export licences or other measures, shall be instituted or maintained by any contracting party on the importation of any product of the territory of any other contracting party or on the exportation or sale for export of any product destined for the territory of any other contracting party.

The wording of Article XI:1 is clear as to the obligation of Members that there is absolute prohibition on quantitative restrictions irrespective of the motives behind the restriction.[59] Three other cases show that the use of Article XI as a defense in restricting products into the territory of a Member is a violation of WTO rules. In the two *Tuna* cases,[60] the United States was held to be in violation of Article XI. Again, in the *US-Shrimp* case, the United States was held to be in violation of Article XI when it placed an embargo on imports of 'dolphin-unsafe shrimp'.[61]

---

[59] See the decision of the Panel on *Quantitative Restrictions Against Imports of Certain Products from Hong Kong*, adopted on 12 July 1983, L/5511, BISD 30S/129.

[60] *United States – Restrictions on Imports of Tuna*, unadopted, 3 September 1991, DS21/R, BISD 39S/155; *United States – Restrictions of Imports of Tuna*, unadopted, 16 June 1994, DS29/R.

[61] *United States – Import Prohibition of Certain Shrimp and Shrimp Products*, WT/DS58/AB/R, adopted on 6 November 1998.

4.6.3 Enforcement Under WTO Legal System

Should any attempt be made to insert a social clause in the WTO agreement, this would likely have an impact on the WTO system. In this section, we review the likely impact and review the arguments by some proponents of using the "general exception" provisions.

4.6.3.1 Impact on the WTO

Firstly, should the WTO be given the responsibility of promoting the observance and ensuring compliance and implementation of core labour standards, it would entail subjecting these labour standards to the WTO's dispute settlement mechanism since unlike the ILO, the WTO has the ability to enforce agreements. This raises the question whether the dispute settlement system is well equipped to handle a legal problem with social connotations.

Secondly, given the history of the labour and trade debate especially from the declaration at the first WTO Ministerial Conference in Singapore, how the issue contributed to the collapse of the third WTO Seattle Ministerial Conference, the reaffirmation of the declaration made in Singapore during the fourth Ministerial Conference at Doha (that the ILO is the competent body to deal with labour issues), and the continuous opposition of developing countries, any discussion of the linkage would likely have a negative impact on the ongoing Doha trade round negotiations. Given the nature of the Doha Round, dubbed the development round, failure to conclude the round would have an adverse impact on the integration of developing countries into the multilateral trading system and thus on their economic development. And failure to promote economic growth will in turn not put the developing countries in a good position to comply with the CLS.

Thirdly, even though there is general agreement that adherence to the core labour standards would positively contribute to improved social conditions, the view of many developing countries is that the CLS should be promoted by the ILO and not the WTO. There is the fear by developing countries opposed to the linkage that adding the CLS to the WTO agenda would overburden the system and have negative consequences on the policy space that they need to develop effective systems commensurate with their level of development.

4.6.3.2 General Exceptions Provisions

GATT 1994 Article XX does provide for certain exceptions to free trade provisions. At first sight, it would appear that Article XX would be the more logical Article for a link between trade and labour standards. Article XX permits a Member to impose barriers to trade, not otherwise permitted under GATT, for certain reasons relating to social policy. Members may impose barriers to trade as an exception under

GATT for measures "necessary to protect human, animal or plant life or health" (Article XX(b)) or measures pertaining to conservation of exhaustible resources (Article XX(g)). The possibility of applying Article XX(d) on "measures necessary to secure compliance with laws or regulations not inconsistent with GATT" to labour standards was discussed during the negotiations of the Havana Charter but was rejected.[62]

Under Article XX(e), countries may bar exports of goods made by prison labour. This has recently been invoked, in the ILO, against Myanmar.[63] However, no other labour standards are itemised in Article XX. It could be argued that the logic supporting the right to bar imports produced by prison labour, for example, could also support the addition of language permitting the barring of imports produced by forced labour. The exceptions under Article XX could also possibly be expanded to include goods produced under conditions that violate other "internationally recognised labour standards", in particular, such as a fundamental human right as freedom of association.[64]

Howse (1999) argues that the idea that issues relating to labour rights are only a matter for the ILO does not take into account the role the WTO has been playing in constraining one important tool available to improve adherence to CLS, which are trade measures expected to be used to punish non-compliance with the CLS. Howse further makes reference to the GATT/WTO jurisprudence in the context of trade and environment. The constraints evoked may go beyond what is needed to avoid the abuse of labour standards to achieve what the critics of the linkage advocate: for protectionist purposes.[65]

Howse also makes reference to the *Turtles* case, which raised the issue of whether trade sanctions could be imposed for environmental reasons. In this case, the Appellate Body upheld the findings of the Panel that the United States measure banning the import of shrimp fished in a manner that threatened sea turtles was justified under Article XX(g).[66]

Article XX provides:

> Subject to the requirement that such measures are not applied in a manner which would constitute a means of arbitrary or unjustifiable discrimination between countries where the same conditions prevail, or a disguised restriction on international trade, nothing in this Agreement shall be construed to prevent the adoption or enforcement by any contracting party of measures:

[62] Brown (2000), p. 6.

[63] Tay (1999), p. 13.

[64] Leary (1996b), p. 204.

[65] Howse (1999).

[66] *United States – Import Prohibition of Certain Shrimp and Shrimp Products*, Report of the Appellate Body, 12 October 1998, WT/DS58/AB/R [hereinafter Turtles]. The Appellate Body found that although the United States conservation scheme itself could be justified in principle under the "conservation of natural resources" exception in Article XX (g), the manner of application of the scheme did not meet certain criteria in the "chapeau" or general preambular provision of Article XX.

(a) necessary to protect public morals;
(b) necessary to protect human, animal or plant life or health;
(c) relating to the importations or exportations of gold or silver;
(d) necessary to secure compliance with laws or regulations which are not inconsistent with the provisions of this Agreement, including those relating to customs enforcement, the enforcement of monopolies operated under paragraph 4 of Article II and Article XVII, the protection of patents, trade marks and copyrights, and the prevention of deceptive practices;
(e) relating to the products of prison labour;
(f) imposed for the protection of national treasures of artistic, historic or archaeological value;
(g) relating to the conservation of exhaustible natural resources if such measures are made effective in conjunction with restrictions on domestic production or consumption . . .

As stated earlier, the proponents of the labour–trade linkage call for the inclusion of social clause in Article XX of GATT. The only reference to labour standards in the GATT/WTO agreements is Article XX(e) (see above). This allows for the prohibition of imports on the ground that the products were manufactured with prison labour. In relation to Article XX(e), Howse argues that the reference to prison labour, in addition to the unambiguous language on labour rights in the Havana Charter, appears to suggest that should GATT XX be intended to include sanctions with regard to labour rights, clear language would have been inserted in this article. Howse adds that the lack of a clear language in the article does not mean the end of the public moral debate, since with the evolution of human rights in an ever changing society the content of public morals could include labour practices as violations of universal human rights.[67]

Another argument concerning Article XX relates to subsection (a), which allows trade measures "necessary to protect public morals". Article XX(a) might be invoked in imposing a trade sanction against products produced with child labour or products originating from countries that deny their workers' rights such as freedom of association or the right to bargain collectively. This is an argument that has continually been at the centre of international trade relations: should a country be allowed to restrict trade to promote public morals?[68]

This raises the issue of whether a trade measure driven by morality is in conformity with the multilateral trade rules. Charnovitz (1998) states that Article XX(a) raises two central questions: (1) what is the type of behaviour that involves public morals, and (2) whose morals can be protected? Although the range of trade

[67] Howse (1999), p. 186.

[68] The panel in the *US-Gambling* case approached the interpretation of 'public morals' exception in Article XIV of GATS by using a dynamic approach. The panel, in its view, stated that the content of the concepts for Members can vary in time and space depending upon a range of factor, including prevailing social, cultural, ethical, and religious values (see paragraph 6.461). The panel indicated that each WTO Member has discretion to determine the practices that would violate the moral code of the community. The panel's reasoning was upheld by the Appellate Body upon appeal. This raises the question whether the public morals debate could apply to the 'public morals' of the importing country with respect to the manner in which goods they import are produced, including goods produced without respect to the CLS.

measures covered by Article XX(a) could include the CLS, there is at present no GATT or WTO jurisprudence on the interpretation of Article XX(a).[69]

In a working paper presented by the International Labour Office for discussion by the Governing Council entitled "The Social Dimensions of the Liberalisation of World Trade",[70] objections were raised concerning the use of Article XX. The Preamble to Article XX contains an injunction against trade restrictions that are a "disguised restriction on international trade". If an exception were added to Article XX for the serious violation of a limited number of fundamental labour standards, a clause could be added requiring reference to the ILO Conventions and monitoring bodies for interpretation and application of the exception in a concrete case. A GATT panel could then assess whether the claimed exception was permissible under Article XX.[71] There are two other general points that should be noted about these attempts to find exceptions within the existing GATT language.

First is that the chapeau of Article XX is also open to different interpretations. The chapeau of Article XX states that any measures should not be applied in a manner that would "constitute a means of arbitrary or unjustifiable discrimination between countries where the same conditions prevail, or a disguised restriction on international trade". It has been emphasised that the measure must first not be a form of arbitrary discrimination. It has also been suggested that the WTO must therefore take pains to try to discern genuine labour concerns from disguised protectionism. The latter should not be excused by reference to Article XX. In contrast, some have suggested that the WTO can and should give more leeway to sincere attempts by nations to legislate their exceptions in the areas of concern identified by Article XX.[72]

Whilst the issue of the linkage, as argued above, has not been incorporated in the WTO legal framework, the argument by Charnovitz merits attention. Charnovitz has raised the issue of the link between trade and public morals and has addressed the question of whether "morality-driven trade measures conflict with international trade rules", based on his extensive discussion of the scope of Article XX(a).[73] Of particular interest to this debate is Charnovitz's discussion on how a moral exception can be applied to products made by indentured children.[74]

Charnovitz makes reference to the 1997 U.S. Congress' ban on imports made by indentured children and makes a distinction between products made by children under forced labour and those who work voluntarily. The question that this raises is how to determine which products are voluntarily made by children and which are made by children working under extreme working conditions. The issue lies at the centre of the debate on why children work in the first place: are many forced to work

[69] For in-depth analysis of Article XX(a), see Charnovitz (1998), p. 689.

[70] ILO.

[71] Leary (1996b), pp. 204–205.

[72] Tay (1999), p. 14.

[73] See Charnovitz (1998), p. 1.

[74] Charnovitz (1998), p. 25.

by their families to supplement family income? We have also raised the question whether most parents given the choice between sending their children to school or to work under hazardous conditions will not choose the former.

In considering the 1997 U.S. Congress decision, it is well documented that on many U.S. farms, whilst children are legally permitted to work at the age of 12, there are children as young as 7 or 8 years who work on farms.[75] Can it be said with certainty that all children who work on family farms do so voluntarily? The evidence collected by organisations such as the Human Rights Watch indicate that during the peak harvest season, children sometimes work up to 14 h, and they earn less than the minimum wage.

In an effort to address this, the Obama administration introduced a bill in September 2009 entitled Children's Act for Responsible Employment (CARE Act, HR 3564) bill, to ensure that all working children are protected equally under the law. However, in April 2012, the administration decided to withdraw the bill under political pressure.[76]

The failure of the CARE Act shows how difficult this issue is, especially given the fact that the major proponents of the linkage issue have not succeeded in keeping children away from hazardous conditions on farms, making it difficult for the U.S. to berate others. This also makes it difficult to determine how a WTO panel can shift through the U.S. position on child labour on farms and, for example, child labour in a country like India in the manufacturing sector. This is irrespective of Charnovitz's argument that interpretation of GATT can be an exception in light of common commitments under *jus cogens* or Diller and Levy's view that there should be harmonisation between international trade rules and international labour and human rights norms.[77]

---

[75] See http://www.hrw.org/support-care. Accessed 10 March 2014. The Fair Labor Standards Act (FLSA) permits children working on farms (but not allowed in any other industry) to work at younger ages, for far longer hours, and under more hazardous conditions than all other working youths.

[76] See http://www.huffingtonpost.com/2012/04/27/white-house-child-labor-agriculture_n_1458701.html. Accessed 30 January 2014. Interestingly, Charnovitz uses India as an example in his analysis. The Indian Government, in August 2012, proposed a ban on employing children under 14. Under the proposed ban, a breach carries a 3-year jail term and a fine of Rs 50,000 (about US$900.00). Should the ban come into effect, it would be a full ban on child labour, following the 1986 Child Labour Act, as amended in 2006. India would then have succeeded in enacting a law totally banning child labour, something the U.S. has not been able to achieve. See Kazmin (2012), p. 5.

[77] Diller Janelle and Levy David (1997), pp. 663–664.

4.7 The Process and Production Method (PPM) Debate

An important area of debate that has a bearing on the labour/trade nexus is the issue of process and production methods (PPMs). PPMs have been defined in broad terms as the activities that are involved in the process of transporting a good market.[78] However, PPMs, which though are the subject of one of the controversies involving trade and environment, have been invoked also in the controversy between trade and labour standards. There is the recognition that the issue of PPMs is crosscutting,[79] going beyond the trade and environment debate to encompass the labour and trade debate.

The impact of the PPM debate on the labour and trade issue is the link between PPMs and sustainable development. In recognition of this linkage, Principle 8 of the Rio Declaration states:

> to achieve sustainable development and a higher quality of life for all people, States should reduce and eliminate unsustainable patterns of production and consumption and promote appropriate demographic policies.[80]

Achieving PPMs-related strategies within a country may not create much of a challenge. However, the challenge is achieving these policies in a globalised world. With the increase in competition between countries, there has been the issue of how to complement the national implementation measures of PPMs with corresponding compliance by trading partners. This is based on the point we raised in Chap. 2 about the fear of a race to the bottom, whereby a country or a number of countries in order to gain competitive advantage might lower costs of production, and that could lead to the lowering of labour standards globally.

4.7.1 *What Are PPMs?*

The PPM term was coined during the Tokyo Round Agreement on Technical Barriers to Trade (TBT).[81] It generally referred to the standards of a product with a focus on the production methods instead of the characteristics of a product.[82]

---

[78] Potts (2008), p. 3. Potts further states that: "Under this definition, a PPM can refer to activities related to the actual production of a good (such as the chemicals used to treat widgets) to the extraction of natural resources for eventual incorporation into goods (harvesting methods applied to timber used in widgets), to trading practices used in bringing goods to market (long-term contracts with timber suppliers in the production of widgets)", p. 3.

[79] OECD Secretariat, Processes and Production Methods (PPMs): Conceptual Framework and Considerations on Use of PPM-Based Trade Measures, OECD/GD(97)137 (1997), p. 7.

[80] See Principle 8 of the Rio Declaration on Environment and Development. UNCEDOR, 11d Sess., Annex, Agenda Item 1, UN Doc. A/CONF.151/26 (1992), p. 8.

[81] Charnovitz (2002), p. 64.

[82] Agreement on Technical Barriers to Trade (1979), GATT, BISD 26S/8, para. 14.25.

PPMs, when applied to the manufacture of goods, can be used either as product related or non-product related.[83] The link between PPMs and the labour standards and trade debate is due to the way goods are produced. That is to say, the objections are less often with the products themselves than the way in which they have been made. This is relevant to the CLS and trade debate since the conditions under which goods are produced have direct bearing on the lives of those involved in the manufacturing process and also their families and the wider society of which they form part.

Whilst PPMs are more of an environmental topic, the issue arises with regard to labour since WTO rules apply only to the regulation of international trade in goods and services, instead of whether or not the goods and services were produced contrary to the ILO standards. In general terms, PPMs refer to the process of production of a good or service. This interpretation includes a number of controversial international trade issues in modern times, for example (1) the health and safety aspects of new technology; (2) resource depletion, both renewable and non-renewable; (3) environmental pollution; and (4) use of child, forced, prison, and slave labour.[84]

4.7.2 The Political Economy of PPMs

The history of the PPM doctrine dates back to the time before the establishment of the WTO, when a series of GATT panel decisions introduced the concept of process and production methods. Under this doctrine, the GATT made it *prima facie* GATT illegal for any government to impose a tax or a regulatory disadvantage on imported products because of the way the goods were produced. The only exception related to the manner of production that had some impact on the characteristics of the product itself. In this case, should a government forbid the sale of imported goods produced with child labour, this would be in violation of GATT Articles III and XI.[85]

The PPM debate has, at its core, the desire of a number of WTO Members to regulate the trade in goods and services at the international level on the basis of the process and manufacturing methods or know-how employed in the production of the goods and services. This raises the issue of adding another layer in the form of safety or environmental concerns in addition to the social clause issue, further complicating the international regulation of trade.

The increased debate on consideration of PPMs has come from consumers mainly in developed countries. Whilst policymakers and producers in the developed world might not be opposed to PPMs within the MTS, there is the realisation

---

[83] OECD (1997).

[84] Read (2005), p. 239.

[85] Hudec (2000), p. 187.

that PPMs would give rise to increased complexity in the regulatory process and leave greater room for disputes. On the other hand, developing countries, just as in the debate on the inclusion of a social clause, are opposed to the inclusion of PPMs in the WTO agenda. This is perceived by developing countries as an attempt to create a harmonisation system based on environmental, technological, and other standards using the high standards in the developed world as benchmarks. Should that be the case, it could have a negative impact on their already unstable market access situation and their special and differential treatment provisions.[86]

4.7.3 GATT/WTO and PPMs

The first time the doctrine was applied was in the first *Tuna/Dolphin* case, and also in the second *Tuna/Dolphin* (the facts of both cases are similar, and based on the same provision of the U.S. Marine Mammal Protection Act (MMPA)).[87] The U.S. banned the import of tuna with the reason that these tunas were produced in a manner resulting in high rates of dolphin mortality. In this case, the ruling of the panel was that the United States import prohibition against tuna harvested in an environmentally unsafe manner violated either GATT Article XI or GATT Article III:4. The case showed that countries cannot differentiate between tuna caught with dolphin excluding devices and tuna caught without protecting dolphins since there was no difference in the quality of the products. The panel in the *Tuna/Dolphin* case further ruled that neither Articles XI and III:4 violations were to be excused under GATT Article XX exceptions for health and conservation ways and that the tuna embargo was prohibited under GATT rules.

The reasoning behind the ruling was that the US could not impose an embargo on imports of tuna products from Mexico on the basis that Mexican regulations on the way tuna was produced did not meet the U.S. standards. Should the U.S. arguments have been accepted, it would have opened the door for other countries to ban imports of a product from another country simply because the importing country has different standards. This would have been in conflict with the establishment of the MTS—to create predictable trade rules.

Hudec (2000) notes that this ruling was criticised by environmental organisations and other groups based on the product-process methods concept. The critics' major complaint was that the PPM doctrine "placed an unwarranted legal burden on all trade measures designed to discourage activities in other countries harmful to the environment, or harmful to other important interests such as human rights or labor rights".[88]

---

[86] See Read (2005), p. 243.

[87] *United States – Restrictions on Imports of Tuna* (DS29/R), GATT Panel Report, circulated on 16 June 1994 (not adopted). US–Tuna II: *United States – Restrictions on Imports of Tuna*, not adopted, 33 I.L.M. (1994), pp. 839–903.

[88] Hudec (2000), p. 188.

In the context of the environment, for example, there are treaties that severely limit trade in endangered species of flora and fauna and impose conditions on transnational trade in hazardous waste.[89] These treaties have been generally accepted, with no challenge to date in the WTO. On the other hand, there is considerable controversy over cases in which it is the PPMs that are considered environmentally harmful or violate labour standards. GATT jurisprudence states that PPMs violate the principle of non-discrimination, which apply to "like products", and a product's likeness is determined by the quality, function, or end-use in the market.[90]

In the *Shrimp/Turtle* case,[91] the issue was U.S. measures banning the import of shrimp that had been fished in a manner that threatened sea turtles, an endangered species. The Panel found the U.S. measures to be discriminatory since the U.S. did not take into account methods other than turtle excluder devices (TEDS) to protect sea turtles. The legal reasoning of the Appellate Body in upholding the Panel report appeared to be a rejection of the two earlier *Tuna/Dolphin* cases on the ruling on Article XX exceptions, stating that the exceptions could be available to governments to regulate imports on the basis of the process by which they were produced. In spite of this, the WTO jurisprudence on the PPMs is indecisive since neither a Panel nor the Appellate Body has been called upon to rule on the correctness of the ruling in the *Shrimp/Turtle* case.[92]

It has been suggested that the GATT rule requiring that "like products" be treated alike means that countries cannot ban products because of their production methods. According to Howse, this view has no basis either in the text of the GATT or the negotiating record for the agreement. He states further that two dispute panels invented the distinction in the 1990s, but neither had its opinion adopted by the membership as a binding ruling. Since then, the Appellate Body of the WTO has suggested that what makes products "like" depends on a case-by-case analysis and will vary from context to context.[93]

From an economic perspective, an externality is an externality[94] whether resulting from the production process for a good or the actual consumption of the end product. In both cases, the GATT permits a country to address the harm in

[89] Convention on International Trade in Endangered Species of Wild Fauna and Flora (www.cites.org) and Basel Convention on the Control of Transboundary Movements of Hazardous Wastes and their Disposal (www.basel.int).

[90] See *Japan – Customs Duties, Taxes and Labelling Practices on Imported Wines and Alcoholic Beverages* (L/6216 – 34S/83), GATT Panel Report, 10 November 1987, paragraph 5.6; *European Communities – Measures Affecting the Prohibition of Asbestos and Asbestos Products* (WT/DS135), Appellate Body Report, adopted on 5 April 2001, paragraphs 101 et seq.

[91] *United States – Import Prohibition of Certain Shrimp and Shrimp Products* (WT/DS58, May 15, 1998), Panel report; WT/DS58/AB/R (October 12, 1998) Appellate Body Report.

[92] Howse (1998).

[93] Howse (1998).

[94] An externality of an economic transaction is the impact on a party that is not directly involved in the transaction.

question by regulation, including bans (provided equal treatment is afforded to both domestic products and imports). Howse gives an example in the environmental context that a shrimp caught in a way that threatens sea turtles is not a "like" product to a shrimp that is caught with turtle-friendly technology; the former creates environmental costs that the latter does not, and this has nothing to do with protectionism.[95]

By way of summary, therefore, the text and charter of the WTO appear to allow and partially support recognition of labour rights in trade rules.[96] This possibility has however not been developed by the WTO. The culture and practice have instead remained focused on trade. This is justified by some as being the WTO's mandate and expertise. Should sanctions be allowed to be imposed, it would entail not only an insertion of a social clause in Article XX but also a change in the rules of origin, fundamental principles of non-discrimination, pushing the WTO further into confusion, a system already ill-equipped to handle something of this nature.

Cottier and Caplazi (2000) postulate that WTO-related measures should only focus on a product-related approach. And the ILO should focus on the implementation of broader policies. In their view, this approach builds on the tradition of the multilateral trading system. A further argument is that this approach would limit the use of CLS for protectionist reasons, and the approach is to bring about a proper balance between the goals of achieving trade liberalisation, market access, and social policy concerns. This, the argument goes, would ease a number of concerns voiced by developing countries that labour standards would be used to promote protectionist import restrictions by developed countries.

According to the GATT–WTO rules, international trade should not be conducted on a discriminatory basis. A further policy option for trade-linked labour standards is the inclusion of relevant labour clauses in regional, subregional, and bilateral trade and investment agreements. The broader emerging trade law regime, in comparison to the multilateral regime, is the regional model with consistent references to labour standards in many of these RTAs. These references are based largely on the 1998 ILO Declaration and the implementation of the standards and rely on domestic arrangements rather than international law.

These arrangements generate only limited pressure to adhere to the international standards. Among the most important agreements of this kind is the North American Agreement on Labor Cooperation (NAALC), which is a side agreement to the North American Free Trade Agreement (NAFTA) of 1994, concerning local enforcement of CLS in Mexico, the United States, and Canada; the US–Jordan Free Trade Agreement; US–Singapore; US–Chile; and others. Labour rights

[95] Howse (1998).

[96] Authors such as Zagel argue that a look at the historical context of Article XX(e) of GATT, for example, appear to suggest that the object and purpose of this provision is meant to prohibit competition of national products produced in the course of normal work, which are normally more expensive than products of prison labour. The Article, in Zagel's view, is not a humanitarian provision in prohibiting products of prison labour. See Zagel (2005), pp. 14–15.

provisions are also incorporated in bilateral agreements of the EU, such as the agreements with South Africa, Chile, and Mexico.

References

Addo, K. (2002). The correlation between labour standards and international trade – Which way forward?'. *Journal of World Trade, 36*(2).

Bassiouni, M. C. (1997). International crimes: *Jus Cogens* and *Obligatio Erga Omnes. Law and Contemporary Problems, 59*(4).

Bidwell, P. W., & Diebold, W. (1949). The United States and the International Trade Organisation. *International Conciliation, 27*, 185.

Brown, D. K. (2000). *International Labor Standards in the World Trade Organization and the International Labour Organization* (Discussion Paper 2000–2003). Department of Economics, Tufts University.

Carter, B. E., Trimble, P. R., & Bradley, C. A. (2003). *International law* (4th ed.). New York: Aspen.

Charnovitz, S. (1998). The moral exception in GATT. *Virginia Journal of International Law, 38.*

Charnovitz, S. (2002). The law of environmental "PPMs" in the WTO: Debunking the myth of illegality. *Yale Journal of International Law, 27*(59).

Cleveland, S. (2003). Why International Labor Standards? In R. J. Flanagan & W. B. Gould (Eds.), *International Labor Standards*. Stanford: Stanford University Press.

Compa, L. A., & Diamond, S. F. (Eds.). (1996). *Human rights, labor rights, and international trade*. Philadelphia: University of Pennsylvania Press.

Cottier, T., & Caplazi, A. (2000). Labour standards and World Trade Law: Interfacing legitimate concerns. In T. Geiser et al. (Eds.), *Arbeit in the der Schweiz des 20. Jahrhunderts: Wirtschaftliches, rechtliche uns soziale Perspektiven*. Bern: Verlag Paul Haupt.

Diller Janelle, M., & Levy David, A. (1997). Child labor, trade and investment: Toward the harmonization of international law. *American Journal of International Law, 91.*

Dörr, O., & Schmalenbach, K. (Eds.). (2012). *Vienna Convention on the law of treaties: A commentary*. Heidelberg: Springer.

Howse, R. (1998). *The Economist*, 2 November 1998.

Howse, R. (1999). The World Trade Organization and the protection of workers' rights, Northwestern School of Law of Lewis & Clark College. *The Journal of Small and Emerging Business Law.*

Howse, R., & Mutua, M. (2000). Protecting human rights in a global economy: Challenges for the World Trade Organization. In H. Stokke & A. Totensen (Eds.), *Human rights in development*. The Hague: Kluwer Law International (Yearbook 1999/2000, The Millennium Edition).

Hudec, R. E. (2000). The product-process doctrine in GATT/WTO jurisprudence. In M. Bronckers & R. Qiuck (eds) *New directions in International Economic Law*, Essays in Honour of John H. Jackson. The Hague: Kluwer Law International.

ILO. 'The Social Dimensions of the Liberalisation of World Trade', Doc. GB. 261/WP/SLD/1 (Working Party on the Social Dimensions of the Liberalisation of International Trade, Int'l Labour Office, Governing Body, 261st Sess., 1994) [hereinafter Social Dimensions].

Kaufmann, C. (2008, February). *Globalisation and core labour rights: What role for the World Bank and the International Monetary Fund?* (NCCR Trade Regulation Working Paper No. 01).

Kazmin, A. (2012). India plans child labour reform. *Financial Times, Europe*, 30 August 2012, Thursday.

Leary, V. (1996a). The paradox of workers' rights as human rights. In L. A. Compa & S. F. Diamond (Eds.), *Human rights, labor rights, and international trade*. Philadelphia: University of Pennsylvania Press.

Leary, V. (1996b). Workers' rights and international trade: The social clause (GATT, ILO, NAFTA, U.S. Laws. In J. Bhagwati & R. E. Hudec (Eds.), *Fair trade and harmonization, prerequisites for free trade?* (Vol. 2). Cambridge: The MIT Press.

Lepard Brian, D. (1993). *The necessity of Opinio Juris in the formation of customary international law.* http://web.law.duke.edu/cicl/pdf/opiniojuris/panel_2-lepard-the_necessity_of_opinio_juris_in_the_formation_of_customary_international_law.pdf. Accessed 9 Apr 2014.

Mathis, J. H. (2002). *Regional Trade Agreements in the GATT/WTO: Article XXIV and the Internal Trade Requirement.* The Hague: T.M.C. Asser Press.

McRae, D. M. (2000). The WTO in international law: Tradition continued or new frontier? *Journal of International Economic Law, 3*(1).

OECD. (1997). *Processes and production methods (PPMs): Conceptual framework and considerations on use of PPM-based trade measures.* OECD/GD(97)137.

Parker, K., & Neylon, L. B. (1989). *Jus Cogens*: Compelling the law of human rights. *Hastings International Comparative Law Review, 12.*

Petersmann, E.-U. (2003). Human rights and the law of the World Trade Organization. *Journal of World Trade, 37*(2).

Potts, J. (2008). *The legality of PPMs under the GATT: Challenges and opportunities for sustainable trade policy.* International Institute for Sustainable Development (IISD).

Read, R. (2005). Process and production methods and the regulation of international trade. In N. Perdikis & R. Read (Eds.), *The WTO and the regulation of international trade: Recent trade disputes between the European Union and the United States.* Cheltenham: Edward Elgar.

Schefer Krista, N. (2010). *Social regulation in the WTO: Trade policy and International Legal Development.* Cheltenham, UK/Northampton, MA, USA: Edward Elgar.

Tay, S. (1999). *Trade, the environment and labor: Texts, concepts, and institutions.* World Bank.

Valticos, N. (1998). International labour standards and human rights: Approaching the year 2000. *International Labour Review, 137*(2).

Vandaele, A. (2005). *International Labour Rights and the social clause: Friends or foes.* London: Cameron May.

Zagel, G. M. (2005). WTO & human rights: Examining linkages and suggesting convergence. *IDLO Voices of Development Jurists Paper Series, 2*(2).

Chapter 5
Unilateral Social Clauses

5.1 Introduction

The linkage between labour standards and international trade, as discussed above, has hinged on the inclusion of a social clause in the WTO Agreement. Whilst the debate is an age-old issue, the United States in particular has made requests for the establishment of a working party on the relationship between the CLS and international trade.[1] Whilst the European Union has not been seen to be making much effort as compared to the United States in establishing the linkage, both the EU and the United States have included the respect for the CLS in their Generalised System of Preferences (GSP) schemes. These unilateral efforts have been instituted due to the lack of support at the international level to establish a linkage.

It is interesting to note that social clauses are not new in international trade agreements. For example, Article XX(e) of GATT 1947 contains a clause allowing Member States to take action in case of goods produced with prison labour. This chapter will review the precedents in other international trade agreements and the unilateral efforts of the United States and the EU under their respective GSP schemes. Finally, we will analyse a form of corporate social responsibility (CSR) called international framework agreements (IFAs), which although not popular is gaining attention as having the prospective to help resolve the age-old linkage issue. The IFA is the only form of CSR that would be considered in this chapter because whilst the others have long been tried—the IFAs signed to date are commitments to respect the CLS—it is beginning to emerge as the agreement with potential.

---

[1] GATT, *Relationship of Internationally Recognized Labour Standards to International Trade*, Communication from the United States, 28 October 1987, and also in 1990.

K. Addo, *Core Labour Standards and International Trade*,
DOI 10.1007/978-3-662-44619-5_5

5.2 Social Clauses in International Trade Agreements: Precedents

The issue of a social clause in international trade agreements is not new. The efforts of the international community in achieving compliance and redressing the grievances of workers would be in line with the mandate given to the ILO in its Constitution: the promotion of "Lasting peace through social justice". A number of international commodity agreements contain a social clause, and this is in contrast to the absence of such a clause in the international trade agreement. GATT 1947, Article XX allows Members to take measures against products produced with prison labour, but this is as far as the social clause goes. However, there appears to be a social dimension in the Preamble to the Agreement Establishing the WTO, which states that the Parties recognise

> ... that their relations in the field of trade and economic endeavour should be conducted with a view to raising standards of living, ensuring full employment and a large and steadily growing volume of real income and effective demand.

In 1987, the U.S., supported by the EU, made an attempt to reach a consensus on the creation of a GATT working party to review the inclusion of labour standards into the GATT. The proposal made by the U.S. for the terms of reference of the working party was

> To examine the possible relationship of internationally recognised labour standards[2] to international trade and to the attainment of the objectives of the General Agreement. In the light of this examination, to consider any proposals and suggestions that may be put forward with respect to issues relating to trade and the observance of internationally recognized labour standards; and to report its findings and conclusions to the Council.

In spite of the lack of consensus on the inclusion of a social clause in the multilateral trade agreement, a number of international commodity agreements, on the other hand, contain a social clause.

For instance, Article 45 of the Sixth International Tin Agreement, 1982, provides:

> Members declare that, in order to avoid the depression of living standards and the introduction of unfair competitive conditions in world trade, they will seek to ensure fair labour standards in the tin industry.

Article 28 of the International Sugar Agreement, 1987, provides:

> Members shall ensure that fair labour standards are maintained in their respective industries and, as far as possible, shall endeavour to improve the living of agricultural and industrial

[2]The international labour standards that the U.S. wanted to address were (1) freedom of association, (2) freedom to organise and bargain collectively, (3) freedom from forced or compulsory labour, (4) minimum age for the employment of children, and (5) measures setting minimum standards in respect of conditions of work. See GATT, Relationship of Internationally Recognized Labour Standards to International Trade, Communication from the United States, 28 October 1987. Quoted in Waer (1996), pp. 26–27.

> workers in the various branches of sugar production and of growers of sugar cane and sugar beet.

Article 53 of the 1987 International Natural Rubber Agreement provides:

> Members declare that they will endeavour to maintain labour standards designed to improve the standards of living of workers in their respective natural rubber sectors.

The International Cocoa Agreement contains a social clause in Article 49 and provides:

> Members declare that, in order to raise the levels of living populations and provide full employment, they will endeavour to maintain fair labour standards and working conditions in the various branches of cocoa production in the countries concerned, consistent with their stage of development, as regards both agricultural and industrial workers employed therein.

Even though there is no evidence of the social clauses in the agreements having been enforced, they are indication of precedents of social clauses in international agreements, and a social clause can only be considered fair by both proponents and critics if it stands a chance of being adopted and will function effectively.[3]

5.3 Unilateral Efforts

According to the GATT–WTO rules, international trade should not be conducted on a discriminatory basis. However, a link between CLS and trade has been established through unilateral, non-reciprocal trade preference schemes. Developed countries have used the Generalised System of Preferences (GSP) to provide reduced or no tariffs for imports from developing countries in return for compliance with CLS. GSP schemes are operated by the United States, Canada, Japan, Norway, Switzerland, Australia, and New Zealand. In the sections below, we analyse the GSP schemes of the United States and the European Union.

A further policy option for trade-linked labour standards is to include relevant clauses in regional, subregional, and bilateral trade and investment agreements. The broader emerging trade law regime in comparison with the multilateral regime is the regional model with consistent references to labour standards. These references are based largely on the 1998 ILO Declaration, and the implementation of the standards relies on domestic arrangements rather than international law. These arrangements generate only limited pressure to adhere to the international standards. Among the most important agreements of this kind is the North American Agreement on Labor Cooperation (NAALC), which is a side agreement to the North American Free Trade Agreement (NAFTA) of 1994, concerning local enforcement of CLS in Mexico, the United States, and Canada; the US–Jordan Free Trade Agreement; US–Singapore; US–Chile; and others. Labour rights

---

[3] See Waer (1996).

provisions are incorporated also in bilateral agreements of the EU. The examples also include agreements with South Africa, Chile, and Mexico.

Failure to establish a link at the multilateral level has led to a linkage through unilateral, non-reciprocal trade preference schemes. The Generalised System of Preferences (GSP) is used in part by developed countries to provide reduced or no tariffs for imports from developing countries that respect the core ILS.

The GATT/WTO rules allow two significant exceptions to the MFN rule. The first concerns the rules under Article XXIV, which permits the creation of FTAs and interim agreements, as discussed in Chap. 6. The other exception allowed under GATT is that developed countries can grant non-reciprocal preferential market access to developing countries under the Generalised System of Preferences (GSP). It is this option of according special market access to developing countries that developed countries have used to impose labour standards on developing countries.

5.3.1 The Enabling Clause

The legal cover of the GSP scheme started with the Decision of the CONTRACTING PARTIES on *Differential and More Favourable Treatment, Reciprocity and Fuller Participation of Developing Countries*, otherwise known as the Enabling Clause. This emerged from the Tokyo Round of Multilateral Trade Negotiations. This clause basically permits developed countries to accord differential and more favourable treatment to developing countries, without according such treatment to other Members of the WTO. In other words, it provides legal cover for, most notably, trade concessions granted to developing countries under the Generalised System of Preferences (GSP) of 25 June 1971, by waiving the provisions of Article I of GATT 1994.

Paragraph 2(c) of the Enabling Clause extends such treatment to regional or global trading arrangements entered into by developing countries for the mutual reduction or elimination of tariffs and non-tariff measures. In other words, agreements entered into between developing and developed countries fall outside the scope of the Enabling Clause.

Before the enactment of the "Enabling Clause", developing countries invoked Part IV of the General Agreement to enter into such preferential trading arrangements.[4] The enactment of the Enabling Clause in November 1979 provided

[4] Part IV, which deals mainly with trade and development, was added to the General Agreement in 1965, at the behest of developing countries. It established the principle of non-reciprocity in trade negotiations between developed and developing countries and provided for special and differential measures intended to promote the trade and development of the less-developed members of GATT. It has been argued by some that it does not create legally enforceable rights. In other words, its provisions are merely hortatory in character. See Kessie (1999, 2000).

developing countries with a permanent legal basis for the formation of preferential trading arrangements.[5]

5.4 U.S. Unilateral Efforts

The GSP policy of the United States, which was inaugurated in 1974, was amended in 1984 to allow duty-free access for selected products provided that the exporting country respects internationally recognised worker rights. These include the CLS and "acceptable conditions of work related to wages, hours of work and health and safety".[6]

The inclusion of labour standard provisions in U.S. trade-related legislation goes as far back as the 1890s. This started with legislation directed against the importation of goods made with prison labour. However, in the 1930s, the U.S. undertook a number of initiatives to ensure that the goods entering the territory of the U.S. were produced according to U.S. domestic fair labour standards. This included the right to organise and bargain collectively. Table 5.1 provides a brief summary of the relevant legislation from 1890.

5.4.1 The United States Generalised System of Preferences

The inclusion of labour clauses in FTAs signed between the United States and other countries is a recent phenomenon in comparison with the incorporation of these labour clauses in the Generalised System of Preferences (GSP) schemes. The GSP scheme in the United States was first adopted as part of the Trade Act of 1974. The GSP scheme provides preferential duty-free access for about 4,800 products from 131 designated beneficiary countries and territories. The process of labour standard inclusion began in 1983 with the Caribbean Basin Initiative (CBI), followed shortly thereafter by the inclusion of labour rights provisions in the GSP when the programme was renewed in 1984. The process continued with the passage of the Andean Trade Preference Act (ATPA) in 1991 and the Caribbean Basin Trade Partnership Act (CBTPA) and Africa Growth and Opportunity Act (AGOA) in 2000. One of the eligibility criteria for benefiting under these non-reciprocal trading

---

[5] The precursor of the Enabling Clause was the January 1979 Decision of the CONTRACTING PARTIES to adopt the Report of the Working Party on Preferential Trading Arrangements. The Decision essentially authorised, contrary to the terms of Article I of the General Agreement, the formation of preferential trading arrangements. Members who invoked this Decision to form or make modifications to an existing arrangement were required to notify the CONTRACTING PARTIES.

[6] Harvey (1996).

Table 5.1 U.S. trade and investment legislation with labour standard provisions (1890–1989)

Year	Act	Labour standard provisions
1890	McKinley Tariff Act	It bans importation of goods, wares, articles, and merchandise manufactured by convict labour
1930	Smoot–Hawley Tariff Act (Section 307)	This bans import of goods produced, mined, or manufactured by convict, forced, or indentured labour. The President is authorised to adjust tariffs to equalise differences in cost of production
1974	Trade Act (Section 301)	The Act grants discretionary power to the President to take all appropriate and feasible action to obtain elimination of unfair practises. The United States Trade Representative (USTR) may initiate investigations of foreign labour practices, or act upon complaints from interested persons. Disputes may be referred to disputes resolution under any applicable trade agreement
1977	International Emergency Economic Powers Act	This Act deals with extraordinary threats to US national security, foreign policy, or economy. It prohibits virtually all foreign economic transactions and allows the President to control assets. It was used in 1985 against South Africa for, inter alia, violations of workers' rights
1983	Caribbean Basin Economic Recovery Act	This provides (under certain conditions) for additional trade preferences to selected Caribbean and Central American countries. One of these conditions is that in granting benefits, the President must take into account the degree to which workers are afforded reasonable workplace conditions and enjoy the right to organise and bargain collectively. There is no ongoing monitoring process or complaints procedure. Ensuing negotiations under the CBI led to significant commitments by several governments such as Honduras, El Salvador, the Dominican Republic, and Haiti
1984	Generalised System of Preferences (renewal)	Following re-authorisation, additional conditions and criteria for preferential treatment were included. It is provided that the President shall not designate any beneficiary country if it has not taken or is not taking steps to afford internationally recognised worker rights to workers in the country (including any designated zone in that country). These rights are defined as (1) right of association, (2) right to organise and bargain collectively, (3) prohibition on the use of any form of forced or compulsory

(continued)

Table 5.1 (continued)

Year	Act	Labour standard provisions
		labour, (4) minimum age for the employment of children, (5) acceptable conditions of work with respect to minimum wages, hours, hours of work, and occupational safety and health. An ongoing monitoring process and complaints procedure exist. Under these provisions, GSP status for particular products, sometimes only for particular products, was withdrawn from a number of countries: e.g., Central African Republic, Chile, Liberia, Myanmar, Nicaragua, Paraguay, Romania, and the Sudan. In June 1993, Mauritania was denied beneficiary status, and the position of Thailand and Indonesia was reviewed
1985	Overseas Private Investment Corporation (renewal)	It was amended to require that investment insurance be withheld from projects in countries not taking steps to adopt and implement laws that extend internationally recognised worker rights. There is ongoing monitoring of progress and complaints procedure. Three countries were removed from eligibility in early 1987. The 1986 Anti-Apartheid Act made it incumbent on US firms employing more than 25 persons in South Africa to follow a code of conduct that includes fair labour standards
1987	US participation in the Multilateral Investment and Guarantee Agency of the World Bank	This made US participation conditional on countries affording internationally recognised workers' rights to their workers
1988	Omnibus Trade and Competitiveness Act	The Act states that the principal negotiating objectives of the US regarding workers' rights are (1) to promote respect for workers' rights to GATT articles; (2) to secure a review of the relationship of workers' rights to GATT articles, objectives, and related instruments with a view to ensuring that the benefits of the trading system are available to all workers; and (3) to adopt as a principle of the GATT that the denial of worker rights should not be a means for a country or its industries to gain competitive advantage in international trade. Impact of this law is as yet difficult to assess
1989	International Development and Finance Act	This Act requires the Export–import Bank to evaluate overseas labour practices before granting assistance

Source: ILO, The Social Clause: Issues and Challenges. See http://actrav.itcilo.org/actrav-english/telearn/global/ilo/guide/hoelim2.htm. Accessed 24 January 2014

arrangements was the condition that countries comply with the internationally recognised labour standards.

In 1984, the United States amended the GSP scheme by adding that a GSP beneficiary country is ineligible if the country has not taken or is not taking steps to afford workers internationally recognised worker rights. Section 502(b)(7) of Title V of the Trade and Tariff Act of 1984 provided that

> [t]he President shall not designate any country a beneficiary developing country under this section if such country has not taken or is not taking steps to afford internationally recognized worker rights in the country, including any designated zone in that country.[7]

The rights, as defined in the law, is provided in Section 502(b)(4). And states that for the purposes of Title V, the term "internationally recognized workers' rights include:

- the right of association;
- the right to organise and bargain collectively,
- prohibition on the use of any form of forced or compulsory labor;
- a minimum age for the employment of children; and
- acceptable conditions of work with respect to minimum wages, hours of work, and occupational safety and health".

Under the GSP law, the President is required to submit an annual report on the protection of internationally recognised workers' rights in each of the beneficiary countries. The monitoring of workers' rights is included in the United States State Department's annual country report on human rights practices. This provision of reporting on labour practices in beneficiary countries in facilitating decisions on the granting or revoking of trade preferences is significant in bringing about compliance with the CLS.

One of the most often raised issue in the GSP annual reviews are on workers' rights. For example, during the period 1985–1991, in the petitions filed with the office of the United States Trade Representative, workers' rights accounted for 121 out of the 192 "country practices". In the following investigations conducted as a result of these petitions, some countries committed themselves to improve their compliance with labour rights. Other countries lost their GSP benefits either through temporary suspension (Burma, Central African Republic, Chile, Maldives, Mauritania, Paraguay, Sudan, and Syrian Arab Republic) or, in extreme cases, permanent termination of benefits (Liberia and Nicaragua).

The GSP schemes operated by the U.S. and Europe have had ambiguous effects. Out of 63 cases reviewed between 1985 and 1995 for labour rights reasons under the U.S. GSP scheme, 12 ended in the withdrawal or suspension of GSP benefits for 10 countries, 51 resulted in a decision that the benefit-receiving country was taking steps to afford worker rights, and 7 cases are still pending (Harvey 1996). Since

[7] United States, Trade and Tariff Act of 1984, Pub. L. 98-573.

1996, benefits have only been suspended for Belarus. In several instances where U.S. trade sanctions were applied or a GSP review was announced, several countries moved to reform their labour code or changed their labour practices.[8] Yet it is also clear that many developing countries resent the conditionality attached to trade assistance programmes.

An analysis of the enforcement of labour rights provisions in the GSP schemes of the U.S. showed that the U.S. Government enforced the unilateral labour rights provisions less on the basis of a fair and consistent assessment of violations than with a view to U.S. foreign policy interests and domestic policies (Greven 2005).

Furthermore, there is little evidence of trade sanctions being used to effectively promote improved labour standards overseas. One recent review conducted by Elliot of countries petitioned under the GSP noted that "the 30 cases ended up being evenly divided between success and failure and, even in these cases it was difficult to know if it was the threat of sanctions or the focus of public attention that was the real motivation for change".[9] Similarly, a recent survey of U.S. economic sanctions used for a wide range of objectives over the 1970s and 1980s showed that they resulted in positive outcomes in less than one case in five.[10]

5.4.2 Impact of United States GSP on Beneficiary Countries

In spite of the criticisms leveled against the lack of effective enforcement of labour standards under the GSP scheme, it appears that the inclusion of labour clauses in the United States GSP scheme has led to some positive results. In several instances where U.S. trade sanctions were applied or a GSP review was announced, several countries moved to reform their labour code or changed their labour practices.

We provide some examples of how the United States GSP regime has induced change.

In the case of Chile, democratic reforms were instituted following the removal of GSP, even though the government did not take the necessary steps to improve the overall labour rights situation.[11]

In Peru, the trade union movement stated that the government gave more careful consideration to the GSP petition against the country than the criticism levelled by the ILO Committee on Freedom of Association and the Committee of Experts.[12]

---

[8] See Greven (2005) for a summary of studies of successes and failures of U.S. and European GSP schemes.

[9] Bates (2000).

[10] Hufbauer, Schott, and Elliot (1990) *Economic Sanctions Reconsidered*, as quoted by Bates (2000), p. 5.

[11] Harvey (1996), p. 5.

[12] Harvey (1996), p. 5.

Further to the filing of two petitions in 1990 and 1991, the Dominican Republic made illegal labour by debt bondage in response to the threat of losing its GSP position for sugar exports.[13]

In Thailand, following a petition filed in 1992, the government instituted labour legislation that included the CLS in state enterprises.[14]

However, the removal of preferential treatment, or even the threat of it, can have undesired or inadvertent effects. This became evident when U.S. trade sanctions were imposed on Bangladesh under the 1992 Child Labour Deterrence Act. Children working in Bangladesh's garment industry were dismissed. But as there were no alternative jobs available to them, they staged a demonstration demanding to be given their jobs back. It was then agreed that their removal from the industry should be more gradual and tied to the availability of employment and educational facilities. The lesson to be learned from this case is that trade sanctions can at best induce a country to change its policy on child labour, but it does not yet resolve the problem. Local action is also required to effectively reduce child labour in socially acceptable ways.[15]

5.5 The European Union's Generalised System of Preferences

5.5.1 Introduction

The GSP scheme of the EU is considered a central component of its strategy towards developing countries. The main thrust of the EU strategy is to promote sustainable development in using trade as an engine in the achievement of both economic and social goals. The European Union (EU) is the world's largest provider of trade preferences in favour of developing countries. After the recommendation by United Nations Conference on Trade and Development (UNCTAD) in 1968 that developed countries adopt generalised systems of trade preferences for exports from developing countries, the European Union became the first to adopt such a preference scheme.

The EU GSP Scheme was first introduced in 1971 and has over the years evolved considerably. In 2006, the EU undertook substantial changes to its GSP scheme (see Table 5.2). The EU's GSP strategy towards developing countries is manifest in its relations with the Africa, Caribbean and Pacific (ACP) group of countries under the Economic Partnership Agreements (EPAs). In addition to this are the GSP schemes in bilateral and other EU RTAs.

---

[13] Harvey (1996), p. 6.

[14] USTR (The President's 1997 Annual Report), p. 186; USTR (The President's 2000 Annual Report), p. 134.

[15] Panagariya (2000), p. 14.

Table 5.2 Evolution of labour provisions in the EU GSP, from 1995 to 2002

Year entered into force	Reference to ILO instruments	Enforcement mechanisms
1995	Convention Nos. 29 and 105	Withdrawal of trade preferences in the case of "systematic and serious violations" of these Conventions
1999	Convention Nos. 29 and 105 (for sanction-based labour provisions) Convention Nos. 87, 98, and 138 (for incentive-based labour provisions)	Withdrawal of trade preferences in case of "systematic and serious violations" of ILO Conventions No. 29 and 105. Additional preferences for effective implementation of ILO Conventions No. 87, 98, and 138
2002	1998 Declaration, all Fundamental Conventions	Withdrawal of trade preferences in case of "systematic and serious violations" of the ILO Fundamental Conventions; additional preferences for effective implementation of the ILO Fundamental Conventions[a]

Source: Ebert and Posthuma (2011)
[a]Since 2006, GSP beneficiaries are to ratify all ILO Fundamental Conventions in order to be eligible for the additional preferences

The EU GSP scheme comprises three separate preference regimes—(a) the GSP: this is the general GSP scheme; under this, developing countries are offered generous tariff reductions; (b) the GSP+: under this programme, the EU offers additional preferences on top of the general GSP to a group of selected developing countries that have ratified and implemented international human, labour, and environmental standards with regard to good governance[16]; and (c) the Everything But Arms (EBA). This is a scheme for least developed countries, under which they are offered duty-free and quota-free market access to all products, except for arms and ammunitions.[17]

5.5.2 The EU's New GSP Scheme

On 31 October 2012, the EU adopted a reformed GSP law (Regulation No 978/2012) to take effect on 1 January 2014 and remain in effect for 10 years. According to the EU, a major reason for the change in regulation is the entry into force of the Lisbon Treaty. This, in the EU's view, necessitated a redesign of the

[16] See Mid-term Evaluation of the EU's Generalised System of Preferences, CARIS, available at http://trade.ec.europa.eu/doclib/docs/2010/may/tradeoc_146196.pdf, p. 16. Accessed 28 January 2014.

[17] Generalised Scheme of Preferences (GSP), European Commission, Directorate-General for Trade, available at http://ec.europa.eu/trade/policy/countries-and-regions/development/generalised-scheme. Accessed 28 January 2014.

GSP scheme to reflect the new institutional arrangement. Under the new arrangement, the role of the European Parliament in trade policy has been enhanced.[18]

Below we provide a brief overview of the key features of the new regulation:

(a) GSP:

- The number of countries that benefit from the preferential access to the EU market is reduced from 176 to 89. The reduction in the number of countries reflects what the EU considers to be countries, which do not require GSP preferences in order to stay competitive.
- Countries that already enjoy preference access to EU markets under an FTA or a special autonomous trade regime: this would affect 34 countries that have signed FTAs with the EU or have other preferential market access arrangements.
- The reformed GSP scheme removes tariff preferences from countries that have been classified by the World Bank as high or upper income economies in the last 3 years.
- Countries that have alternative market access arrangement for developed markets: included in this arrangement are the 33 countries with their own market access regulation.
- Institution of a graduation mechanism of competitive sectors: the product sections under the graduation mechanism are expanded from 21 to 32. According to the EU, this will ensure that graduation is more objective since the products in the categories are very homogenous. Furthermore, the graduation threshold will increase from 15 to 17.5 % (for textiles, from 12.5 to 14.5 %).[19]

(b) GSP+ (below we discuss in detail the impact of the GSP+ on the labour and trade linkage):

- Under the new regulation, the EU has the objective of furthering the promotion of core human and labour rights and also environment and good governance. To achieve this, the EU has reinforced the incentive scheme for countries to join the GSP+ scheme.
- Countries that enjoy preferences under this part of the scheme are not subject to graduation.
- The EU at the same time has enhanced its monitoring mechanisms to ensure that those rights and principles are upheld.[20]

---

[18] See factsheet: The EU's new Generalised Scheme of Preferences (GSP), at http://trade.ec.europa.eu/doclib/docs/2013/february/tradoc_150582.pdf, p. 2. Accessed 28 January 2014.

[19] The EU's new Generalised Scheme of Preferences (GSP), at http://trade.ec.europa.eu/doclib/docs/2013/february/tradoc_150582.pdf, p. 6. Accessed 28 January 2014.

[20] The EU's new Generalised Scheme of Preferences (GSP), at http://trade.ec.europa.eu/doclib/docs/2013/february/tradoc_150582.pdf, p. 9. Accessed 28 January 2014.

(c) EBA:

- The new regulation is intended to lead to the strengthening of the effectiveness of the EBA scheme. The beneficiaries under EBA will be reduced, leading to a reduction in competition.

The EU states that the new scheme will enhance stability and predictability. According to the EU, both importers and exporters need stability and predictability in order to use the GSP preferences. So instead of the 3-year cycle for review, the new scheme has a lifespan of 10 years. The EU has also instituted a 1-year transition period for beneficiary countries to make the necessary changes. The EU has also stated that beneficiaries under the general GSP scheme will only be removed if they are listed as high or upper-middle income 3 years in a row. The EU acknowledges that there are many procedures that operators need to take into account, which was not well highlighted under the old regulation. In the new regulation, the EU has provided more detailed information for the purpose of transparency. Finally, even though the new scheme will take effect on 1 January 2014, the EU has published the legal texts and rules 1 year in advance to give operators ample time to familiarise themselves.

5.5.3 Tariff Preferences Under the Special Incentive Arrangement (GSP+)

A country benefits from the schemes by providing information on their domestic labour legislation and its implementation and monitoring. Should there be evidence of a violation of the CLS by any country under the GSP scheme, the EU reserves the right to withdraw the benefits. In 2004, the EU proposed a new regulation for trade policy on tariff preferences for the period 2005–2008. Included in the proposal were simpler and more flexible rules, extending the range of duty-free products to 7,200, and a focus on a smaller number of countries, preferably LDCs, with vulnerable and poorly diversified economies. To benefit under the scheme and be granted trade preferences, a country has to show that it is actually conforming to the CLS instead of mere ratification of the ILO Conventions.

In the subsections below, we discuss the EC Council Regulation (EC) No. 2501/2001, which required adherence to the CLS in light of the analysis of the case that India brought under the WTO dispute mechanism. In this case, India contested the tariff concessions granted by the European Communities to 12 developing countries under its GSP scheme. It should be noted that the new Council Regulation 978/2012 builds on the 2001 regulation and has even enhanced it to further promote the ILO core labour standards. The two regulations are considered separately from the other two parts of the scheme because of the link by the EU under this part (GSP+) of the GSP arrangement between increased trade and respect for the ILO core labour standards.

5.5.3.1 The Provisions of the 2001 and 2012 GSP+ Scheme

The EU, since the middle of the 1990s, aims through its 'incentive labour clause' at helping countries that apply the CLS through the provision of preferential benefits for making inroads in including social policy in their trade policy. The EU–GSP schemes make explicit reference to the CLS and apply these to countries in Latin America, Asia and the Pacific, Africa, the Caribbean basin, Central and Eastern Europe, and the Commonwealth of Independent States. The European Union has, since January 2002, adopted a new GSP policy that doubles the tariff reduction for countries that respect the CLS, as well as environmental standards, human rights, and the control of drugs. As mentioned above, this regulation has been reformed and the section on the special incentives of GSP+ has been further strengthened.

The GSP scheme (Council Regulation No. 2501/2001) that was challenged by India at the WTO is the Generalised Tariff Preferences for the period from 1 January 2002 to 31 December 2004.[21] After the expiry of this Regulation, the EU adopted Council Regulation No 980/200536. This Regulation entered into force on 1 January 2006 and expired on 31 December 2008. In order to ensure the continuity of the GSP scheme, a new Regulation was adopted by the Council on 22 July 2008 (Council Regulation (EC) No 732/2008) to cover the period from 1 January 2009 to 31 December 2011. This scheme will then be replaced by Council Regulation 978/2012.

The GSP+ scheme of 2501/2001 provided for preferential market access to designated beneficiary countries. The scheme has four "Special Incentives Arrangements", relating to least developed countries:

- to combat drug production,
- to combat drug trafficking,
- to protect labour rights, and
- to protect the environment.

Under this scheme, the EU adopted what Hepple (2005, p. 102) terms as a 'carrot and stick' approach to CLS. The carrot is the 'special incentive arrangement for the protection of labour rights'. For a beneficiary country to qualify, the country must show that its national legislation incorporates the essence of the standards in ILO Conventions 29 and 105 on forced labour, 87 and 98 on the freedom of association and the right to collective bargaining, 100 and 111 on non-discrimination in respect of employment and occupation, and 138 and 182 on child labour (see Chap. 2 for in-depth review of the Conventions).[22] The 'stick' is the temporary withdrawal of

[21] Council Regulation (EC) No. 2501/2001 of 10 December 2001, Official Journal of the European Commission 31.12.2001. The ILO Conventions are also stated in the new regulation of 31 October 2012, Regulation No 978/2012.

[22] Council Regulation 2501/2001, Article 14(2), and the new Council Regulation No 978/2012, Article 9 and Annex VIII.

preferential arrangements in respect of all or of certain products that originate from a country benefiting under the scheme.

The newly adopted scheme (978/2012) includes the four special incentive arrangements, plus respect for good governance. The EU's adoption of this scheme was in part due to the ruling of the Panel and Appellate Body in the case brought by India, challenging the EU special preferences for selected developing countries that were actively implementing anti-narcotics programmes. The ruling in that case was that it is permissible to differentiate among non-LDCs as long as the distinctions among countries are based on a "widely-recognised development, financial, [or] trade need".[23] In order to comply with the ruling of the Dispute Settlement Mechanism (DSM), the EU in this new scheme provided for greater preferences for vulnerable non-LDCs meeting specific widely recognised criteria, including the ratification and implementation of international conventions on human and labour rights, good governance, and the environment.

The enhanced scheme is intended to be used by the EU as a lever to make certain that implementation achieves two main objectives: (a) does not deteriorate and (b) improves over time. The EU through this scheme will engage in regular dialogue with the beneficiary countries (at the moment 15 countries) as a means of following up and, in some cases, temporarily redrawing the tariff concessions. The EU considers this approach to be 'progressive improvement', given the fact that changes have to be made to fully implement some of the 27 Conventions that are complex and involve adjustment costs.[24]

The special incentive arrangements under 2501/2001 was meant to provide greater market access to the designated beneficiary countries, compared to those that are eligible under the General Scheme. For the countries that apply and receive the special incentives for labour and environment, they also receive an additional reduction in duties to the extent of five percentage points (which makes it a total of 8 (3.5 + 5) percentage points). According to the EU, the primary objective of the GSP is to contribute to the reduction of poverty and the promotion of sustainable development and good governance. The preferential tariff rates, when exporting to the EU market, enable developing countries to participate more fully in international trade and generate additional export revenue to support them in developing industry, create jobs, and thereby reduce poverty.[25]

With respect to the new scheme (978/2012), countries in order to qualify must meet three criteria[26]:

---

[23] European Communities—Conditions for the Granting of Tariff Preferences to Developing Countries, WT/DS246/AB/R, adopted 20 April 2004, paragraph 164.

[24] See factsheet: The EU's new Generalised Scheme of Preferences (GSP), at http://trade.ec.europa.eu/doclib/docs/2013/february/tradoc_150582.pdf, p. 13. Accessed 1 February 2014.

[25] See http://ec.europa.eu/trade/issues/global/gsp/index_en.htm. Accessed 2 February 2014.

[26] See Article 9 of REGULATION (EU) No 978/2012 OF THE EUROPEAN PARLIAMENT AND OF THE COUNCIL of 25 October 2012, applying a scheme of generalised tariff preferences and repealing Council Regulation (EC) No 732/2008.

1. They must not only ratify the 27 Conventions listed in Annex VIII but also take the necessary steps towards their implementation.
2. The countries must also give an undertaking that they will maintain the ratification and the implementing legislation and measures. They should also accept regular monitoring and review of the implementation record in accordance with the implementation provisions of the relevant conventions.[27]
3. A beneficiary country should be considered vulnerable, in which case it is not classified by the World Bank as a high-income country during 3 consecutive years; the country's exports to the EU are heavily concentrated in a few products. Its five largest sections of GSP-covered imports into the EU market represent more than 75 % in value of its total GSP-covered exports and has a low level of exports to the EU, covering less than 1 % in value of the total GSP covered imports.[28]

5.5.3.2 The WTO Decision on the India GSP Case

In 2003, India complained under the WTO dispute settlement procedures about the special incentive arrangements. India challenged preferential tariff treatment accorded by the European Communities to 12 beneficiary countries (not including India) pursuant to the European Communities' special arrangements to combat drug production and trafficking (the "Drug Arrangements"), as provided in Council Regulation (EC) No. 2501/2001 of 10 December 2001. It is important to note that India initially challenged the European Union's labour rights clauses in its GSP programme. India later withdrew its claim under the labour rights clause.[29]

5.5.3.3 Panel Report

Before the Panel, India claimed that the European Communities' (EC) Drug Arrangements are inconsistent with the most-favoured-nation (MFN) principle embodied in Article I:1 of GATT 1994. India further argued that the Drug Arrangements are not justified by the Enabling Clause. The Panel found that (1) India has demonstrated that the tariff preferences under the Special Arrangements to Combat Drug Production and Trafficking (the "Drug Arrangements") provided in the EC's GSP scheme are inconsistent with Article I:1 of GATT 1994; (2) the EC has failed to demonstrate that the Drug Arrangements are justified under paragraph 2(a) of the Enabling Clause, which requires that the GSP benefits be provided on a "non-

[27] Factsheet: The EU's new Generalised Scheme of Preferences (GSP), at http://trade.ec.europa.eu/doclib/docs/2013/february/tradoc_150582.pdf, p. 14. Accessed 2 February 2014.

[28] The EU's new Generalised Scheme of Preferences (GSP), at http://trade.ec.europa.eu/doclib/docs/2013/february/tradoc_150582.pdf, p. 14. Accessed 2 February 2014.

[29] *European Communities – Conditions for the Granting of Tariff Preferences to Developing Countries*, WT/DS246/AB/R, adopted 20 April 2004 (hereinafter India GSP).

discriminatory" basis; and (3) the EC has failed to demonstrate that the Drug Arrangements are justified under Article XX(b) of GATT 1994 since the measure is not "necessary" for the protection of human life or health in the EC, nor is it in conformity with the Chapeau of Article XX.

5.5.3.4 Appellate Body Report

The European Communities filed a Notice of Appeal challenging the Panel's legal conclusion that the Drug Arrangements are inconsistent with Article I:1 of GATT 1994. A summary of the Appellate Body Report is as follows.

The Appellate Body upheld two of the Panel's findings: (1) the Enabling Clause operates as an exception to Article I:1 of the GATT 1994, and (2) the Enabling Clause does not exclude the applicability of Article I:1 of the GATT 1994. The Appellate Body modified, however, one of the Panel's findings with respect to the relationship between Article I:1 of the GATT 1994 and the Enabling Clause. The Appellate Body found that the complaining party is obliged not only to claim inconsistency with Article I:1 of the GATT 1994 but also to raise the relevant provisions of the Enabling Clause that the complaining party argues are not satisfied by the challenged measure.

Based on these findings, and because the EC did not appeal any other aspect of the Panel's reasoning with respect to Article I:1, the Appellate body found that it need not rule on the Panel's conclusion as to the consistency of the challenged measure with Article I:1 of GATT 1994.

The Appellate Body reversed the Panel's legal interpretation of paragraph 2 (a) of the Enabling Clause and footnote 3 thereto, by concluding that, in granting differential tariff treatment, preference-granting countries are required, by virtue of the term "non-discriminatory", to ensure that identical treatment is available to all similarly situated GSP beneficiaries, i.e., to all GSP beneficiaries that have the same "development, financial and trade needs" to which the treatment in question is intended to respond. With respect to the consistency of the challenged measure with the Enabling Clause, the Appellate Body upheld, albeit for different reasons, the Panel's conclusion that the European Communities failed to demonstrate that the challenged measure was justified under paragraph 2(a) of the Enabling Clause.[30]

5.5.3.5 The Relevance of the Appellate Body Decision

Analysing the case from a broader point of view, the significance of this decision is twofold. Firstly, the case has dispelled the concern that an unfavourable outcome would prejudice the EU and U.S. GSP schemes that developing countries currently

[30] See http://www.wto.org/english/tratop_e/dispu_e/cases_e/ds246_e.htm. Accessed 2 February 2014.

have access to. There was the uneasiness among EU and U.S. officials that should the panel's original finding on non-discrimination be upheld, their respective drug eradication programmes and other special GSP tariff benefits could be put at risk. Secondly, the Appellate Body in its ruling noted that the EC's "special incentive arrangements for the protection of labour rights" and the "special incentive arrangements for the protection of the environment", which were not at issue in this case, in contrast to the drug arrangements, included detailed provisions setting out the procedure and substantive criteria that apply to a request by a country to become a beneficiary. The statement of the Appellate Body on the reference to labour-related preferences contains an *obiter dictum*, which states:

> Articles 10 and 25 of the Regulation, which relate specifically to the Drug Arrangements, provide no mechanism under which additional beneficiaries may be added to the list of beneficiaries under the Drug Arrangements as designated in Annex I . . . This contrasts with the position under the 'special incentive arrangements for the protection of labour rights' and the 'special incentive arrangements for the protection of the environment', which are described in Article 8 of the Regulation. The Regulation includes detailed provisions setting out the procedure and substantive criteria that apply to a request by a beneficiary under the general arrangements described in Article 7 of the Regulation (the 'General Arrangements') to become a beneficiary under either of those special incentive arrangements.[31]

This could indicate, *prima facie*, that these arrangements are WTO compatible, implying that WTO Members are free to include sustainable development concerns in their GSP schemes provided they meet the relevant conditions and are justified under the relevant WTO rules. The decision of the Appellate Body also gives some indication as to how a future WTO panel might approach the protection of labour rights in trade issues.[32]

5.6 Impact of European GSP Scheme on Beneficiary Countries

According to the EU, its GSP is the most widely used of all developed-country GSP systems.[33] In this respect, when reviewed from the labour standard perspective, due to the strong linkage between benefitting from the preferences and ratification and implementation of the CLS, it has the probability of making a major impact in adherence to the CLS.

It is worthy to note that the development of the EU GSP from a sanctions based approach to the twofold "carrot and stick" approach involving the imposing sanctions is when a beneficiary violates the labour provisions to temporary withdrawal

[31] Appellate Body Report, *EC – Tariff Preferences*, para. 182.

[32] See, generally, Bartels (2007), pp. 869–886.

[33] EC (2012).

of a country from the list of GSP+ beneficiary countries and enjoying additional preferences in the event of ratification and full implementation of the CLS. Also worthy to note is that instead of the EU developing its own criteria for labour standards, it has consistently referred to the ILO core conventions. Even though it initially made reference to only some of the ILO core labour standards it has since the adoption of the 1998 ILO Declaration on FPRW, it has since 2002 included all the eight CLS.

In 2010, the EU commissioned the Centre for the Analysis of Regional Integration at the University of Sussex (CARIS) to undertake a midterm review of the GSP scheme.[34] The results of the analysis by CARIS were that, on the whole, the scheme has been successful. The report showed that imports that benefitted from the GSP scheme were significant and in 2009 amounted to €60 billion. This was equivalent to more than 9 % of the total EU imports from all beneficiary countries. It should be noted that the 9 % import varies across categories of beneficiaries, with preferential imports accounting for 8 % of total imports from GSP countries, 20 % of total imports from GSP+ countries, and 32 % of total imports from EBA beneficiaries.[35]

The report also showed that there is evidence of GSP preferences increasing the trade and investment climate in beneficiary countries. The report also highlighted the general attractiveness of the scheme due to the high utilisation rate of the preferences but showed that there was room for improvement, with about utilisation rate of 53 % for GSP countries, 69 % for EBA countries, and 85 % for GSP+ countries.[36] Concerning the impact of the GSP+, the CARIS report concluded that this arrangement has had a positive impact on the ratification of the CLS. The report stressed the need for a system to monitor progress in implementation.[37]

The EU GSP+ scheme appears to constitute a more positive approach to development and sustainability since it is likely to have the greatest impact on making trade work for development and, in turn, adherence to the CLS. The preferences can be temporarily withdrawn where there is a 'serious and systematic violation' of any of the CLS. The approach in the GSP scheme very much reflect the EU's view regarding conditionality and the offering of carrots in order to establish a positive relationship between trade and labour standards.

The *EC-GSP* case most likely had an impact on the EU providing detailed information on the procedures (temporary withdrawals, safeguards, etc.). This detailed structure of the GSP scheme, in particular the GSP+, makes it useful for developing countries since it sets out detailed provisions on the procedure and substantive criteria that apply to a request by a country to become a beneficiary. Also, the section on temporary withdrawal is very detailed.

---

[34] Gasiorek et al. (2010).

[35] EC (2012),

[36] EC (2012).

[37] Gasiorek et al. (2010). The inclusion of a regular monitoring system in the new GSP scheme could be attributed to the findings in the CARIS report.

The use by the EU of combining the positive and negative labour rights conditionalities has the advantage of minimising trade distortions. This is important for developing countries as they have to make great efforts to comply with the conditionalities. The difference between positive conditionality and negative conditionality is stated by Brandtner and Rosas:

> While trade sanctions may sometimes fulfill an important symbolic function and may be reasonably effective (as the prospect of economic loss does have a dissuasive effect), they should not be resorted to lightly. Resorting to "carrots" may well prove to be a more attractive way of "forcing people to be free".[38]

In spite of the likelihood of the GSP+ programme having a positive impact on compliance with the CLS, the CARIS report noted some limitations. The first is that like the basic GSP, the GSP+ programme does not cover 1,200 of the EU's tariff lines that have non-zero MFN tariff rates. The EU has classified some products (beef and other meats, dairy products, some processed fruits and vegetables, oils, and processed sugar) as very sensitive and as such not covered by the GSP+ programme. Second, the report found that there may be some limitations in relation to the application of rules of origin. Third, the implementation of some of the 27 conventions that beneficiary countries are required to comply in order to be eligible for the GSP+ may not be an immediate development priority in many low-income countries and may distract attention and effort from other possibly higher priority reforms needed to accelerate growth and poverty reduction.[39]

In all, the positive conditionality in the GSP+ scheme in relation to the CLS, in spite of some limitations, has the potential to not only promote the ratification of the core conventions of the ILO but also ensure their effective implementation. The link established by the EU between trade and the CLS, and by extension development, provides a glimpse into how a multilateral system could work to make trade work for development: what could be termed as a trade instrument with a social dimension.

5.7 International Framework Agreements

Whilst the unilateral efforts discussed above are initiated by governments, a new form of transnational social dialogue has developed, which has the potential to redress the imbalance in employer–employee relationship and to establish more collaborative relations between multinational companies (MNC) and their workers worldwide. With the advent of globalisation, embodying developments in the economic, political, and societal spheres, the development of international framework agreements (IFAs) could assist in addressing the issue of the global "race to the bottom" by equalising an MNC's labour costs irrespective of the country in

[38] Brandtner and Rosas (1999), p. 722.

[39] Gasiorek et al. (2010), p. 19.

which it operates. In which case, countries known for lack of adherence to the CLS or weak labour protections might be able to benefit from the MNC's compliance.[40]

Given the growing relevance of IFAs as a form of CSR, but a bilateral agreement from which management and labour could reap entirely new forms of social regulation, we will in this section, and for the purposes of this chapter, only discuss the impact of the IFAs as the only initiative on the global industrial relations or form of CSR, which in our opinion can help bridge the gap between compliance with the CLS and increased international trade.

An IFA is defined as a bilateral company-related agreement that an MNC and a Global Union Federation (GUF) negotiate as a way of establishing an ongoing relationship and of ensuring that the company respects the same labour standards across all the countries in its global production system.[41] By December 2012, 80 IFAs had been signed between MNCs and GUFs.[42] This marks an increase trend in the signing of IFAs from the first signing in 1988 between the French company Danone (known then as BSN) and the International Union of Food, Agricultural, Hotel, Restaurant, Catering, Tobacco and Allied Workers' Associations (IUF).

In this era of globalisation, with no international framework to regulate the process and difficulty of regulating especially capital, as it flows across borders, and especially to low-income countries with a history of lack of adherence to the CLS, or without the capacity to enforce the CLS, unions saw the relevance of promoting cross-border solidarity in the interests of workers. And as mentioned above, avoid the pitting of workers in different countries against one another in a competitive environment and avoid the so-called "race to the bottom".[43] The question that the present IFAs could help to address, particularly from the perspective of global unions is, how labour can be protected in this new and emerging global context.

5.7.1 IFAs and Corporate Social Responsibility

In recent times, many MNCs have, through their own initiatives and pressure from the international community, started a form of corporate self-regulation as part of their business model, termed as corporate social responsibility (CSR). CSR initiatives have been based on a sustainable development approach, encompassing the three pillars of economic viability, social responsibility, and environmental protection. Through their CSR or voluntary initiatives, MNCs consider the impact of their operations in the countries they operate.

---

[40] Coleman (2010), pp. 633–634.

[41] Papadakis (2011a), p. 277.

[42] Papadakis (2011b), p. 1.

[43] Coleman (2010), p. 605.

These voluntary initiatives have been grouped into five broad categories: (1) - management-driven, unilateral corporate codes of conduct and statements on business ethics; (2) public-private initiatives, for example the United Nations Global Compact, European CSR Alliance, the ILO and International Finance Corporation (IFC) Better Work Programme, with the assistance of other international organisations in the implementation phase; (3) the International Organization for Standardization with their ISO quality guidelines, such as labelling, for example, ISO 8000 (data quality) and ISO 26000 on social responsibility[44]; (4) multi-stakeholder initiatives such as the Ethical Trade Initiative (ETI), Social Accountability SA 8000, Fair Labour Association (FLA); and (5) IFAs.[45]

Even though all the five categories of CSR have important functions in this era of globalisation, the IFAs stand out as the only initiative that is the outcome of direct negotiations between MNCs and GUFs[46] and has the potential to ensure that MNCs will respect the ILO CLS they have committed themselves to.

Whilst the argument can be made that IFAs are scarce in the area of CSR, they are a novel approach to enforce that the promises made to comply with the CLS are kept. The IFAs signed to date make explicit reference to the ILO fundamental standards (freedom of association and collective bargaining, non-discrimination, and elimination of child labour and forced labour). The IFAs also touch on other important management-labour issues on employment, wages, working time, health and safety, training, and restructuring.[47] The IFAs have the potential to create the enabling environment to build a more cooperative, collaborative relationship that allows management and unions to work to achieve the principles outlined in the IFA.

5.7.2 *Expectations from IFAs*

From the perspective of management, IFAs, in addition to establishing a good working relationship with labour and improving its creditability for shareholders and investors, also could create the right conditions to boost the competitiveness of an MNC on the global market. In addition, IFAs could be a means of introducing cross-border policies and avoid time consuming processes of conducting parallel

[44] See: http://www.iso.org/iso/catalogue_detail?csnumber=42546. Accessed 5 March 2014. "ISO 26000:2010 is intended to assist organizations in contributing to sustainable development. It is intended to encourage them to go beyond legal compliance, recognizing that compliance with law is a fundamental duty of any organization and an essential part of their social responsibility. It is intended to promote common understanding in the field of social responsibility, and to complement other instruments and initiatives for social responsibility, not to replace them."

[45] Papadakis (2011b), pp. 1–2.

[46] Papadakis (2011b), p. 2.

[47] Papadakis (2011a), p. 279.

negotiations in each country where an MNC is present.[48] The compliance with CLS could signal to consumers, clients, governments, and nongovernmental organisations that it is adhering to the ethical standards and could show the company's commitment to CSR.

On the part of unions, IFAs facilitate global coordination, by assisting the local and global unions to cooperate. This boosts their ability not only to negotiate effectively but also to effectively implement the principles outlined in the IFAs. The IFAs have created the right conditions for unions to bring about better democratic industrial and improved social dialogue among their members and their relationship with the management. This in turn could lead to better working conditions across the global production and value chains.[49]

At a time when the densities of unions globally are declining, the IFAs when used effectively could bolster their numbers and help unions overcome the economic and political obstacles to unionisation. IFAs could also strengthen the role of unions as promoters of effective labour regulations at the local, regional, and international levels. The increase in the number of unions could raise the awareness of the positive impact of freedom of association on development.[50]

Since the issue of compliance with CLS has more to do with the private sector in each country, the signing of IFAs moves the burden of governments to monitor compliance to the unions and management. Since the IFAs contain the commitment to respect the CLS in every country an MNC operates in, even countries that have not ratified some of the core conventions (and even if they are ILO Members, as stated in the ILO 1998 Declaration) are required to respect, promote, and realise in good faith the CLS, in the industries that sign onto IFAs. Compliance with the CLS could boost the image of the countries and could make them attractive for FDI.

In summary, the expectation of IFAs is the promise by MNCs to respect the CLS and allow the exercise of these rights and principles at work. Unions, on the other hand, also promise not to be involved in negative publicity campaigns that could damage the reputation of MNCs and thereby affect their profitability.[51] For both parties, the signing of IFAs signals their willingness to engage in social dialogue as a means of addressing the issues of concern to them and lead to the establishment of a system of sound industrial relations.[52] This could be seen as a sharp contrast to the CSR initiatives, which normally is a pledge by management to address issues of public interest through an adjustment of its internal governance structure on a unilateral basis.[53]

---

[48] Welz (2011), p. 59.

[49] Papadakis (2011b), p. 3.

[50] In Chap. 3, we discussed the impact of freedom of association on development. Should unions be able to organise freely, this could help in the realisation of the benefits of freedom of association.

[51] Coleman (2010), p. 603.

[52] Papadakis (2011a), p. 279.

[53] Papadakis (2011a).

5.7.3 Impact of IFAs on the Labour and Trade Linkage

In spite of the fact that IFAs are new instruments in the world of industrial relations and has the potential to encourage and promote social partnerships and dialogue in the global value chain system, the fact remains that they are not widespread and are more prevalent in Europe than in other parts of the world. Irrespective of these facts, the present IFAs are a benchmark for future IFAs (when it becomes widespread) and from the literature appears to generate hope among both policymakers and academics, on one hand, and, on the other, among MNCs and GUFs that IFAs could be a force for good in the promotion of sound industrial relations and form a framework at the enterprise, local, and global levels, in ensuring the adherence to the CLS across the world of work.[54]

The potential impact of IFAs on industrial relations has been well researched.[55] The evidence on the implementation, effectiveness, and impact of IFAs appears to be positive. On the issues of whether: (1) the extent to which the provisions in the IFAs studied have been implemented; (2) promote sound industrial relation between the parties; (3) provide a framework for workers to organise at both the national and global level; (4) provide a framework for the resolution of disputes; (5) paves the way for solidarity across borders; and (6) IFAs are effective tools in cases of restructuring, the evidence is that IFAs are beneficial in promoting workers' organisation, helps in increasing union coverage and contributes to labour-management disputes, in particular, in countries where they do not have the tradition of industrial relations.[56] The cases that have been documented have all shown to a consideration degree how the IFAs were instrumental in the resolution of disputes, and have provided frameworks that have served to promote global social dialogue, especially in times of industrial change.[57]

In evaluating IFAs and how it could impact on the labour standards and trade linkage, it should be borne in mind that IFAs are different from the so-called traditional forms of collective agreements. IFAs are generally agreements that are, in principle, intended to be a framework to ensure the harmonious relationship between MNCs and GUFs, with particular reference to the respect for the CLS throughout the operations of an MNC.

[54] Papadakis (2011a), pp. 281–282.

[55] See, for example, Papadakis (2008, 2011a, b), Riisgard (2004); Riisgard (2005), Stevis (2010a, b) and Telljohann et al. (2009).

[56] Papadakis (2011a), pp. 295–296.

[57] See Welz (2011), Papadakis (2011a, b), Stevis (2010a), Telljohann et al. (2009), and Riisgard (2004), *supra* note 48.

5.7.4 Binding Nature of IFAs

However, the question remains as to the legal binding nature of IFAs. Are IFAs only considered "soft law" enforced through cooperation by the parties and only a gentleman's agreement, making their binding nature only dependent on their effective implementation?[58]

Whilst the GUFs and MNCs consider IFAs to be a way of improving industrial relations and a mechanism for collaborative relationship, research conducted on many IFAs conclude that IFAs do not provide for detailed provisions on how to monitor compliance and also how to resolve disputes over alleged breaches of the principles outlined in the agreement.[59] In fact, it has been stated that IFAs "scarcely recognize that there will be disputes on this scale".[60] Even though the agreements provide for unions to be heard, they do not provide detailed procedures for conflict resolution.[61]

Most of the literature on the binding nature of IFAs assumes that these agreements are not legally enforceable in the countries in which they are signed.[62] For example, the law in the United Kingdom presumes that collective agreements are not legally enforceable, and the origin of this presumption lies in common law. However, under European law, it cannot be assumed that such agreements are not binding since an agreement concluded under the umbrella of a European Works Council (EWC) may make it difficult to deny the legal effects, assuming "all other EWC agreements in the jurisdiction in question are legally binding".[63]

Although there are no cases to date that have been brought before a court of law on the binding nature of IFAs,[64] Coleman (2010) has considered the legal enforceability of IFAs. Her consideration of this issue is the approach taken under the traditional principle of U.S. federal contract law.[65] She examined the extent to which IFA agreements could be enforced in the federal courts in the United States. Through this approach, Coleman drew a parallel between IFAs and the employer neutrality agreements in the course of the recognition of a union at the workplace.[66]

[58] Papadakis (2011a), p. 282.

[59] Coleman (2010), p. 609.

[60] Ewing (2008), p. 220.

[61] Coleman (2010), p. 609, states that under the enforcement mechanisms of IFAs, "Agreements that do address compliance generally take one of three approaches: (1) management is responsible for ensuring compliance and the unions have a mandate to report violations; (2) management and trade union representatives form a monitoring group responsible for implementing and monitoring the agreement and addressing disputes and violations; or (3) reports evaluating implementation and compliance are presented and discussed at the annual European Works Council".

[62] See Ewing (2008), pp. 224–225; Papadakis (2011a), p. 282; Rudikoff (2005).

[63] Ewing (2011), p. 10.

[64] As at September 2013.

[65] Coleman (2010), p. 617.

[66] Coleman (2010), p. 616.

Coleman contends that IFAs are contracts that could be enforced in federal courts in the U.S. under Section 301 of the Labor Management Relations Act (LMRA) as a labour contract.[67] She further argues that U.S. courts can exercise jurisdiction over MNCs and GUFs since the agreements are, under contract law, supported by consideration from both parties. She refutes the argument that an IFA is voluntary, as if they are a "gratuitous promise by the company".[68] This, she states, is based on a company agreeing to respect the CLS and a GUF agreeing not to participate in activities that would negatively impact on the company, damage its reputation, and adversely affect profitability.[69] She concludes by stating:

> The language of the IFAs demonstrates the parties' intent to be bound by the agreement and their assent to the agreement. Codes of conduct use the same language to create legally binding agreements between MNCs and their suppliers, and ILO declarations and recommendations show the existence of meaningful content to these rights. IFAs are supported by adequate consideration and are not simply gratuitous promises on the MNCs' part.[70]

Within the ILO, there is no formal mechanism for complaints whereby violations of the CLS as contained in the 1998 Declaration can be raised, and by extension an enforcement mechanism for violations of the principles in IFAs. Article 26 of the ILO Constitution allows for the filing of complaints with the ILO in cases where a Member is not satisfied with the effective observance of another Member in respect of any of the Conventions. These complaints can only be brought by a Member against another. However, in cases of violations of freedom of association, complaints can be brought by workers' and employers' organisations.[71] The void in an enforcement mechanism for CLS as outlined in the 1998 Declaration needs to be filled if IFAs are to be effective mechanisms in ensuring compliance with the CLS.

In the concluding remarks of her study of the Coordinadora Latinoamericana de Sindicatos Bananeros (COLISIBA) and the IUF–Chiquita Framework Agreement, Riisgard stated: "In summary, the case *shows an agreement with potential*, in relation to social dialogue and local organizing. In practice *this potential has been exploited only to a low degree*, but after merely a year it had achieved several positive results . . ." (italics added).[72] Given the potential of IFAs and their likelihood of shaping the emerging cross-border industrial relations,[73] we will consider in Chap. 9 how an ILO/WTO enforcement mechanism built on the IFA framework (an agreement with potential) could hold the key to the resolution of the contentious issue of the labour standards and international trade linkage.

---

[67] Coleman (2010), p. 603.

[68] Coleman (2010).

[69] Coleman (2010).

[70] Coleman (2010), p. 634.

[71] ILO (2012), para. 86.

[72] Riisgard (2005), p. 730.

[73] Papadakis (2011a), p. 297.

References

Bartels, L. (2007). The WTO legality of the EU's GSP+ arrangement. *Journal of International Economic Law, 10*(4).

Bates, J. (2000, April). *International Trade and Labor Standards*. Progressive Policy Institute, Policy Report. http://www.dlcppi.org/texts/trade/standards.htm. Accessed 27 Jan 2014.

Brandtner, B., & Rosas, A. (1999). Trade preferences and human rights. In P. Alston et al. (Eds.), *The EU and human rights*. Oxford: Oxford University Press.

Coleman, S. (2010). Enforcing International Framework Agreements in U.S. Courts: A contract analysis. *Columbia Human Rights Law Review, 41*(2).

Ebert, F. C., & Posthuma, A. (2011). *Labour provisions in trade arrangements: Current trends and perspectives, International Institute for Labour Studies*. Geneva: International Labour Organization.

EC. (2012). Draft Commission Staff Working Document: Trade as a driver of development. http://ec.europa.eu/governance/impact/ia_carried_out/docs/ia_2011/sec_2011_0536_en.pdf. Accessed 3 Feb 2014.

Ewing, K. D. (2008). International regulation of the global economy—The role of Trade Unions. In B. Bercusson & C. Estlund (Eds.), *Regulating labour in the wake of globalisation: New challenges, new institutions*. London: Hart.

Ewing, K. D. (2011). Global framework agreements in context: UK and US. *Journal of the International Centre for Trade Union Rights, 18*(2).

Gasiorek, M., Gonzalez, J. L., Holmes, P., Parra, M. M., Rollo, J., Wang, Z., et al. (2010). *Final report on the mid-term evaluation of the EU's generalised system of preferences*. Centre for the Analysis of Regional Integration (CARIS). http://trade.ec.europa.eu/doclib/docs/2010/may/tradoc_146196.pdf. Accessed 3 Mar 2014.

Greven, T. (2005). Social standards in bilateral and regional trade and investment agreements (Occasional Papers No. 16). Geneva: Friedrich-Ebert-Stiftung.

Harvey, P. J. (1996). *U. S. GSP labour rights conditionality: 'Aggressive Unilateralism' or a forerunner to a multilateral social clause?* International Labour Rights Fund Publications. www.laborrights.org/publications/usgsp.html. Accessed 22 Jan 2014.

Hepple B. A. (2005). *Labour laws and global trade*. Hart Publishing.

ILO. (2012). *Handbook of procedures relating to international labour Conventions and Recommendations*. Geneva: ILO.

Kessie, E. K. (1999). Developing countries and the World Trade Organization – What has changed? *World Competition, 22*(2).

Kessie, E. K. (2000). Enforceability of the legal provisions relating to special and differential under the WTO Agreements. *The Journal of World Intellectual Property, 3*(6).

Panagariya, A. (2000). *Trade-labor link: A post-Seattle analysis*. College Park: University of Maryland.

Papadakis, K. (Ed.). (2008). *Cross-border social dialogue and agreements: An emerging global industrial relations framework?* Geneva: International Institute of Labour Studies.

Papadakis, K. (2011a). Globalizing industrial relations: What role for International Framework Agreements? In S. Hayter (Ed.), *The role of collective bargaining in the global economy*. Cheltenham: Edward Elgar.

Papadakis, K. (2011b). *Shaping global industrial relations: The impact of International Framework Agreements*. Basingstoke: Palgrave Macmillan.

Riisgard, L. (2004). *The IUF/COLISIBA-CHIQUITA framework agreement: A case study* (ILO Working Paper No. 94). Geneva: International Labour Office.

Riisgard, L. (2005). International Framework Agreements: A new model for securing workers rights? *Industrial Relations: A Journal of Economy & Society, 44*(4).

Rudikoff, L. P. (2005). *International Framework Agreements: A collaborative paradigm for labor relations* (Global Law Working Paper 01/05). http://www.law.nyu.edu/global/workingpapers/2005/ECM_DLV_015787. Accessed 10 Mar 2014.

Stevis, D. (2010a). *International Framework Agreements and global social dialogue: Lessons from the Daimler case* (Employment Working Paper No. 46). Geneva: International Labour Office.

Stevis, D. (2010b). *International Framework Agreements and global social dialogue: Parameters and prospects* (Employment Working Paper No. 47). Geneva: International Labour Office.

Telljohann, V., da Costa, I., Müller, T., Rehfeldt, U., Zimmer, R. (2009). European and International Framework Agreements: practical experiences and strategic approaches. http://www.eurofound.europa.eu. Accessed 6 Mar 2014.

Waer, P. (1996). Social clauses in international trade: The debate in the European Union. *Journal of World Trade, 30*(4).

Welz, C. (2011). A qualitative analysis of International Framework Agreements: Implementation and impact. In K. Papadakis (Ed.), *Shaping global industrial relations: The impact of International Framework Agreements*. Palgrave Macmillan: Basingstoke.

Chapter 6
Regional Trade Agreements and the Interface Between Labour Standards and International Trade

6.1 Introduction

More than four decades ago, John Jackson wrote:

> As the general incidence of all tariffs and other trade barriers decline world-wide, assuming the trend of the last twenty years continues, the problem of preferential arrangements may fade in importance.[1]

Contrary to Jackson's statement, regionalism has grown in strength and regional trade agreements (RTAs) are seen as an integral part of the multilateral trading system (MTS) and account for almost half of world trade and operate alongside the trade agreements of the WTO. In 1995, when the WTO was established, only three members (Japan, Korea, and Hong Kong) out of the original 120 members belonged to an RTA.[2] By the end of 2013, with 159 Members the number of countries not part of any RTA was very few.

As at September 2013, about 500 RTAs had been notified to the GATT/WTO.[3] According to the WTO, during the period 1948–1994, the GATT received 124 notifications of RTAs (relating to trade in goods). However, since the establishment of the WTO, there has been a marked increase in the number of RTAs notified. Since 1995, over 400 additional arrangements covering trade in goods or services have been notified.[4] This indicates the increase in the number of RTAs since the establishment of the WTO, and this in spite of the success of the Uruguay Round negotiations.

---

[1] Jackson (1969), p. 623.

[2] Sapir (1998), p. 718.

[3] For more information on RTAs notified to the GATT/WTO, see http://www.wto.org/english/tratop_e/region_e/regfac_e.htm. Accessed 6 March 2014.

[4] http://www.wto.org/english/tratop_e/region_e/regfac_e.htm.

K. Addo, *Core Labour Standards and International Trade*,
DOI 10.1007/978-3-662-44619-5_6

This increase in part could be attributed to the inadequacy of the MTS to address in a coherent manner issues of global concern such as the definition of international standards, restrictions on business practices of cartels, setting of the rules for investment and competition policy. The MTS has not been able to effectively tackle issues such as immigration and under the General Agreement on Trade in Services (GATS), Mode 4 (temporary movement of natural persons). However, the MTS has implemented the Trade Related Intellectual Property Rights (TRIPS) agreement, by moving beyond trade liberalisation to establish worldwide standards.[5] The rise in the number of RTAs raises the question of whether RTAs may be allowed to precede multilateral agreements and serve as a testing ground for multilateral solutions.

Although the multilateral trading system and the regional integration agreements share the common goal of trade liberalisation, trade liberalisation is not the only objective for which states enter into regional arrangements. Some countries have entered into RTAs for geopolitical reasons, and for some other countries, RTAs could act as a stepping stone to the multilateral system. Whilst there is no clear answer as to the extent to which regional integration agreements have influenced the multilateral trade system, it cannot be denied that recent regional developments have major implications for the multilateral system. This influence is in two main areas. First, the growth of regionalism may at times stimulate progress at the multilateral level. Second, regionalism may serve as laboratories for the multilateral trade system.[6]

In this section, we will carry out an analysis of the legal implications of regional trade agreements under WTO rules to determine the legality of these agreements. It is not intended in this section to provide a definite answer as to the extent of influence of regional trade agreements on the multilateral system but merely to provide a framework of analysis from which policymakers could take cue in resolving the contentious issue of the relationship between labour standards and international trade. Before we examine the influence of RTAs on the MTS, it is necessary to first discuss the momentum that RTAs have gained in recent times.

6.2 The Rise of Regionalism

The proliferation of regional trade agreements (RTA) in recent times has put into question the viability and effectiveness of the multilateral trading system, whose cornerstone is the non-discrimination principle. It is estimated that over half of world trade is being conducted on a preferential basis. This trend raises the question whether the multilateral trading system embodied in the World Trade Organization (WTO) is capable of regulating international trade relations among countries in the

---

[5] Bail (1997), p. 842.

[6] Demaret (1997), p. 832.

twenty-first century. It could be argued that it is the dissatisfaction with the WTO that has motivated a number of countries to turn to bilateral/regional trade agreements to underpin their trade policy.

The criticism is often made that it takes too long to negotiate new agreements in the WTO, given the different levels of development of its Members, and that agreements reached usually represent the lowest common denominator. The Uruguay Round was expected to have been concluded in 4 years, but it took almost 8 years to finalise. It should be borne in mind, however, that it was during the Uruguay Round that the number of RTAs notified to the GATT increased.

Box 6.1: The Motives for Regionalism

The spread of regionalism, including among countries that have traditionally avoided this approach, is due to a range of factors, including:

- a concern not to be left out of the growing web of preferential deals;
- a belief in the business community that, as product cycles get shorter and multilateral negotiating cycles get longer, quicker results may be obtained regionally;
- the desire to use regional liberalisation as a catalyst for domestic reform;
- a concern on the part of government to use bilateral deals to promote underlying political or strategic objectives;
- or to pursue non-trade concerns, for example, related to core labour standards or protection of the environment. It is sometimes suggested that developing countries pursue RTAs for market access gains while developed countries seek deeper integration. This is too stark a distinction. Developed countries too have market access goals (including via regulatory issues like trade facilitation), while developing countries have a stake, via institution-building, in deeper integration, Cottier (1998).[7]

The increase in RTAs leads to the questions as to whether the surge indicates that countries are losing faith in the multilateral trading system and placing their hopes and aspirations in bilateralism and regionalism and whether trade policy officials believe that bilateralism and regionalism offered a better route to global trade liberalisation. Did countries during the Uruguay Round see RTAs as an insurance policy in the event that the Round failed?

The failure of the WTO Ministerial Conference in Seattle (1999) added to the uncertainty about the MTS, as it was during the Uruguay Round negotiations.

[7] Other reasons put forward are the following: to increase market access, to promote investment, to shield against unfair use of trade remedies, to guard against slowed multilateral liberalisation, to increase support for multilateral liberalisation, to achieve "WTO-plus" levels of integration, to solidify domestic reforms, to increase competitiveness in global markets, to increase clout in international negotiations, to achieve economic stability, and to meet other strategic goals. For a full discussion of these reasons, see Lynch (2010), p. 2.

Countries, which historically were in full support of the multilateral approach, have entered into RTAs. Does this again indicate that their confidence in the MTS is waning? Adding to all this was again the failure of WTO Members in Cancun (2003) to reach an agreement. The United States, for example, stated its intentions plainly after the Cancun meeting that it would promote free trade globally, regionally, and bilaterally,[8] but more specifically it stated its intention to conclude more bilateral deals—a promise that it has kept, considering the number of bilateral agreements it has entered into.

In recent times, doubts have been cast on the Doha declaration made by trade ministers at Doha, Qatar, that the Doha Development Agenda launched in 2001 would be completed in 3 years. As at September 2013, WTO Members were still in negotiations on the modalities for the successful launch of the Doha Work Programme. However, some have expressed the view that the proliferation of RTAs should not be cause for alarm since the two approaches to global free trade are not mutually exclusive.[9]

Whilst a number of studies have concluded that the two approaches to the liberalisation of trade are complementary and mutually supportive,[10] the former Director General of the WTO, Mr. Mike Moore, cautioned against the proliferation of regional trade agreements and highlighted the threat it poses to the multilateral trading system.[11] The view of the Director General cannot be disputed, given the nature of some of the agreements being concluded and the signatories of such agreements. The proposed Free Trade for the Americas (FTAA) and the North Asian Free-Trade Area linking Japan, China, and South Korea, if implemented, would remove a sizeable proportion of world trade from the aegis of the WTO with far-reaching implications for the multilateral trading system.

Economists agree, however, that regional trade agreements could be building blocks for the multilateral trading system if they embrace the principles of open

[8] Zoellick (2002), p. 20.

[9] Bergsten (2000), pp. 19–21. See further, De Melo and Panagariya (1992), p. 1.

[10] Studies carried out by WTO, the Organisation for Economic Cooperation and Development (OECD), the International Monetary Fund (IMF), and the World Bank have all indicated that regionalism has on the whole been very supportive of the multilateral trading system. They argue that the fact that there has not been any tension between multilateralism and regionalism to date owes much to political restraint and the simplicity of some of the agreements that were notified to the GATT.

[11] See speech ("Globalizing Regionalism: A New Role for MERCOSUR in the Multilateral Trading System", pp. 1–2) by the Director General of the WTO, Mr. Mike Moore, delivered in Buenos Aires on 28 November 2000, pp. 1–2: "In the 1990s, it was widely assumed that building complementary regional and multilateral institutions was the only way to grapple with the complexities of a fast-changing international economy. But in the wake of Seattle – and our inability so far to launch a new global trade round – has the time come to question that easy assumption? Is there a risk that regionalism is becoming a stumbling-block, more than a building block, for the new WTO? Draining energy from multilateral negotiations? Fragmenting international trade? And creating a new international dis-order characterized by growing rivalries and marginalization and the possibility of hostile blocks?".

regionalism. In other words, they contend that if regional trading blocs eschew protectionism and reduce barriers to the trade of third countries, it could provide a boost for the multilateral trading system.[12] Under WTO law, there is no obligation on parties to regional trade agreements to reduce barriers to the trade of third countries. Their main obligation is to ensure that barriers to the trade of third countries are not increased. In other words, the decision as to whether to embrace open regionalism and reduce barriers to the trade of third countries is a voluntary one.

However, because of political pressures, many regional trading arrangements insist on reciprocity before reducing barriers to the trade of third countries. Thus, whilst reduction of trade barriers among the parties to a regional trade agreement could generate some efficiency gains and increase the welfare of the participating countries, the impact of the agreement on third countries is far from certain. Considering the impact on poor countries, Jagdish Bhagwati has pointed out that "Everyone loses out but the poor countries suffer the most because their companies are least prepared to deal with the confusion".[13] Bhagwati further added that "where a significant power such as the U.S. or the European Union is involved in an agreement, it almost always sneaks in reverse preferences – and trade-unrelated issues such as patent protection and labour standards – that exact a heavy cost on developing countries".[14]

In spite of such comments as stated by Bhagwati on the impact of RTAs on developing countries, especially the least developed, the findings of a case study conducted on the impact of the membership of Zambia and Mauritius in Common Market for Eastern and Southern Africa (COMESA) and Southern Africa Development Cooperation (SADC) provide some indication of how RTAs can assist to support and facilitate the participation, in this case, of developing countries in the WTO. Bilal and Szepesi stated:

> [W]hile RTA Membership had little direct impact so far on the preparation and conduct of the WTO negotiations . . . regional groupings can play a much needed role in the WTO preparations through indirect means . . . By raising awareness, by training, by providing a platform for the exchange of views and information, and by stimulating trade capacity building initiatives, COMESA and the SADC have contributed to a better preparation of their member countries on trade issues, which have had positive spillovers on their participation in the WTO.[15]

The two opposite views of the impact of regionalism shows the need for striking a balance between the countries that form a regional group and those outside that group. This calls for WTO Membership in working with the WTO Secretariat to ensure that the Members adhere to the WTO rules. The Understanding of Article XXIV, for example, states in the preamble:

---

[12] Freund and Emanuel (2010).

[13] Bhagwati (2001).

[14] Bhagwati (2001).

[15] Bilal and Szepesi (2005), pp. 389–390.

> [T]he purpose of regional trade agreements should be to facilitate trade between the constituent territories and not to raise barriers to the trade of other Members with such territories; ... in their formation or enlargement the parties to them should to the greatest possible extent avoid creating adverse effects on the trade of other Members.[16]

The Ministerial Declaration in the Doha Development Round negotiations adopted on 14 November 2001 called for Members negotiating with the aim of further clarifying and improving the rules that apply to RTAs. In spite of the failure by the WTO Membership to successfully complete the Doha negotiations to date, Members have agreed to a new transparency mechanism.

Whilst the debate on the impact of RTAs at the WTO has been contentious at times, in recent times it appears the debate is taking a different turning. The shift is more from the costs and benefits analysis to how RTAs can be a force for good. In this respect, the Director General of the WTO, Pascal Lamy, notes:

> I find the debate about whether regionalism is a good or bad thing sterile. This is not the point. We need to look at the manner in which RTAs operate, and what effects they have on trade opening and on the creation of new economic opportunities ... We often think and talk about how regionalism might be hurting multilateralism, either by bolstering discriminatory interests, or perhaps by fostering an anti-trade-openness posture, if regionalism is seen as a way of building protectionist structures behind enlarged closed markets ... what I would like to do is turn the question around. I would like to ask what the WTO might do to help avoid a situation in which these negative aspects of regional agreements prevail, and ultimately to promote multilateralization.[17]

Further to the Director General's quote above, in his speech to the African Union Summit on 29 January 2012, he stated that WTO Members should use multilateral trade negotiations and the WTO system as impetus for greater regional integration. He added that "there is absolutely no contradiction between accelerating regional integration and deepening the multilateral trading system".[18]

The apparent shift in the age old view on the impact on RTAs could also be related to the reluctance of WTO Members to challenge the consistency of RTAs with the multilateral rules under the dispute settlement system. Pauwelyn provides three reasons for which he considers why WTO Members refrain from this challenge. First, he states that with the exception of Mongolia, all WTO Members have entered into one or more RTAs. And that any Member should have an interest in clarifying or tightening the rules under Article XXIV as this might work against their own RTA agenda. Second, WTO Members might not have confidence in panels to make binding decisions on the complexity of Article XXIV compliance. Finally, should an RTA not liberalise 'substantially all the trade' among their members and thereby violates Article XXIV, a third party might not have the incentive to raise the issue of inconsistency since, in his view, this could result in more discrimination.[19]

---

[16] Preamble of the Understanding to Article XXIV. See WTO website.

[17] Lamy (2007).

[18] Lamy (2012).

[19] See Paulwelyn (2009), p. 369.

Pauwelyn further states that the experience of the dispute system to date indicates that panels and the Appellate Body avoid making decisions on Article XXIV. He cites the cases of (1) *Turkey-Textiles*,[20] where the panel and the Appellate Body, without providing in-depth analysis, gave the presumption that the EC-Turkey customs union was in line with GATT Article XXIV, (2) the WTO case law under the Safeguards Agreement also suggest that the panel and the Appellate Body avoid ruling under Article XXIV, and (3) the panel decision in *Brazil-Tyres*[21] case is another example in avoiding an examination of RTAs as the panel did not rule on the exclusion for MERCOSUR imports under Article XXIV.[22]

Given the political and legal reality that RTAs are here to stay,[23] it is no wonder that there has been a change in attitude towards RTAs in the multilateral system. The opinion of Director General of the WTO above provides a clear indication that the time for a change in approach in the international community on RTAs has arrived.

Pauwelyn recommends that there is the need for a shift in focus from WTO law from "hierarchy and supremacy over RTAs to one of mutual recognition, accommodation and respect".[24] He proposes that (1) the focus should be on integrating developments in regionalism into WTO activities and also allow panels under the dispute system to interpret and apply WTO rules with respect to RTAs and (2) instead of emphasis on Article XXIV, RTA trade negotiators should work to achieve complementarity with other WTO Agreements in order to "preserve the integrity of both systems".[25]

The proposals by Pauwelyn in light of developments in the "world" of increasing regionalism is all the more timely, views that we subscribe to, given our observation that RTAs in spite of their apparent weaknesses and also possible negative impact on the multilateral system has a potential for good, especially in successfully resolving the CLS and trade debate. And as mentioned above, in light of recent financial crises and likely difficult employment creation prospects globally, the efficacious mixture of political, legal, economic, social, and moral policies holds the key to addressing the difficult issues, which bear on the linkage issues.

---

[20] *Turkey – Restrictions on Imports of Textile and Clothing Products*. The report of the Panel as modified by the Appellate Body, was adopted on 19 November 1999, WT/DS34/R.

[21] *Brazil – Retreaded Tyres* Panel Report, Brazil—Measures Affecting Imports of Retreaded Tyres, WT/DS332/R, adopted 17 December 2007, as modified by Appellate Body Report WT/DS332/AB/R.

[22] *Brazil – Retreaded Tyres* Panel Report.

[23] *Brazil – Retreaded Tyres* Panel Report.

[24] *Brazil – Retreaded Tyres* Panel Report, p. 370.

[25] *Brazil – Retreaded Tyres* Panel Report.

6.3 Legal Basis for RTAs Under the Multilateral System: GATT/WTO Rules on RTAs

Policies relating to regional trade arrangements start with the most-favoured-nation (MFN) obligation. This principle is stated in Article I of GATT 1994—that there should be no discrimination between like products/services originating in or destined for different countries and that each trading partner gets immediately and unconditionally the best treatment given to any other trading partner. The importance of this principle in multilateral relations is undisputed.

The Appellate Body in *EC-Tariff Preferences* stated that the MFN principle is a 'cornerstone of the GATT' and 'one of the pillars of the WTO trading system'.[26] Before the *EC-Tariff Preferences* ruling, the Appellate Body ruled in an earlier case: "For more than fifty years, the obligation to provide most-favoured-nation treatment in Article I of the GATT 1994 has been both central and essential to assuring the success of a global rules-based system for trade in goods."[27]

The report of a committee commissioned by the WTO in 2004 highlights the situation of how widespread RTAs have become. The Sutherland Report on *The Future of the WTO* on MFN and the RTAs stated:

> [N]early five decades after the founding of the GATT, MFN is no longer the rule; it is almost the exception. Certainly, much trade between the major economies is still conducted on an MFN basis. However, what has been termed the 'spaghetti bowl' of customs unions, common markets, regional and bilateral free trade areas, preferences and an endless assortment of miscellaneous trade deals has almost reached the point where MFN treatment is exceptional treatment.[28]

This statement buttresses the reality of the prevalence of RTAs in the global economy making the MFN obligation that has been the cornerstone of the GATT and a major pillar of the multilateral trading system less predominant.

6.4 Relevant Multilateral Rules on Regional Trade Agreements

Members of GATT/WTO can form regional trading arrangements pursuant to Article XXIV of GATT 1994, Article V of the GATS, or the Decision on Differential and More Favourable Treatment, Reciprocity and Fuller Participation of Developing Countries ("the Enabling Clause"). Where the conditions of these

---

[26] Appellate Body Report, *EC – Tariff Preferences*, para. 101.

[27] Appellate Body Report, *US – Section 211 Appropriations Act*, para. 297. See also Appellate Body Report, *Canada – Autos*, para. 69.

[28] Report by the Consultative Board to the Director General Supachai Panitchpakdi, *The Future of the WTO: Addressing Institutional Challenges in the New Millennium* (hereinafter the 'Sutherland Report') (WTO, 2004), para. 60.

Articles cannot be fulfilled, a waiver could be obtained from the Members under Article IX of the Marrakesh Decision Establishing the WTO to establish a regional trading arrangement, such as the Lomé Convention.

Analysis of the relevant provisions of Article XXIV demonstrate that the WTO rules pertaining to RTAs have been interpreted so broadly and inconsistently that it is difficult to state categorically what the obligations of Members are under the rules of the WTO. Further to this is also the lack of a coherent body of jurisprudence to guide Members who wish to form regional trading arrangements. Under GATT, the Working Parties established to examine the consistency of regional trade agreements with the relevant multilateral trade rules were open to all Members, including those whose agreements were being examined. In other words, the processes of examination to test the consistency of the agreements with the multilateral rules were not free from extraneous considerations such as national pride and politics.

An examination of some of the reports of the Working Parties reveal that in trade arrangements involving developing countries, the Working Parties were influenced by considerations relating to development.[29] So far as it was perceived that the agreement might assist the countries to increase their participation in the multilateral trading system, little regard was given as to whether the multilateral disciplines had been adhered to by the parties.

It is further argued that same holds true for agreements involving developed countries. Since the European economic integration in the 1950s and 1960s was seen as necessary to halt the spread of communism, the United States and other major non-European trading nations did not insist on full compliance with the terms of Article XXIV, as they thought that for geopolitical reasons it was necessary in the interest of world peace and security to have a stable and prosperous Western Europe.[30] Thus, notwithstanding the difficulties that some Members had with the Treaty of Rome, the six original members of the EEC were not vigorously challenged when they implemented their agreement. Doubts about the consistency of the Treaty of Rome with the rules of the GATT/WTO still lingers on as the Treaty was never given a clean bill of health by the GATT. This has, to some extent, set the stage for differing interpretations given to the provisions of Article XXIV by Members of the WTO.

Having discussed the rise of regionalism, we now turn our attention to the issue of the legal implications of these agreements under WTO rules. This analysis is relevant if RTAs are being recommended as testing grounds for the multilateral system.

---

[29] Kessie (2001).

[30] Frankel (1997), p. 5. See further, Snape et al. (1993), p. 6.

6.5 Examination of the Relevant Sections of Article XXIV

To ensure that the formation of a regional trading arrangement does not worsen a Member's terms of trade, WTO rules lay down a number of conditions that have to be complied with by countries wishing to form such arrangements. The Article that regulates regional trade arrangements is Article XXIV of GATT 1994 and the Provisions of the Understanding on the Interpretation of Article XXIV of the GATT 1994. This Article essentially provides legal cover for Members of the WTO to form or join customs unions or free trade areas, provided that their "purpose [is] to facilitate trade between the constituent territories and not to raise barriers to the trade of other contracting parties with such territories".[31] Paragraph 8 of Article XXIV makes it clear that the WTO rules only apply to customs unions, free trade areas, and interim agreements for the formation of free trade areas and customs unions. Thus, the rules do not cover agreements establishing common markets and economic unions.[32]

A customs union is defined as the "substitution of a single customs territory for two or more customs territories, so that (1) duties and other restrictive regulations of commerce (except where necessary, those permitted under Articles XI, XII, XIII, XIV, XV and XX) are eliminated with respect to substantially all the trade between the constituent territories of the union or at least with respect to substantially all the trade in products originating in such territories, and (2) subject to the provisions of paragraph 9, substantially the same duties and other regulations of commerce are applied by each of the members of the union to the trade of territories not included in the union".

By way of comparison, a free trade area is defined as "a group of two or more customs territories in which the duties and other restrictive regulations of commerce (except where necessary, those permitted under Articles XI, XII, XIII, XIV, XV and XX) are eliminated with respect to substantially all the trade between the constituent territories of the union or at least with respect to substantially all the trade in products originating in such territories".

Thus, the basic difference between a customs union and a free trade area is that whilst under the former the parties are obliged to apply "substantially the same duties and other regulations of commerce", they are not obliged to do so in a free trade area. Put simply, each constituent member has the right to retain its external tariffs on the trade of non-constituent members.

The guiding principle is stated in Article XXIV:4. It provides that the formation of a free trade area or a customs union should lead to the creation of trade between the constituent territories and not raise barriers to the trade of third countries. Article XXIV:5 is intended to operationalise this broad principle as it provides that the general incidence of duties and regulations of commerce should not be increased or made more restrictive after the formation of the free trade area or

[31] See Article XXIV: 4 of the General Agreement.

[32] See Frankel (1997), pp. 13–17.

customs union. Article XXIV:6 lays down procedures for compensating third countries in the event of a country breaching the rule laid down in Article XXIV:5. Article XXIV:7 obliges parties to regional trade agreements to notify their agreements to the WTO for examination to determine whether they are consistent with WTO rules. Article XXIV:8 obliges parties to a free trade area or a customs union to liberalise substantially all the trade between themselves, and in the case of a customs union, they should apply substantially the same duties and other regulations of commerce.

On face value, the rules appear to be very clear, but in reality they are ambiguous. Professor Jackson has observed that Article XXIV incorporates "criteria that are so ambiguous or so unrelated to the goals and policies of GATT Contracting Parties that the international community was not prepared to make compliance with the technicalities of Article XXIV the *sine qua non* of eligibility for the exception from other GATT obligations".[33] This situation has been taken advantage of by WTO Members that have interpreted the rules in a manner more favourable to them.

Jackson's observation indicates the starting point for this situation. He stated:

> Article XXIV of GATT contains one of the most troubled provisions of GATT ... [T]he most important of these provisions (Article XXIV, paragraphs 4 through 10) establishes an exception to GATT obligations for regional arrangements that meet a series of detailed and complex criteria.[34]

Whilst the Committee on Regional Trade Agreement (CRTA) is expected to review and determine the consistency of agreements with the relevant rules of the WTO, it has not been able to make decisions due to the consensus rule that requires that decisions should be taken by all WTO Members. In effect, parties to the regional trade agreements being examined would have to agree that their agreement is inconsistent with the rules of the WTO before the Committee could take a definitive decision. Since this is unlikely, it could be said that the WTO does not exercise any effective control over regional trade agreements. To make up for the loophole in WTO rules and practice, Members of the WTO are increasingly being tempted to have recourse to the dispute settlement mechanism to challenge the consistency of regional trade agreements with the rules of the WTO.

During the years of the GATT, there was the implicit understanding that a Member could not have recourse to the dispute settlement mechanism to challenge the overall consistency of an agreement with the rules of the WTO. This was perceived to fall exclusively within the jurisdiction of the Working Parties, which were established to examine the agreements. It was thought, however, that a

---

[33] Jackson (1969), p. 587.

[34] Jackson (1969), pp. 575–576. See further the unadopted panel report in *EEC-Member States' Import Regimes for Bananas*, June 3, 1993, DS32/R, para. 358: "The Panel noted that Article XXIV:5 to 8 permitted the Contracting Parties to deviate from their obligations under other provisions of the General Agreement for the purpose of forming a custom union ..."

Member could use the dispute settlement procedures to challenge an aspect of the agreement that was inconsistent with WTO rules.

In the case between India and Turkey,[35] the Appellate Body held that it and the panels have the jurisdiction to determine the overall consistency of regional trade agreements with WTO rules. Some Members of the WTO have criticised the decision of the Appellate Body and accused it of usurping the functions of the CRTA.

6.5.1 *Analyses of the Legal Implications of Regional Trade Agreements Under WTO Rules*

As stated above, the legal basis for the formation of customs unions and free trade areas is Article XXIV. GATT 1994 allows members to deviate from the MFN principle. Members are allowed to form or join customs unions or free trade areas. The basis for the formation of regional integration agreements is Article XXIV.4, which states:

> The contracting parties recognize the desirability of increasing freedom of trade by the development, through voluntary agreements, of closer integration between the economies of the countries parties to such agreements. They also recognize that the purpose of a customs union or a free-trade area *should be to facilitate trade between the constituent territories and not to raise barriers to the trade of other contracting parties with such territories* (italics added).

[35] *Turkey – Restrictions on Imports of Textile and Clothing Products*. The report of the Panel, as modified by the Appellate Body, was adopted on 19 November 1999, WT/DS34/R, hereinafter *Turkey – Textiles*. On 6 March 1995, the Turkey–EC Association Council adopted Decision 1/95 to conclude the association agreement between Turkey and the EC. Article 12(2) of the Decision states: "In conformity with the requirements of article XXIV of the GATT Turkey will apply as from the entry into force of this Decision, substantially the same commercial policy as the Community in the textile sector including the agreements or arrangements on trade in textile and clothing." Following this, Turkey in January 1996 imposed quantitative restrictions on imports from India on 19 categories of textiles and clothing products. In 1998, India filed a complaint against Turkey claiming that the restrictions imposed by Turkey were inconsistent with Turkey's obligations under Articles XI and XIII of GATT and were not justified by Article XXIV of GATT, which did not authorise the imposition of discriminatory QRs, and that the restrictions were inconsistent with Turkey's obligations under Article 2 of the ATC. India also claimed that the restrictions appeared to nullify or impair benefits accruing to it directly or indirectly under GATT and the ATC. Turkey did not deny India's clam that the quantitative restrictions were inconsistent with its obligations under Articles XI and XIII of the GATT 1994 and Article 2.4 of the Agreement on Textiles and Clothing. However, Turkey argued that the quantitative restrictions were justified under Article XXIV. The Panel found that Turkey's imposition of the quantitative restrictions were inconsistent with Articles XI and XIII. The Panel also found that Turkey's measures were new restrictions, which did not exist at the time of the entry into force of the ATC, and, thus, were prohibited by Art. 2.4. In its ruling on appeal, the Appellate Body agreed with the Panel's ruling that Turkey's measures were not justified under Article XXIV.

This provision makes it clear that WTO Members can form WTO-consistent regional groupings. As compared to the other WTO provisions regulating regional trade agreements, much has been written about Article XXIV of the GATT 1994. It is generally perceived as lacking in clarity and not providing sufficient guidance to Members wishing to form free trade areas or customs unions. Over the years, WTO Members have given differing and conflicting interpretations of the main provisions of Article XXIV. The reports of Working Parties established to examine the consistency of regional trade agreements with GATT/WTO rules were mostly inconclusive and did not provide sufficient guidance to WTO Members.

In the *Turkey-Textiles* case, the Panel and the Appellate Body provided valuable insight on the main requirements of Article XXIV. According to the second sentence of Article XXIV:4, the purpose of a free trade area or a customs union should be to create trade among the parties to the agreement and not to raise barriers to the trade of third parties. This implies that WTO Members are obliged not to use regional trading arrangements as instruments to discriminate against the trade of nonparties to the agreement. The agreement is expected to create trade between the parties and not result in substantial trade diversion of trade from third countries. However, the relationship between Article XXIV:4 and the other provisions of Article XXIV has raised a number of issues.

6.5.2 The Scope of Article XXIV:4 and Its Relationship with Other Provisions in Article XXIV of GATT 1994

There has been a long debate on the issue as to whether the requirements of Articles XXIV:4 and XXIV:5–9 are mutually exclusive or supportive in the sense that parties to regional trade agreements are not expected to comply with the conditions set out in those articles without any clear result. Hong Kong, in a communication to the Committee on Regional Trade Agreements, stated that "[t]he uncertainty is whether this provision should be regarded as being in the nature of a preamble or whether the injunction "not to raise barriers to the trade of (third parties)" can be applied objectively".[36]

During the review of the Treaty of Rome by a subgroup of the Working Party, members of the European Economic Community (EEC) provided forceful arguments that the only requirements that had to be complied with by Members wishing to form free trade areas or customs unions were paragraphs 5–9 of Article XXIV, as paragraph 4 thereof did not lay down any positive obligation on Members.[37]

---

[36] See WTO Document WT/REG/W/31; 18 November 1998, p. 1.

[37] The Working Party Report (L/778) was adopted on 29 November 1957: see GATT, (BISD) (1958) Sixth Supplement, para. 2, pp. 70–71. In the examination of the North American Free Trade Agreement by the Committee on Regional Trade Agreements, the representative of the European Communities said that according to Article XXIV:4, "it was permissible to form free trade

The interpretation provided by the EEC was not shared by some members of the Working Party, who were of the view that the second sentence of paragraph 4 created a separate obligation in addition to those laid down in paragraphs 5–9.[38]

The apparent reason for the divergent opinions is that if paragraph 4 is accepted as imposing a separate and an additional obligation, members of a customs union or a free trade area may be obliged not to raise barriers to the trade of any individual Member of the WTO. Put differently, in assessing the impact of a customs union or a free trade area, an aggregated analysis is to be avoided as it may conceal the real impact of the agreement on individual countries. The difficulty in determining the relationship between paragraphs 4 and 5–9 is succinctly summarised by Professor Kenneth Dam:

> The relationship between paragraph 4 and paragraphs 5 through 9 is. . .a fertile source of controversy. If an agreement clearly complies with paragraph 4, is it automatically to be considered as meeting the standards of paragraphs 5 through 9? Or does paragraph 4 really contain only introductory language, and, in view of the word "accordingly", are the substantive rules to be found in paragraphs 5 through 9? Perhaps there are two complementary or additive sets of standards—the "purpose" test of paragraph 4 and the form requirement of the following paragraphs. The number of ways in which paragraph 4 can be related to paragraphs 5 through 9 is limited only by the number and the ingenuity of lawyers involved in the interpretation of Article XXIV.[39]

During the Uruguay Round, negotiators had the opportunity to clarify the scope of this provision and its relationship with other provisions of Article XXIV but failed to state in clear and unambiguous language what the obligations of Members are under the Article. Indeed, it could possibly be argued that the Understanding compounded the murky situation by providing that "[c]ustoms unions, free trade areas, and interim agreements leading to the formation of a customs union or free trade area, to be consistent with Article XXIV, must satisfy, inter alia, the provisions of paragraphs 5–8 of that Article". Proponents of a broader interpretation of the terms of Article XXIV:4 have seized upon the use of the words "must satisfy, inter alia, the provisions of paragraphs 5, 6, 7 and 8" to bolster their argument that in addition to the specified articles, there are other obligations that have to be satisfied by Members wishing to form customs unions or free trade areas, including those specified in Article XXIV:4.

Even though the argument has some merit, there is nothing in the terms of the Understanding that confirms that Article XXIV:4 lays down a separate and distinct obligation that has to be complied with by Members. If the Members so intended, they could have expressly stated so. The panel in *Turkey-Textiles* held that Article XXIV:4 did not lay down a separate obligation in and of itself.[40] The fundamental

agreements or customs unions, provided Members did so in a way that did not harm others or undermined the broad, non-discriminatory architecture of the multilateral trading system": see WT/REG4/M/2; 21 February 1997; para. 22, p. 6.

[38] See GATT, Sixth Supplement, The Working Party Report (L/778), para. 3, p. 71.

[39] See Dam (1970), p. 278.

[40] *Turkey – Textiles*, WT/DS34/R, para. 9.126, p. 131.

issue in that case was whether Article XXIV of GATT 1994 obligated Members of the WTO that are parties to a regional trade arrangement (customs union) to have the same commercial policy towards third countries and, if it did, whether it justified the introduction of quantitative restrictions prohibited by GATT 1994 and the Agreement on Textiles and Clothing and Article XI of GATT 1994.

Turkey argued that Article XXIV:4 did not create a separate obligation that had to be complied with by Members wishing to form regional trade arrangements. Turkey submitted that the consistency of measures adopted by parties to a regional trading arrangement had "to be determined by reference to Article XXIV:5 to Article XXIV:8 of GATT and not to other GATT provisions".[41]

India argued that whilst Members of the WTO were free to enter into regional trade arrangements, they still had to respect other WTO disciplines. In other words, a Member is not exempted from its WTO obligations simply because it has entered into a regional trade arrangement with another country, be it a Member of the WTO or not. The guiding principle laid down in Article XXIV:4 had to be respected by all Members entering into regional trade arrangements; otherwise, WTO rules would be abused and rendered ineffective.[42]

India's argument was supported by several countries that had participated in the proceedings as third parties. The Panel, however, was not swayed by these arguments, as is evident from the following passage:

> [w]hile not expressed as an obligation, paragraph 4 (and its elaboration in the fifth paragraph of the Preamble of the GATT 1994 Understanding on Article XXIV) argues against an interpretation of paragraph 5(a) that would read into that paragraph an exception to GATT rules that prohibit specific trade barriers.[43]

This view of the Panel was endorsed on appeal by the Appellate Body:

> Paragraph 4 contains purposive, and not operative, language. It does not set forth a separate obligation itself but, rather, sets forth the overriding and pervasive purpose for Article XXIV which is manifested in operative language in the specific obligations that are found elsewhere in Article XXIV. Thus, the purpose set forth in paragraph 4 informs the other relevant paragraphs of Article XXIV, including the chapeau of paragraph 5. For this reason, the chapeau of paragraph 5, and the conditions set forth therein for establishing the availability of a defence under Article XXIV, must be interpreted in the light of the purpose of customs unions set forth in paragraph 4. The chapeau cannot be interpreted correctly without constant reference to this purpose.[44]

Regardless of the views of the Panel and the Appellate Body, it cannot be taken as settled that Article XXIV:4 does not create a separate obligation that has to be respected by WTO Members wishing to form regional trading arrangements. Although the views of the Appellate Body are treated with respect by WTO

[41] *Turkey – Textiles*, para. 6.32, p. 37.

[42] *Turkey – Textiles*, para. 6.47, p. 39.

[43] *Turkey – Textiles*, para. 9.123, p. 131.

[44] *Turkey – Textiles*. The Appellate Body report was adopted on 19 November 1999, WT/DS34/AB/R, para. 57, p. 15.

Members, it is expressly stated in Article IX:2 of the Marrakesh Agreement Establishing the WTO that "[t]he Ministerial Conference and the General Council shall have the exclusive authority to adopt interpretations of this Agreement and of the Multilateral Trade Agreements". Thus, the views of the Appellate Body are not binding on the entire membership of the WTO. Indeed, as is stated in Article 19.2 of the Dispute Settlement Understanding (DSU), "in their findings and recommendations, the panel and Appellate Body cannot add to or diminish the rights and obligations provided in the covered agreements."

Similarly, it is provided in Article 14 of the DSU that "[a]n Appellate Body report shall be adopted by the DSB and unconditionally accepted by the parties to the dispute". In other words, Members that were not parties to the dispute are not under any obligation to accept the report. It is well established under GATT/WTO law that the views of previous panels are not binding on subsequent panels. They are merely of persuasive effect and not required to be followed.

6.5.3 *Review of WTO Rules Relating to Regional Trading Agreements: Examination of Article XXIV:5, 7, & 8 of GATT 1994*

Article XXIV of the GATT 1994 lays down five broad obligations that have to be complied with by WTO Members wishing to form free trade areas or customs unions. Breach of any of these conditions could potentially render an agreement inconsistent with the relevant rules of the WTO.

6.5.3.1 Relevant Provisions of Article XXIV

Tariffs Should Not Be Higher After the Formation of the Customs Union or Free Trade Area: Article XXIV:5

One of the cardinal principles of the WTO is that tariffs and regulations of commerce should not be higher or more restrictive after the formation of the free trade area or customs union. In the case of free trade areas, Article XXIV:5 (b) provides that "the duties and other regulations of commerce maintained in each of the constituent territories and applicable at the formation of such free-trade area ... shall not be higher or more restrictive than the corresponding duties and other regulations of commerce existing in the same constituent territories prior to the formation of the free-trade area".

This provision has been the subject of differing interpretations among WTO Members. Some Members argue that the words "maintained" and "applicable" demonstrate that it is the applied rates of duty that have to be taken into account in the examination of the consistency of an agreement with Article XXIV of GATT

1994. Others disagree and insist that it is the bound rates that have to be taken into account. In any event, the disagreement is moot as in many instances, the parties to free trade agreements do not usually change their external tariffs vis-à-vis third parties. It is this flexibility that distinguishes free trade areas from customs unions. In the case of the latter, the parties are required to have substantially the same duties and other regulations of commerce towards third countries,

The basic objective of this provision is to prevent WTO Members from increasing barriers to trade when they form free trade areas. In *Turkey-Textiles*, the Appellate Body held that under certain circumstances, Article XXIV:5 could provide legal cover for measures that are inconsistent with WTO rules:

[I]n a case involving the formation of a customs union, this 'defence' is available only when two conditions are fulfilled. First, the party claiming the benefit of this defence must demonstrate that the measure at issue is introduced upon the formation of a customs union that fully meets the requirements of sub-paragraphs 8 (a) and 5(a) of Article XXIV. And, second, that party must demonstrate that the formation of that customs union would be prevented if it were not allowed to introduce the measure at issue. Again, both these conditions must be met to have the benefit of the defence under Article XXIV.[45]

In this case, both the Panel and Appellate Body held that the quantitative restrictions on textile and clothing products introduced by Turkey upon the entry into force of its customs union agreement with the European Union were not justified as it could have resorted to less trade-restrictive measures such as rules of origin to achieve its objective.

Transitional Period for the Creation of a Free Trade Area or Customs Unions Should Normally Not Exceed Ten Years: Article XXIV:5(c)

Article XXIV:5(c) of the GATT 1994 provides that where the agreements do not establish fully-fledged free trade areas or customs unions upon their entry into force, the restrictions on trade between the parties should be eliminated within a "reasonable period of time". The lack of sufficient guidance resulted in widely varying transitional periods. It took, for example, over 30 years for the European Communities and Turkey to establish their customs union. Many GATT contracting parties that pushed for strengthened disciplines on interim agreements for the creation of free trade areas and customs unions saw the lack of consistency as unsatisfactory. As a response, it was agreed during the Uruguay Round that "[t]he "reasonable period of time" referred to in paragraph 5(c) of Article XXIV should exceed 10 years only in exceptional cases. In cases, where Members parties to an interim agreement believe that 10 years would be insufficient, they shall provide a full explanation to the Council for Trade in Goods of the need for a longer period."[46]

---

[45] WT/DS34/AB/R, para. 45.

[46] Paragraph 3 of the Understanding on the Interpretation of Article XXIV of the GATT 1994.

Notification of Agreements Establishing Free Trade Areas and Customs Unions

Article XXIV:7 of the GATT 1994 mandates that WTO Members deciding to enter into a customs union or free trade or an interim agreement leading to the formation of such a union or area to "promptly notify the...[WTO] and...make available to...[it] such information regarding the proposed union or area as will enable... [it] to make such reports and recommendations to. .. [Members] as they may deem appropriate". It would appear that WTO Members are obliged to notify their agreements to the WTO before implementing them. Prior notification is intended to give the WTO the opportunity to review the agreement and recommend any necessary changes before its implementation.

In practice, however, very few agreements are notified to the WTO before their implementation. This could be attributed to a number of reasons. First, the GATT/WTO has not in the past been able to come to unanimous decisions in its review of regional trade agreements. Positive consensus is needed to make recommendations for changes, and since the parties to the agreement under review participate in the process, the review process always ends in a deadlock. It is interesting to note that the Treaty of Rome, which established the European Economic Community in 1957, has not been explicitly approved by the GATT/WTO. Knowing perfectly well that the WTO would not be in a position to make recommendations or suggest changes to their agreement, parties have tended not to treat their notification obligations very seriously. Second, prior examination and approval of a regional trade agreement by the WTO before its implementation could create some political difficulties for a number of countries as it gives the impression that WTO can overrule national parliaments and administrations.

The notification obligation imposed by Article XXIV:7 of the GATT 1994 is not very onerous and should not pose any great difficulties for countries. To facilitate the examination process, the Committee on Regional Trade Agreements has developed a standard format for the notification of agreements. There have been proposals in the context of the negotiations to streamline the examination process. As reported to the Trade Negotiations Committee (TNC) by the Chairman of the Negotiating Group on Rules, work is advanced in the Group on transparency of regional trade agreements.

Agreement Should Substantially Cover All the Trade Between the Parties: Article XXIV:8 of the GATT 1994

According to Article XXIV:8 of the GATT 1994, agreements establishing free trade areas and customs unions must cover "substantially all the trade between the constituent territories ...". This provision is seen as one of the most controversial provisions in the GATT. It is the view of some WTO Members that this provision obliges parties to free trade agreements and customs unions to include all major sectors of economic activity in the coverage of the agreement. They argue that agreements, which exclude agriculture, fisheries, and other sensitive sectors, are not consistent with Article XXIV of the GATT 1994. Among the countries that subscribe to this view are Australia and the United States, although it is interesting to note that the free trade agreement between the two countries did not provide unrestricted market access for all agricultural products. Tariff rate quotas were established for certain products, including dairy products, beef, sugar, cotton, and peanuts.[47]

The most vocal of the opposing group is the European Communities, which have long argued that the words "substantially all the trade" do not mean all the trade between the parties should be liberalised. They point out that to hold otherwise would be to ignore the ordinary meaning of the word "substantially". Proponents of this view believe that the test in Article XXIV:8 of the GATT 1994 will be satisfied if a substantial proportion of the parties' trade is covered by the agreement.[48] In other words, what is determinative is the volume of trade liberalised and not whether any major sector of economic activity is excluded. In submissions to GATT Working Parties, some contracting parties argued that the test would be satisfied if 80 % of the trade between the parties was covered by the agreement. Other contracting parties that insisted that the agreements should not exclude the agricultural sector did not accept this view.[49]

The Understanding on the Interpretation of Article XXIV that was adopted during the Uruguay Round failed to definitively resolve the issue. It merely provided in its preamble that regional trade agreements could contribute to the expansion of world trade if the agreements extended to all trade and diminish world trade if they excluded major sectors from their coverage. The issue was partly resolved by the Appellate Body in the *Turkey-Textiles* case, where it held that both the quantitative and qualitative aspects should be considered when determining whether an agreement satisfied the "substantially all the trade" requirement. The Appellate Body further upheld the long-held view of the European Communities that the words "substantially all the trade" did not mean that all the trade between the parties had to be liberalised. Without giving any benchmark, it held that the test required something considerably more than merely some of the trade between the parties:

> Sub-paragraph 8(a)(i) of Article XXIV establishes the standard for the internal trade between constituent members in order to satisfy the definition of a 'customs union'. It requires the constituent members of a customs union to eliminate 'duties and other restrictive regulations of commerce' with respect to 'substantially all the trade' between them. Neither the GATT Contracting Parties nor the WTO Members have ever reached an agreement on the interpretation of the term 'substantially' in this provision. It is clear, though, that 'substantially all the trade' is not the same as all the trade, and also that

[47] WT/REG/W/22; 30 January 1998.

[48] The Working Party Report (L/4064) was adopted on 30 October 1974: see GATT, **Basic Instruments and Selected Documents** (BISD) (1975) 21st Supplement, para. 16, p. 80.

[49] See WTO Document, WT/REG/W/17/Add.1, *supra* note 121. See further Communication from Australia in WTO Document WT/REG/W/25.

> 'substantially all the trade' is something considerably more than merely some of the trade. We note also that the terms of sub-paragraph 8(a)(i) provide that members of a customs union may maintain, where necessary, in their internal trade, certain restrictive regulations of commerce that are otherwise permitted under Articles XI through XV and under Article XX of the GATT 1994. Thus, we agree with the Panel that the terms of sub-paragraph 8(a)(i) offer 'some flexibility' to the constituent members of a customs union when liberalizing their internal trade in accordance with this sub-paragraph. Yet we caution that the degree of 'flexibility' that sub-paragraph 8(a)(i) allows is limited by the requirement that 'duties and other restrictive regulations of commerce' be 'eliminated with respect to substantially all' internal trade.[50]

This provision can have significant implications for countries that are negotiating RTAs. If the view is taken that no sector of economic activity can be excluded or that the agreement should cover a minimum percentage of trade between the parties, it could make it difficult for countries to protect their sensitive sectors.

The Application of Substantially the Same Duties and Other Regulations of Commerce in the Case of Customs Unions

According to Article XXIV:8(a)(ii), parties to an agreement establishing a customs union must apply substantially the same duties and other regulations of commerce vis-à-vis third parties. In *Turkey-Textiles,* both the Panel and Appellate Body held that the parties are not obliged to apply the same duties and other regulations of commerce. They have the flexibility to apply different tariffs and other regulations of commerce on a limited number of products:

> subparagraph 8(a)(ii) establishes the standard for the trade of constituent members with third countries in order to satisfy the definition of a 'customs union'. It requires the constituent members of a customs union to apply 'substantially the same' duties and other regulations of commerce to external trade with third countries. The constituent members of a customs union are thus required to apply a common external trade regime, relating to both duties and other regulations of commerce. However, subparagraph 8(a)(ii) does not require each constituent member of a customs union to apply the same duties and other regulations of commerce as other constituent members with respect to trade with third countries; instead, it requires that substantially the same duties and other regulations of commerce shall be applied.[51]

The term "substantially all the trade" has raised a lot of controversy. Two schools of thought have emerged concerning the proper interpretation of the term: first, the quantitative approach and, second, the qualitative approach.

[50] WT/DS34/AB/R, para. 48.

[51] WT/DS34/AB/R, para. 49.

6.5.3.2 The Quantitative Approach

Those who support this approach are of the view that the test in Article XXIV:8 requires parties to regional trade agreements to liberalise a significant proportion of the trade between them. In the examination of the Treaty Establishing the European Economic Community, the representatives of the six participating countries expressed the view that the test would be satisfied if 80 % of the volume of trade between the parties was liberalised.[52] This view was not shared by a majority of the members of the Working Party, who preferred a flexible approach under which each case would be examined on its merits:

> Many members of the Sub-Group said that each case of a proposed customs union or free-trade area had to be considered on its merits and that it was, therefore, inappropriate to fix a general figure of the percentage of trade which could be subjected to internal barriers without running counter to the definition in paragraph 8(b) of Article XXIV. A matter to be considered was whether the provisions of a free-trade area pointed towards a gradual increase of barriers affecting the trade between the constituent parties or a gradual reduction of such barriers. Moreover, any calculation of the percentage of trade not freed from barriers would need to take account of the fact that this trade would be, or would have been, larger if the trade had been allowed to flow freely. Some members of the Sub-Group thought that it would be unrealistic to apply the same criterion to a free-trade area such as that existing ... [among developing countries] and to a free-trade area the members of which were highly industrialized countries accounting for a large percentage of world trade.[53]

Whilst the quantitative approach has some positive aspects, by offering insight into the level of liberalisation of the trade between the parties, it has some conspicuous drawbacks. It could provide parties to regional trade agreements with the opportunity to maintain barriers in the so-called sensitive sectors such as agriculture and textiles and clothing. It appears that the selectivity associated with the quantitative approach appears to be its main weakness. Australia, for example, has stated:

[52] The Working Party Report (L/778) was adopted on 29 November 1957: see GATT, (BISD) (1958) Sixth Supplement, para. 33, p. 100. In the examination of the North American Free Trade Agreement by the Committee on Regional Trade Agreements, the representative of the European Communities said that according to Article XXIV:4, "it was permissible to form free trade agreements or customs unions, provided Members did so in a way that did not harm others or undermined the broad, non-discriminatory architecture of the multilateral trading system": see WT/REG4/M/2, 21 February 1997, para. 22, p. 6. See further the report of the Working Party in the examination of European Communities—Agreements with Portugal that was adopted on 19 October 1973: see GATT, Basic Instruments and Selected Documents (BISD) (1974), Twentieth Supplement, para. 16, p. 176. The representative of the EC observed that "no exact definition of the expression ['substantially all the trade'] existed and that the precise figures would vary from case to case according to several factors. At any rate, percentages were established as a general indicator of the trade covered by the Agreement and were not to be regarded as a conclusive factor."

[53] GATT; **BISD**, Sixth Supplement, para. 34, p. 100.

> At first glance, it might seem advisable to use actual trade statistics and trade flows in an assessment of the extent to which the substantially-all-trade criterion has been met. There are, however, some difficulties associated with this. Participants in several working parties established to examine free trade agreements and customs unions have recognized that any calculation of the percentage of trade not freed from barriers would need to take account of the fact that this trade would be, or would have been, larger than if the trade had been allowed freely ... [S]imply looking at trade flows does not take account of the dynamics at work before the conclusion of an arrangement, its implementation and the situation prevailing once it has been fully implemented.[54]

To reduce the selectivity associated with the quantitative approach, Australia suggested that the figure proposed by the EEC be increased to 95 % and that consideration should be given to using the Harmonized Commodity Description and Coding System as a benchmark for determining whether the arrangements meet the target figure:

> [S]ubstantially all the trade' should be defined as coverage by a free trade agreement or an agreement or an agreement establishing a customs union of 95 per cent of all the six-digit tariff lines listed in the Harmonized System. This approach would ensure that there is sufficient flexibility to set aside product areas that for one reason or another cannot yet be traded between the partners free of restrictions ... One advantage of proceeding in this way is that it would not be necessary to discover the extent to which trade in a given product may have been affected by other measures in place. Additionally, it is unlikely that this approach would permit the carving-out of any major sector because of the strong possibility that the permitted exemptions would have to be spread out over a range of potentially sensitive sectors ... [T]his type of approach ... has the great advantage of being easily verifiable without requiring complex econometric work.[55]

Notwithstanding its simplicity and ease of application, the Australian proposal has not been approved by the Committee on Regional Trade Agreements. It could be argued that the Australian suggestion has no textual basis and would appear to be reading too much into the language agreed by the Members of the WTO. The choice of 95 % appears to be arbitrary and seems to have no regard for the ordinary meaning of the phrase 'substantially all the trade'. As has been pointed out by the European Communities, substantial does not mean 'all', and Members have the flexibility to decide which sectors they wanted to carve out of their trade agreement.[56] Presumably, the argument could be made that approval of the Australian proposal by the Committee on Regional Trade Agreement would mean that Members had taken the decision, albeit indirectly, to amend the provisions of Article XXIV of GATT 1994.

---

[54] WT/REG/W/22; 30 January 1998, para. 8, p. 3.

[55] WT/REG/W/22; 30 January 1998, paras 10–13.

[56] In the joint examination of the interim agreements between the European Communities and the Czech Republic, Hungary, Poland, and the Slovak Republic, the representative of the European Communities stated that "the word 'substantially' qualified the phrase 'all the trade'. A free trade area did not mean complete free trade; otherwise the word 'substantially' was meaningless": see WT/REG1/M/2; 3 October 1997, para. 14, p. 4.

6.5.3.3 The Qualitative Approach

Proponents of this approach argue that for the test in Article XXIV:8 to be satisfied, the regional trade agreement should not exclude any major sector of economic activity. The principal objective of this group is to ensure that the so-called sensitive sectors such as agriculture and textiles and clothing are not carved out of any agreement. They argue that the fact that these two sectors usually account for a small proportion of the trade flows between the constituent territories is not reason for them to be excluded. They see their exclusion as nothing more than a protectionist response to the demands of special interest groups.

In a communication from Australia to the Committee on Regional Trade Agreements, Australia argued for a combination of the two approaches, as each has its strengths and weaknesses:

> The CRTA might therefore consider what the respective advantages and disadvantages of the qualitative and quantitative approaches are. Some threshold questions in such a consideration could be the definition for the purposes of Article XXIV of a sector or a major sector, and what percentage figure could legitimately be considered to cover substantially all trade. Both approaches have their advantages. That of the qualitative approach is that it leaves out no major sector. This is important particularly where a reduced amount of trade in a sector takes place because of other policies in place. The quantitative approach sets a benchmark which can be verified against the statistical evidence. A successful solution to this problem probably will combine elements of both schools, provided one accepts that a certain level of discipline is desirable.[57]

Subsequent to this communication, Australia proposed a formula that would ensure that parties to regional trade agreements actually liberalise trade between themselves across all sectors:

> Our proposal is that "substantially all the trade" should be defined as coverage by a free trade agreement or an agreement establishing a customs union of 95 per cent of all the six-digit tariff lines listed in the Harmonized System. This approach would ensure that there is sufficient flexibility to set aside product areas that for one reason or another cannot yet be traded between the partners free of restrictions. One advantage of proceeding in this way is that it would not be necessary to discover the extent to which trade in a given product may have been affected by other measures in place. Additionally, it is unlikely that this approach would permit the carving out of any major sector because of the strong possibility that the

[57] WT/REG/W/18; 17 November 1997, paras 10–12, p. 2. See further communication from Hong Kong to the CRTA, WT/REG/W/19, dated 17 November 1997, paras 14–16, p. 3: "[t]he meaning of the word 'substantially' is imprecise. It obviously means less than quite close to the whole, but how close it approaches completeness is far from clear. It is also open to discussion whether the meaning of 'substantially' should be interpreted quantitatively, qualitatively, or both... It is also for consideration whether a single definition or threshold for the word 'substantially' should be pursued in numerical terms...[T]he expressed purpose of a customs union 'to facilitate trade between constituent territories and not to raise barriers to trade of other contracting parties with such 'territories' should also have an impact on the consideration of this issue."

> permitted exemptions would have to be spread out over a range of potentially sensitive sectors ... [This] workable definition ... has the great advantage of being easily verifiable without requiring complex econometric work.[58]

Whilst a number of countries have expressed support for the Australian proposal, others also believe that the figure of 95 % is arbitrary and fail to see how the proposal would ensure that regional trade agreements remain supportive of the multilateral trading system. Australia accepts that the figure of 95 % is arbitrary but argues that since "substantially all the trade" does not mean all the trade between the parties, "the criterion, expressed numerically, therefore has to be below 100 per cent...The higher the figure is, the more it will contribute to trade liberalisation between the parties."[59]

To date, the CRTA has not adopted the Australian proposal, notwithstanding the realisation that the lack of a workable definition of the phrase "substantially all the trade" was partly responsible for the slow progress being made by the CRTA in evaluating the consistency of agreements with the relevant multilateral trade rules.

6.6 Agreements Notified Pursuant to the Enabling Clause

The Decision of the CONTRACTING PARTIES on Differential and More Favourable Treatment, Reciprocity and Fuller Participation of Developing Countries, known as the Enabling Clause, emerged from the Tokyo Round of Multilateral Trade Negotiations. This clause basically permits developed countries to accord differential and more favourable treatment to developing countries, without according such treatment to other Members of the WTO. In other words, it provides legal cover for, most notably, trade concessions granted to developing countries under the Generalized System of Preferences (GSP) of 25 June 1971 by waiving the provisions of Article I of GATT 1994.

Paragraph 2(c) of the Enabling Clause extends such treatment to regional or global trading arrangements entered into by developing countries for the mutual reduction or elimination of tariffs and non-tariff measures. Thus, agreements entered into between developing and developed countries fall outside the scope of the Enabling Clause. The consistency of such agreements with WTO disciplines

---

[58] WT/REG/W/22; 30 January 1998, paras 10–13, p. 3. In its response to a comment as to whether or not the figure of 95 % would apply to the trade of all the parties to a regional trade agreement, Australia replied as follows: "The figure of 95 per cent would apply to any arrangement regardless of the number of parties. Between them, the parties would be able to exempt 5 per cent of all six-digit tariff lines as listed in the Harmonised system (HS) from the requirement spelt out in GATT Article XXIV:8. How they would share out the 5 per cent would reflect the particular circumstances of the economies involved. The actual division of the available tariff lines would be done through negotiations between the prospective parties to the arrangement. In the same vein, if, for example, three economies were to participate, each would be entitled to a notional 1.66 per cent of exceptions." WT/REG/W/22/Add.1; 24 April 1998, para. 3, pp. 1–2.

[59] WT/REG/W/22/Add.1; 24 April 1998, para. 2, p. 1.

would have to be examined under the provisions of Article XXIV of GATT 1994 or Article V of GATS, unless a waiver is obtained pursuant to the provisions of Article IX of the WTO Agreement.

Before the Enabling Clause was enacted, developing countries invoked Part IV of the General Agreement to enter into such preferential trading arrangements.[60] The enactment of the Enabling Clause in November 1979 provided developing countries with a permanent legal basis for the formation of preferential trading arrangements.[61] The members of ASEAN, which had, for example, notified their preferential trading arrangement under Part IV in 1978, re-notified their agreement under the Enabling Clause.

6.6.1 Requirements Under the Enabling Clause

Developing countries wishing to invoke the Enabling Clause to form preferential trading arrangements are required to comply with a number of conditions. The first is that the arrangement should be designed to facilitate and promote the trade of developing countries and not to raise barriers to or create undue difficulties for the trade of any other contracting parties. This requirement mirrors what is spelt out by paragraph 4 of Article XXIV of the General Agreement. Given the reluctance of many developed countries to challenge agreements notified pursuant to the Enabling Clause, it is unclear what this requirement really means. Could it be argued that it is merely a general statement that does not create an obligation on developing countries, or should it be interpreted as an obligation on parties to such arrangements not to raise barriers to the trade of any individual Member, whether developed or developing?

If the ruling of the Appellate Body on the scope of Article XXIV:4 in the *Turkey-Textiles* case is taken into consideration, then presumably it could be said that the corresponding provision in the Enabling Clause does not create any obligation on developing countries entering into preferential trading arrangements. The problem with this argument is that the Enabling Clause does not contain any comparable provisions to Article XXIV:5 of the General Agreement, which according to the Appellate Body spells out the obligations to be complied with by members of a

[60] Part IV, which deals mainly with trade and development, was added to the General Agreement in 1965, at the behest of developing countries. It established the principle of non-reciprocity in trade negotiations between developed and developing countries and provided for special and differential measures intended to promote the trade and development of the less-developed members of GATT. It has been argued by some that it does not create legally enforceable rights. In other words, its provisions are merely hortatory in character.

[61] The precursor of the Enabling Clause was the January 1979 Decision of the CONTRACTING PARTIES to adopt the Report of the Working Party on Preferential Trading Arrangements. The Decision essentially authorised, contrary to the terms of Article I of the General Agreement, the formation of preferential trading arrangements. Members that invoked this Decision to form or make modifications to an existing arrangement were required to notify the CONTRACTING PARTIES.

customs union or a free trade area. Should the absence of this equivalent provision in the Enabling Clause be interpreted as meaning that there is no obligation to be complied with by developing countries entering into regional integration agreements? According to Crawford and Laird (2000), the Enabling Clause gives developing countries *carte blanche* when it comes to concluding regional trade agreements.[62]

Whilst a literal interpretation of the Enabling Clause may lead one to this conclusion, it is doubtful whether the CONTRACTING PARTIES to the GATT intended to give developing countries a free rein. When read in context, it could be argued that whilst the requirements for developing countries are relatively very weak, their agreements are nevertheless expected to meet a certain threshold. It is debatable whether the test would be satisfied if evidence can be adduced to show that intra-regional trade among the participating countries has increased. Should there be an increase in intra-regional trade—but there is also evidence to the effect that the trade agreement has led to the diversion of trade from nonmember countries—how should such a situation be addressed? These are issues that merit attention since for an RTA to support the multilateral process, it should contribute to the overall trade creation and not divert trade. Or should there even be direct diversion, the percentage of trade creation should far outweigh the trade diversion in order qualify as welfare enhancing.

The Enabling Clause envisages that developing countries entering into preferential trading arrangements may reduce both tariffs and non-tariff barriers to the trade of partner countries. Whereas it requires that the reduction of non-tariff barriers be done according to guidelines provided by Members, it does not contain a similar provision for the reduction of tariff barriers. As observed by the WTO Secretariat:

> Paragraph 2(c) [of the Enabling Clause] clearly treats tariffs differently from non-tariff measures, with no specific criteria set out for the mutual reduction or elimination of tariffs, while action on non-tariff barriers is to be governed by criteria or conditions that may be prescribed by the contracting parties.[63]

A further obligation to be fulfilled by developing countries invoking the Enabling Clause to form a preferential trading arrangement is to ensure that their agreement does not impede the MFN reduction or elimination of tariff and non-tariff trade restrictions. It is quite difficult to delineate the scope of this requirement, but a literal reading would suggest that if the conditions prevailing in the participating countries are conducive, then they should not hesitate to extend the benefits to other Members of the GATT/WTO. It may be recalled that during the Kennedy and Tokyo Rounds of Trade Talks, the members of the EEC extended some of the benefits they had granted to each other on an MFN basis.

---

[62] See Crawford and Laird (2000), p. 13.

[63] WTO Secretariat (1995), p. 18.

6.6.2 *The Enabling Clause and Article XXIV*

One issue upon which no agreement has been reached is whether the Enabling Clause could be relied upon to form fully fledged customs unions or free trade areas. As noted by the WTO Secretariat:

> During past debates in the GATT, it had been argued on one side that the Enabling Clause was not appropriate to deal with such RTAs which took the form of either FTAs, customs unions or interim agreements, but rather Article XXIV. On the other side, it was said that trade agreements among developing countries were covered by the Enabling Clause [regardless of the provisions of the agreement].[64]

The examination of the agreement establishing MERCOSUR brought this problem to the fore. At the heart of the dispute is how to define the relationship between the Enabling Clause and Article XXIV of the General agreement. There are two schools of thought on this issue. The first school is of the view that the Enabling Clause provides developing countries with an alternative legal basis for the formation of regional trading arrangements. In which case, they can rely on the provisions of the Enabling Clause to form customs unions or free trade areas. The second school, on the other hand, argues that the Enabling Clause cannot be relied upon to form such agreements as it only provides legal cover for the exchange of preferences covering a narrow range of products. According to the WTO Secretariat:

> The Enabling Clause does not contain any reference to Article XXIV, an omission which has left unclear whether the Enabling Clause applies in situations where that Article does not, or affects the terms of the application of that Article, or represents, for developing countries, a complete alternative to the Article. Indeed, views differ as to whether the Enabling Clause provides an appropriate basis for all regional arrangements among developing countries or, as some governments maintain, was not intended to cover arrangements of major significance that, up to 1979, would have been handled under Article XXIV.[65]

It would appear that where the agreement is entered into by medium-income and high-income developing countries, pressure would be exerted on the countries for an examination of their agreement under the provisions of Article XXIV. The case of MECORSUR[66] provides such an example. The parties argued initially that since all of them were developing countries, their agreement should be examined under the provisions of the Enabling Clause, as opposed to the provisions of Article XXIV. Some countries challenged this assertion, and it was eventually agreed that the standard terms of reference for the examination of agreements had to be amended. As a result, the terms of reference for the Working Party are as follows:

> To examine the Southern Common Market Agreement (MERCOSUR) in the light of the relevant provisions of the Enabling Clause and of GATT 1994, including Article XXIV, and to transmit a report and recommendations to the Committee on Trade and Development for submission to the General Council, with a copy of the report transmitted as well to the

[64] WTO Secretariat (2000), footnote 74 and accompanying text, p. 15.

[65] WTO Secretariat (1995), p. 18.

[66] This is an RTA comprising of Argentina, Brazil, Paraguay and Uruguay.

Council for Trade in Goods. The examination of the Working Party will be based on a complete notification and on written questions and answers.[67]

The cases following the MERCOSUR agreement have not followed this precedent. The parties to the Common Market for Eastern and Southern African States (COMESA) notified the Agreement under the Enabling Clause, and no challenge was raised as to the proper legal basis for the examination of the agreement. The implicit acceptance by the Committee on Trade and Development of the right of the COMESA member countries to notify under the Enabling Clause seems to buttress the speculation that only agreements entered into by medium- and high-income developing countries may attract challenges from other Members of the WTO.

6.7 The Impact of the *Turkey-Textiles* Case on the CLS and Trade Debate

The ruling of the panel and Appellate Body in the *Turkey-Textiles* case offers useful lessons for the labour standard and trade debate as the rulings provide a number of details on the legal limitations of RTAs. The relevance of the *Turkey-Textiles* jurisprudence helps in addressing the questions raised earlier: whether the dispute settlement mechanism of the WTO is the appropriate forum to adjudicate on a possible case scenario on the linkage between labour standards and trade and also whether an issue that has social ramifications should be decided by a joint committee of ILO and WTO rather than a panel on only points of law. The other point is whether a party should be allowed to use the WTO dispute settlement mechanism to challenge the decision(s) of the joint committee. Further to this is the issue of whether a multilateral approach vis-à-vis a regional approach is best situated to address the contentious issue of the linkage.

Before we consider the issues that rise from the linkage debate, it is important to note that the panel in *Turkey-Textiles* case considered Turkey's proposition that Article XXIV is *lex specialis* to the WTO and thus constitutes a self-contained regime. The panel did not agree with this reasoning. According to the panel, the WTO is a single undertaking and Article XXIV is part of it.[68]

---

[67] WT/COMTD/5/Rev.1; 25 October 1995. During the years of the GATT, agreements notified under the Enabling Clause were not thoroughly examined. Normally, after notifying the CTD in writing of the formation of the regional trading arrangement, one of the parties would officially introduce the agreement in the next meeting of the CTD. Any interested contracting party could ask questions or express its opinion on the agreement. There was usually no Working Party examination of agreements notified pursuant to the Enabling Clause, hence the reluctance of developing countries to allow the examination of their agreements under Article XXIV, under which Working Parties were routinely established to examine the consistency of agreements with the multilateral rules.

[68] WT/DS34/R, paras 9.186–9.187, p. 147.

6.7.1 Issues in the Turkey-Textiles *Case*

At the heart of Turkey' case was the conception that Article XXIV constitutes a distinct regime that allows parties to an RTA to seek a waiver from the obligations it owes to other WTO Members. This appears to be an important issue that was addressed, the extent to which the creation of an RTA exempts WTO Members from their obligations. Whilst the panel made reference to the Article XXIV exemption by linking it to the MFN or non-discriminatory principle in Article I, the Appellate Body, in reference to the relevance of the chapeau of paragraph 5 of Article XXIV, broadened the scope of the exemption:

> The Appellate Body interpreted "shall not prevent" to mean "shall not make impossible". The Appellate Body then stated that: [T]hus, the chapeau makes it clear that Article XXIV may, under certain conditions, justify the adoption of a measure which is inconsistent with certain other GATT provisions, and may be invoked as a possible "defence" to a finding of inconsistency.[69]

The Appellate Body further made it clear that whilst Article XXIV could justify a derogation in a matter that involves the formation of a customs union, this defence is only available when two conditions are met, namely:

> First, the party claiming the benefit of this defence must demonstrate that the measure at issue is introduced upon the formation of a customs union that fully meets the requirements of sub-paragraphs 8(a) and 5(a) of Article XXIV. And, second, that party must demonstrate that the formation of that customs union would be prevented if it were not allowed to introduce the measure at issue. Again, both these conditions must be met to have the benefit of the defence under Article XXIV.[70]

The panel also introduced a new mechanism in determining the measures that may be permitted under an RTA arrangement. The panel made reference to Article 41 of the Vienna Convention governing the conditions under which parties to a multilateral agreement may modify the agreement as between themselves.[71] The panel referred to the *EC-Bananas III* case, in which both the panel and Appellate Body concluded that unless the rights of parties to the Lomé Convention are explicitly authorised by a waiver, the parties to the Convention could not alter their rights and obligations as WTO Members. The panel applied this reasoning to the case and concluded that even though it is not an issue before the panel, should the Turkey-EC association agreement have required Turkey to adopt all EC trade policies, this requirement would not be sufficient reason for Turkey to be exempted from its WTO obligations.[72]

The first issue is whether, as Turkey argued in this case, a Panel could not review the consistency of its agreement with the provisions of Article XXIV since the

---

[69] WT/DS34/AB/R, para. 45, p. 11.

[70] WT/DS34/AB/R, para. 58, p. 16.

[71] Article 41 of the VCLT in relation to RTAs is discussed in Chap. 4.

[72] WT/DS34/R, paras 9.182, p. 145.

matter was still before the Committee on Regional Trade Agreements. The Panel rejected Turkey's argument that it could not examine the challenged measures by basing itself on the provisions of paragraph 12 of the Understanding on the Interpretation of Article XXIV. The Panel held that this provision authorised panels to examine the consistency of a measure or measures that may have been adopted by parties to a regional trade agreement:

> We understand from the wording of paragraph 12 of the WTO Understanding on Article XXIV, that panels have jurisdiction to examine "any matters 'arising from' the application of those provisions of Article XXIV". For us, this confirms that a panel can examine the WTO compatibility of one or several measures "arising from" Article XXIV types of agreement...This indicates that, although the right of WTO Members to form regional trade arrangements is "an integral part" of the set of multilateral disciplines of GATT and now WTO, the DSU procedures can be used to obtain a ruling by a panel on the WTO compatibility of any matters arising from such regional trade arrangements...[T]he term "any matters" clearly includes specific measures adopted on the occasion of the formation of a customs union or in the ambit of a customs union...[We conclude] that a panel can assess the WTO compatibility of any specific measure adopted by WTO Members at any time and we cannot find anything in the DSU, Article XXIV or the 1994 GATT Understanding on Article XXIV that would suspend or condition the right of Members to challenge measures adopted on the occasion of the formation of a customs union.[73]

With respect to the wider issue as to whether a panel could examine the overall consistency of a regional trade arrangement with the provisions of Article XXIV, the Panel held that the CRTA was properly placed to examine that issue as there were many factors that had to be taken into account, and which presumably could not be undertaken by panels:

> [W]e note that the...CRTA has been established, inter alia, to assess the GATT/WTO compatibility of regional trade agreements entered into by Members, *a very complex undertaking which involves consideration by the CRTA, from the economic, legal and political perspectives of different Members, of the numerous facets of a regional trade agreement in relation to the provisions of the WTO. It appears to us that the issue regarding the GATT/WTO compatibility of a customs union, as such, is generally a matter for the CRTA*. ...[I]t is arguable that a customs union (or a free-trade area) as a whole would logically not be a "measure" as such, subject to challenge under the DSU (emphasis added).[74]

6.7.2 Appellate Body Review

On appeal, the Appellate Body affirmed the decision of the Panel and indicated, however, in *obiter dicta*, even though the parties had not raised the issue on appeal, that the Panel cited a previous ruling by stating that the Panel was wrong in

---

[73] *Turkey – Textiles*. The report of the Panel, as modified by the Appellate Body, was adopted on 19 November 1999, WT/DS34/R, paras 9.50–9.51, pp. 112–113.

[74] *Turkey – Textiles*, paras 9.52–9.53, p. 114.

assuming that the dispute settlement procedures of the WTO cannot be used to challenge the overall consistency of a regional trade arrangement with the provisions of Article XXIV:

> [T]he Panel...did not address the question of whether the regional trade arrangement between Turkey and the European Communities is, in fact, a "customs union" which meets the requirements of paragraphs 8(a) and 5(a) of Article XXIV. The Panel maintained that "it is arguable" that panels do not have jurisdiction to assess the overall compatibility of a customs union with the requirements of Article XXIV. We are not called upon in this appeal to address this issue, but we note in this respect our ruling in *India – Quantitative Restrictions on Imports of Agricultural, Textile and Industrial Products* on the jurisdiction of panels to review the justification of balance-of-payments restrictions under Article XVIII:B of the GATT 1994...The assumption by the Panel that the agreement between Turkey and the European Communities is a "customs union" within the meaning of Article XXIV was not appealed. Therefore, the issue of whether this arrangement meets the requirements of paragraphs 8(a) and 5(a) of Article XXIV is not before us.[75]

It can be inferred from the language used by the Appellate Body that it considered that recourse can be made to the dispute settlement procedures to challenge the overall consistency of an agreement with the provisions of Article XXIV and also measures imposed by Members to safeguard their balance-of-payments problems.[76] This view of the Appellate Body has been criticised by some Members of the WTO and academics. In the run-up to the Seattle Ministerial Conference, India tabled a proposal that would have made it clear that it is "only the Committee of Balance-of-payments [which] shall have the authority to examine the overall justification of BOP measures".[77]

The decision of the Appellate Body that the dispute settlement procedures could be invoked to challenge the overall consistency of regional trade agreements with the provisions of Article XXIV and also the compatibility of measures adopted by Members to safeguard their balance-of-payments position pursuant to Article XVIII:B of the GATT 1994 has been criticised by Roessler. According to Roessler, the Appellate Body should have deferred to the respective WTO political bodies or alternatively exercised judicial restraint. In arrogating to itself those extensive powers, the Appellate Body has violated key principles of international law and its own jurisprudence by interpreting widely the provisions (footnote 1 to the BOP Understanding and paragraph 12 of the Article XXIV Understanding) that it claims confer authority on panels to make those decisions:

> Whatever the correct interpretation of the terms "application of", the question remains whether the DSU assigning competence to panels can be interpreted as overriding the

[75] *Turkey – Textiles*, para. 60, pp. 16–17. The Appellate Body report, together with the Panel report, as modified by the Appellate Body report, was adopted on 19 November 1999, citing WT/DS90/AB/R, adopted 22 September 1999, paras 80–109.

[76] Roessler (2000), p. 7. He notes that: "[t]his ruling [of the Appellate Body] implies that ... [it] is of the view that panels are competent to examine the overall consistency of a regional trade agreement."

[77] See paragraph 21 of the Draft Ministerial Conference Text; JOB (99)/5865/Rev.1); 19 October 1999.

> provisions of other agreements assigning competence to the WTO's political bodies. It is recognised in international law that "as a general rule, anybody possessing jurisdictional powers has the right in the first place itself to determine the extent of its own jurisdiction". When an organ of the WTO determines its own jurisdiction, it thus exercises its right to interpret the provision of the WTO Agreement conferring authority upon it. In doing so, it must pursuant to Article 31 of the Vienna Convention on the Law of Treaties take into account not only the terms of the provision attributing powers to it, but also the context in which this provision appears. That context comprises those provisions of the WTO Agreement that attribute related powers to other bodies. An analysis of the terms of those jurisdictional provisions may lead the WTO organ to the conclusion that not only it but also other organs could claim jurisdiction over the matter at issue. Such a conflict must be resolved in good faith in the light of the institutional structure that the framers of the WTO Agreement have set up to realise the purposes of the WTO. The principles of the interpretation of the Vienna Convention of the Law of Treaties thus suggest that the judicial organs of the WTO cannot determine their jurisdiction exclusively on the basis of the provisions of the DSU.[78]

Roessler further reasons that the ruling of the Appellate Body undermines the balance of rights and obligations of WTO Members and expressly contradicts Article 3.2 of the DSU, which provides that "[r]ecommendations and rulings of the DSB cannot add to or diminish the rights and obligations provided in the covered agreements". By giving undue weight to the procedural rights of complainants, the Appellate Body ignored the rights of defendants to have their measures evaluated by the appropriate WTO body:

> Article 3.2 of the DSU states the obvious, namely that the complainant's rights under the DSU cannot diminish the rights of the defendant under other WTO agreements. The procedural rights of Members under the DSU are thus clearly subsidiary to those conferred by the WTO agreements: a complainant may resort to the DSU only to enforce the obligations of the defendant under other WTO agreements, not however to diminish the rights of the defendant under those agreements. *This implies that a panel cannot determine its jurisdiction in a manner that diminishes those rights. Article 3.2 of the DSU obliges them to exercise judicial restraint whenever a WTO Member attempts to resort to the DSU for the purpose of negating another Member's procedural rights under another WTO agreement*[79] (emphasis added).[80]

The view expressed by Roessler (as shown in italics) appears to add weight to the view that should the decision-making process of the various WTO bodies, including the CRTA and the BOP Committee, be incapable of yielding conclusive results, there would be a strong incentive for some Members to resort to the dispute settlement procedures to challenge the legality of measures that they deem to be in conflict with the provisions of the WTO Agreement.

The issue to be addressed, in this context, is whether it is desirable for panels to determine the consistency or otherwise of regional trade agreements with the provisions of Article XXIV.

---

[78] Roessler (2000), pp. 7–8.

[79] Roessler (2000), p. 8.

[80] Roessler (2000), p. 8.

6.7.3 The Dispute Settlement Mechanism and the Scope of Review on the Overall Consistency of Regional Trade Agreements with the Provisions of Article XXIV

WTO Members had, until the recent decisions of the Appellate Body in *India-Quantitative Restrictions* and *Turkey-Textiles*, assumed that it was only the CRTA that could evaluate the overall consistency of regional trade agreements with the provisions of Article XXIV. This has led to continued efforts at reforming the examination process in order to produce conclusive results. The establishment of the CRTA in 1996 is a clear indication that the Members did not intend that panels should examine the overall consistency of RTAs with the provisions of Article XXIV.

Given the establishment of the CRTA, it is not likely that WTO Members had any intention of giving panels the authority to evaluate the overall consistency of regional trade agreements with the provisions of Article XXIV. Should that be the case, it would mean that a situation of an incoherent way of determining the consistency of agreements with the relevant multilateral trade rules would develop. With the proliferation of regional trade agreements and the desire of WTO Members to ensure that the relevant rules are complied with, Members would not want an *ad hoc* procedure for determining such an important issue. The DSB cannot establish a panel unless it is specifically requested to do so by a Member. In which case, if panels are to have the sole authority of determining the consistency of agreements with the relevant multilateral trade rules, it would lead to a situation whereby many countries would get away with implementing or maintaining inconsistent agreements unless they were challenged by other Members before a panel.

Since it important to ensure that regional trade agreements are supportive of the multilateral trading system and given the need to safeguard the rights of nonparticipating countries, it is unlikely that Members of the WTO would create a mechanism that could lead to an unpredictable system for evaluating agreements. In this regard, the comments made by the Premier of New South Wales concerning the necessity of a Bill of Rights to safeguard the fundamental rights of citizens are relevant to the debate:

> Courts operate within an adversarial process. *Matters only arise before them when there is a dispute and judgments are made on the basis of particular facts. Decisions are therefore piecemeal in nature and cannot take into account all issues relevant to determining policy.* The material before the courts is limited by rules of evidence and procedure. A court is not an appropriate forum for making these decisions[81] (italics added).

As previously noted, a panel is likely to approach the issue of consistency of a regional trade agreement with the relevant multilateral trade rules from a strictly legal perspective. It is unlikely to take into account the dynamic and static effects of the agreement. An agreement that simply complies with the rules of the WTO may

[81] Carr (2001), p. 17.

not necessarily further the objectives of the multilateral trading system by creating trade for the benefit of third countries. In this respect, the Panel in *Turkey-Textiles* noted that the issue of GATT/WTO compatibility of regional trade agreements is a "very complex undertaking which involves consideration by the CRTA, from the economic, legal and political perspectives of different Members, of the numerous facets of a regional trade in relation to the provisions of the WTO".[82]

The view expressed by the panel is pertinent to the development of a legal framework for resolving possible future conflicts on the labour standard and trade debate since, as already stated, in addition to the economic, legal, and political perspectives mentioned by the panel, the linkage issue has also the social perspective to factor in. In this respect, because of its specific functions and the narrowly defined terms of reference, it can be stated that if the WTO dispute settlement mechanism is not well positioned to determine the overall consistency of regional trade agreements with the relevant multilateral trade rules, how much more so the linkage issue with much broader issues to consider.

6.7.4 *Concurrent Jurisdiction Debate*

Whereas the Panel's view in the *India-Quantitative Restrictions* case that there could be concurrent jurisdiction as far as the determination of the consistency of agreements with the relevant multilateral trade rules concerned is plausible, it is extremely unlikely that Members intended to have such a duopoly, given the uncertainties it could produce.[83] It is feasible to envisage the situation where a panel and the CRTA may come to different conclusions regarding the consistency of an agreement with the relevant multilateral trade rules. As previously noted, a panel is more likely to approach the issue of consistency of an agreement with the

---

[82] *Turkey – Textiles*, para. 9.52, p. 114.

[83] "It is possible that a panel and the BOP Committee could examine successively the issue of whether the same balance-of-payments measures are justified under Article XVIII:B. If there has been no decision in the BOP Committee or General Council at the time of the panel's consideration of the issue, the issue of conflict does not arise at the panel stage, which is the situation in this case. While the BOP Committee and the General Council have considered the justification of India's balance-of-payments measures at issue in this case, they made no determinations and reached no agreed conclusions. Even if this Panel were to decide that India's measures are not justified, nothing would prevent the Committee and the General Council from reaching different conclusions on the basis of new, different facts, in which case the Council could take a decision on a phase-out period under paragraph 13 of the 1994 Understanding on Balance-of-Payments Provisions. Moreover, what Members accepted in the DSB could be modified in the General Council. The discretionary competence of the General Council to waive India's obligations under Article IX of the WTO Agreement would remain unaffected. Similarly, a decision by the Panel that India's measures were justified as of November 1997 would not preclude re-examination by the BOP Committee or the General Council of India's measures in the future": WT/DS90/R, para. 5.93, p. 153.

multilateral trade rules from a narrow perspective, whilst the CRTA is more likely to take into consideration broader factors such as the static and dynamic effects of the agreement and how it would facilitate global trade for the benefit of nonparticipating countries.

Whilst the Panel is correct in asserting that it would be rare for such a situation to happen, the mere possibility that it could happen does not do much to increase the confidence of Members and private business operators in the multilateral trading system.

The lack of confidence in the dispute settlement mechanism is likely to be exacerbated if the General Council or any of its subsidiary Committees were to exercise its competence and reverse the ruling of a panel or the Appellate Body on an issue that has created legitimate expectations in the private sector. The following scenario is, for example, likely to damage the confidence of private business operators in the multilateral trading system.

Let us assume that a panel issues a ruling finding a regional trade agreement to be consistent with the relevant multilateral trade rules, which encourages private companies from foreign countries to invest in the new free trade area. If the CRTA was unable to conclusively agree on the consistency of the agreement or was to find the agreement to be inconsistent with WTO rules, it could affect significantly the business interests of private parties, who may have no recourse to have their grievances redressed at the multilateral level.

References

Bail, C. (1997). Comments, in *Regionalism and multilateralism after the Uruguay round: Convergence, divergence and interaction*. Brussels: European University Press.

Bergsten, F. (2000). East Asian regionalism: Towards a tripartite world. *The Economist*, 15 July.

Bhagwati, J. (2001). A costly pursuit of free trade. *Financial Times*, 6 March 2001.

Bilal, S., & Szepesi, S. (2005). How regional economic communities can facilitate participation in the WTO: The experience of Mauritius and Zambia. In P. Gallagher, P. Low, & A. Stoler (Eds.), *Managing the challenges of WTO participation: 45 case studies*. Cambridge: Cambridge University Press.

Carr, B. (2001). Only people – not bills – protect rights. *The Australian*, 9 January 2001, Tuesday.

Crawford, J. A., & Laird, S. (2000). *Regional Trade Agreements and the WTO*. Paper presented at a meeting of the North American Economic and Finance Association, Boston, 6–9 January.

Cottier, T., & Caplazi, A. (1998). Labour standards and world trade law: Interfacing legitimate concerns. In T. Geiser, H. Schmid, & E. Walter-Busch (Eds.), *Arbeit in der Schweiz des 20. Jahrhunderts. Wirtschaftliche, rechtliche und soziale Perspektiven*. Berne/Stuttgart/Wien: Verlag Paul Haupt.

Dam, K. (1970). *The GATT: Law and International Economic Organization*. Chicago: University of Chicago Press.

De Melo, J., & Panagariya, A. (1992). *The new regionalism in trade policy*. Washington: World Bank.

Demaret, P. (1997). The reciprocal influence of multilateral and regional trade rules: A framework of analysis. In P. Demaret, J. F. Bellis, & G. Jiménez (Eds.), *Regionalism and multilateralism after the Uruguay round, convergence, divergence and interaction*. Brussels: European Interuniversity Press.

Frankel, J., (1997). *Regional trading blocs in the world economic system*. Washington: Institute for International Economics.

Freund, C., & Emanuel, O. (2010). *Regional Trade Agreements* (CEP Discussion Paper No. 961). London: London School of Economics and Political Science.

Jackson, J. (1969). *World trade and the law of the GATT*. New York: Bobbs-Merrill.

Kessie, E. K. (2001). The World Trade Organization and Regional Trade Agreements: An analysis of the relevant rules of the WTO (Unpublished Doctor of Juridical Science thesis manuscript. On file with the author).

Lamy, P. (2007). *Proliferation of regional trade agreements "breeding concern"*. In Speech of the Director General at the opening of the 2007 Conference on Multilateralizing Regionalism, Geneva, 10 September 2007. www.wto.org/english/news_e/sppl_e/spple67_e.htm. Accessed 6 Mar 2014.

Lamy, P. (2012). *Use multilateral trade negotiations and the WTO system as impetus for greater regional integration*. In Speech of the Director General at the African Union summit on 29 January 2012 in Addis Ababa, Ethiopia. http://www.wto.org/english/news_e/sppl_e/sppl214_e.htm. Accessed 7 Mar 2014.

Lynch, D. A. (2010). *Trade and globalization: An introduction to Regional Trade Agreements*. Lanham, USA: Rowman & Little- field Publishers Inc.

Paulwelyn, J. (2009). Legal avenues to 'multilateralizing regionalism': Beyond Article XXIV. In R. Baldwin & P. Low (Eds.), *Multilateralizing regionalism: Challenge for the global trading system*. Cambridge: Cambridge University Press.

Roessler, F. (2000). *The institutional balance between the judicial and the political organs of the WTO*. Paper presented at the Conference on "Efficiency, Equity and Legitimacy: The Multilateral Trading System at the Millennium", John F. Kennedy School of Government, Harvard University, Cambridge, MA, 1–2 June.

Sapir, A. (1998). The political economy of EC regionalism. *European Economic Review, 42*.

Snape, R. H., Adams, J., & Morgan, D. (1993). *Regional Trade Agreements: Implications and options for Australia*. Canberra: Department of Foreign Affairs and Trade.

WTO Secretariat. (1995). *Regionalism and the World Trading System*. Geneva: WTO.

WTO Secretariat. (2000). Synopsis of "Systemic" issues related to Regional Trade Agreements. WT/REG/W/37; 2 March.

Zoellick, R. (2002). Unleashing the trade winds. *The Economist*, 5 December.

Chapter 7
Regional Trade Agreements and Labour Provisions

7.1 Labour Provisions in Regional Trade Agreements

With the increasing failure to include labour standards in the WTO, the second best option in the opinion of the proponents has been to include labour standards in regional and bilateral trade agreements. In this chapter, we would examine labour standard clauses in some regional trade agreements,[1] specifically trade agreements signed by the United States, the European Union, and Canada with other countries. This chapter will also highlight other relevant free trade agreements with social clauses.

We would like to, as mentioned earlier, reiterate here that the analyses will mainly focus on the North America Free Trade Agreement (NAFTA) side agreement: the North America Agreement on Labor Cooperation (NAALC). The objective for focusing on the NAALC is that it is about the only FTA that has adjudicated labour disputes. The emphasis on the NAALC does not in any way indicate that the FTAs signed by the European Union (EU), Canada, and other countries are not relevant to the discussion of the linkage between the CLS and international trade in FTAs, but rather all the agreements fit into the overall debate in finding a common ground for the resolution of this contentious issue.

From the time of GATT until the 1990s, there was no trade agreement with a labour provision. However, by 2011, trade agreements with labour provisions had risen to 47. Of these trade agreements, about two-thirds contain labour provisions with reference to four categories of CLS. According to research carried out by the ILO, whereas only four per cent of all trade agreements that came into force between 1995 and 1999 included labour provisions, the figure rose to about one-third of all trade agreements signed between 2005 and 2011.[2]

---

[1] Space will not allow us to consider all RTAs with the labour provisions entered into to date. As such, we will review a selection of such RTAs.

[2] ILO (2012), pp. 100–101.

K. Addo, *Core Labour Standards and International Trade*,
DOI 10.1007/978-3-662-44619-5_7

As at 2011, approximately 120 countries were covered by at least one trade agreement and about 50 countries were covered by two trade agreements. Out of these countries, about 20 have signed trade agreements with labour provisions that include trade measures. Some of these labour provisions are either included in the body of the trade agreement or contained in a side agreement.

7.2 United States of America RTAs with Labour Provisions

Since it signed its first free trade agreement with Israel in 1985, the United States has negotiated FTAs with 20 countries such as Canada, the North American Free Trade Agreement (NAFTA, with Canada and Mexico), Jordan, Chile, Singapore, Australia, Morocco, Bahrain, and Oman; the CAFTA-DR regional trade agreement with the Dominican Republic and the five Central American countries (Costa Rica, El Salvador, Guatemala, Honduras, and Nicaragua), Peru, Colombia, Panama, and South Korea.

According to Bolle, the agreements with the last six Central American countries is a reflection of bipartisan agreement on the language on labour standards as indicated in the *New Trade Policy With America*, which was agreed between the former president G.W. Bush administration and Congress on 10 May 2007. This policy is important in United States labour relations with its trading partners as it advocates two key labour provisions: first, the need for a fully enforceable commitment that countries signing FTAs with the United States will adopt, maintain, and enforce in their national laws and practice, the basic international labour standards as stated in the 1998 ILO Declaration. Second is the commitment to use identical enforcement provisions for labour and commercial disputes.[3]

With respect to free trade agreements entered into by the United States, we would examine the North American Free Trade Agreement (NAFTA) and the US–Jordan, Singapore, Chile, and Peru Free Trade Agreements.

Bolle has categorised the labour and enforcement provisions in the various agreements into four models. These four models are highlighted below:

Model 1—the parties under NAALC agree to enforce their own labour laws and standards. The only enforceable provision with sanctions under the Agreement is found in Article 29(1), which states that "... persistent pattern of failure ... to effectively enforce its occupational safety and health, child labor or minimum wage technical standards". This must be trade related and also covered by mutually recognised labour laws. Comparing the main agreement with the side agreement, the side agreement has different enforcement procedures from the main agreement. Furthermore, there are limits placed on monetary enforcement

[3] See Bolle (2008), p. 3.

assessments, with the suspension of benefits for non-compliance. The main agreement has no monetary assessments.

Model 2—the U.S.–Jordan FTA, unlike NAALC, incorporated a number of labour provisions in the main agreement, which include Parties agreeing "not to fail to effectively enforce its labour laws ... in a manner affecting trade".[4] Under this Agreement, the commercial and labour provisions share the same dispute settlement procedures. This makes the labour and commercial provisions equally enforceable.

Model 3—the seven trade agreements with 12 different countries, that is, Chile, Singapore, Australia, Morocco, Bahrain, Oman, and the CAFTA-DR countries (Costa Rica, El Salvador, Guatemala, Honduras, Nicaragua, and the Dominican Republic) contain only one enforceable labour provision, which states that each party "shall not fail to effectively enforce its labour laws ... in a manner affecting trade between the Parties". Labour laws in all the agreements are defined as "a Party's statutes or regulations ... that are directly related to" the United States list of worker rights that are internationally recognised. All seven agreements share many of the same procedures for labour and commercial disputes. Whereas limit on monetary penalties are placed on labour disputes, there are no limits placed on commercial disputes. For both types of disputes, suspension of benefits is used only as a last recourse.

Model 4—the new Trade Policy for America included four enforceable labour concepts as template language to be included in pending FTAs and future FTAs in identical form. The concepts are (1) a fully enforceable commitment that Parties to free trade agreements would adopt and maintain in their laws and practices as stated in the ILO Declaration, (2) a fully enforceable commitment prohibiting FTA countries from lowering their labour standards, (3) new limitations on "prosecutorial" and "enforcement" discretion (i.e., countries cannot defend failure to enforce laws related to the five basic core labour standards on the basis of resource limitations or decisions to prioritise other enforcement issues), and (4) the same dispute settlement mechanisms or penalties available for other FTA obligations (such as commercial interests).[5]

The Agreements under this Model have the same dispute settlement provisions for both labour and commercial disputes. The labour provisions are fully enforceable. The template language also includes a footnote that states: "The obligations set out in Article 17.2, as they relate to the ILO, refer only to the ILO Declaration." Whilst the agreement of May 10, 2007, is silent on this issue, it appears to suggest that Parties would be held only to the principles of the ILO Declaration but not to the conventions of the ILO. It is important to note that the New Trade Policy with America only deals with goods for export (Table 7.1).

[4] See Article 6.4 of the U.S.–Jordan FTA.

[5] Text of Congress Administration Trade Deal, *Inside U.S. Trade*, May 11, 2007; and *Trade Facts: Bipartisan Trade Deal*. Office of the USTR, Bipartisan Agreement on Trade Policy, May 2007.

Table 7.1 United States FTAs with labour rights and social provisions

FTA	Date entered into force on	Labour rights and social provisions in Agreement	Model
US/Oman FTA	1 January 2009	• Labour rights and labour issues are included in chapter 16 • Labour rights and labour issues are also developed in Annex 16-A (Labour Cooperation Mechanism)	3
US/Peru FTA	1 February 2009	• Labour rights and labour issues are included in chapter 17	4
US/South Korea FTA	15 March 2012	• Labour rights and labour issues are included in chapter 19 • Labour rights and labour issues are also developed in Annex 19-A entitled "Labour Cooperation Mechanism", and the protection of labour rights is confirmed in a public letter	4
US/Panama FTA or TPA (trade promotion agreement)	7 July 2007	• Labour rights and labour issues are included in chapter 16	4
US/Morocco FTA	1 January 2006	• Labour rights and labour issues are included in chapter 16	3
US/Bahrain FTA	August 2006	• Labour rights are included in chapter 15 • Labour Cooperation Mechanism in Annex 15-A	3
US/Colombia FTA	15 May 2012	• Labour rights and labour issues are included in chapter 17	4
US/Australia FTA	1 January 2005	• Labour rights are included in chapter 18, page 236 of the final text	3
CAFTA-DR (Central American and Dominican Republic FTA)	5 August 2005	• Labour rights are included in chapter 16	3
US/Chile FTA	1 January 2004	• Labour rights and labour issues are included in chapter 18	3
US/Singapore FTA	1 January 2004	• Labour rights and labour issues are included in chapter 17 and in Annex 17-A, pages 207 to 211	3
US/Jordan FTA	17 December 2001	• Labour rights and labour issues are included in chapter 6	2
North American Free Trade Agreement (NAFTA)	1 January 1994	This contains the North American Agreement on Labor Cooperation (NAALC) text	1

Source: ILO (see http://www.ilo.org/global/standards/information-resources-and-publications/free-trade-agreements-and-labour-rights/WCMS_115531/lang--en/index.htm#P61_3885. Accessed 27 March 2014, and Bolle (2008))

7.3 United States of America's Motives for Promoting FTAs

The reasons for the United States entering into the free trade agreements are threefold: economic, political, and social. First, the economic reasons were to expand sales opportunities for U.S. companies exporting to Mexico, enhance North American international competitiveness by permitting companies to set up operations where it would be most profitable economically, without distortions caused by trade or investment barriers. In addition, "level the playing field" by protecting U.S. jobs and wages from what some consider unfair competition from low-wage foreign producers.

Second is the political reasoning for doing so. The U.S. appears to be leaning more towards countries that have moved toward market economies and democracy, which then makes them both political and commercial allies of the United States.[6] The U.S. also sees the FTAs as a means to increase transparency in corporate governance, legal systems, and due process in the partner countries and a means to strengthen the local economies.[7]

Third, in addition to the economic and political reasons are the social considerations. The labour provisions in recent agreements are indications of the U.S. commitment to uphold the rights of workers. The FTAs are built on the U.S. traditional support for and promotion of labour standard conventions adopted by the ILO. The U.S. Congress has grappled with the issues raised by arguments for and against the linkage between trade and labour standards. Two issues tend to have emerged: (1) whether these agreements balance the promotion of worker rights with trade and investment opportunities for businesses and (2) if the labour provisions in the agreements are the proper models for future trade agreements.[8] As discussed below, the U.S.–Jordan Agreement was the first to incorporate labour provisions in the body of an FTA. This provision has raised debate in the U.S. Congress as to whether worker rights provisions should, in the future, be included in free trade agreements or that the U.S.–Jordan model should be a one-time occurrence.

Whereas the NAFTA agreement had labour provisions in a side agreement, the U.S. agreements with Jordan, Chile, and Singapore have labour provisions incorporated in the body of the agreements.[9] Table 7.3 shows a comparison of the four

---

[6] Hubbard (2005), p. 55.

[7] Hubbard (2005), p. 55.

[8] Bolle (2003a).

[9] The labour provisions in the U.S.–CAFTA Free Trade Agreement are identical with the U.S.–Chile Free Trade Agreement but then somewhat similar to the U.S.–Singapore Free Trade Agreement. Labour obligations in CAFTA are part of the core text of the trade agreement and include provisions that commit CAFTA countries to provide workers with improved access to procedures that protect their rights. It provides a three-part cooperative approach. The Agreement requires that all parties shall effectively enforce their own domestic labor laws, which, however, may not be in line with international standards. They will work with the ILO to improve existing

agreements. We intend in this section to examine only the labour provisions under NAFTA and the U.S.–Jordan, U.S.–Singapore, U.S.–Chile, and U.S.–Peru Free Trade Agreements. A comparison of the labour provisions in both NAFTA and U. S.–Chile agreements are made in Table 7.3. The reason for this comparison is to show how the provisions in model 1 evolved to the provisions in model 2 as an indication of the evolution of labour provisions from the start. Also in Table 7.3, we undertake a comparison of the key provisions under the four models and the agreements that fall under each to provide a full picture of the evolution of labour provision process.

7.4 Review of United States of America Free Trade Agreements and Labour Rights

The section below reviews one free trade agreement each from models 1–3 and two agreements from model four.

7.4.1 North American Free Trade Agreement (NAFTA)

On 1 January, 1994, the agreement signed between the United States, Canada, and Mexico, known as the North America Free Trade Agreement (NAFTA), entered into effect. NAFTA is the largest and most comprehensive trade agreement signed to date. NAFTA is the first agreement to include labour provisions in a trade agreement. Originally, labour issues were not to be part of the agreement. The main agreement only mentions labour issues in the preamble. In the text are listed reasons for signing the agreement such as job creation, improved working conditions, and the protection and enforcement of basic workers' rights. With regard to labour issues, this was as far as the agreement went. NAFTA was not intended to address labour issues within the body of the agreement.[10]

However, during the NAFTA debates in the U.S. Congress, organised labour intensified its efforts since it was believed at that time that a considerable number of jobs in the U.S. would be lost to a low-wage country like Mexico. The critics of the agreement alleged that an estimated 500,000 U.S. jobs and even more would be lost to Mexico.[11] In an attempt to allay the fears of organised labour, President Clinton agreed to negotiate a supplemental agreement to NAFTA, which became known as the North American Agreement on Labor Cooperation (NAALC).

---

labor laws and enforcement. Furthermore, strategies will be to improve workers' rights (consultations, training programmes, financial resources, and public participation).

[10] Joe (1995), p. 451.

[11] Church (1993), p. 41. Quoted in Joe (1995), p. 451.

7.4.1.1 NAALC: Precedent for Labour Standards in Trade Agreements

The NAALC came into effect on 1 January 1994, the same time as the parent agreement after the leaders of the three countries had agreed to its final form in September 1993.[12] The Agreement created a multinational enforcement and review system that allows each country to monitor how the others enforce their national labour laws. NAALC holds the potential in effectively ensuring that the rights of workers are protected in the NAFTA countries, at the same time making possible the expansion of trade among the countries. Murphy (1995) states that the NAALC reaffirms NAFTA's goals as set forth in the Preamble to the creation of an expanded, secure market for the Parties' goods whilst enhancing the Parties' competitiveness in the global market and helping in the creation of new employment opportunities.[13]

NAALC provides an avenue for employers, employees, unions, and governments to work to promote workers' rights. The signatories expect to achieve the goals of the Agreement through the publication and dissemination of information concerning job training, union activity, and labour law.

The NAALC, though it is not the first attempt to link the right of workers and trade agreements, broke new ground in the history of trade agreements by creating labour-related obligations and establishing sanctions for failure to fulfil them in certain cases. The agreement represented an attempt to balance the differing interests of foreign and domestic labour forces and governments of all countries. The aim of the NAALC is to promote labour standards by obliging each party to enforce its domestic labour laws and ensure that the labour laws provide for high-quality standards, but the Agreement does not issue mandates. The Agreement is clear on the sovereignty of the three nations and goes further to confirm the primacy of each nation's domestic labour law. It affirms "full respect for each Party's constitution" and accepts the "right of each Party to establish its own domestic labor standards".[14]

In this respect, NAALC does not require or push for the harmonisation of the three countries' laws. As it is stated in Annex 1 of the Agreement, NAALC's goals "are guiding principles that the Parties are committed to promote ... but do not establish common minimum standards".[15]

The agreement promotes mutual obligation and mutual responsibility. The NAALC established an infrastructure with a governing body and an administration to encourage interaction between the three countries.

The NAALC has 11 labour principles:

1. freedom of association and protection of the right to organise;
2. the right to bargain;

---

[12] See North American Agreement on Labor Cooperation, September 13, 1993, United States of America–Mexico–Canada [hereinafter NAALC] (stating final draft of labour agreement).

[13] See Preamble of NAALC.

[14] See NAALC Article 2.

[15] See NAALC Annex 1.

3. the right to strike;
4. prohibition of forced labour;
5. labour protection for children and young persons;
6. minimum employment standards, such as minimum wages and overtime pay, covering wage earners, including those not covered by collective agreements;
7. elimination of employment discrimination on the basis of such grounds as race, religion, age, sex, or other grounds as determined by each party's domestic laws;
8. equal pay for men and women;
9. prevention of occupational injuries and illnesses;
10. compensation in cases of occupational injuries and illnesses; and
11. protection of migrant workers.[16]

These principles go far beyond the core labour rights embodied in the 1998 ILO Declaration. The NAALC calls on all three governments to improve performance regarding all these rights and standards. There is, however, no enforceable obligation to do so. In fact, the parties to the NAALC are not even explicitly prohibited from weakening their labour law: Article 3 of the NAALC recognises "the right of each Party to establish its own domestic labor standards, and to adopt or modify accordingly its labor laws and regulations".[17]

The side agreement not only defines labour laws as laws and regulations that are directly related to the eleven rights; it also demands that these rights provide for "high labor standards" to be harmonised among the three parties and that they should be continually improved over time. The agreement states that a prerequisite determination should be made to effectively enforce a member's domestic law before a claim can be brought against any of the other parties under the dispute resolution mechanism.[18] The agreement allows any person with a recognised interest under the law to submit complaints or petitions to any of the three parties.[19] However, only three areas fall under this provision, namely child labour, minimum wage and technical labour standards, and occupational safety and health. The agreement does not allow for complaints to be brought in cases relating to freedom of association, right to bargain collectively, and forced labour.

Enforcement provisions in the agreement involve a three-tiered structure that excludes fines or sanctions outside the realm of child labour, minimum employment standards, and occupational health and safety. In the case of freedom of association and the right to collective bargaining, the agreement only allows for ministerial consultations between the labour ministers.

[16] See Article 49 of NAALC.

[17] See Article 3 of NAALC.

[18] See Article 2 of NAALC.

[19] See Article 27.1 of NAALC.

Box 7.1: The Three-Tier System

- The first tier is limited to NAO review and ministerial oversight. A committee of experts cannot evaluate the enforcement of labour principles in this tier, and no penalties are provided for non-compliance. The labour principles in this tier are freedom of association, collective bargaining, and the right to strike.
- In the second tier are principles subject to NAO review, ministerial consultations, and evaluation by a committee of experts. This does not call for arbitration of disputes and does not require the imposition of penalties. Included in this tier are forced labour, gender pay equity, employment discrimination, compensation in case of injury or illness, and protection of migrant labour.
- The labour principles in the third tier—child labour, minimum wages, and occupational safety—receive the full treatment: NAO review, ministerial consultations, evaluation and arbitration, and eventually monetary penalties (Hufbauer and Schott 2005, p. 123).

The agreement permits the creation of a Commission on Labour Cooperation, which is made up of a ministerial council (the three labour ministers) and a secretariat. The Commission mainly deals with cooperative endeavours and studies, and an institutional structure has been set up to deal with complaints on non-enforcement of each country's domestic labour laws ("submissions"). The NAOs in each member's labour department or ministry have the duty to receive and process submissions from civil society with respect to the non-enforcement of labour law in any of the three countries. However, the submissions are not limited in scope, i.e., in matters affecting only trade.

Under the agreement, the NAOs are obliged, if requested, to provide information from any of the other NAOs. Basing their review on the information collected, a NAO can request ministerial consultations. If these consultations do not resolve the issue, no further action can be taken for problems involving freedom of association, the right to bargain collectively, or the right to strike. With respect to the other rights, a three-person evaluation committee of experts (ECE) can be appointed to work out a report for review by the ministerial council, including recommendations to improve compliance.

Finally, a five-member arbitration tribunal can be appointed. In cases of child labour, minimum employment standards, and occupational safety and health, a "persistent pattern of non-enforcement" can ultimately result in monetary assessments (fines)—which will be paid into a fund to improve enforcement of labour law in the offending country or, if those are not paid, trade sanctions. Both fines and trade sanctions are capped at 0.007 % of the volume of trade between the two countries (or US$20 million, whichever is lower). Critics of these cumbersome, quasi-diplomatic enforcement procedures have pointed out that it will take more than 30 months to reach this final stage.

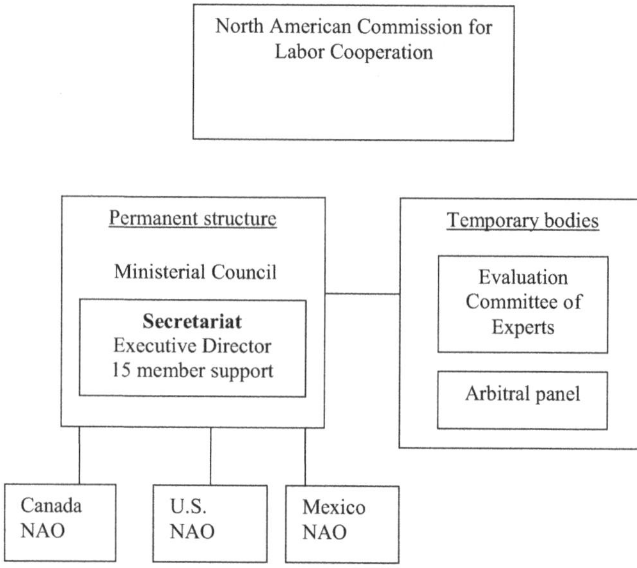

Fig. 7.1 Institutional structure of NAALC. *Source*: GAO-01-933 North American Free Trade Agreement

In spite of the fact that the initial focus of the agreement was to ensure that Mexico's labour laws were in line, the agreement has a noteworthy feature—reciprocity. This has led to complaints filed against U.S. labour practices. On the whole, the process is similar to that of the process at the ILO, where members use diplomatic pressure and moral suasion (Fig. 7.1).

7.4.1.2 Obligations of the Three Parties Under NAALC

The parties, in signing the NAALC, are obliged to undertake six obligations under "Part Two" of the side agreement. First, the parties accepted the general commitment in Article 2 in establishing and maintaining high labour standards, which should be consistent with high-quality and productivity workplaces. Further, under this obligation, the parties are to continue to strive in improving those standards in their labour laws and regulations.[20] This obligation is significant as it has formed the basis for a number of complaints.

Second, the parties are to "promote compliance with, and effectively enforce its labour law through appropriate government action". This entails seven points listed under Article 3. These are appointing and training inspectors; monitoring compliance and investigating suspected violations, including through on-site inspections; seeking assurances of voluntary compliance; requiring record keeping and

[20] See Article 2 of Part Two of NAALC.

reporting; encouraging the establishment of worker-management committees to address labour regulation of the workplace; providing or encouraging mediation, conciliation, and arbitration services; or initiating, in a timely manner, proceedings to seek appropriate sanctions or remedies for violations of its labour law.[21]

The third obligation concerns private action ensuring that private parties have access to procedures for the enforcement of domestic labour law and collective agreements. The fourth obligation deals with the enforcement of labour laws that are fair, equitable, and transparent. In achieving this, each party has to guarantee procedural due process. Parties are to guarantee open hearings, the right to present information and evidence, and the right to written decision based on the evidence in respect of which the parties were given the opportunity to be heard. The Agreement provides for impartial and independent tribunals and courts and appropriate remedies for the enforcement of labour rights, including compliance agreements, fines, penalties, imprisonment, injunctions, or emergency workplace closures.[22]

The fifth obligation is a requirement on transparency. Each party is required to publish or otherwise make available to interested parties its laws, regulations, procedures, and administrative rulings of general application.[23] The final obligation is that each party is to promote public awareness of its domestic labour law. This should include making public information available on enforcement and compliance procedures and promoting public education regarding labour laws.[24]

7.4.2 *Labour Provisions in the United States–Jordan FTA (U.S.–Jordan FTA)*

The U.S.–Jordan FTA went into effect on 17 December 2001. This agreement for the first time broke new ground by the inclusion of multiple workers' rights provisions in the body of the free trade agreement rather than in a side agreement, as it was the case under NAFTA.[25] The agreement covers a number of areas such as services, protection of intellectual property rights, and dispute settlement.

The US–Jordan FTA was signed on 24 October 2000 by the Clinton administration but entered into force on 17 December 2001. The agreement was the third free trade agreement signed by the U.S. The agreement covers substantive issues such as trade in services, electronic commerce, intellectual property rights, balance

[21] The obligations of each party under Article 3 do not extend to a party enforcing the laws of another party.

[22] Article 5 of NAALC.

[23] Article 6 of NAALC.

[24] Article 7 of NAALC.

[25] Labour provisions are also included in such agreements as the US–Singapore and US–Chile Free Trade Agreements.

of payments, rules of origin, environmental provisions, and a transparent dispute settlement process.

However, it is in the area of labour standard provisions that the agreement has come to be seen as ground breaking. The labour provisions in the agreement do not require either country to adopt any new labour laws. Each country is allowed to retain the right to set and change its own labour standards. The two countries affirmed the significance of not waiving or derogating from their labour laws as a way to encourage trade. Under the agreement, the labour provisions in this agreement were more substantive in nature than the provisions under NAFTA since the negotiators made enforceable labour standards go beyond the core labour standards under ILO jurisdiction.

The agreement specifies two sets of provisions over labour issues: labour provisions (Article 6) and dispute settlement provisions (Article 17). The agreement specifically lists freedom of association, the right to collective bargaining, minimum age, prohibition of forced or compulsory labour, minimum age for employment of children, and conditions of work as the relevant key principles.[26] The labour provisions in the agreement are an indication of the parties' commitment to the core labour standards as enunciated by the ILO and internationally recognised worker rights as defined by the U.S. Trade Act of 1974 (as amended). The labour provisions in the agreement are a confirmation that in the pursuit of free trade, the rights of workers can be protected.[27] In fact, the preamble to the agreement states that the parties "desire to promote higher labor standards by building their respective international commitments and strengthening their cooperation on labor matters" and also wish to "promote effective enforcement of their respective ... labor laws". Specifically, Article 6.1 of the agreement states:

> The parties affirm their obligations as members of the International Labor Organization ("ILO") and their commitments under the ILO Declaration on Fundamental Principles and Rights at Work and its Follow-up. The Parties shall strive to ensure that such labor principles and the internationally recognized labor rights set forth in paragraph 6 are recognized and protected by domestic law.

The agreement provides for resolution of disputes that may arise as a result of (a) interpretation of the agreement, (b) alleged failure of a Party to carry out its obligations under the agreement, and (c) measures taken by a Party that severely distort the balance of trade benefits accorded by the agreement or substantially undermine fundamental objectives of the agreement.

The agreement provides for a period of 270 days or about 9 months in case a Party intends to pursue a dispute. The Party would have to send a request for

---

[26] Included in the conditions of work is minimum wages. This principle is not included in the ILO core labour standards and appears to address the concern of lawmakers and trade unions that increased trade could result in decrease in wages, which could adversely affect U.S. workers, the so-called race to the bottom.

[27] http://www.whitehouse.gov/news/releases/2001/09/20010928-12.html. Accessed on 2 April 2014.

consultations to a contact point. If the Parties fail to resolve the matter within 60 days of the submission, either party could refer the matter to the Joint Committee to be resolved within 90 days or within a period specified by the Joint Committee. The Panel is requested to present a report containing its findings of fact and its determination, and this is nonbinding. Should the dispute not be resolved within 30 days after the report of the Joint Committee, the affected Party shall be entitled to take "any appropriate and commensurate measure".

According to Elliot (2003), the U.S.–Jordan model provides a risk because of the unclear language of the dispute settlement provisions. She argues that the labour standard text in the agreement is weak, making it unlikely that any dispute would get as far as allowing a Party to take "any appropriate and commensurate measure". The only "shall" is found in Article 6(3b), where each party is required to strive to ensure that their laws provide for consistency of their labour standards with internationally recognised labour rights in a way that does not affect trade relations.[28]

In comparing (see Table 7.2) the U.S.–Jordan Free Trade Agreement with that of the side agreement under NAFTA, it could be argued that the U.S.–Jordan FTA better advances the correlation between the protection of worker rights and trade far beyond that contained in the NAALC. This is achieved in the U.S.–Jordan agreement in two ways: (a) including worker rights provisions in the body of the agreement and (b) allowing either Party the right to take "any appropriate and commensurate measure" if the dispute procedures do not lead to resolution. Bolle (2003b) has stated that the influence of the U.S.–Jordan agreement is seen in the language re-authorising the U.S. Trade and Promotion Authority, and this would go a long way in permitting the inclusion of similar provisions in new trade agreements to include provisions similar to those in the Jordan agreement in the body of the agreement.[29]

7.4.3 Labour Provisions in the United States–Singapore Free Trade Agreement (U.S.–Singapore FTA)

The United States, after the conclusion of the U.S.–Jordan agreement, stated its intention to negotiate a free trade agreement with Singapore. The U.S.–Singapore FTA went into effect on 1 January 2004. The wide-ranging nature of this agreement is similar in many respects to that of the U.S.–Jordan FTA. The agreement has, in effect, eliminated tariffs on trade in goods between the two countries. The agreement also covers trade in services, market access, investment measures, rules of origin, government procurement, the environment, intellectual property rights, licensing of professionals, capital controls, telecommunications, and dispute settlement.

[28] Elliot (2003), p. 15.

[29] Bolle (2003b).

Table 7.2 Comparison of key provisions of U.S.–Jordan FTAs and NAFTA

Provision	Jordan Free Trade Agreement, Article 6	NAFTA (P.L. 103–182)
Location of the labour provisions	In the body of the agreement	In the labour side agreement
Definition of worker rights	**"Internationally Recognized Worker Rights" from Trade Act of 1974** (P.L. 93-618 as amended by Sec. 503 of P.L. 98-573): a) right of association; b) right to organize and bargain collectively; c) prohibition of forced or compulsory labor; d) minimum age for employment of children; e) acceptable conditions re: minimum wages, hours; and occupational safety and health. **"Core Labor Standards" from the International Labor Organization (ILO)**: a) freedom of association; b) right to organize and bargain collectively; c) prohibition on the use of forced labor; d) prohibition of exploitative child labor; e) prohibition of employment discrimination.	**"Internationally Recognized Worker Rights" from Trade Act of 1974 (at left), plus the following additions:** f) the right to strike; g) minimum employment standards relating to overtime pay; h) elimination of employment discrimination; i) equal pay for men and women; j) compensation in cases of occupational injuries and illnesses; k) protection of migrant workers.
Basic labour requirements	a) All countries must enforce their own labor laws and standards in trade-related situations.	All countries must enforce own labor laws and standards in trade-related situations and shall strive toward the entire list of worker rights.
	b) Each Party shall strive to "*not waive or otherwise derogate from*" its laws as an encouragement for trade.	No comparable provision
Worker rights subject to dispute resolution	All of them	Only three standards out of 11 (for child labor, minimum wages, and occupational safety and health) are enforceable through dispute settlement and ultimately sanctions.
	No similar provision	Dispute resolution may be undertaken only for failure to enforce one's own worker rights laws and regulations, and if alleged failure to enforce is trade related and

(continued)

Table 7.2 (continued)

Provision	Jordan Free Trade Agreement, Article 6	NAFTA (P.L. 103–182)
		covered by mutually recognized labor laws.
Enforcement body and dispute resolution procedure	Each country shall designate an office to serve as a contact point on the agreement.	Trade ministers (the Ministerial Council) meet occasionally, supported by a 15-member Secretariat to resolve issues with consultation and persuasion.
	Any issue not resolved through consultation within 60 days may be referred to a **Joint Committee**, and, if still not resolved within 90 days, to a **Dispute Settlement Panel** chosen by the parties.	In each country a **National Administrative Office (NAO)** oversees the law; Then an: **Evaluation Committee of Experts (ECE)** and subsequently an **Arbitral Panel (AP)** are appointed as needed to debate cases.
Ultimate penalties	If the issue is still not resolved in 30 days, after the panel reports, the affected party may take *any appropriate and commensurate measure.*	The AP may issue a monetary assessment; and if this is not paid, issue sanctions. **Maximum penalties:** suspension of NAFTA benefits to the amount of the monetary penalty (which may be no greater than NAFTA benefits from tariff reductions) for 1 year.

Source: Congressional Research Service (2001)

The labour provisions under the Singapore agreement are, in many respects, similar to the labour provisions in the Jordan agreement. The agreement marked the second time that labour standard provisions was included in the main body of the agreement. Under the agreement, both signatories stated their obligations as Members of the ILO and that they will ensure that their labour laws provide for labour standards that are consistent with internationally recognised labour standards. Just as in the U.S.–Jordan FTA, the U.S.–Singapore agreement contains language that requires the parties to effectively enforce their own domestic labour laws[30] and not weaken or reduce domestic labour protection as a means to encourage trade or investment.[31] Whereas the reference to investment is absent in the U.S.–Jordan FTA, the U.S.–Singapore FTA makes reference to investment.[32] The Singapore

[30] US–Singapore FTA, Article 17.1(1).

[31] US–Singapore FTA, Article 17.2(1)(a).

[32] Article 17.2(2) provides: "The Parties recognize that it is inappropriate to encourage trade or investment by weakening or reducing the protections afforded in domestic labor laws. Accordingly, each Party shall strive to ensure that it does not waive or otherwise derogate from, or offer to waive or otherwise derogate from, such laws in a manner that weakens or reduces adherence to the internationally recognized labor rights referred to in Article 17.7 as an encouragement for trade with the other Party, or as an encouragement for the establishment, acquisition, expansion, or retention of an investment in its territory."

agreement includes a reference to the rights recognised as fundamental by the ILO, as well as the so-called internationally recognised labour rights, which are not all recognised as fundamental by the ILO. Just as in the U.S.–Jordan FTA, there is a reference to "acceptable conditions of work with respect to minimum wages, hours of work and occupational safety and health".[33] The U.S.–Singapore FTA, as in the case of the Jordan agreement, does not include the "elimination of discrimination against different categories of workers on the basis of gender, ethnicity, etc." as a part of the core labour standards, which the ILO Declaration considers as fundamental.

The minimum wage, as used in the U.S.–Singapore FTA, refers in the case of Singapore to the wage guidelines provided by the National Wages Council (NWC) gazetted under the Employment Act.[34] With respect to the U.S., statutes and regulations referred to the acts of the U.S. Congress or regulations promulgated pursuant to an act of the U.S. Congress that are enforceable, in the first instance, by action of the federal government.[35]

Annex 17A of the agreement calls for the establishment of a "Labor Cooperation Mechanism". This, according to the agreement, is recognition that cooperation is needed to provide enhanced opportunities to improve their labour standards and to further advance the parties' common commitments. This includes the June 1998 ILO Declaration on Fundamental Principles and Rights at Work and its Follow-up.[36] The functions of the Labor Cooperation Mechanism, among others, include establishing priorities for cooperative activities on labour matters, exchanging information with regard to labour law and practice, and finding ways to improve labour law and practice in each signatory country.[37] The cooperative mechanism is also tasked with undertaking activities on the fundamental rights and how to effectively apply them, managing labour relations, and providing unemployment assistance programmes and other social safety net programmes.[38]

Dispute settlement under the U.S.–Singapore FTA is similar to that of the U.S.–Jordan FTA. In both cases, the dispute resolution mechanisms allow for consultations to be followed by a Panel report and attempt by a Joint Committee to help settle the dispute. In spite of this, a complaining party is entitled to take unilateral action. However, in the U.S.–Singapore dispute settlement proceedings after consultations and the issuance of a Panel report, the matter is referred back to a Joint

[33] See US–Singapore FTA, Article 17.7(2)(e).

[34] US–Singapore FTA, Article 17.7(2)(a).

[35] US–Singapore FTA, Article 17.7(2)(b).

[36] See US–Singapore FTA, Annex 17A(1).

[37] US–Singapore FTA, Annex 17A(2).

[38] US–Singapore FTA, Annex 17A(3).

Committee for eventual resolution.[39] Should the Joint Committee fail to resolve the matter or should a party fail to execute an agreed upon resolution, instead of the complaining party taking unilateral action, the complaining party could request that the Panel be reconstituted to impose an "annual monetary assessment" at a cap of US$15 million a year.[40] This marks a difference from the U.S.–Jordan FTA, which allows the complaining party to take action when it deems it appropriate and commensurate.

7.4.4 *Labour Provisions in the United States–Chile Free Trade Agreement (U.S.–Chile FTA)*

The U.S.–Chile FTA is the first agreement between the US and a South American country. It is interesting to note that Chile is not a major trading partner of the U.S. but became attractive for an FTA due to its commitment to free trade and its political and economic stability in the South American region. The agreement was signed on 3 September 2003 and followed the precedent already established under the U.S.–Jordan and US–Singapore FTAs—the incorporation of labour provisions in the body of the agreement. In the preamble of the agreement, both parties resolved to increase employment opportunities and strive for the improvement of working conditions and living standards. They also resolved to protect, enhance, and enforce basic workers' rights.[41]

Under the agreement, both parties reaffirmed their obligations as ILO members and committed themselves to recognise and legally protect labour principles and rights as defined in the 1998 ILO Declaration on Fundamental Principles and Rights of Work and its Follow-up.[42] The labour rights in the U.S.–Chile FTA are the same as those listed in the US–Jordan FTA.[43]

The agreement commits both signatories to effectively enforce their individual labour laws through a sustained and recurring course of action or inaction, in a manner that affects trade between the two countries.[44] The agreement also recognises the right of each party to exercise discretion with respect to issues of compliance and to make decisions on the allocation of resources to enforcement concerning labour matters that are deemed to have higher priorities.[45]

As it is in the U.S.–Singapore FTA, the U.S.–Chile FTA does not allow the parties to waive or derogate from the internationally accepted labour principles as a

[39] US–Singapore FTA, Articles 17.4–17.6.

[40] US–Singapore FTA, Annex 20A.

[41] See Preamble of US–Chile FTA.

[42] US–Chile FTA, Article 18.1.

[43] US–Chile FTA, Article 18.8.

[44] US–Chile FTA, Article 18.21(a).

[45] US–Chile FTA, Article 18.21(b).

way to encourage trade and investment with the other party.[46] However, with reference to minimum wages, the U.S.–Chile FTA states that the setting of standards and levels of the minimum wages should not be subjected to obligations under the agreement and that each party's obligations under the agreement relate to the enforcement of the level of the minimum wage agreed upon by the member.[47]

The agreement created a "Labor Affairs Council" to oversee the implementation of and review of the agreement, which includes the activities of the "Labor Cooperation Mechanism,[48] similar to the U.S.–Singapore FTA. All decisions of the Council are to be taken by mutual agreement of both parties and are to be made public. Any of the parties can request consultations with the other party concerning issues in the labour chapter. The FTA provides a clear schedule for resolution of issues before the matter is referred to other bodies.[49]

Should the Council fail to reach an agreement on a matter under consultation within 60 days, the complaining party may request consultations with the offices of the Commission of Good Offices, Conciliation and Mediation. If no agreement is reached, then four members on the labour roster are selected to resolve the dispute.[50] The U.S.–Chile FTA is different from the U.S.–Jordan FTA in the sense that whereas the U.S.–Jordan FTA permits appropriate and commensurate measures to be taken in case of violation of any of the labour provisions in case a dispute cannot be resolved, the U.S.–Chile FTA does not allow either party to have recourse to the dispute settlement mechanisms on any issue than the enforcement of the party's domestic labour laws in a matter affecting trade between the parties. The issues to be considered as affecting trade consists of only five out of the eight labour standards stated in the agreement (child labour—two labour standards, forced labour, standards on freedom of association and acceptable conditions of work).

The U.S.–Chile FTA is similar to the U.S.–Singapore on the imposition of a monetary assessment adjusted for inflation at a cap of US$15 million annually. The monetary assessment is to be paid in equal quarter instalments into a fund established by the Commission to be invested in improving labour law enforcement. Should the party complained against fail to meet the payments, then the other party is permitted to take action, which includes the suspension of tariff benefits without affecting the benefits of third parties.[51]

The FTA also recognises the importance of cooperation in enhancing opportunities to further advance common commitments. Such commitments include the ILO Declaration and compliance with ILO Convention on the elimination of the worst form child labour (Convention No. 182). In order to achieve this, the FTA includes a Labor Cooperation Mechanism (LCM). The LCM provides a framework

---

[46] US–Chile FTA, Article 18.2.2.

[47] US–Chile FTA, Article 18.8(e).

[48] US–Chile FTA, Article 18.4.

[49] US–Chile FTA, Article 18.6.

[50] US–Chile FTA, Article 18.7.1.

[51] US–Chile FTA, Article 22 and Annex 22.

for the labour ministries of the two countries to work together in improving systems of administration and ensuring the enforcement of labour laws. Article 18.4 under the Labor Chapter of the FTA states that a contact point should be established that will serve as a contact point for the LCM. The labour ministries of both Parties are to carry out the work of the LCM. The activities of the LCM include the establishment of priorities for cooperation; the development and periodical review of a work programme for technical assistance in accord with the priorities set; the exchange of information on labour policies and the importance of observing and effectively applying labour law and practices in the territories of both Parties; the exchange of information on and the encouragement of the best labour practices and advance understanding of, respect for, and effective implementation of the ILO principles as stated in the Declaration; promotion of the collection and publication of comparative data on labour standards, labour market indicators, and activities on enforcement; arrangement for sessions periodically to review cooperate activities to be in a position to provide direction for future activities; and, finally, development of suggestions for each ministry for consideration.

7.4.5 Labour Provisions in the United States–Peru Trade and Promotion Agreement (U.S.–Peru FTA)

The U.S.–Peru Trade Promotion Agreement (TPA) was signed between the two countries on 12 April 2006. The agreement went into effect in February 2009. The TPA marks the first agreement signed under the deal struck between the U.S. Congress and the G.W. Bush administration—the "New Trade Policy for America". Even though both are not each other's major trading partners, trade between the U.S. and Peru constituted for both countries a strategic as well as an economic agreement. In the words of the former U.S. trade representative Rob Portman, "[a]n agreement with Peru is a key building block in our strategy to advance free trade within our hemisphere." And the Peruvian President Alejandro Toledo also stated: "[w]e have reached an agreement where Peru came out the winner."[52]

In 2007, Peruvian exports to the U.S. were 19 %, whilst U.S. exports to Peru were 17.7 % of total Peruvian imports. Whilst this constituted a trade imbalance for the U.S., in 2008 the U.S. exports to Peru resulted in a trade balance for the U.S. For the U.S., the TPA would ensure that eighty per cent of the exports of consumer and industrial goods to Peru and about two-thirds of U.S. farm exports to Peru will be duty free upon entry into force of the TPA. The TPA is comprehensive in that it covers all the areas of trade under the WTO agreement in addition to agreements on

[52] Quoted in "U.S., Peru Strike Free-Trade Agreement", *The Washington Post*, Thursday, December 8, 2005, p. D06. In the President's view, practically all of Peruvian goods would enter the U.S. market duty free.

government procurement, competition policy, labour, environment, textiles, and apparel.

As with all other agreements entered into by the United States, with the exception of NAALC, the labour obligations of the TPA are included in the core text. Under the terms of the agreement, each party is required to adopt and maintain in its statutes and regulations the labour rights as stated in the ILO Declaration. The rights, as stated in the TPA, refer only to the ILO Declaration.[53] This has been seen as controversial and has been criticised by labour groups that the TPA does not require Peru to comply with the other international standards as laid down by the ILO but only the core labour standards. Each party is required not to derogate from the agreement in a manner that would affect trade or investment between the parties.[54]

On the issue of enforcement, each party is expected not to fail to effectively enforce its labour laws in accordance with Article 17.2.1 (the ILO Declaration), in addition to the party's own labour laws. This obligation is enforceable through the TPA dispute settlement procedures.[55] The TPA also contains procedural guarantees that persons with legally recognised interest in a particular issue would have appropriate access to tribunals and that workers and employers also have a fair, equitable, and transparent access to labour tribunals. Each party is also requested to promote a public awareness programme of its domestic labour laws.[56]

The TPA calls for the establishment of a "Labor Affairs Council" at the cabinet level or equivalent representatives of the parties. The responsibilities of the Council are to "oversee the implementation of and review progress" of the labour section of the TPA. The Council is also to develop general guidelines for the parties' consideration and resolution of issues.[57] Any party can request consultations with the other party on labour issues by a written request to the contact point of the other party.[58]

The TPA has a section on labour cooperation and capacity-building mechanism. The aim of this is the pursuit of bilateral and regional activities on labour issues, which include the rights under the ILO Declaration, compliance with ILO Convention 182 on the elimination of the worst forms of child labour; labour administration to strengthen the institutional capacity of labour administrations and labour tribunals; establishment and strengthening of alternative labour dispute resolution mechanisms in resolving labour disputes; improvement of social dialogue among workers, employers, and governments; cooperation to improve occupational safety and ensure health compliance; mechanisms and best practice to protect and promote the rights of migrant workers; programmes for social assistance and training;

---

[53] See U.S.–Peru Trade Promotion Agreement (TPA), Article 17.2.1 and footnote 2.

[54] TPA, Article 17.2.2.

[55] TPA, Article 17.3.1.

[56] TPA, Article 17.4.

[57] TPA, Article 17.5.

[58] TPA, Article 17.6.

development of programmes to promote new employment opportunities; and development of programmes on gender issues.[59]

The TPA has an extensive section on dispute settlement. Under the provisions of the dispute settlement procedures, should the parties fail to resolve an issue (which includes labour issues), with clear deadlines for resolution, any of the parties could then request in writing a meeting with the Commission (comprising of cabinet-level representatives). Should the Commission fail to resolve a matter, a party may request in writing the establishment of an arbitral panel. The TPA provides rules on the qualifications of panellists, panel selection, rules of procedure, third party participation, the role of experts, the initial report of the panel, the final report of the panel, how to implement the final report of the panel, and rules on non-implementation, which could lead to the suspension of benefits. Should the party complained against eliminate the nonconformity or the nullification or impairment found by the panel, the dispute settlement section provides for rules on review of parties compliance (Tables 7.2 and 7.3).

7.5 European Free Trade Agreements with Labour Provisions

The European Union (EU),[60] which began in the 1950s first as a coal and steel trade agreement, has today expanded in scope and size. It is now a customs union and is a single market in both goods and services trade. In addition to the free movement of workers within the Union, the EU has also developed a Social Charter, which states the fundamental workers' rights to be adhered to by all EU members. The approach adopted by the EU in its regional and bilateral arrangements is based on social development objectives encompassed in a cooperative framework. Whilst the EU recognises and promotes social rights and tends to improve cooperation, the agreements also include specific issues such as gender and health. It is important to note that the EU does not pursue a trade sanction-based approach as a means of getting its trading partners to adhere to the CLS. Rather, its approach is to offer additional tariff preferences to its trading partners to effectively implement the UN and ILO human/labour rights international conventions.

Included in the European Community Charter of Basic Social Rights are the following:

A. the right to freedom of association and collective bargaining;
B. the right of men and women to equal treatment;

---

[59] TPA, Annex 17.6.

[60] The members of the European Union (EU are) Austria, Belgium, Denmark, Finland, France, Germany, Greece, Ireland, Italy, Luxembourg, the Netherlands, Portugal, Spain, Sweden, the United Kingdom, and the newly acceded members Croatia, Cyprus, Czech Republic, Estonia, Hungary, Latvia, Lithuania, Malta, Poland, Romania, Slovakia, and Slovenia.

Table 7.3 Key labour aspects of U.S. Trade Agreements in all models

Agreement	NAFTA (1994)	U.S.–Jordan (2001)	U.S.–Chile (2004)/ Singapore (2004)/Australia (2005)/Morocco (2006)/Bahrain (2006)/Central America–Dominican Republic (CAFTA-DR) (2006)/Oman (2009)	U.S.– Peru (2009)/Korea (2011)/Panama & Colombia (not yet in force)
Model	1	2	3	4
Location of Provisions	In a side agreement	In the body of the agreement	In the body of the agreement	In the body of the agreement
Reference to ILO instruments	No	ILO 1998 Declaration	ILO 1998 Declaration, Convention No. 182 (worst forms of child labour)	ILO 1998 Declaration, Convention No. 182 (worst forms of child labour)
Basic labour provisions	Each Party: 1. Strives to improve domestic standards along 11 labor principles (which include ILO core labor standards and U.S. internationally recognized worker rights).	Each Party: 1. Strives to ensure that ILO labor principles and internationally recognized worker rights are protected by domestic law;	1. Same as in U. S.–Jordan	1. Same as in U. S.–Jordan
	2. Agrees to effectively enforce its own labor laws in a manner affecting trade.	2. Shall not fail to enforce its own labor laws in a manner affecting trade;	2. Same as in U. S.–Jordan	2. Same as in U. S.–Jordan.
	3. Retains discretion in allocating enforcement resources.	3. Retains discretion in allocating enforcement resources;	3. Same as in U. S.–Jordan.	3. Same as in U. S.–Jordan.
	4. No similar provision to item 4 as in models 2–4.	4. Agrees not to waive or derogate from domestic labor law to encourage trade.	4. Agrees not to waive or derogate from domestic labor law to encourage trade or investment.	4. Agrees not to waive or derogate from domestic labor law to encourage trade or investment.

(continued)

Table 7.3 (continued)

Agreement	NAFTA (1994)	U.S.–Jordan (2001)	U.S.–Chile (2004)/ Singapore (2004)/Australia (2005)/Morocco (2006)/Bahrain (2006)/Central America–Dominican Republic (CAFTA-DR) (2006)/Oman (2009)	U.S.– Peru (2009)/Korea (2011)/Panama & Colombia (not yet in force)
	5. May not undertake labor law enforcement in the other's territory.	5. No provision	5. Similar to NAFTA	5. Similar to NAFTA
	6. Is entitled to private remedies and procedural guarantees. Each Party	6. No provision	6. Similar to NAFTA	6. Similar to NAFTA
Labour provisions subject to panel proceedings and sanctions	Sanctions are authorized for failure to effectively enforce one's own occupational safety and health, child labor, or minimum wage standards in a manner that is trade-related and covered by mutually recognized labor laws.	Sanctions are authorized for all labor provisions.	Sanctions are authorized only for sustained failure to enforce one's own labor laws in a manner affecting trade.	Sanctions are authorized only for sustained failure to enforce one's own labor laws in a manner affecting trade.
Enforcement mechanism and maximum penalty	During first year of agreement: $20 million; thereafter 0.007 % of total trade between parties; maximum penalty for failure to pay fine: suspension of NAFTA benefits to the amount of the monetary enforcement assessment.	The affected party may take any appropriate and commensurate measure.	$15 million annually; for failure to pay: suspension of benefits to the equivalent dollar value	Regular trade sanctions or monetary assessment under the regular dispute settlement mechanism of the agreement

Source: Congressional Research Service [See Bolle (2009), CRS-6 and Ebert and Posthuma (2011)]

C. the improvement of living and working conditions;
D. the right to information, consultation, and participation;
E. the protection of children and adolescents in employment;
F. the right to freedom of movement;
G. employment and remuneration;
H. the right to social protection;
I. the right to vocational training;
J. the right to health and safety in the workplace;
K. the protection of elderly persons;
L. the protection of persons with disabilities.

Due to the scope and nature of the European Union, it appears to be one of the best examples of incorporating social concerns, in particular rights of workers in economic integration agreements. It is important to note that the EU started as a social and economic integration and as a way to secure peace and social equality in the aftermath of the Second World War.

The impression the EU has given in other parts of the world on the incorporation of labour standards in trade agreements appears to be positive, making some advocate that it is a model to follow.[61] In spite of this positive picture, the EU has been criticised for not doing enough, in terms of labour standards, when negotiating trade agreements with other countries.[62] The examples given are the EU trade agreements with Mexico and also with South Africa, which have no provisions on the promotion or protection of labour standards.

Grynberg and Qalo (2006) argue that since the U.S. had already entered into NAFTA with Mexico and that the labour standard provisions under NAALC is applicable on an MFN basis (in this case applicable to the EU), there was no need to include labour standard provisions in the European Communities (EC)–Mexico agreement. They argue further that if the EU was serious about including labour standards in trade agreements, the EU would have made concerted efforts to consolidate the labour provisions in NAALC by strengthening those provisions in the EC–Mexico FTA.[63]

In this subsection, we will consider five trade agreements signed by the EU with other countries. One of the agreements has provisions on cooperation in the social field, which encompasses the social responsibility that the parties bear towards

[61] See Brecher and Costello (1994).

[62] For example, the Trade Union Congress (TUC) states that even though the EU has made positive statements about the need to include labour standards in trade agreements, the EU seems to be less inclined to push strongly for it. According to the TUC, the reasons given by the EU is that developing countries object on the ground that any inclusion of workers' rights is only a protectionist ploy and a move to undermine the competitive advantage of the developing countries. See http://www.tuc.org.uk/international/tuc-13751-f0.cfm. Accessed 11 March 2014.

[63] For a discussion of the history of EU initial caution in including labour provisions in RTAs and the developments that have led to the change in the EU approach to integrating economic and social dimensions of trade and development as is the case in recent RTAs, see Kenner (2011).

workers. The other is the first agreement between the EU and another trading partner that makes reference to labour standards.

Earlier trade agreements entered into by the EU focused on dialogue and cooperation at the governmental level. However, the more recent agreements, such as the EU–CARIFORUM States Partnership Agreement, Republic of Korea, Colombia, and Peru, have established a more wide-ranging institutional mechanism that involves social partners and other stakeholders in implementing the labour provisions in the agreements. This makes a major improvement in the EU approach to the inclusion of labour standards in its trade agreements.

7.5.1 Euro-Mediterranean Association Agreements

In 1995, the EU started the "Barcelona process", a partnership with the countries of the Southern Mediterranean.[64] The negotiations led to the replacement of the 1970s Cooperation Agreements with the Mediterranean partners. The agreements all have provisions on "cooperation in the social field".[65] This section of the agreement deals with social matters and state that the parties agree to undertake regular dialogue to realise the objectives. The cooperation in the social field includes equal treatment of workers, social domain concerning living and working conditions of migrants, migrations, and social protection. The agreements provide for dialogue with respect to "social problems of post-industrial societies such as unemployment, rehabilitation of disabled people and vocational training". The association agreements do not make reference to the ILO labour standards, but reference is made to respect for democratic principles and fundamental human rights as set out in the Universal Declaration of Human Rights, which the agreements consider a significant element.[66] Grynberg and Qalo (2006) argue that even though the core labour standards cannot be compared to the Universal Declaration of Human Rights (UDHR) since the CLS are more detailed, the reference nonetheless constitutes specifications that, in their view, relate to UDHR.[67] For example, the UDHR calls for the abolition of child labour and sets a basic minimum age for young ones in employment.[68]

[64] The countries are the People's Democratic Republic of Algeria (2001), the Arab Republic of Egypt (2004), the Hashemite Kingdom of Jordan (2002), the State of Israel (2000), the Kingdom of Morocco (2000), the Republic of Tunisia (1998), Lebanon (2002), and the Palestinian Authority (1997).

[65] Article 74 of the EU–Algeria Association Agreement, Article 71 of the EU–Morocco and EU–Tunisia Association Agreements, Article 65 EU–Egypt and EU–Lebanon Association Agreements, and Article 62 of the EU–Jordan Association Agreement.

[66] Article 2 of the EU–Algeria, EU–Morocco, EU–Tunisia, EU–Egypt, EU–Israel, EU–Jordan, EU–Lebanon and EU–Palestine Association Agreements.

[67] Gyrnberg and Qalo (2006), p. 642.

[68] Article 2(3) of the Universal Declaration of Human Rights Convention.

Under the terms of the agreements, the parties reserve the right to prohibit or restrict the importation or exportation of goods on grounds of public morality, public policy, or public security; for the protection of health and life of human, animals, or plants, among others, the agreement provides that the prohibitions and restrictions do not constitute arbitrary discrimination or disguised restriction on trade.[69] The prohibitions and restrictions stated in the agreements are similar to those stipulated in GATT Article XX (General Exceptions). Without explicitly referring to labour standards, the inclusion in the agreements to prohibition and restriction of goods on public morality grounds could include, for example, goods produced with child labour.

The settling of disputes under the association agreements is uncomplicated. The agreement requires the Association Council to settle disputes by means of a decision in relation to the application or interpretation of the agreements. Should the Council fail to reach a decision, then either party may appoint an arbitrator and the Association Council will appoint a third arbitrator. The decision of the arbitrators is by a majority vote.[70] Under the terms of the agreement, if a party fails to fulfil its obligation under the agreement, the other party can take "appropriate measures". However, the agreement requires the complaining party to give priority to measures that least disturb the functioning of the agreement.[71]

7.5.2 European Community–Chile Association Agreement (EC–Chile FTA)

On 18 November 2002, the EC and Chile signed a free trade agreement that established a political and economic association covering a wide range of areas, such as services, investment, government procurement, competition, intellectual property, and dispute settlement. The agreement comprises three pillars: political dialogue, cooperation, and trade. The building blocks of the agreement are the respect for democratic principles and fundamental human rights and the promotion of sustainable economic and social development.[72]

---

[69] Article 26 of EU–Egypt Association Agreement, Article 27 of EU–Algeria, EU–Israel, EU, Jordan and EU–Lebanon Association Agreements, Article 28 of EU–Morocco and EU–Tunisia Association Agreements, Article 24 of EU–Palestine Association Agreement and Article 67 of EU–Algeria Association Agreement.

[70] Article 62 of EU–Egypt Association Agreement, Article 75 of EU–Israel Association Agreement, Article 97 of EU–Jordan Association Agreement, Article 82 of EU–Lebanon Association Agreement, Article 67 of the EU–Palestine Agreement, Article 100 of the EU–Algeria Association Agreement and Article 86 of the EU–Morocco and the EU–Tunisia Association Agreements.

[71] Article 86 of EU–Egypt Association Agreement, Article 79 of EU–Israel Association Agreement, Article 101 of EU–Jordan Association Agreement, Article 86 of EU–Lebanon Association Agreement, Article 70 of the EU–Palestine Agreement, Article 104 of the EU–Algeria Association Agreement, Article 90 of the EU–Morocco and Article 70 the EU–Tunisia Association Agreements.

[72] EC–Chile Association Agreement, Article 1(1) and (2).

The preamble of the Association Agreement makes reference to the respect for democratic principles and fundamental human rights based on the UN Universal Declaration of Human Rights. The preamble also makes reference to the need to promote economic and social progress. These ideals are also repeated in Title I, Article 1. Under Article 16(1), the Agreement, in addition to mentioning the need to strengthen their respective institutional capacity to support "democracy, the rule of law and respect for human rights and fundamental freedoms", reference is also made to promoting social development, which the parties' state should work hand in hand with economic development. The need to work to reinforce social and economic development bodes well for adherence to the CLS, which to effectively achieve entails working on both the social and economic fronts.

Also in Article 44 of the agreement under Title V, Social Cooperation, the parties once again indicate their recognition of the importance of social development, which is put on equal level with economic development. For the first time in EC trade agreements, reference is made in Article 44 to the promotion of the relevant conventions of the ILO with particular mention of the core labour standards.[73] Furthermore, under Article 44, priority is given to the promotion of human development, poverty reduction, and the fight against social exclusion. The article also includes the promotion of the role of women, development and modernisation of labour relations, development of an efficient health service, and promotion of job creation.[74]

The formulation of the "Social Cooperation" section under Title V under the Agreement appears to be more of a promotional nature rather than enforceable rights. Whilst the parties agree to cooperate on social issues, there is no reference to consultations on the interpretation and application of the issues raised and on how to achieve the priorities under this section.

The dispute settlement system in the Agreement is built on the WTO dispute settlement system. Article 183 provides for consultations between the parties. Articles 184–188 also provide for elaborate procedures, appointment of arbitrators, information and technical advice, arbitration panel rulings, and compliance of the rulings. Given the nature of the dispute settlement procedures, it is not clear how the social issues raised under Title V could be enforced.

The EC–Chile FTA can be differentiated from the U.S. FTAs in that the trading partners are not required to incorporate labour standards in their domestic laws nor do the EC expect its trading partners to recognise labour standards that do not form part of the ILO core labour standards.

[73] EC–Chile Association Agreement, Article 44.1 states: "The Parties recognise the importance of social development, which must go hand in hand with economic development. They shall give priority to the creation of employment and respect for fundamental social rights, notably by promoting the relevant conventions of the International Labour Organisation covering such topics as the freedom of association, the right to collective bargaining and non-discrimination, the abolition of forced and child labour and equal treatment between men and women."

[74] EC–Chile Association Agreement, Article 44.4.

7.5.3 EU–ACP Agreement (The Cotonou Agreement and the Economic Partnership Agreements)

The Cotonou Agreement signed on 23 June 2003 in Cotonou, Benin, is a successor to a series of agreements called the Lomé Conventions. The Cotonou Agreement brings together the EU and 79 countries from Africa, the Caribbean and the Pacific (ACP). The new Cotonou Agreement builds on the expired Lomé Convention, dating back from 1975 and provided for development cooperation and trade preferences for the former colonies of the EC Member States.

The EU–ACP relationship, in fact, dates back to the formation of the EC, and the trade preferences were contained in successive Yaoundé Conventions. The idea behind the EU's trade policy with the ACP countries is that its former colonies need help to export their products. The EU–ACP cooperation began in 1958, when six members of the then EC granted unilateral aid to the overseas countries and territories that were placed under its jurisdiction. These arrangements were made to address a broad range of development issues, including financial aid, good governance, and sustainable development. The Agreements are non-reciprocal and provide for preferential access to the EU market for Members of the ACP countries.

The Cotonou Agreement maps out ACP–EU relations up to 2020 (with a revision scheduled every 5 years). It provides for a framework in three main areas:

- political dialogue,
- development support,
- economic and trade cooperation.

The Cotonou Agreement established a framework agreement for the conclusion of Economic Partnership Agreements (EPAs)[75] and has as one of its objectives the economic, cultural, and social development of the ACP countries. The Agreement entered into force on 8 June 2003 and is to be superseded by the EPAs. The non-reciprocal arrangement was granted a waiver by the WTO Membership and was meant to expire in 2008. The trade provisions were to be renegotiated between 2002 and 2008, leading to the establishment of FTAs in line with GATT Article XXIV.

The Agreement has five pillars: a political dimension, participatory approaches, poverty reduction, a framework for economic and trade cooperation, and a reform of financial cooperation (on aid assistance). The Agreement provided under Articles 9, 13, and 26 on human rights and committed "Parties [to] undertake to promote and protect all fundamental freedoms and human rights, be they civil and political, or

---

[75] The ACP Group of countries have been divided into seven negotiating configurations: five in Africa (Southern African Development Community (SADC), Eastern and Southern Africa (ESA), East African Community (EAC), Economic Community of West African States and Mauritania (ECOWAS), Economic Community of Central African States (CEMAC), plus the Democratic Republic of Congo and São Tomé and Príncipe. For the Pacific is the Pacific Islands Forum (PIF) and for the Caribbean, the Caribbean Forum of Caribbean States (CARIFORUM).

economic, social and cultural". In the event of non-compliance, the Agreement provides under Article 96 a review mechanism and also the possibility of "appropriate measures".

The Lomé Convention that expired in February 2000 introduced new commitments such as the promotion of human rights and respect for democracy into the agreement. The Cotonou Agreement, in addition to the human rights dimension, broadened the scope with the inclusion of provisions relating to labour standards. The labour standard clauses are contained in Article 50 and provides as follows:

7.5.3.1 Trade and Labour Standards

1. The Parties reaffirm their commitment to the internationally recognised labour standards, as defined by the relevant International Labour Organisation (ILO) Conventions, and in particular the freedom of association and the right to collective bargaining, the abolition of forced labour, the elimination of worst forms of child labour and non-discrimination in respect to employment.
2. They agree to enhance cooperation in this area, in particular in the following fields:
   - exchange of information on the respective legislation and work regulation;
   - the formulation of national labour legislation and work regulation;
   - educational and awareness-raising programmes;
   - enforcement of adherence to national legislation and work regulation.
3. The Parties agree that labour standards should not be used for protectionist trade purposes.

The Trade and Labour Standards clause provides general provisions on trade-related areas and states that the EC shall support the ACP countries' efforts to strengthen their capacity to handle all areas related to trade, including improving and supporting the institutional framework.

The Agreement under Article 98 on dispute settlement provides that any dispute arising from the interpretation or application of this Agreement between one or more Member States of the Community, on the one hand, and one or more ACP countries, on the other hand, shall be submitted to the Council of Ministers and that each party may appoint an arbitrator. Should one or both parties fail to do so, either party may ask the Secretary General of the Permanent Court of Arbitration to appoint the second arbitrator. The parties to the dispute shall be bound by measures necessary to carry out the decision.

It is important to note that in both the clauses on human rights and trade and labour, reference is made to the international human rights law and to the ILO Conventions. Article 50(3) states that labour standards should not be used for protectionist purposes. This is very important for the ACP countries since one of the major arguments against the inclusion of a social clause in the WTO Agreement is the fear that developed countries would use the labour standard clauses to protect their industries.

The labour standard provisions in the Cotonou Agreement whilst not creating further obligations beyond the parties' commitment to the ILO Conventions, provide for cooperation and capacity building. Article 55 provides for development of finance cooperation aimed at supporting and promoting the efforts of ACP countries to achieve the objectives set out in the Agreement by providing adequate financial and technical assistance. This is similar to the provisions in the U.S.–CAFTA-DR and Colombia Agreements. The Cotonou Agreement further provides for educational and awareness-raising programmes. Article 26 refers to the rights of children and, in particular, mentions primary education as an area of cooperation. Article 44 also states that the EU shall support the ACP countries to strengthen their capacity to handle all areas that are trade related. This goes beyond the provisions in the United States FTAs in protecting children rights and provision of education.

7.5.4 EU–CARIFORUM States Partnership Agreement

On 15 October 2008, the EU signed an Economic Partnership Agreement (EPA) with the CARIFORUM States.[76] The CARIFORUM Economic Partnership Agreement, as discussed in the section above, is part of the Economic Partnership Agreements that the EU is negotiating with the African, Caribbean and Pacific countries in order to resolve the issue of compatibility of EU Agreements with the ACP Group of Nations with the WTO since under WTO rules, developed countries are required to treat all developing countries equally under the MFN principle and not to give more favourable treatment to only those countries that, for example, EU has historical or cultural ties with, as it was the case under the Cotonou trade arrangements.

Negotiations leading to the signing of the Partnership Agreement dates back to April 2004, when the EU launched a comprehensive and far-reaching agreement with an ambitious plan covering the full range of trade issues such as, competition, public procurement, innovation and intellectual property, environment, protection of personal data, and social aspects—under which labour standard issues fall.

EU-CARIFORUM Agreement is the first trade agreement to be concluded under the overall framework of the EPAs and signifies the start of new trade relations between the EU and the CARIFORUM countries, which both the EU and the CARIFORUM countries see as a comprehensive agreement with strong develop-

[76] The CARIFORUM States are Antigua and Barbuda, the Commonwealth of the Bahamas, Barbados, Belize, the Commonwealth of Dominica, the Dominican Republic, Grenada, the Republic of Guyana, the Republic of Haiti, Jamaica, Saint Christopher and Nevis, Saint Lucia, Saint Vincent and the Grenadines, the Republic of Suriname, and the Republic of Trinidad and Tobago.

ment dimensions and components.[77] The Agreement has been hailed as using "the tools of trade and investment liberalisation to contribute to the realization of broader policy goals: sustainable development and regional integration in the Caribbean area".[78]

7.5.4.1 Respect for Core Labour Standards

The preamble of the Partnership Agreement reaffirms the signatories' commitment to the respect for human rights, democratic principles, and the rule of law. Also in the preamble, the signatories consider the need to promote economic and social development as a means of promoting "a stable and democratic political environment". The preamble then considers the importance of respect for the ILO CLS when it states:

> CONSIDERING the need to promote economic and social progress for their people in a manner consistent with sustainable development by respecting basic labour rights in line with the commitments they have undertaken within the International Labour Organisation ...[79]

Labour standards are considered in chapter 5 of the Agreement entitled 'Social Aspects'. Article 191(1) states:

> The Parties reaffirm their commitment to the internationally recognised core labour standards, as defined by the relevant ILO Conventions, and in particular the freedom of association and the right to collective bargaining, the abolition of forced labour, the elimination of the worst forms of child labour and nondiscrimination in respect to employment. The Parties also reaffirm their obligations as members of the ILO and their commitments under the ILO Declaration on Fundamental Principles and Rights at Work and its Follow-Up (1998).

The Parties also reaffirm their commitment in Article 191(2) to the UN Economic and Social Council on Full Employment and the ILO Decent Work Agenda. The Parties further provide a link between international trade and full and productive employment as a means of achieving decent work for all sections of society. It is also interesting to note in Article 191(3) that the Parties show recognition of the beneficial role of the CLS and decent work in achieving economic efficiency and concludes this section by showing the need for policy coherence between trade policies and employment and social policies.

Whilst recognising the importance of respect for the CLS, the Agreement in Article 192 also recognises the right of each of the signatory countries to regulate and also establish social regulations and labour standards in accordance with their

---

[77] See the views of the EU and CARIFORUM at http://www.caricom.org/jsp/community_organs/epa_unit/epa_in_context.jsprespectively. Accessed on 5 April 2014.

[78] Zampetti (2011), pp. 179–180.

[79] Preamble of the Economic Partnership Agreement between the CARIFORUM States, of the one part, and the European Community and its Member States, of the other part.

developmental priorities and each of the signatory countries having the freedom to adopt or modify their relevant laws and policies. Also important is that even though each of the Parties have that freedom, each "shall (*making it mandatory,* italics added) ensure that its own social and labour regulations and policies provide for and encourage high levels of social and labour standards consistent with the internationally recognised rights set forth in Article 191 and shall strive to continue to improve those laws and policies".

The Agreement in Article 193 also provides for upholding the levels of protection by stating that the Parties, in order to attract FDI, should not lower the level of protection as stipulated in domestic social and labour legislation and not derogate from the legislation. Article 194 provides for the need for a regional dimension in promoting decent work as a means of boosting the individual regulatory processes with emphasis on the regional approach.

Article 195 provides for a consultation and monitory process through their respective domestic processes, as well as the mechanisms set up under the Agreement. The Agreement calls for the set-up of the CARIFORUM-EC Consultative Committee on social issues contained in Articles 191–194. The Consultative Committee can, if it so wishes, submit oral and written recommendations to the Parties on social issues. Parties have the liberty to seek advice from the ILO on social issues, and Parties may also request consultations with other Parties with respect to the interpretation and application of Articles 191–194.

The provision for consultations is for a period of 3 months, which can be extended to 6 months when the advice of the ILO is sought. Should the matter not be resolved through consultations, any Party can exercise its right to request that a Committee of Experts be convened to review the matter. The Committee is expected to present to the Parties its report within a period of 3 months. Further to this is the section on cooperation, which the Parties consider to be important in order to achieve the social and labour issue components of the Agreement (Article 196). This Article calls for cooperation in four areas, namely (1) exchange of information, (2) formulation of national social and labour legislation, (3) educational and awareness-raising programmes, and (4) enforcement of adherence to national legislation and work regulation.

7.5.4.2 Dispute Settlement System

The Agreement in Part III between Articles 202 and 223 contains very detailed procedures on dispute avoidance and settlement. However, Article 204(6) indicates that a Party cannot bring a dispute with respect to the interpretation and application of issues under 'Social Aspects' (under which respect for the CLS fall), "unless the procedures of Article 189(3), (4) and (5) and Article 195(3), (4) and (5), respectively have been invoked and the matter has not been satisfactorily resolved within 9 months of the initiation of the consultations. Consultations pursuant to those provisions shall replace those which would have been required under this Article." In this respect, the consultations undertaken under Article 195 would substitute the consultations under the dispute settlement chapter. It is important to note that in the event of a dispute involving the interpretation of social issues, the penultimate sentence of Article 213(2) provides that "appropriate measures shall not include the suspension of trade concessions . . ."

The EPA dispute settlement system is very much based on the WTO dispute settlement system. The consultation, panel, and compliance stages are in large part based on the WTO system. A review of the dispute settlement system under this agreement indicates the predisposition towards negotiating solutions to the issues that might arise rather than litigation. However, should a dispute be brought under the system, the procedures provide for an "expeditious, equitable and effective means to resolve . . ."[80] In respect of recourse to the dispute settlement should the Committee of Experts fail to resolve issues on CLS and also the fact that Article 213 (2) does not allow a party to suspend trade concessions, it is indicated that the parties should consider compliance with the CLS as merely a developmental issue that does not require the use of trade measures to resolve.

The CARIFORUM–EU Economic Partnership Agreement like the EC–Chile Association Agreement only commits the Parties to respect the ILO CLS. The affirmation of the Parties' commitment to the CLS is based on the fact that all the signatories are also Members of the ILO and are bound by the ILO Declaration of Fundamental Principles and Rights at Work, which encompass the CLS. What is interesting is the link between trade and the respect for the CLS and the aim of promoting decent work at the regional level. The emphasis on the link between respect for the CLS, decent work, and economic efficiency at both the national and regional levels indicates the extent to which the Parties are prepared to work towards the overarching aim of the Partnership Agreement in achieving sustainable development.[81]

7.5.5 EU–Republic of Korea FTA

On 6 October 2010, the European Union and the Republic of Korea (South Korea) signed a free trade agreement. With the ratification of the agreement by both the EU

[80] Brown (2011). Brown also provides an in-depth review of the dispute settlement system of the CARIFORUM–EU Agreement.

[81] A number of issues have been raised as to how the EPA would contribute to CARIFORUM countries' development. For example, the Economic Commission for Latin America and the Caribbean (ECLAC) has conducted an analysis of the implications of the EPA. The report conducted showed that when the EPA is implemented, it would pose some challenges for the region. Furthermore, the report also states that according to preliminary estimates, the CARIFORUM countries stand to lose as much as US$300 million annually in tariffs should they resort to the GSP scheme, with far reaching implications. In the view of the ECLAC, further study needed to be undertaken to determine the exact nature of the impact. See ECLAC (2008).

Parliament and the South Korean National Assembly, the agreement went into effect on 1 July 2011.

The Agreement is very comprehensive and includes liberalisation of tariffs, non-tariff barriers, and services. In addition, the agreement includes new disciplines such as competition policy. Although areas such as intellectual property is not new, the parties have undertaken commitments that build on or even deepen commitments that they have already committed to at the multilateral level (the so-called WTO-plus provisions). The Agreement also has a chapter on workers' rights and environmental standards.

The Parties in the preamble of the Agreement reaffirms their commitment to the Universal Declaration of Human Rights and also their commitment to sustainable development with reference to economic, social, and environmental dimensions as a means of reducing poverty, full and productive employment, and decent work. The preamble also mentions the desire of the parties to strengthen "development and enforcement of labour and environmental laws and policies" as a means of promoting basic workers' rights and sustainable development . . ."[82]

Under chapter one, Article 1.1(h), the Parties whilst seeking to promote FDI, specifically states that there should be no lowering or reducing of labour standards in the application and enforcement of the labour laws of the Parties.

7.5.5.1 Respect for the Core Labour Standards[83]

Labour standards are considered under chapter 13, entitled "Trade and Sustainable Development". Article 13.1 defines the scope of the "trade-related aspects of

[82] Preamble of Free Trade Agreement between the European Union and its Member States, of the one part, and the Republic of Korea, of the other part.

[83] Prior to the signing of the EU–Korea FTA, the Republic of Korea's memberships of the ILO in 1991 and the OECD in 1996 have positively influenced its labour relation record. As at March 2011, Korea had not ratified the fundamental ILO Conventions: 87 and 98 on Freedom of Association and the effective recognition of the right to collective bargaining. The history of improving the industrial relations climate in the country started after the Asian financial crisis of 1998. This led in part to the creation of a Tripartite Commission of government officials, employers, and workers. The creation of the Tripartite Commission was a milestone in industrial relations in Korea and would not have been possible due to the hostile nature of the relationship between the government and labour. The compromise reached by the Tripartite Commission in the areas of reform and the resulting social compact was important in that it improved the government's ability to manage the financial crisis and thus played a role in Korea overcoming the crisis. The case of industrial relations in Korea during the financial crisis shows how labour activities run in sharp contrast to the general belief that globalisation strengthened the power of employers vis-à-vis employees. In the South Korean case, developments rather strengthened the power of labour through increased union activity. This is an example of how organised union activities, in conjunction with international organisations, notably the ILO, can in a period of crisis turn it into an opportunity in bringing about changes for the better and helping to resolve the contentious issue of the linkage between labour standards and economic development and, in particular, international trade. See also Kim and Kim (2003).

labour". The footnote to that Article provides more clarification on the scope by stating that labour as referred to in the Agreement "includes issues relevant to the Decent Work Agenda and 2006 Ministerial Declaration of the UN Economic and Social Council on Full Employment and Decent Work".[84]

Under the Agreement, both Parties recognise the right of each to establish their own levels of labour protection and also to adopt or even modify their laws and policies to ensure that those laws and policies encourage high labour protection.[85] The Parties also state that they "recognise the importance of international cooperation and agreements on employment and labour affairs as a response of the international community to economic, employment and social challenges and opportunities resulting from globalisation".[86] This recognition is important as acknowledgement by the Parties of the impact of globalisation on employment and its attendant social effects. What is also interesting is the latter part of Article 13.4, where the Parties commit themselves to consulting and cooperating on trade-related labour and employment issues.[87]

In Article 13.4(2), the Parties once again make reference to the 2006 Ministerial Declaration of the UN Economic and Social Council on Full Employment and Decent Work whilst recognising that the key elements of sustainable development are full and productive employment and decent work for all. The Parties' commitment of using international trade in a way that boosters full and productive employment and decent work is a laudable objective that if included in a multilateral agreement with a clear link between trade and compliance with the CLS could contribute to sustainable development and probably assist in the efforts of achieving decent work, especially during crisis such as the recent financial crisis, as a way to lessen the social impact on many people.

In Article 13.4(3), both sides commit themselves by virtue of their membership of the ILO to the ILO 1998 Declaration on Fundamental Principles and Rights at Work. This Article further states that the Parties would effectively implement the ILO Conventions that they have ratified. Interestingly, the Parties commit themselves to making continued and sustained efforts in ratifying fundamental ILO Conventions, "as well as the other Conventions that are classified as 'up-to-date' by the ILO".[88]

7.5.5.2 Dispute Settlement

In settling any dispute arising under the "Trade and Sustainable Development" section (Chapter 13), Article 13.16 provides that "[f]or any matter arising under this

[84] See footnote 84 of the EU/Korea FTA.
[85] Article 13.3 of the EU/Korea FTA.
[86] Article 13.4 of the EU/Korea FTA.
[87] Article 13.4 of the EU/Korea FTA.
[88] Article 13.4 of the EU/Korea FTA.

Chapter, the Parties shall only have recourse to the procedures provided for in Articles 13.14 and 13.15".[89]

Article 13.14 states that in any matter with respect to the provisions under Chapter 13, either party may request consultations with the other party, including the communications of the Domestic Advisory Group(s),[90] by sending a written request to the contact point of the other Party, with consultations to commence promptly in resolving the issue(s). The composition of the Domestic Advisory Group(s) is very interesting for Article 13.12(5) calls for a balanced representation of independent representative organisations such as civil society of environmental organisations, labour groups and business organisations, and other relevant stakeholders.

Article 13.14(2) states that the parties are to make every effort in reaching a satisfactory resolution of the issue. The inclusion of the resolution of the matter to reflect the activities of the ILO "so at to promote greater cooperation and coherence between the work of the Parties and these organisations" shows the importance that the parties attach to work of organisations such as the ILO. The Article also provides for seeking the advice of organisations or bodies in the resolution of the matter.

It is only when a party considers that the matter should be further discussed that the party could request that the Committee on Trade and Sustainable Development be convened to consider the matter.[91] Further to the satisfactory resolution of the matter, Article 13.15 provides for a party to request that a Panel of Experts be convened to examine the matter. This provision is available only after 90 days of the delivery of a written request for consultations. The parties can make submissions to the Panel of Experts and the Panel is to seek information and advice from the parties, the Domestic Advisory Group(s),[92] and international organisations, as stipulated in Article 13.14, if the Panel deems this to be appropriate.

The EU–Korea FTA is a clear example of the EU approach to resolving labour issues within trade agreements. The agreement only provides for resolution of any matter arising under the labour section through consultations and does not provide for sanctions. his is also evident in the CARIFORUM agreement. However, the approach adopted by the EU, especially in the agreement with Korea, whereby ensuring compliance through the set-up of "civil society groups" comprising of a mix of business, labour, and environmental organisations opens a new chapter in making sure that matters on labour, which we have argued above is a combination of many issues, is resolved in a coherent manner. This policy coherence approach to resolving, in particular, labour issues provides a good framework for resolving an issue that cuts across a plethora of other issues and disciplines (Table 7.4).

---

[89] Articles 13.14 and 13.15 are respectively entitled: "Government consultations" and "Panel of Experts".

[90] Article 13.12(2) calls for the establishment of Domestic Advisory Group(s) on sustainable development in the implementation of Chapter 13. The composition of the Domestic Advisory Group(s) is very interesting.

[91] Article 13.14(3).

[92] Article 13.15(1).

Table 7.4 EU trade agreements with labour provisions

Name and date of entry into force of the trade agreements	Reference to ILO instruments	Scope of provisions
Trade Agreements with the Palestinian Authority (1997), Morocco (2000), Israel (2000), Algeria (2005), Cameroon (2009)	No	Cooperation and/or dialogue on selected issues related to labour standards
Trade Agreement with Chile (2003)	Fundamental Conventions	Commitment to give priority to the respect for basic social rights, including through the promotion of ILO Fundamental Conventions and social dialogue Cooperation on various labour and social issues
Trade Agreements with South Africa (2000), ACP Countries (2003)	Fundamental Conventions	Reaffirms the parties' commitment to the ILO's CLS Cooperation on various labour and/or social issues
Trade Agreement with the CARIFORUM Countries (2008)	1998 Declaration, Fundamental Conventions	Commitment on (1) ensuring compliance with ILO CLS, (2) not weakening or failing to apply national labour legislation to encourage trade or investment Cooperation, and (3) monitoring framework with stakeholder participation, optional ILO consultation Framework for amicable solution of differences—if the dispute cannot be solved through consultation, appropriate measures other than on trade sanctions may be taken (e.g., readjustment of cooperation activities)

Source: Ebert and Posthuma (2011)

7.6 Regional Trade Agreements of Canada with Labour Provisions

The first free trade agreement that Canada signed was in 1989 with the United States, which has since been superseded by NAFTA, signed in 1994 to include Mexico. Since 1997, Canada has signed eight regional trade agreements, but only six are in force.

The Canadian agreements follow the model of the NAALC, whereby the labour provisions are not included in the main agreement but in a side agreement (Labour Cooperation Agreements). Below, we provide a brief overview of the labour provisions in three agreements (Canada FTAs with Chile (1997), Costa Rica (2002), and Colombia (2011)).

In the sections below, we will review under each of the three agreements the preambles and the scope of the labour provisions. But we will jointly review the segments under labour institutions and agencies, dispute settlement mechanisms, and enforcement mechanisms. The reason for this is that even though the preambles and labour provisions segments are similar, it is instructive to point out certain provisions that are important and unique to each of the agreements. Under the other segment, the labour institutions and agencies and dispute settlement and enforcement mechanisms follow a similar pattern.

7.6.1 Canada–Chile Free Trade Agreement (CCFTA)

Canada and Chile signed a free trade agreement on 5 December 1996, and the agreement came into force on July 1997. As already stated above, the labour provisions are included not in the text of the agreement but rather as a side agreement. This agreement was the first Canada RTA with a labour side agreement after NAALC.

The agreement does not make reference to any ILO instrument, nor does it directly mention the CLS or the ILO 1998 Declaration, but it defines "labour law" in Article 44, as referred to in Article 3(1),[93] to include 11 labour principles similar to the labour principles under NAALC.

The Parties in the preamble of the labour cooperation agreement state their desire to "build on their respective international commitments and to strengthen their cooperation on labour matters".[94] The text indicates that even though the agreement came into force before both Parties signed onto the ILO 1998 Declaration, their commitments to respect and promote the principles in the Declaration applies under this agreement. It is important to note that whilst the Parties state that each should "promote compliance with and effectively enforce its labour law through appropriate government action",[95] the earlier statements in the preamble are an indication of how to achieve that.

In the preamble, the Parties resolved to promote in line with the laws in each of their countries to strengthen "labour–management cooperation to promote greater dialogue between worker organizations and employers ..." The preamble further states that the Parties are resolved to "encouraging consultation and dialogue between labour, business and government". This part of the preamble is closely aligned with the tripartite system of the ILO. And it is further reinforced by the work of the ministerial Council under the auspices of "The Canada–Chile Commission on Labour Cooperation" in Part Three of the side agreement. Article 11 of the side agreement under "Cooperative Activities" provides a list of such

[93] Article 3(1) states: "Each Party shall promote compliance with and effectively enforce its labour law through appropriate government action ..."

[94] Preamble of the Canada–Chile Free Trade Agreement.

[95] Article 3(1) of Canada–Chile Free Trade Agreement.

cooperative activities to be carried out between the Parties, and this includes activities under "labour–management relations and collective bargaining procedures".

It is important to note that in Article 11(2), the Parties agree that in carrying out the cooperative activities referred to in Article 11(1), attention should be given to "the economic, social, cultural and legislative differences between them". This appears to respond to any issue that could arise as to how two countries with different levels of economic and social development could be cooperative on labour issues.

7.6.2 Canada–Costa Rica Free Trade Agreement

The Canada–Costa Rica FTA came into force on 1 November 2002. Just as in the case of the FTA with Chile, the labour provisions of the FTA are contained in a side agreement. In the preamble of the Agreement, the Parties recalled their resolve to not only "create new employment opportunities and improve working conditions and living standards" but in doing so to also "protect, enhance and enforce basic workers' rights".[96]

The Preamble also acknowledges the importance of technical cooperation in labour issues; this, the Parties acknowledge, would ensure that the strategies formulated in achieving economic and social development would reinforce sustainable development. The Parties also stated their recognition of the fact that there are differences in "their respective levels of development and sizes of their economies". As in the case of the Canada–Chile side agreement, Article 12, in conjunction with Annex 3 of this Agreement on "Cooperative Activities", provides the framework to achieving the objectives of the Agreement. The activities to be carried out in Annex 3 are very important for labour standards compliance in a developing country such as Costa Rica in strengthening institutional capacity; strengthening and improving labour inspectorates; strengthening the sections dealing with social security, gender issues, people with disabilities, and young persons; and, finally, modernising the systems of alternative dispute resolution.[97]

Under the objectives of the Agreement, the Parties state their desire to "promote to the maximum extent possible, the labour principles and rights set out in Annexes 1 and 2". Whilst Annex 1 refers to the ILO 1998 Declaration, Annex 2 lists additional labour principles, namely "minimum employment standards; prevention of occupational injuries and illnesses; and compensation in cases of occupational injuries or illnesses".

---

[96] See Preamble to Agreement on Labour Cooperation between the Government of Canada and the Government of the Republic of Costa Rica.

[97] Annex 3 of the Agreement on Labour Cooperation between the Government of Canada and the Government of the Republic of Costa Rica.

7.6.3 Canada–Colombia Free Trade Agreement

The Canada–Colombia FTA came into force on 15 August 2011, making it the fourth FTA between Canada and a South American country. Similar to the other agreements, the labour provisions are in a side agreement. The preamble of the Agreement recalls the resolve of the Parties to "protect, enhance and enforce basic workers' right; strengthen cooperation on labour matters; and build on their respective international commitments on labour matters".

The Parties state their recognition of the importance of "encouraging consultation and dialogue between labour, business and government".[98] This, as in the Costa Rica FTA, is a clear indication of the Parties' recognition of the importance of using the ILO tripartite system to strengthen labour relations. The Parties also recognised the importance of corporate social responsibility and also of "coherence between labour and economic objectives". This is important in ensuring that economic development goes hand in hand with social progress.

The Agreement makes reference to the ILO 1998 Declaration. In addition to the fundamental principles and rights at work, the Parties have also added two other principles,[99] which they state relate more closely to the ILO's Decent Work Agenda. In order for Colombia to better meet its obligations under the labour accord, the Agreement in Article 9 on "Cooperative Activities" provides a list of possible areas of cooperation, and Annex 1 also provides activities directly related to the achievement of the accord's objectives.

7.6.4 Canadian FTAs with Chile, Costa Rica, and Colombia: Labour Institutions and Dispute Settlement Mechanisms

All three Agreements call for the establishment of a Ministerial Council of ministers responsible for labour affairs to oversee and promote the implementation of the labour agreement. The councils are assisted by a National Secretariat or Point of Contact of each of the parties, and these Secretariats or Points of Contact may set up an advisory committee (in the case of Canada–Chile FTA) or a national labour committee (in the case of Canada–Colombia FTA). Whereas the FTAs with Chile

[98] Preamble of the Agreement on Labour Cooperation between the Government of Canada and the Government of the Republic of Colombia.

[99] Article 1(e.) acceptable conditions of work with respect to minimum wages, hours of work and occupational health and safety, and (f.) providing migrant workers with the same legal protections as the Party's nationals in respect of working conditions.

and Colombia set out the specific requirement for the Council to meet, the Costa Rica FTA does not.

The three Agreements have articles on ministerial consultations, whereby either Party may request in writing to hold consultations regarding any of the obligations under the Agreement. Should the matter not be successfully resolved at the ministerial level, the Agreements make provision for Evaluation Committee of Experts (Chile) or for Review Panels (Costa Rica and Colombia) to consider the complaint, with elaborate rules of procedure.

7.6.4.1 Dispute Resolution

All the three Agreements provide for the resolution of disputes; however, the Chile and Colombia FTAs have more elaborate rules of procedure than the Costa Rica FTA, from consultation, selection of Panel members, implementation of final report to compliance or review of implementation.

The Canada–Chile FTA provides for an enforcement mechanism of fines not greater than US$10 million, which must be paid into a fund to improve or enhance the labour law enforcement in the Party complained against. In the case of the Canada–Colombia FTA, the amount of the assessment is not to exceed US$15 million annually. Both Agreements provide a list of factors upon which the determination must be based[100]:

a. (*in the case of Canada–Chile FTA*) the pervasiveness and duration of the Party's persistent pattern of failure to effectively enforce its occupational safety and health, child labour or minimum wage technical labour standards and (*in the case of Canada–Colombia FTA*) the pervasiveness and duration of the Party's failure to comply with its obligations within the meaning of subparagraph 2(b) of Article 17;
b. the reasons for the Party's failure to comply with such obligation, including, where relevant, its failure to observe the terms of an action plan;
c. the level of compliance that could reasonably be expected of the Party given its resource constraints;
d. the efforts made by the Party to begin remedying such non-compliance after the final report of the panel, including through the implementation of any mutually agreed action plan; and
e. any other relevant factors.

[100] The language in both FTAs is similar with only few differences. We only provide the original language for both FTAs under (a), but for (b) to (e) we only use the language in the Canada–Colombia FTA, which is also similar to the Canada–Peru FTA.

Table 7.5 Canada FTAs with labour provisions

Name and date of entry into force of the agreements	Reference to ILO instruments	Labour obligations	Enforcement mechanisms[a]
Trade Agreement with Chile (1997)	No	Striving for a high level of national labour laws in the area of CLS, as well as minimum working conditions[b] and migrant rights Enforcement of national labour laws in these areas	Fine up to US$10 million (for the non-application of national labour law in the area of child labour, occupational safety and health, and minimum wages)
Trade Agreement with Costa Rica (2002)	ILO 1998 Declaration	Striving for a high level of national labour laws in the area of CLS and promotion of minimum working conditions[b] and migrant rights Enforcement of national labour laws in these areas	Only modification of labour cooperation activities (in the case of the non-application of national labour law in the areas)
Trade Agreements with Peru (2009), Colombia (2011), Jordan, and Panama (not yet in force)	ILO 1998 Declaration, Convention No. 182[c]	Respect for CLS, minimum working conditions,[b] and migrant rights Enforcement of national labour law in these areas[d]	Fine up to US$15 million (in the case of Jordan: unlimited) for violations relating to issues covered by the ILO 1998 Declaration; to be paid into a special labour rights fund

Source: Ebert and Posthuma (2011)
[a]The enforcement mechanism only applies to "trade-related" matters
[b]For the purposes of this table, the term "minimum working conditions" is used to describe labour standards regarding hours of work, minimum wages, and occupational safety and health
[c]The Convention is mentioned in the context of labour cooperation under this agreement
[d]These agreements additionally preclude the Contracting States from encouraging trade or investment through weakening of labour law against the labour principles contained in the agreement

In the case of the Canada–Costa Rica FTA, there is no provision for monetary assessments. Under Article 23(5), the Agreement only provides:

> If the panel determines that the Party that was the object of the request has not remedied its persistent pattern of failure to effectively enforce its labour law directly related to principles and rights set out in Annex 1, the Party that made the request may take reasonable and appropriate measures, exclusive of fines or any measure affecting trade, but including the modification of cooperative activities pursuant to Article 12, to encourage the other Party to remedy that persistent pattern, in keeping with the panel's determinations and recommendations.

Table 7.5 provides an overview of the Canadian FTAs with labour provisions.

7.7 Selection of Other Regional Trade Agreements with Labour Provisions

Apart from the RTAs signed by the USA, the EU, and Canada, which are the most prominent trade agreements with labour provisions, a number of agreements signed by African, Asian, Latin American, and Caribbean countries contain some form of labour provisions. In the sections below, we review briefly these trade agreements with labour provisions.

7.7.1 Asian Trade Agreements with Labour Provisions

Out of the eight trade agreements reviewed in this section, five have labour provisions contained in a labour side agreement or in a memorandum of understanding. Four of these agreements make specific reference to the ILO 1988 Declaration and six provide for cooperation in labour issues through the exchange of information on joint projects. Further to the cooperation of activities, seven of the agreements contain provisions that discourage each of the signatories to weaken their labour laws in order to improve their trade and investment positions.

Ebert and Posthuma (2011)[101] have identified two main models with respect to the form and legal consequences in their review of the Asian trade arrangements with labour provisions. The first model is the agreements that have the labour provisions in a side agreement or in memoranda of understanding. Some of these agreements do not create legal obligations in case of breach of the agreement. For example, the agreement between New Zealand and Thailand states: "This Arrangement will not legally bind the Participants."[102] However, it should be noted that the agreement provides that should there be differences between the participants regarding the interpretation of the arrangement, the participants "will endeavor to resolve the differences through consultation within the Labour Committee".[103] Similarly, the memorandum of understanding on labour cooperation attached to the Trans-Pacific Strategic Economic Partnership Agreement[104] provides: "[T]he Parties will make every effort to reach a consensus on the matter through co-operation, consultation and dialogue."[105]

[101] Ebert and Posthuma (2011).

[102] Section 4, paragraph 4.1 of the Arrangement on Labour between New Zealand and the Kingdom of Thailand.

[103] See Section 3, paragraph 3.7 on Institutional Arrangements.

[104] The parties to the agreement are the Governments of Brunei Darussalam, the Republic of Chile, New Zealand, and the Republic of Singapore.

[105] See Article 5(2) of the memorandum of understanding on labour cooperation attached to the Trans-Pacific Strategic Economic Partnership Agreement.

The second model identified by Ebert and Posthuma is the agreements that have the labour provisions in the body of the trade agreement. These agreements[106] do not only contain promotional labour provisions but also have conditional labour provisions. In these three agreements, should any dispute arise over the interpretation and application of the labour provisions, submission may be made under the regular dispute settlement procedures.

The Association of Southeast Asian Nations (ASEAN) treaty of 1992 presents a distinctive case. Even though the treaty does not contain labour provisions, ASEAN members in 2007 adopted a plan of action on national occupational safety and health frameworks (OSH) "as an additional priority area in the ASEAN Labour Ministers work programme".[107] The plan of action called on members to adopt ILO standards in the development of each member's national OSH profile and to bring it in line with internationally recognised best practices. The plan of action also recommended the establishment of a common ASEAN checklist based on ILO standards and internationally acknowledged best practices.[108]

The plan of action also called for improved capacity building efforts and knowledge sharing with stakeholders, such as companies and employees in putting into operation the national OSH strategy and programme. This, in addition to the regional cooperation efforts and international cooperation, is a sign of the ASEAN members' recognition of the importance not only of cooperation but also of working with the other two arms of the ILO tripartite system (employers and workers) in the effective implementation of the plan of action.

7.7.2 *African Trade Agreements with Labour Provisions*

Four trade agreements in Africa contain labour provisions. The labour provisions in these agreements are only of a promotional nature and do not contain minimum labour standards, nor do they oblige the signatories to enforce their national labour laws. The agreements only focus on cooperation in labour issues. Table 7.6 provides in a table form these agreements. The SADC agreement contains a section entitled "Work and Employment" and has a tripartite commission on labour and social affairs. In 2003, the tripartite commission adopted the Social Charter on Fundamental Labour Rights in Southern Africa, with the objective of facilitating

[106] Three Agreements, Japan–Philippines Economic Partnership Agreement (JPEPA), Nicaragua–Republic of China (Taiwan) Free Trade Agreement, and Agreement on Free Trade and Economic Partnership between the Swiss Confederation and Japan, as shown in Table 5.5, fall within this category.

[107] Plan of Action on National Occupational Safety and Health Frameworks for ASEAN (see http://www.aseansec.org/20917.pdf. Accessed 10 April 2014.

[108] Plan of Action on National Occupational Safety and Health Frameworks for ASEAN, paragraph 6.1.2.

Table 7.6 Asian FTAs with labour provisions

Name and entry into force of the trade agreements	Reference to ILO instruments	Commitment to certain minimum labour standards	Non-encouraging of trade or investment through weakening labour laws	Cooperation on labour issues	Institutional arrangements	Consultation mechanisms in case of differences
New Zealand–Thailand Trade Agreement (2005)[a]	1998 Declaration	Yes	Yes	Yes	Labour Committee	Yes
Chile–China Trade Agreement (2006)[a]	No[b]	No	No	Yes	No	No
Trans-Pacific Partnership Agreement (2006)[a]	1998 Declaration	Yes	Yes	Yes	No	No
New Zealand–China Trade Agreement (2008)[a]	1998 Declaration	No	Yes	Yes	No (but senior official meetings)	No (but discussions of labour issues of mutual concern possible)
Japan–Philippines Economic Partnership Agreement (2008)	Yes (refers to the internationally recognised labour standards)	No	Yes	No	No	Yes[c]
Taiwan, China–Nicaragua Trade Agreement (2008)	No (but the labour principles contain all the CLS)	Yes	Yes	Yes	Labour Affairs Committee	Yes[c]
Japan–Switzerland Trade Agreement (2009)	No	No	Yes	No	No	Yes[c]
New Zealand–China Trade Agreement (to enter into force in 2011)[a]	1998 Declaration	No	Yes	Yes	National contact points	Yes

Source: Ebert and Posthuma (2011)

[a]The labour provisions are contained in a labour side arrangement or memorandum of understanding

[b]However, the preamble of this agreement refers to the objectives of the ILO

[c]The labour provisions of this agreement are subject to the regular dispute settlement mechanism, which may as a last resort entail the suspension of trade benefits

Table 7.7 Sub-Saharan African FTAs with labour provisions

Name and date of entry into force of the trade agreements	Reference to ILO instruments	Scope of provisions
Southern African Development Community (SADC) (1992)[a]	Yes	Provision of regional framework for cooperation to ensure that the tripartite structure is retained and to promote the formulation of and harmonisation of legal, economic, and social policies and programmes
Treaty of the Economic Community of West African States (ECOWAS) (1993, revised in 2005)[b]	No	Cooperation regarding labour law harmonisation and the promotion of women's professional organisations
Agreement Establishing the Common Market for Eastern and Southern Africa (COMESA) (1994)[c]	No	Cooperation regarding employment conditions and labour law
Treaty for the Establishment of the East African Community (EAC) (2000)[d]	No	Cooperation on employment and working conditions with an emphasis on gender equality, including the abolition of discriminatory law and practice

Source: Ebert and Posthuma (2011)

[a]Members are Angola, Botswana, the Democratic Republic of the Congo, Lesotho, Malawi, Mauritius, Mozambique, Namibia, Seychelles, South Africa, Swaziland, Tanzania, Zambia, and Zimbabwe

[b]Members are the Republic of Benin, Burkina Faso, the Republic of Cabo Verde, the Republic of Cote D'Ivoire, the Republic of Gambia, the Republic of Ghana, the Republic of Guinee, the Republic of Guinee Bissau, the Republic of Liberia, the Republic of Mali, the Republic of Niger, the Republic of Nigeria, the Republic of Senegal, the Republic of Sierra Leone, and Togolese Republic

[c]Members are Burundi, Comoros, D.R. Congo, Djibouti, Egypt, Eritrea, Ethiopia, Kenya, Libya, Madagascar, Malawi, Mauritius, Rwanda, Seychelles, Sudan, Swaziland, Uganda, Zambia, and Zimbabwe

[d]Members are Burundi, Kenya, Rwanda, Tanzania, and Uganda

consultations among social partners in order to achieve harmonious labour relations (Tables 7.7 and 7.8).[109]

7.7.3 *Chile Trade Agreements with Labour Provisions*

As discussed above, the Latin American region has witnessed a gradual evolution of labour provisions in trade agreements. However, the experience of Chile within this

[109] Lazo (2009), p. 23. This article can be accessed at http://www.iadb.org/intal/intalcdi/PE/2009/04460.pdf. Accessed on 10 April 2014.

Table 7.8 Latin America and Caribbean FTAs with labour provisions

Name and date of entry into force of the trade agreement	Specific instruments	Reference to ILO instruments	Commitments to certain minimum labour standards	Framework for Labour Cooperation or Monitoring
Treaty on the Caribbean Community and Common Market (CARICOM) (1973)	Text of the Revised Treaty (1997)	No	No	Technical Cooperation within the Council for Human and Social Development
	Charter of Civil Society for the Caribbean Community of 1995	No	Yes (including freedom of association, child labour, working conditions, and occupational safety and health)	Review of progress by the Secretary General
	Declaration of Labour and Industrial Relations Principles of 1998	"International Labour Conventions"	Yes (covering numerous areas of labour law, including CLS)	No
Cartagena Agreement on the Andean Community (1988)	Andean Instrument on Occupational Safety and Health (1999, as revised in 2004)	No	Yes (in the area of occupational safety and health)	Technical assistance through a Labour Committee, assistance in case of differences regarding the interpretation of the Andean Instrument
Southern Common Market (MERCOSUR) 1991)	Social-Labour Declaration (1998)	1998 Declaration	Yes (covering numerous areas of labour law, including CLS)	Dialogue, cooperation, and review of progress by the Social Labour Commission

Source: Ebert and Posthuma (2011)

region stands out. Chile has entered into a number of trade agreements by incorporating the labour provisions in the body of the agreement as a side agreement, signed memoranda of understanding on labour issues, or an observer in the labour institutes of MERCUSOR. With the exception of Africa, Chile has entered into at least one trade agreement with labour provisions with a country in each continent. We have already discussed the Chilean trade agreements with labour provisions entered into with the United States of America, the EU, Canada, and China. Even noteworthy is the fact that Chile has entered into trade agreements with labour provisions not only with developed countries but also with other developing countries.

The agreements with developing countries mostly contain the same references, as found in Chile's agreement with developed countries. The agreements entered

Table 7.9 Chilean FTAs with labour provisions

Name and date of entry into force of the trade agreement	Reference to ILO instruments	Commitments to certain minimum labour standards	Non-encouraging of trade or investment through weakening labour law	Cooperation on labour issues	Specific institutions	Consultation mechanisms in case of differences
Chile–Panama Trade Agreement (2008)[a]	1998 Declaration	Yes	Yes	Yes	National Contact Point; Joint Labour Cooperation Committee	Yes
Australia–Chile Trade Agreement (2009)	1998 Declaration	No	No	Yes	National Contact Point	No
Chile–Colombia Trade Agreement (2009)	1998 Declaration	Yes	Yes	Yes	National Contact Points, High-Level Meetings	Yes
Peru–Chile Trade Agreement (2009)[a]	Yes[b]	Yes[b]	Yes	Yes	Joint Labour and Migration Cooperation Committee	No
Chile–Turkey Trade Agreement (to enter into force in 2011)	1998 Declaration	Yes	Yes	Yes	Working groups or subcommittees dealing with labour cooperation may be established	No

Source: Ebert and Posthuma (2011)

[a]The labour provisions are contained in a labour side arrangement or memorandum of understanding

[b]This text additionally refers to the UN International Convention on the Protection of the Rights of All Migrant Workers and Members of Their Families of 1990

into by Chile are all of a promotional nature and do not contain conditions for provisions for incentive or sanction mechanisms. Table 7.9 provides an overview of the trade agreements with labour provisions entered into by Chile. The Chilean agreements with the United States, the EU, Canada, China, and its membership in the Trans-Pacific Partnership Agreement has not been included in this table since we have already discussed them above.

References

Bolle, M. J. (2003a). *Free trade agreements with Singapore and Chile: Labor issues*. CRS Report for Congress, CRS-1-3, Updated 12 September 2003.

Bolle, M. J. (2003b). *Jordan–U.S. free trade agreement: Labor issues*. CRS Report for Congress, CRS-5, Updated 1 July. http://assets.opencrs.com/rpts/RS20968_20030527.pdf. Accessed 10 Feb 2014.

Bolle, M. J. (2008). *Overview of labor enforcement issues in free trade agreements*. CRS Report for Congress, Code RS22823, 29 February 2008.

Brecher, J., & Costello, T. (1994). *Global village or global pillage: Economic reconstruction from the bottom up*. Cambridge, MA: South End Press.

Brown, C. A. (2011). Dispute avoidance and settlement. In A. B. Zampetti & J. Lodge (Eds.), *The CARIFORUM–EU economic partnership agreement: A practitioners' analysis*. The Netherlands: Kluwer Law International.

Church, G. J. (1993). It's just that close. *Time*, 15 November 1993.

Ebert, F. C., & Posthuma, A. (2011). *Labour provisions in trade arrangements: Current trends and perspectives, International Institute for Labour Studies*. Geneva: International Labour Organization.

ECLAC. (2008). *The CARIFORUM–EU economic partnership agreement (EPA): An assessment of issues relating to market access, safeguards and implications for regional integration*. 26 October 2008. http://www.eclac.org/publicaciones/xml/9/35129/L.181.pdf. Accessed 6 Apr 2014.

Elliot, K. A. (2003). *Labor standards and the free trade area of the Americas* (WP 03-7). Washington, DC: Institute for International Economics.

Grynberg, R., & Qalo, V. (2006). Labour standards in the US and EU preferential trading arrangements. *Journal of World Trade, 40*(4).

Hubbard, G. (2005). CAFTA: A win–win case. *Businessweek*, 4 July 2005.

Hufbauer, G. C., & Schott, J. J. (2005). *NAFTA revisited: Achievements and challenges*. Washington, DC: Institute for International Economics.

ILO. (2012). *Fundamental principles and rights at work: From commitment to action*. ILC, 101st Session, Geneva.

Joe, H. J. (1995). *Immigration and labor, NAFTA and beyond: A new framework for doing business in the Americas*. Dordrecht: Martinus Nijhoff.

Kenner, J. (2011). Labor clauses in EU preferential trade agreements – An analysis of the Cotonou Partnership Agreement. In K. Bagwell & P. Mavroidis (Eds.), *Preferential trade agreements: A law and economic analysis*. Cambridge: Cambridge University Press.

Kim, D.-O., & Kim, S. (2003). Globalization, financial crisis and industrial relations: The case of South Korea. *Industrial Relations, 42*(3).

Lazo, G. P. (2009). *Trade agreements and their relation to labour standards: The current situation* (Issue Paper No. 3). Geneva: International Centre for Trade and Sustainable Development.

Murphy, B. S. (1995). NAFTA's North American agreement on labor cooperation: The present and the future. *Connecticut Journal of International Law, 10*.

Zampetti, A. B. (2011). Environment, social aspects and institutional provisions. In A. B. Zampetti & J. Lodge (Eds.), *The CARIFORUM–EU economic partnership agreement: A practitioners' analysis*. The Netherlands: Kluwer Law International.

Chapter 8
The Impact of Regional Trade Agreements on the Labour-Trade Debate

8.1 Introduction

Can RTAs act as a stimulus or a laboratory for the multilateral system? This chapter examines this in light of the labour provisions in the RTAs discussed. In this chapter, the emphasis is on the NAFTA side agreement (NAALC) since it is about the only RTA that has heard labour disputes. We will review the implications of the NAALC on labour rights protection in North America and how it has impacted on the labour standards and trade debate. This chapter also tries to answer the question as to whether RTAs advance workers' rights by examining labour enforcement under both the CAFTA-DR and U.S.–Cambodia Textile Agreements. Finally, the chapter discusses the limits of regionalism in addressing the linkage issue.

8.2 The Influence of RTAs on the Multilateral System

The surge in the number of RTAs in recent times has raised the question as to whether they are building blocks or stumbling blocks for the multilateral system. This proliferation has also raised the issue of the effectiveness of the multilateral system on which the principle of non-discrimination is built. This recent surge in the number of RTAs has been distinguished from the earlier RTAs, which failed to make an impact on the world scene. The recent RTAs have succeeded and are making an impact. It is estimated that a greater percentage of the world trade is being conducted on a preferential basis, making some observers see the break-up of world trade into regions. Whilst this trend may raise concerns, recent studies by the Organization for Economic Cooperation and Development (OECD) and the WTO suggest that RTAs may complement rather than threaten the multilateral trade system. It is against this backdrop of complementarities that it is argued that

K. Addo, *Core Labour Standards and International Trade*,
DOI 10.1007/978-3-662-44619-5_8

regional trade agreements could act as a stimuli and laboratory for the multilateral system in effecting compliance with ILO core labour standards.

8.2.1 RTAs as Stimulus for the Multilateral System

The formation of the European Economic Community (EEC) in 1958, which was a political formation in ensuring that no wars would be fought in Europe, was supported by the United States. The Americans also supported the formation of the EEC common customs tariffs by proposing a round of talks on liberalisation in the GATT so as to keep the momentum in the multilateral direction. The Kennedy Round was thereafter opened and brought about a worldwide reduction of custom duties. After the 1973 enlargement of the European Community, the Tokyo Round was also started. This round (the last before the Uruguay Round) brought about tariff reductions worth more than $300 billion, even more than all the previous six rounds put together. The adoption of the European Community (EC) of the Single Market initiative to turn a free trade area into a true common market, with its plans on further expansion, contributed in part to the United States' conversion to regionalism and its revival in South America and the launching of the Asian-Pacific Economic Cooperation (APEC).[1]

The fear of a "Fortress Europe" and European resistance to American proposals at a General Agreement on Tariffs and Trade (GATT) ministerial conference in Geneva for a new round of multilateral negotiations in Geneva in 1982 contributed significantly to the development of regionalism in North America. The thinking was that if the road towards multilateralism is obstructed, then other roads needed to be explored. The American response was initiating regional agreements with Israel (U.S.–Israel Free Trade Agreement) and an agreement with the Caribbean countries (Caribbean Basin Initiative). The real shift in policy was the agreement with Canada, resulting in the Canada– U.S. Free Trade Agreement (CUSFTA). The spread of regionalism in the developing world was to contribute to the shift in policy, when Mexico entered into negotiations with the U.S. and Canada, which resulted in the North America Free Trade Agreement (NAFTA).

This surge in regionalism served as a warning that unless GATT was revised, the organisation of world trade could be divided into regional trading blocs. This no doubt led to the successful completion of the Uruguay Round. This completion significantly broadens the coverage of the multilateral trade system and should increase the role played by the rule of law in the conduct of world trade. From all indications, regionalism may well have provided a stimulus to multilateral liberalisation.[2]

---

[1] Demaret (1997), p. 832.

[2] Demaret (1997), p. 832.

8.2.2 RTAs as Laboratories for the Multilateral System

The issue of whether a regional trade agreement could act as a pilot project for the multilateral system in an area is dependent on how best the policies formulated are put into practice and the fastest way to achieving that goal. The experience of the multilateral system has shown how slow and awkward it can be to negotiate separately with more than 100 countries. Some authors have argued that the costs of negotiation rise with the number of countries involved so that it is easier for a smaller group of countries to negotiate an agreement.[3] With a common policy, they can then enter multilateral negotiations as a group. Regional integration in effect reduces the number of countries participating in multilateral negotiations since the number of policy proposals submitted is few and allows for in-depth deliberations. This would probably increase the efficiency of the negotiations and make a satisfactory worldwide agreement more likely. The experience of the EU is a notable example. It is worthwhile to note from the onset that the regional experiment will only succeed if the political will is there and the economic framework is right.

In addition, the adoption and implementation of policies at the regional level will enable regional partners to learn by doing or gain experience through a trial and error basis. This could then serve as a testing ground for implementation at the multilateral level. The experience gained at the governmental level will help to adapt to new policies and practices and create the enabling environment to implement multilateral agreements. Furthermore, the success of implementation at the regional level could act as motivation for the multilateral system to follow. In effect, RTAs could provide testing grounds or test laboratories for the multilateral system.

A way to determine whether the regional models like European Union or NAFTA have acted as laboratories in the past or could serve the multilateral system in the future could be examined from a general standpoint.

8.2.2.1 General Standpoint

The European Union has been hailed as a model in achieving liberalisation and, although not a perfect model since the EU aims at achieving not only economic integration but also political integration, nevertheless provides a yardstick that could measure the influence of RTAs on the multilateral trading system. The EU has shown how trade liberalisation in its entirety can be achieved, e.g. free movement of goods, services, capital, natural and legal persons, and the parallel enforcement of competition rules. The European Court of Justice is also an indication of how important the enforcement of rules and adherence to the rule of law is taken. This helps achieve harmonisation and promote mutual recognition.

[3] Demaret (1997), p. 832.

The EU portrays a more balanced institution and shows how unequal economic partners could harmoniously work together in achieving their goals and are able to bargain on the same level. In short, the EU is an example of how level the playing field could be made. A notable example is how poorer members of the EU have been able achieve higher standards and the rapid acceleration of income growth by the adoption of minimum standards and mutual recognition.

The NAFTA agreement, though not a completely perfect model since in its present form it cannot accommodate many new members, shows how countries with unequal economic development could work towards liberalisation and the reduction in tariffs to the benefit of their economies, although some critics see the union dominated by the largest economy, the United States of America.

The examples of the EU, NAFTA, and other regional agreements are case studies for the multilateral system. In spite of the shortcomings of RTAs and the legal controversy surrounding their compliance with Article XXIV of the General Agreement on Tariffs and Trade (GATT), RTAs are examples in that they help facilitate the mobility of both capital and labour. The proliferation of regional trade agreements has helped to enhance the competitiveness of open economies and to provide labour market flexibility, by bringing countries at various levels of economic development together. The EU with the admission of ten East European countries in 2004 took this process further.

8.3 The U.S. Trade Act of 2002

On 6 August 2002, President George W. Bush signed the United States Trade Act of 2002 into law.[4] The Trade Act provides the President with trade promotion authority to negotiate new trade agreements with United States trading partners. The Trade Act stipulates that the U.S. Congress can only vote up or down on any trade agreement that the President sends to Congress and that Congress could not amend the agreement. The authority that Congress gave the President is sometimes referred to as "fast track" authority as it is meant to streamline approval of trade agreements. The relevance of this Act is the link that it creates for the promotion of the ILO core labour standards by establishing a link between trade and workers' rights.

Although non-discrimination is not mentioned in the definition provided in the Trade Act, it should be noted that the Trade Act provides protection in three other areas described as "acceptable conditions of work with respect to minimum wages, hours of work, and occupational safety and health".

The Trade Act of 2002, Section 2102 provided details of 17 principal negotiating objectives for agreements signed under the fast-track authority. Among these

[4] The Trade Act of 2002 (Public Law 107–210), 19 U.S.C. 3801 (U.S. Trade Promotion Authority Act).

objectives are provisions on labour and the environment. The Trade Act of 2002, section 2103 provides that the principal negotiating objectives of the United States with respect to labour and the environment are

- to ensure that a party to a trade agreement with the United States does not fail to effectively enforce its environmental or labor laws, through a sustained or recurring course of action or inaction, in a manner affecting trade between the United States and that party after entry into force of a trade agreement between those countries;
- to recognize that parties to a trade agreement retain the right to exercise discretion with respect to investigatory, prosecutorial, regulatory, and compliance matters and to make decisions regarding the allocation of resources to enforcement with respect to other labor or environmental matters determined to have higher priorities, and to recognize that a country is effectively enforcing its laws if a course of action or inaction reflects a reasonable exercise of such discretion, or results from a bona fide decision regarding the allocation of resources, and no retaliation may be authorized based on the exercise of these rights or the right to establish domestic labor standards and levels of environmental protection;
- to strengthen the capacity of United States trading partners to promote respect for core labour standards . . .;
- to strengthen the capacity of United States trading partners to protect the environment through the promotion of sustainable development;
- to reduce or eliminate government practices or policies that unduly threaten sustainable development;
- to seek market access, through the elimination of tariffs and nontariff barriers, for United States environmental technologies, goods, and services; and
- to ensure that labor, environmental, health, or safety policies and practices of the parties to trade agreements with the United States do not arbitrarily or unjustifiably discriminate against United States exports or serve as disguised barriers to trade.[5]

Pursuant to Section 2102 of the Trade Act of 2002, the President of the United States is obligated to prepare a number of reports to the U.S. Congress such as a United States Employment Impact Review, Labor Rights Report, and Laws Governing Exploitative Child Labor Report. These reports are submitted to the Committee on Ways and Means of the House of Representatives and the Committee on Finance of the Senate. These reports are issued under authority from the President by the United States Department of Labor in consultation with the U.S. Secretary of State and the United States Trade Representative. The reports are to describe the entire relevant legal framework, including national laws and international conventions and practices for the protection of workers' rights,

[5] Section 2103(11) of Trade Act 2002 Public Law 107–210—August 6, 2002, 19 USC 3801.

including the administration of labour law, labour institutions, and the system of labour justice of a signatory country.

The relevant sections of the Trade Act of 2002 are, for example, Section 2105(c)(5), which requires the President to review and report to Congress on the impact of future trade agreements on U.S. employment, including labour markets. This Section provides that the President shall

> review the impact of future trade agreements on United States employment, including labor markets, modeled after Executive Order 13141 to the extent appropriate in establishing procedures and criteria, report to the Committee on Ways and Means of the House of Representatives and the Committee on Finance of the Senate on such review, and make that report available to the public.

The Trade Act of 2002, under Section 2102(c)(8) on labour rights, also requires that the President shall

> [i]n connection with any trade negotiations entered into under this Act, submit to the Committee of Ways and Means of the House of Representatives and the Committee on Finance of the Senate a meaningful labor rights report of the country, or countries, with respect to which the President is negotiating.

Finally, the Trade Act of 2002 Section 2102(c)(9) on laws governing exploitative child labour provides that the President shall

> with respect to any trade agreement which the President seeks to implement under trade authorities procedures, submit to the Congress a report describing the extent to which the country or countries that are parties to the agreement have in effect laws governing exploitative child labor.

Since 2003, the United States Department of Labour, in consultation with the Secretary of State and the United States Trade Representative, has issued eight reports on the United States Employment Impact Review pursuant to section 2102(c)(5). Under section 2102(c)(8) on Labour Rights Reports, nine reports have since 2003 been issued. Pursuant to section 2102(c)(9) on Laws Governing Exploitative Child Labour, nine reports have been issued.

The fact is that countries that have entered into FTAs with the United States are aware that such reports would be issued about their compliance with their national laws and international conventions could act as a preventive mechanism to ensure observance (and the recent report of the ILO CEACR is evidence of the efforts that such countries are making towards compliance with the CLS). In the writing of such reports, the United States officials would have to enter into dialogue with the government officials of signatory countries. To this extent, a greater degree of collaboration is required by the signatory countries, thus creating the opportunity to use trade policy to help workers and influence and monitor labour rights in these countries.

8.4 Implications of NAALC on Labour Rights Protection in North America

In 2002, the Office of the United States Trade Representative (USTR), in its report on NAALC during its eighth anniversary, stated:

> The NAALC has contributed to transparency and public debate on labor law and enforcement issues that, to a large extent, did not exist before. In fact, neither bilateral nor trilateral cooperative efforts to improve worker rights were nearly as pronounced as they have been since NAFTA and the NAALC.[6]

With this assertion, the USTR painted a positive picture of the impact of the NAALC on labour relations in North America. The report further stated that the NAALC is a unique tool for tripartite cooperation, which aims at promoting labour standards, compliance with labour laws, and the enforcement of those laws in each of the signatory countries.

Further to the 2002 report, the 2004 report on "NAFTA at ten" again stated the important role of the NAALC, in that the side agreement has added a social dimension to the main agreement. The report listed two main achievements: (1) how the enforcement of labour laws in the signatory countries has been greatly enhanced and (2) how the agreement has helped establish institutions and created a formal process through which the public can raise concerns about the enforcement of labour law directly with governments.[7]

The USTR stated further that through NAALC, more than 50 trilateral cooperative programmes have been carried out. These include conferences, seminars, technical exchanges focusing on labour relations, occupational safety and health, workplace equity, and workforce development.[8]

The role of the NAALC in ensuring protection of labour rights in North America has received mixed results. Some authors claim that the NAALC is important in the provision of innovative and potentially effective means of ensuring that workers' rights in the NAFTA signatory countries are protected whilst at the same time facilitating the expansion of trade among the signatories.[9] Others have concluded that the NAALC has not in effect achieved the intended results whilst acknowledging that the process should not entirely be discredited.[10] The reviews of the NAALC raises the questions as to whether the NAFTA side accord has had any impact in North America and, if so, whether the process, even with its deficiencies, could constitute "an important first step" in the provision of an effective and

[6] See report of "NAFTA at Eight" at http://www.ustr.gov/archive/assets/Trade_Agreements/Regional/NAFTA/asset_upload_file374_3603.pdf. Accessed on 12 April 2014.

[7] "NAFTA at Eight" at http://www.ustr.gov/archive/assets/Trade_Agreements/Regional/NAFTA/asset_upload_file374_3603.pdf and also "NAFTA at Ten" at www.ustr.gov. Accessed 12 April 2014.

[8] NAFTA at Ten at www.ustr.gov.

[9] See Murphy (1995), p. 407.

[10] See, for example, LaSala (2001), pp. 346–347.

efficient means of workers' protection under a multilateral approach.[11] Before we discuss this, we first examine labour enforcement under NAALC and review some of the submissions filed with the NAOs.

8.5 Labour Enforcement Under NAALC

8.5.1 NAALC: The Dispute Resolution Process

The aim for the different investigating and consulting apparatus, as already stated above, is to ensure that each Party complies with its duty to enforce its own domestic law. However, the monitoring process is not intended to be adversarial. Article 20 of the Agreement states that the Parties "shall make every attempt through cooperation and consultations to resolve any matter" arising under the Agreement.[12] Foremost, the responsibility for resolving disputes falls on the three NAOs. In this respect, Article 16(3) states that "[e]ach NAO shall provide for the submission and receipt . . . of public communications on labor law matters arising in the territory of another Party. Each NAO shall review such matters, as appropriate, in accordance with domestic procedures."[13] In spite of the article couched in political language, the role of the NAOs is clear: they are required to accept and, if appropriate, investigate allegations that another Party is not enforcing its domestic labour law as required by the Agreement.

The NAOs' jurisdiction to investigate such allegations is expansive, covering all matters relating to "labor law", as defined by the Agreement.[14] The decision whether to accept a submission is left to the discretion of each NAO.[15] For example, in the case of the United States NAO, a submission is accepted when a complaint is filed: (1) which relates to labour law matters in another Party's territory and

---

[11] Murphy (1995), p. 406.

[12] NAALC, Article 20.

[13] NAALC, Article 16(3).

[14] Article 49 defines labour law as "laws and regulations, or provisions means laws and regulations, or provisions thereof, that are directly related to: (a) freedom of association and protection of the right to organize; (b) the right to bargain collectively; (c) the right to strike; (d) prohibition of forced labor; (e) labor protections for children and young persons; (f) minimum employment standards, such as minimum wages and overtime pay, covering wage earners, including those not covered by collective agreements; (g) elimination of employment discrimination on the basis of grounds such as race, religion, age, sex, or other grounds as determined by each Party's domestic laws; (h) equal pay for men and women; (i) prevention of occupational injuries and illnesses; (j) compensation in cases of occupational injuries and illnesses; (k) protection of migrant workers".

[15] NAALC, Article 16(3).

(2) where a review would further the objectives of the Agreement.[16] The United States NAO, through the Agreement and U.S. regulations, is given broad discretion in its determination of whether an investigation of Canadian or Mexican enforcement of labour laws is appropriate in a particular case.

Should an NAO decide that a complainant has adequate ground for bringing a complaint, it may conduct an investigation to determine whether the allegation (s) have merit.[17] Each NAO, in so doing, follows the procedures established by its own country. In the case of the United States, the investigation may include hearings and written submissions.[18]

Article 21 of NAALC permits an NAO as part of its investigations to seek assistance of the NAO in the country being investigated regarding the requested country's labour law, administration of those laws, and labour market conditions in the country.[19] The rationale behind this provision is to encourage consultations between the different NAOs. This provision permits the NAO conducting the investigation to seek all the necessary information to enable it to determine whether the country under investigation is enforcing its domestic laws in an effective manner. The NAO consulted is under obligation, when requested, to promptly provide any publicly available data or information relating to its domestic laws, procedures and policies, proposed changes to its laws, and any clarifications and details requested.[20]

In the event of the completion of its investigation the NAO determines that the Party under investigation failed to comply with its obligations under the Agreement, the NAO may recommend consultations by the Ministerial Council under Article 22 of the Agreement.[21] The Agreement still at this high level seeks to resolve complaints in an amicable way through consultation and cooperation among the Parties.[22]

---

[16] See Murphy (1995). Revised Notice of Establishment of U.S. National Administrative Office and Procedural Guidelines, 59 Fed. Reg. 16,660, 16,661 (1994). In determining whether these prerequisites are met, the NAO will consider (1) whether the subject of the complaint alleges matters that are "inconsistent" with a Party's obligations under the Agreement, (2) whether the matters at issue "demonstrate" a pattern of non-enforcement of labor law by another Party, (3) whether there has been harm to the person or organisation submitting the request, and (4) whether appropriate relief has been sought in the domestic courts of the Party complained about. 59 Fe. Reg. 16,661. The NAO must decide whether to accept a submission for review within 60 days of its filing.

[17] NAALC, Article 21(1).

[18] See 59 Fed. Reg. 16,662. The U.S. NAO was the first to conduct investigations under Article 16. The submissions that fall under this article are discussed in this chapter.

[19] NAALC, Article 21(1).

[20] NAALC, Article 21(2)

[21] NAALC, Article 22. In the case of the United States, the U.S. NAO "shall" recommend that the Secretary of Labour request consultations in the Council of Ministers on the matter if the NAO determines that the matter has not been satisfactorily resolved by the NAO's investigation. 59 Fed. Reg. 16,662.

[22] Canada, for example, may not request (1) consultation under Article 22, (2) the establishment of an Evaluation Committee of Experts (ECE) under Article 23, (3) consultations under art. 27, (4) the initiation of procedures under Article 28, or (5) the establishment of a panel as far as a complaining party under art. 29, for any government or province, which has not agreed to be bound by NAALC. See NAALC, Annex 46, paras 1 and 3. See Murphy (1995).

In case the ministerial consultations do not arrive at a resolution or if the Council of Ministers determines that it would be helpful to call on outside expertise to assist in the resolution of the issue at the centre of the dispute, the Agreement provides that any Party may request the creation of an ad hoc Evaluation Committee of Experts (ECE).[23] The ECE should be comprised of three members, all experts in labour matters or "other appropriate disciplines", which are independent of all three signatories and the Secretariat.[24]

Article 23(2) of NAALC states the aim of the ECEs as follows:

> The ECE shall analyze, in the light of the objectives of this Agreement and in a nonadversarial manner, patterns of practice by each Party in the enforcement of its occupational safety and health or other technical labor standards as they apply to the particular matter considered by the Parties under Article 22.

Under Article 23, the ECE is only to be convened in a matter that is trade related, covered by the signatories' mutually recognised labour laws. Where a matter has been previously dealt with in an ECE report "in the absence of such new information as would warrant a further report",[25] the NAALC stipulates that no ECE should be convened. However, for the ECE to carry out its duties under Article 23(2), it is entitled to solicit information from the Secretariat, each Party's NAO, organisations outside that have relevant experience, and the larger public.[26]

Article 25 sets out the timeline for the issuance of reports by an ECE. It states that an ECE must issue its report 120 days after its establishment. The report is to include details of its investigation, its conclusions, and any recommendations it chooses to make. The report is then to be given to the Ministerial Council in a draft form. When the countries involved in the dispute have had the opportunity to respond to the draft report, the ECE may modify its report and publish the final report.[27]

Upon the publication of the final ECE report, the Agreement also provides that the parties consult each other. Should the succeeding consultations not bring about a resolution of the matter, either Party may call for the establishment of an Arbitral Panel, which the Council has to approve by a two-thirds vote.[28] The Arbitral Panel is to consist of five members who are drawn from rosters of experts maintained by the Commission.[29] The Parties in the dispute are to appoint a chairman within 15 days, and the chairman should not be a citizen of either Party.[30] The four other

[23] NAALC, Article 23(1).

[24] NAALC, Article 24.

[25] NAALC, Article 23(4).

[26] NAALC, Article 24(1)(e).

[27] NAALC, Articles 25(1) and (2).

[28] NAALC, Article 29(1). This provision prevents the Party under investigation from stopping the formation of the Arbitral Panel.

[29] NAALC, Articles 30 and 32.

[30] NAALC, Article 32(1)(b).

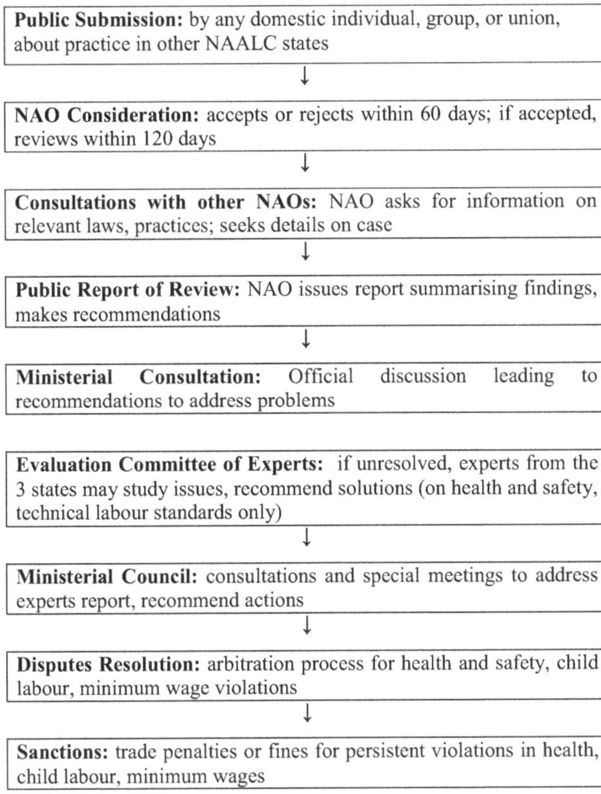

Fig. 8.1 NAALC submission process. *Source*: Finbow (2006), p. 68

openings on the Panel are filled by each Party selecting two members who are citizens of the other country[31].

The NAALC has procedural rules similar to that of the WTO dispute settlement system. In the case of the NAALC, the Parties at least have the right to one hearing before the Panel. They also have the prospect of making initial and rebuttal written submissions (Fig. 8.1).[32] The Panel is expected to present its initial findings 180 days after it has been convened. The report should contain the Panel's findings of fact and its determination as to whether there has been a persistent pattern of failure by the party complained against in enforcing its labour laws.[33] In so doing, the Panellists may submit separate opinions on issues should they not arrive at a unanimous decision.[34] The Party complained against can submit written comments

[31] NAALC, Article 32(1)(c).

[32] NAALC, Article 33(1).

[33] NAALC, Article 36(2).

[34] NAALC, Article 36(3).

on the Panel's initial report within 30 days after the presentation of the initial report.[35] The Panel, after consideration of the complaining Party's written comments, can reconsider its findings, request the views of the Party that filed the complaint, or make any further examination that it deems fit on its own initiative or based on the request of the disputing Party.[36]

In making its final determination as to whether a Party complained against has been effective in enforcing its labour laws, the Panel under Article 49(1) is supposed to give the particular country broad discretion. Article 49(1) states that for the purposes of this Agreement

> A Party has not failed to "effectively enforce its occupational safety and health, child labor or minimum wage technical labor standards" or comply with Article 3(1) in a particular case where the action or inaction by agencies or officials of that Party:
> (a) reflects a reasonable exercise of the agency's or the official's discretion with respect to investigatory, prosecutorial, regulatory or compliance matters; or
> (b) results from *bona fide* decisions to allocate resources to enforcement in respect of other labor matters determined to have higher priorities.

This definition at the Panel stage rules out a finding of persistent failure to enforce labour standards when there is evidence that a country has exercised reasonable discretion in public policy decisions regarding resource allocation. The Agreement does not state what would constitute reasonable exercise of a Party's discretion.

Should a Panel determine that there has been a persistent pattern of failure, the Agreement under Article 38 similar to other good dispute settlement mechanisms contains provisions for the enforcement of Arbitral Panel rulings. The Agreement states that "the disputing Parties may agree on a mutually satisfactory action plan, which normally shall conform with the determinations and recommendations of the panel".[37] In case the Parties are not able to agree on a mutually satisfactory action plan within 60 days of the final report, or the complaining Party is of the view that the other Party has not fully complied with the agreed upon action plan, the disputing Party may request the reconvening of the Panel.[38]

In the reconvened Panel, the Panel is to determine whether the plan proposed by the Party complained against is sufficient to remedy the failure. If the Panel is of the view that the plan is not sufficient, the Panel is to establish a new plan and may, where it deems fit, impose a monetary enforcement assessment against the offending Party.[39] In essence, the monetary assessment is a fine against the Party complained against "to improve or enhance the labor law enforcement in the Party complained against, consistent with its law".[40] If however the Party complained

---

[35] NAALC, Article 36(4).

[36] NAALC, Article 36(5).

[37] NAALC, Article 38.

[38] NAALC, Article 39(1).

[39] NAALC, Article 39(4).

[40] NAALC, Annex 39.3, p. 1519.

against fails to pay the monetary assessment, the complaining Party can suspend trade benefits to the Party complained against under NAFTA.[41]

Even though the Agreement allows for sanctions, the nature of the Agreement is not to punish Parties that violate the Agreement but to seek a solution through consultations and cooperation among the signatories. This approach tends to be more political, which although can be frustrating to a complainant in the private sector is well-suited to resolving issues among nation-states.[42] It is generally acknowledged that litigation, especially a prolonged one, as could be the case in a dispute between two states is detrimental to the maintenance of friendly relations. This invariably is also detrimental to conducting business with its attendant effects on economic prosperity. In maintaining long-term economic and political relations, the process under NAALC, even if in the strict legal sense does not resolve a child labour or minimum wage dispute, is good in terms of the long-term benefits of increasing the welfare of workers through increased economic activity. The major argument is that trade tends to be a means to achieving the level of economic development that will make parents send their children to school and also make industry pay better wages.

Box 8.1: Resolution of Disputes: North American Agreement on Labor Cooperation (NAALC)

- Phase I: Ministerial Consultations
- Phase II: Evaluation Committee of Experts (ECE) (300 days)
  - Draft Report (120 days) submitted shall be for the consideration by the Council (30 days).
  - The Final Evaluation Report shall be presented to the Council (60 days), should be published (30 days).
  - Parties shall present written responses to ECE's recommendations (90 days).
  - Final Report and Parties' written responses shall be considered at the next regular session of the Council.
- Phase III: Arbitral Panel (540 days)
  - If there is no resolution in a regular session, Parties may request in writing more consultations (60 days).
  - If Parties fail to resolve the matter, any Party may request a special session of the Council (20 days).

(continued)

[41] NAALC, Annex 41B, Article 41.

[42] The Agreement makes provision for resolving private sector disputes under Chapter 11 of NAFTA.

Box 8.1 (continued)

- If Council cannot resolve the matter within 60 days, the Council may convene an Arbitral panel (180 days to present an Initial Report after the last panellist is selected).
- The Parties may submit within 30 days written comments on the Panel's Initial Report.
- Final Report shall be made 60 days after the presentation of the Initial Report. If in its Final Report the panel determines a "persistent pattern of failure to effectively enforce . . ." the Parties may agree on an Action Plan consistent with the recommendations of the panel.
- Review of implementation: if Parties do not agree on an Action Plan or on whether it is being fully implemented, the panel can be reconvened (60–120 days; 180 days). If the panel determines that the Plan has not been agreed/fully implemented, a "monetary enforcement assessment" can be imposed (90 days after the panel has been reconvened).

The possible remedies for enforcement of the 11 labour provisions are a set of seven steps in three distinct "levels of treatment" (step I: initial acceptance and investigation by the NAO, step II: Ministerial consultations, step III: after the ECE has conducted its investigation, it issues different recommendations for each labour principle, as shown in Table 8.1).

8.5.2 *Review of Selected Cases*

This section examines some of the labour disputes brought under NAALC to determine the effectiveness of the dispute resolution under NAFTA. The NAALC labour proceeding is more designed as a fact-finding and dispute avoidance proceeding than as a dispute settlement proceeding. It does not give binding decisions. Under NAALC, when a conflict occurs, the NAO may request consultations with NAO as long as the subject matter of the dispute is covered under the NAALC.[43] Even though the NAALC is intended to resolve all disputes through negotiation, a party that is not satisfied may request additional proceedings.

As at September 2013, 37 submissions had been filed under the NAALC.[44] Out of these, 23 were filed with the U.S. NAO.[45] Twenty-one of these submissions

[43] NAALC, Article 21(1). When NAOs consult, they are under obligation to provide information on any law or procedures and to explain disputed matters. See *id.* at art. 21(2). Each NAO can exercise its right to be involved in any negotiations. See *id.* at art. 21(3).

[44] http://www.dol.gov/ilab/programs/nao/status.htm. Accessed 15 April 2014.

[45] The U.S. NAO's name was changed to Office of Trade Agreement Implementation (OTAI) in 2004. A further change in name occurred in December 2006 to the Office of Trade and Labor Affairs (OTLA).

Table 8.1 NAALC labour principles and levels of treatment

Labour Principles	NAO Review & Report	Optional Ministerial Consultations	Evaluation Committee of Experts (ECE)	Council Review of ECE Report	Post-ECE Ministerial Consultations	Arbitral Panel	Fines or Suspension of NAFTA Benefits
Freedom of association/ right to organise a union	X	X					
Right to bargain collectively	X	X					
Right to strike	X	X					
Prohibition of forced labour	X	X	X	X			
Non-discrimination	X	X	X	X			
Equal pay	X	X	X	X			
Workers' compensation	X	X	X	X			
Migrant worker protection	X	X	X	X			
Child labour protection	X	X	X	X	X	X	X
Minimum employment standards (minimum wage)	X	X	X	X	X	X	X
Safety and health	X	X	X	X	X	X	X

Source: U.S. National Administrative Office, U.S. Department of Labor

involved allegations against Mexico and two against Canada. In Mexico, nine submissions had been filed and involved allegations against the United States. In the case of Canada, six submissions had been filed, with three of them allegations against Mexico and four against the United States.

Out of the 23 submissions filed with the U.S. NAO, 18 involved issues of freedom of association and 9 of the submissions concern issues of the right to bargain collectively. Two of the submissions concerned the use of child labour, one raised issues of pregnancy-based gender discrimination, three involved the right to strike, six concerned minimum employment standards, and eight raised issues of occupational safety and health. Four submissions filed with the U.S. NAO were withdrawn by the submitters before hearings were held or the review process was completed. The U.S. NAO has held hearings on ten submissions, and eight of these submissions have gone on to ministerial-level consultations. The U.S. NAO has rejected the review of seven submissions.[46]

The five submissions accepted by the Mexican NAO have resulted in ministerial-level consultations, and one submission accepted by the Canadian NAO has also resulted in ministerial-level consultations. Three submissions have been declined for review by the Canadian NAO.[47]

Below, we review some of the cases filed with the NAOs of the three signatories to NAALC. Only some of the cases that were accepted for review are discussed here.[48]

8.5.2.1 U.S.A. OTLA (Formerly NAO)

U.S. NAO Submission No. 2005-03 (HIDALGO) (October 14, 2005)[49]

On 14 October 2005, the Federación de Trabajadores Vanguardia Obrera de la Confederación Revolucionaria de Obreros y Campesinos (FTVO-CROC), with support from the U.S. Labor Education in the Americas Project and the Washington Office on Latin America, filed submission 2005-03 with the OTLA. The submission alleged that the Government of Mexico had failed to fulfil its obligation under Article 3 of the NAALC for not effectively enforcing its labour laws with respect to freedom of association and protection of the right to organise, the right to bargain collectively, and the right to strike.

---

[46] http://www.dol.gov/ilab/programs/nao/status.htm. Accessed 15 April 2014.

[47] http://www.dol.gov/ilab/programs/nao/status.htm. Accessed 15 April 2014.

[48] Summary of all the NAO public reports can be found at http://www.dol.gov/ilab/programs/nao/status.htm#iic4. Accessed 15 April 2014.

[49] Public Report of Review of Office of Trade and Labor Affairs, Submission 2005-03, see http://www.dol.gov/ilab/media/reports/nao/publicrep2005-3.htm. Accessed 15 April 2014.

The FTVO-CROC further alleged that the Mexican government did not effectively enforce the country's labour laws in that it failed to conduct required on-site inspections to detect and remedy labour law violations with respect to forced labour, child labour, minimum employment standards, discrimination at the workplace, and occupational safety and health, and also under Article 5 of NAALC concerning fair, equitable, and transparent labour tribunal proceedings.[50]

The aim of the FTVO-CROC submission was to acquire collective bargaining rights for workers at the Rubie's de Mexico (Rubie's) facility in the State of Hidalgo in Mexico.

The OTLA accepted the submission for review on the grounds that the allegations raised issues on labour law matters in Mexico and that the review of the submission would further the purposes of NAALC.

The findings of the OTLA were that

(i) Even though the FTVO-CROC not always followed proper legal procedures in its representation of interested workers at Rubie's, nevertheless there were problems with the way Mexican labour authorities handled the process. The report also stated that there were a number of problems concerning the administrative procedures for allowing the registration of collective bargaining agreements and rights. The OTLA highlight a number of areas of concern, such as, rejection on technical grounds of union petitions; unjustified deals as a result of ineffective communication between federal and state labour authorities, and lack of transparency on how to recognise unions and collective bargaining agreements.
(ii) The OTLA found that the Mexican government failed to conduct the period checks from 1998 to 2005 as stated in the Federal Labour Law.
(iii) Though inspections were eventually conducted in May 2005, there were inconsistencies between federal and local labour authorities in the processes and application of the country's labour laws.
(iv) Whilst the allegation on discrimination was not substantiated, the OTLA found that pregnancy testing was used as part of the employment application process at the company till July 2005.[51]

The OTLA, pursuant to Article 21 of NAALC, recommended consultations between the OTLA and the Mexican NAO on the issues that had an impact on the enforcement of labour laws in addressing the issues raised in the submission under Articles 3 and 5 of the NAALC.

The recommendation of the OTLA was that:

---

[50] See Public Report of Review of Office of Trade and Labour Affairs, Submission 2005-03 at http://www.dol.gov/ilab/media/reports/nao/publicrep2005-3.pdf. Accessed 15 April 2014.

[51] *Ibid.*

(i) Measures should be taken to comply with procedural requirements under Mexican labour law, and also measures taken to prevent unjustified delays and to improve coordination between federal and state authorities in respect of the administration of labour justice procedures;
(ii) There was the need for transparency in the union representation process, which includes the creation of a publicly available registry of unions and collective bargaining agreements;
(iii) That the Mexican government should devote resources to the periodic inspection of workplaces so that the labour law violations as stated in the submission would be adequately addressed.

U.S. NAO Submission No. 2003-01 (PUEBLA) (September 30, 2003)[52]

This submission was filed on 30 September 2003 by the U.S.-based United Students Against Sweatshops (USAS) and Mexican-based Centro de Apoyo al Trabajador (CAT). The submitters were later joined by the Canada-based Maquiladora Solidarity Network (MSN).

The NAO accepted to review the submission on 5 February 2004, and it related to issues on the labour laws in Mexico. The NAO agreed to review as it felt it would further the objectives of the NAALC. The submission raised the following issues: freedom of association and the protection of the right to organise, the right to bargain collectively, occupational safety and health, and minimum employment standards. Further issue was respect to access for workers to fair, equitable, and transparent labour tribunal proceedings.

The submitters alleged that in 2000 and also in 2003, management and government officials were informed about the workers' rights violations at the Matamoros Garment S.A. de C.V. and Tarrant Mexico S.R. de C.V. manufacturing factories in the Mexican state of Puebla.

The workers in both factories made efforts at forming unions, but they were informed that they had union representation, which they did not know about. Based on their belief that the so-called existing unions were not acting in their interest, the workers made efforts at forming separate or independent unions. In their attempts to file their unions' registration, the Local Conciliation and Arbitration Board of Puebla, their registration petitions were denied.

Upon review of the submission, the NAO found that there was an overall lack of knowledge and transparency about legal requirements, the processes that are required for filing complaints, how the government goes about its inspection processes and reporting requirements, and government assistance available to workers.

In the course of the review process, the requests by the U.S. NAO under Article 21 of the NAALC to hold consultations with the Mexican NAO consultations were

[52] See http://www.dol.gov/ILAB/media/reports/nao/pubrep2003-1.htm. Accessed 16 April 2014.

declined. The U.S. NAO thought such consultations were beneficial for the general public in the state of Puebla and in Mexico as a whole, on how to improve outreach efforts as a way of educating workers, employers, and government officials and how to improve transparency on legal requirements.

The NAO ruled that pursuant to Article 22 of the NAALC, there was the need to hold ministerial consultations between the two governments on issues of freedom of association, minimum employment standards, and occupational safety and health.

U.S. NAO Submissions No. 940001 and 940002 (HONEYWELL & GENERAL ELECTRIC) (February 14, 1994)[53]

The two cases were filed separately in 1994 but were eventually reviewed together by the U.S. NAO. The two cases involved allegations of deprivation of workers of their right to be represented by unions of their choice. On 14 February 1994, the International Brotherhood of Teamsters (IBT) filed a complaint against Honeywell with the United States National Administration Office (U.S. NAO) (Submission No. 940001). On the very same day, the United Electrical, Radio and Machine Workers of America (UE) filed a separate submission with the U.S. NAO against General Electric. In both cases, the unions' complaint alleged that workers had been dismissed for union activity. Under the Mexican Constitution, Mexican Federal Labour Law, and ILO Convention 87 (Mexico is Member of the ILO), such discrimination is illegal.[54]

The IBT submission was, in respect of events, relating to the Honeywell factory in Mexico. According to IBT, Honeywell fired approximately 23 production workers, almost all of whom had expressed an interest in joining the Union of Workers of the Steel, Metal, Iron and Related Industries. In their submission, the IBT stated that the workers were made to sign resignation forms to collect their severance pay; in so doing, the workers were made to waive their ability to file claims protesting the dismissals against Honeywell.

In the General Electric case, the UE submission was in relation to allegations on freedom of association and the right to organise (Submission No. 940002). According to the union, General Electric used different intimidating tactics, such as the dismissal of approximately 11 employees in order to restrict the workers from

[53] U.S. Department of Labor, U.S. National Administration Office Report of Review, NAO Submission No. 940001 (October 12, 1994); U.S. Department of Labour, U.S. National Administration Office Report of Review, NAO Submission No. 940002 (October 12, 1994).

[54] See Befort and Cornett (1996), p. 269. The authors argued that contrary to the assumption that Mexican labour laws are inadequate to protect workers' interests or that these laws are inadequately enforced, Mexican labour laws provide the same basic rights and protection to its workers just as the U.S. law provides to U.S. workers. The authors further argue that, in many ways, Mexican labour law is more protective of workers than U.S. law. Furthermore, the authors argue against the proposition that the Mexican government had deliberately manipulated labour standards downward with a view to achieving a trade advantage at pp. 269–272.

organising an independent union. Further to this, the UE submission also contained allegations concerning health and safety standards and the failure of the company to pay the workers for overtime work, as stipulated by law.

On 15 April 1994, the U.S. NAO gave notice that the submissions had been accepted for review. The U.S. NAO held public hearings on 12 September 1994 and issued its report on 12 October 1994. In its findings and recommendations, the U.S. NAO, regarding the scope of its jurisdiction, stated that "... the NAO is not an appellate body, nor is it a substitute for pursuing domestic remedies". Importantly, it stated its purpose as follows: "Rather, the purpose of the NAO review process including public hearing, is to gather as much information as possible to allow the NAO to better understand and publicly report on the Government of Mexico's promotion of compliance with, and effective enforcement of, its labor law through appropriate government action, as set out in Article 3 of the NAALC."

In its findings, the NAO acknowledged the dearth of practical knowledge in each of the three signatory countries about the legislation of the other countries on the right of freedom of association and the right to organise. The NAO recommended that the three countries work together to develop cooperative programmes, such as educational seminars and programmes on the rights of association and organising. The NAO concluded that it would not recommend ministerial consultations on these matters under Article 22 of the NAALC.

U.S. NAO Submission No. 940003 (SONY) (August 16, 1994)[55]

On 16 August 1994, four workers' rights and human rights organisations, headed by the International Labor Rights Education and Research Fund (ILRERF) filed a submission with the U.S. NAO.[56] The submission concerned the operations of a subsidiary of the Sony Corporation in Mexico and involved allegations concerning freedom of association and the right to organise. The U.S. NAO accepted the submission for review and held a public hearing on 13 February 1995. The four organisations alleged that (1) workers were dismissed in retaliation for union organising activity, (2) a union delegate election was flawed since there was insufficient notice of election and an open vote rather than secret ballot, (3) workers protesting the election in front of the plant were dispersed by police using physical force, (4) a petition for registration of an independent union was rejected by a labour tribunal on improper and hyper-technical grounds, and (5) the Mexican government violated its obligations under the NAALC and under ILO Conventions

---

[55] U.S. Department of Labor, U.S. National Administration Office Report of Review, NAO Submission No. 940003 (April 11, 1995).

[56] The four organisations were the International Labour Rights Education and Research Fund, the American Friends Service Committee, the National Association of Democratic Lawyers, and the Coalition for Justice in the Maquiladoras.

87 and 98, which guarantee freedom of association and the right to collective bargaining.[57]

On 11 April 1995, the U.S. NAO issued its report. The NAO, in conducting its review, "considered whether Mexico promoted compliance with, and effective enforcement of, its labor laws that guarantee the right of association and the right to organize freely and prohibit the dismissal of workers because of efforts to exercise those rights (Article 3); whether Mexico ensured that persons have appropriate access to, and recourse to, tribunals and procedures under which labor laws and collective agreements can be enforced (Article 4); and whether Mexico ensured that its tribunal proceedings for the enforcement of its labor law are fair, equitable and transparent (Article 5)".[58]

The U.S. NAO found that the Mexican authorities failed to adequately enforce their labour laws. The NAO also found that (1) it may have been because of union organising activities that workers discharges may have occurred, (2) allegation of police violence and other incidents during the strike raised important questions concerning the enforcement of Mexican labour law, (3) internal union activities were questionable, and (4) the Mexican authorities may have used "technicalities" to frustrate the organising efforts of independent unions.[59] The U.S. NAO concluded its report, stating:

> Given that serious questions are raised herein concerning the workers' ability to obtain recognition of an independent union through the registration process with the local CAB, and as compliance with and effective enforcement of the laws pertaining to union recognition are fundamental to ensuring the right to organize and freedom of association, the NAO recommends that ministerial consultations are appropriate to further address the operation of the union registration process.[60]

Further to the NAO report, Mexico accepted the U.S. request for consultations. U.S. Secretary of Labor Robert Reich and Mexican Secretary of Labour Santiago Onate agreed on an implementation agreement, which was signed on 26 June 1995. The two parties agreed to implement a series of activities to educate all the parties on labour laws dealing with union registration.[61] It was also agreed that officials from the Mexican Department of Labour and Social Welfare would meet with Sony representatives and plant and local labour authorities to further discuss the case.[62]

On 29 March 1996, in a letter addressed to the U.S. Secretary of Labor, the submitters in the case subsequently requested that the ministerial consultations be reopened. They based their argument on the fact that the problems raised in the

---

[57] The U.S. NAO did not accept for review allegations regarding minimum employment standards.

[58] Public Report of Review: NAO Submission No. 940003 (1995), pp. 24–25.

[59] See Public Report of Review: NAO Submission No. 940003 (1995), pp. 26–32.

[60] Public Report of Review: NAO Submission No. 940003 (1995), p. 32.

[61] See U.S. National Administrative Office, Report on Ministerial Consultations on NAO Submission No. 940003 (June 7, 1996).

[62] See U.S. Department of Labour, U.S.–Mexico Agreement on Ministerial Consultations (June 26, 1995).

original submission continued. The Secretary of Labor declined to reopen ministerial consultants but directed the NAO to conduct a follow-up review of the issues raised in the submission, and a related Mexican Supreme Court Decision, and submit a report to him. The NAO conducted the follow-up review as directed, and a report was issued on 4 December 1996.

The NAO in its follow-up report reviewed the current situation of the workers involved in the union organisation efforts as reported in Submission No. 940003 and also initiatives in Mexico to change its labour law. In the report of 4 December 1996, the NAO on the situation of the workers wrote that it had learned from a representative of one of the submitting organisations that the workers dismissed remained unemployed. With respect to the initiatives to changes in the Mexican labour law, the NAO commissioned a study to ascertain the implications of the decisions of the Mexican Supreme Court in two cases. Based on the NAO's review by the legal experts, the follow-up report concluded:

> The two Supreme Court decisions, the Principles of the New Labor Culture, and the proposal for changes to the Federal Labor Law indicate that potentially significant developments continue to take place in Mexico in a wide range of labor matters, including labor legislation, labor-management relations, labor-government relations, and within labor organisations themselves. The extent of the impact of the developments discussed above, however, remains to be seen.

8.5.2.2 Mexico NAO

Mexico NAO Submission No. 9803 (DECOSTER EGG) (August 4, 1998)[63]

On 4 August 1998, the Mexican Confederation of Labour (CTM) filed a submission alleging labour law violations in the United States, which was accepted by the Mexican NAO. The submission was in respect of alleged ineffective enforcement of labour law at the DeCoster Egg Farm in Turner, Maine, USA. The submission alleged that the Mexican workers at the farm did not receive the same legal protections as U.S. workers in terms of general working conditions. The petitioners alleged that failure by the U.S. government to guarantee the enforcement of laws designed to protect them has led to serious violations of their rights with respect to minimum employment standards, elimination of employment discrimination, prevention of occupational injuries and illnesses, and compensation in cases of occupational injuries and illnesses.

On 3 December 1999, the report issued by the Mexican NAO addressed matters relating to the effective enforcement of U.S. labour law based on the submission received. The petitioners alleged that the violations were in respect of five of the principles included in Annex 1 of the NAALC, namely protection of migrant workers (principle 11), minimum employment standards (principle 6), elimination

[63] See Secretariat of Labor and Social Welfare, Mexico National Administration Office, Submission No. 9803 (December 3, 1999).

of employment discrimination (principle 7), prevention of occupational injuries and illnesses (principle 9), and compensation in cases of job-related injuries and occupational illnesses (principle 10).

The NAO in its report recommended that ministerial consultations be held and stated the purpose of the consultations as follows:

> After reviewing Mexican Public Communication 9803, the Mexican NAO, pursuant to Article 22 of the North American Agreement on Labor Cooperation, recommends that the Secretary of Labor and Social Welfare of Mexico request Ministerial Consultations with the Secretary of Labor of the United States. The purpose of the Ministerial Consultations will be to obtain further information on the steps that the U.S. Government is taking to ensure that Mexican migrant agricultural workers enjoy the same legal protection as its nationals; and that they enjoy the respect of their rights in matters of: minimum employment standards; elimination of employment discrimination; safety and health (prevention and compensation for job-related accidents and illnesses). [sic]

On May 18, 2000, a ministerial agreement was signed between the U.S. Labor Secretary and the Mexican Secretary of Labor and Social Welfare. Under the agreement, the U.S. Department of Labor agreed to host a public forum on June 5, 2002, in Augusta, Maine, which was co-sponsored by the State of Maine Department of Labor. Government officials, employer representatives, educators, legal counsellors, advocates, and other service providers in Maine discussed working conditions and treatment of migrant and agricultural workers in the state of Maine. Consistent with the ministerial agreement, U.S. and Mexican labour officials explored ways of promoting and protecting the rights of migrant and agricultural workers in the United States.

Mexico NAO Submission No. 9501 (SPRINT)[64]

On 9 February 1995, for the first time a Mexican trade union filed a complaint against the United States. The trade union—the Independent Union of Telephone Workers of the Republic of Mexico, which was working closely with the Communication Workers of America—coordinated in filing this complaint. The submitters accused the United States for failing to promote NAALC principles relating to freedom of association and the right to organise. The complaint arose as a result of the dismissal of 235 workers in the context of their campaign to organise a union by the Communication Workers of America at a Sprint Spanish language telemarketing facility in California. The submitters further claimed that Sprint's subsequent closure of the facility's operations was to prevent the union from being formed. The complaint also raised the issue of the slow pace of the National Labor Relations Board (NLRB) reviews and the low level of fines available under U.S. law.[65]

---

[64] See Secretariat of Labor and Social Welfare, Mexico National Administration Office, Submission No. 9501 (May 31, 1995).

[65] According to Adams and Singh (1997), American unions had made attempts to address these problems within the American labour law for some time.

The case was the first effort to use the NAALC as a new tool to address the problems. The intention then was not only to benefit Mexican workers in protecting them from American social dumping but also to benefit American workers through public awareness of the inadequacies in the enforcement of the United States labour law.

The submitters sought the reinstatement of the 235 workers and a mandate that Sprint comply with U.S. labour laws by allowing workers to organise freely. The Sprint management denied the allegations on the ground that the closure of the facility was based solely on economic reasons and was in no way related to the union activity.

The Mexican NAO, in accordance with Article 16(3) of the NAALC, proceeded with its review of the submission. The NAO focused its review on the U.S. legislation that protects and promotes the principle of freedom of association and the right to organise. The review principally focused on the procedures that guarantee access to union representation and collective bargaining.

The report of the Mexico NAO after its investigation stated that "[a]fter studying matters related to U.S. labor legislation related to Public Submission 9501/NAOMEX, particularly under the rubric of freedom of association and the right of workers to organize, the NAO of Mexico is concerned about the effectiveness of certain measures intended to guarantee these fundamental labor principles". The NAO recommended ministerial consultations in accordance with Article 22 of the NAALC on the basis that it considered it necessary to further study the effects on the two principles of freedom of association and the right to organise workers of the sudden closure of a plant.

The NAO found that certain NAALC principles were violated, which it put in very diplomatic language. The NAO report stated:

> In view of the above, the NAO of Mexico emphasized in its analysis the possible problems in the effective application of U.S. law, which could arise when an employer refuses to negotiate collectively with a union elected as the exclusive representative of the workers in the bargaining unit, or where the employer refuses to permit that an election take place. Specifically, the NAO, in light of the information obtained, was unable to assess with complete certitude the effects on the rights of workers when an employer, suddenly, closes the place of work.

On 18 July 1995, the workers dismissed from the Sprint plant appeared before an Administrative Law Judge, arguing that the company closed its facility as a way to hinder the formation of a union, which violated U.S. laws guaranteeing freedom of association and the right to organise. The judge found that the Sprint company violated section 8(a)(1) of the National Labor Relations Act when it interfered with rights of employees under the Act.[66] The judge further ruled that the facility's closure was undertaken for lawful business decisions. The workers appealed the case to the National Labor Relations Board. On 27 December 1996, the Board partially disagreed with the Administrative Law Judge and ordered that the workers

[66] The National Labor Relations Act, 29 U.S.C. 151 (1996).

be reinstated with back pay.[67] The Sprint Corp. appealed this decision to the Federal Courts. On November 25, 1997, the U.S. Court of Appeals for the District of Columbia reversed the NLRB and ruled that Sprint closed the facility for legitimate financial reasons.[68]

As part of the Ministerial Consultations Agreement between the U.S. Secretary of Labor and the Mexican Secretary of Labour and Social Welfare, the U.S. Department of Labor held a public forum in San Francisco, California, to allow interested persons an opportunity to convey their concerns about the effects of sudden plant closings. The Labour Secretaries further instructed the trinational Labor Secretariat to conduct a study on the effects of sudden plant closing on the principle of freedom of association and the right of workers to organise in the three countries. The study was completed and released on 9 June 1997.

8.5.2.3 Canada NAO

Canada NAO Submission No. 98-1 (ITAPSA or Echlin Case) (April 6, 1998)[69]

On 6 April 1998, the United Steelworkers of America (Canadian National Office), in concert with 11 other unions and 31 nongovernmental organisations in Canada, the United States of America, and Mexico, filed this submission. This submission was the first to be received by the Canadian NAO. The NAO accepted the submission for review on 4 June 1998. In their submission, the petitioners accused the Mexican government of violating 2 of the 11 labour principles set out in the NAALC: freedom of association and protection of the right to organise, as well as prevention of occupational injuries and illnesses, at the Ciudad de los Reyes, Mexico State, auto parts factory owned at the time by Echlin. The case was substantially similar to the one filed with the U.S. NAO in December 1997. One difference between the case filed in Canada and the one submitted in the United States was that the former included the allegation that Mexico had violated article 2 of the NAALC, regarding "high labor standards", whilst this charge was not made in the case filed before the U.S. NAO.[70]

---

[67] See LCF, Inc., d/b/a La Conexion Familiar and Sprint Corp. and Communications Workers of America, Dist. 9 & Local 9410, AFL-CIO, 322 N.L.R.B No. 137 (December 27, 1996).

[68] *LFC, Inc. v. NLRB*, 129 F.3d 1276 (D.C. Cir. 1997).

[69] See the Office for Inter-American Labour Cooperation, Labour Branch, Submission No. 98-1, at www.ustr.gov.

[70] U.S. NAO Submission No. 9703 (ITAPSA) was filed on December 15, 1997, by the Echlin Workers Alliance, a group of unions from the United States and Canada, which includes the Teamsters; the United Auto Workers; the Canadian Auto Workers; UNITE; the United Electrical, Radio and Machine Workers of America; the Paperworkers; and the Steelworkers. Twenty-four additional organisations, including nongovernmental organisations, human rights groups, and labor unions from the three NAFTA countries, are cited as concerned organisations in the

The Canadian NAO published two reports on the submission. The first part of the report published on 11 December 1998 addressed specifically the freedom of association, collective bargaining, and labour tribunal issues. The second part of the report published on 12 March 1999 addressed the health and safety issues.

In its first report, the Canadian NAO concluded that freedom of association is a constitutional right in Mexico. The report further indicated that this constitutional right is reinforced by Mexican federal law and provisions of international treaties incorporated into domestic law. According to the NAO, the information it received suggested that Mexico did not conform to four obligations (Articles 2, 3, 4, and 5) under the NAALC. The NAO recommended that the Canadian Minister of Labour seek consultations with the Mexican Secretary of Labour and Social Welfare.[71]

In its second report, the Canadian NAO stated that based on the information it received regarding hazardous substances, it appears "that Mexico may not have met its obligations under Article 3(1)(b) of the NAALC to ensure that:

- chemical safety date sheets are readily available to workers;
- hazardous substances are labeled in Spanish, and
- workers exposed to hazardous substances are provided with adequate personal protective equipment".[72]

The NAO recommended that the Canadian Minister of Labour engage the Mexican Secretary of Labour "in a cooperative dialogue on responsible care and international best practices to protect workers who process, adapt or use asbestos in the production of goods".[73]

submission. Subsequently, the AFL-CIO, the CLC (of Canada), and the UNT (of Mexico) joined the submission. The submission alleged violation of freedom of association at the Itapsa export processing plant in Ciudad de los Reyes in the State of Mexico. The submitters alleged that when workers at the facility attempted to organise an independent union, they faced intimidation and harassment from the company and the existing union, the Confederation of Mexican Workers (CTM), including threats of physical violence and job loss. The submitters alleged that Mexican government authorities are aware of the situation and have taken no remedial action. In terms of occupational safety and health, the submission alleged that workers were exposed to asbestos and other toxic substances without adequate personal protective equipment (PPE). The NAO accepted this submission for review on January 30, 1998. The NAO issued its public report on this submission on July 31, 1998, recommending ministerial level consultations on the freedom of association and the safety and health issues raised.

[71] Review of Public Communication CAN 98-1 (Part I), Report issues pursuant to The North American Agreement on Labour Cooperation, December 11, 1999, p. 3.

[72] Review of Public Communication CAN 98-1 (Part II), Report issues pursuant to The North American Agreement on Labour Cooperation, March 12, 1999, p. 3.

[73] Review of Public Communication CAN 98-1 (Part II), Report issues pursuant to The North American Agreement on Labour Cooperation, March 12, 1999, p. 3.

8.5.3 General Discussion of the NAALC Submissions

In this section, we intend to provide a general overview of the NAALC submissions and the reports of the NAOs. A check of all the submissions shows that the U.S. and Mexico NAOs have been agreeing to review cases concerning labour principles such as freedom of association and the right to collective bargaining. These two labour principles are in the first tier (see Box 8.1 above) under the three-tier system. The NAALC does not allow disputes concerning freedom of association to progress past the ministerial oversight stage. In allowing a review of such cases, the NAO has put the spotlight on issues that would normally not have been given much attention.

Out of the 37 submissions filed by the end of September 2013, 14 had been recommended for ministerial consultations. In so doing, the NAOs have implicitly shown that there are some basis to the accusations brought against the employers and governments in question. Even though the mandate of the NAOs and the negotiations and actions that result from the ministerial consultations have been criticised as not adequate, pressure is put on governments and companies to bring about changes for the better. It appears that this process is having some positive effect. A good example is that of Mexico, where some transnational companies have taken steps to bring their actions in compliance with Mexican labour laws. As a result of the criticisms after the review of the Sony case (U.S. NAO Submission No. 940003), the Mexican Conciliation and Arbitration Boards have come under pressure to deliver so as to meet public demand.[74] Commenting on this, Lance Compa has stated that the NAO review process, irrespective of impossibility of sanctions, has

> forced the companies and the government to review their own actions and to have subordinate officials explain their decisions to superiors. On stage, they had to explain corporate conduct and governmental administration, and to defend themselves in the court of public opinion and political judgment, where the overall worth of NAFTA and the side accords will ultimately be settled. . . . [E]asy access for trade union and worker complainants to a public review and a public hearing on the types of issues raised in the first NAO cases might, on the other hand, make companies more careful in their employment policies where union organizing is underway, and make Mexican labor law authorities more evenhanded in their treatment of independent unions and more assertive on behalf of workers discharged for organizing.[75]

Even though the labour principle involved in the Sony case was in the first tier—a non-sanctionable principle—the NAO provision of a forum giving worker representatives the opportunity to demand compliance with labour rights under a trade agreement has great benefits for industrial relations in all the signatory countries. The conduct of the NAO in reviewing cases has been compared to the ILO in the

[74] See Adams and Singh (1997), p. 177.

[75] Compa (1995), p. 178. Compa reports that in the General Electric case (U.S. NAO Submission No. 940002), the company after an internal review offered to reinstate a number of the workers dismissed. See Compa (1995), n. 140, p. 178.

taking up of labour rights issues.[76] Even where the actions are not sanctionable, the provision of a forum for promotion of workers' rights has helped tilt the balance of power, which used to be solely within the confines of management.

The public forums are an important step in ensuring that the public is informed of the workings of multinationals in their countries and other NAFTA countries, making the companies accountable, which without the NAO process would not have been possible. This is a view that has been recognised by both the critics and supporters of NAALC. We state here the views of one critic and supporter. Ian Robinson, one of the foremost critics of the side accord, has stated:

> On this view, perhaps the most useful role the Labour Accord can play in the near future is to give labour rights and standards advocates an institutional focus for increasing public awareness of what is happening to worker rights in the NAFTA countries, thereby helping to increase public pressure on governments to perform better in these areas. Public NAO hearings, such as those in the United States, will facilitate this outcome.[77]

The view of a supporter of NAALC is similar to that of Robinson above:

> Although the Agreement provides for sanctions only in rare circumstances, the process by which NAALC determines whether a country is fulfilling its obligations under NAALC is conducted publicly. Since no one likes to have his or her dirty laundry aired in public, these proceedings could indirectly lead to better enforcement of the Parties' labor laws and, consequently, better observance of those rules by companies.[78]

An evaluation of the effectiveness of the NAOs' review process has shown that the process has been in furtherance of the objectives of the NAALC, mostly through consultation and cooperation. The process has been on the whole an attempt to improve the working condition and living standards in each of the signatory countries.[79]

In spite of the criticisms levelled against the review of cases, there have been attempts made at drawing attention to workers' rights. The NAOs have limited power in the review of cases, but by holding public forums, the NAO process has the potential to exert public pressure on the governments and multinationals to adhere to the 11 principles in the Agreement and has the potential to increase public awareness of the plight of workers and bring about a change for the better. Such change would entail making employers follow not only the letter of the law but also the spirit of the law. In any case, the NAO process is ensuring a change in industrial relations by empowering workers' representatives to speak up against bad labour practices.

---

[76] Compa (1995), p. 148.

[77] Robinson (1995), p. 491.

[78] Murphy (1995), p. 423.

[79] NAALC Agreement, Article 1.

8.6 Impact of NAALC

We have stated above that the NAALC has received mixed reviews; however, the issue of great concern to many developed countries is whether with increasing trade the comparative advantage that many developing countries enjoy in terms of lower costs of production would erode. Can the NAALC example provide a solution or a blueprint in reconciling the issues of labour standards and international trade? In effect, what lessons can the NAALC provide for a multilateral framework?

It is the growth in world trade that has raised concerns about the plight of workers in developing countries and the effect it is having on workers in developed countries. This growth in world trade is bound to continue, and so would the concerns with workers' rights. This makes the example of NAALC important in the development of a multilateral structure that would improve working conditions in developing countries whilst addressing the concerns of workers in developed countries. In reviewing the NAALC model, it is relevant to examine the shortcomings and strengths in light of the views of the critics and advocates in determining the extent to which the model can be used as a blueprint.

8.6.1 Critics of NAALC

One of the main criticisms of the NAALC is the lack of harmonised international labour standards. The NAALC does not call for harmonised labour laws or the establishment of North American labour standards.[80] With their different levels of development, it would not be in the interest of the less developed to be put at par with the developed, in which case it cannot be expected that Mexico would have the same level of labour standards as the U.S. and Canada.

A key criticism of the NAALC is that its provisions limit the extent to which one state can punish the other for labour rights violations, and as such its enforcement mechanism is constrained.[81]

The focus of the NAALC is that each country "promote compliance with, and effective enforcement by each Party of, its labor law".[82] It appears that this approach was what the three countries were prepared to agree upon, due to diverse stages of labour law development. With the United States as the dominant economic power, acceptance by Canada and Mexico on harmonisation of labour laws

[80] Article 1 of Annex 1 states: "The following are guiding principles that the Parties are committed to promote, subject to each Party's domestic law, but do not establish common minimum standards for their domestic law. They indicate broad areas of concern where the Parties have developed, each in its own way, laws, regulations, procedures and practices that protect the rights and interests of their respective workforces."

[81] Nolan Garcia (2011), p. 41.

[82] Article 1 (f) of NAALC.

would appear as if they were succumbing to U.S. pressure. This is also coupled with the view in Canada and Mexico that their labour laws are more protective of workers' rights than the labour laws in the U.S. The case of the labour accord has been compared by Finbow (2006) as a multilateral enforcement model, which in his view

> [D]oes not try to create common standards across all nations, encourage voluntary adherence to ILO standards or threaten countries with loss of trade privileges to compensate for poor working conditions. Instead, it calls on each nation to enforce it own labour laws. The principal means to encourage enforcement is public consultations and publicity, to put pressure on domestic actors. This model respect sovereignty by making national laws and enforcement paramount. It produces limited, gentle pressure to improve standards through investigation, consultation and publication. Countries are expected to provide impartial, effective law enforcement, and to voluntarily improve standards.[83]

The focus of the NAALC on national law has been criticised as insufficient because of the lack of compliance of domestic standards with international core standards. Others point to the fact that in some developing countries, labour law language is sometimes overly rigid and that these countries would do better with improved protection of core rights rather than pressure to enforce their rigid legislation on working conditions.[84]

Organised labour during the NAALC debate stated that companies that choose to remain in the U.S. rather than relocate to Mexico will use their new-found leverage to bring down the wages of U.S. workers. In their view, these lower wages will in turn reduce the U.S. living standards.[85] Furthermore, critics expressed concerns over the Mexican government's anti-union activities. According to some pro-labour experts, the Mexican government dominates unions and directly intervenes in the collective bargaining process through intimidation of the workers.[86] The critics cited examples of police harassment of a union leader and Presidential approval for the revocation of a collective agreement.[87]

With respect to NAALC, some critics pointed out that the Agreement addresses issues that are not problems and ignores issues that are problems.[88] The central criticism is on the limited ability to enforce violations of an individual Party's labour laws. In addition, among the standards subject to enforcement action, it does not include the right to organise, collective bargain, and strike action. According to the AFL-CIO, the NAALC was a step backwards and the Agreement actually weakened existing remedies under U.S. law for addressing labour rights and standards.[89] The argument was that the principle of "national enforcement of

83 Finbow (2006), p. 26.

84 Norton and Bloodworth (1995), p. 451.

85 Norton and Bloodworth (1995).

86 Norton and Bloodworth (1995).

87 Norton and Bloodworth (1995).

88 Norton and Bloodworth (1995).

89 Norton and Bloodworth (1995).

national law" could provide an open door for a party to lower the labour standards enshrined in its national legislation. The view is that the NAALC did not provide a guarantee that the levels of labour rights protection would be sustained in the long term in the signatory countries. Furthermore, the agreement did not provide for the possibility of renegotiation in the event of the weakening of a party's labour law provisions.

Another of the shortcomings of the NAALC highlighted by the critics is the division of the labour principles into three tiers. According to the NAALC, only three labour principles (minimum wage, child labour, and health and safety standards) can be subject to arbitration and a state would only face sanctions when it fails to enforce these three labour principles. The labour principles of key importance to trade unions (freedom of association, collective bargaining, and the right to strike) are omitted from provision of sanctions and can only be subject to review and ministerial consultation, and not even to independent evaluation or arbitration.

8.6.2 *Supporter's Response*

In response to what had been named the "pauper labor" argument, proponents of NAFTA argued that wages are not the only factor influencing a company's choice of geographic location.[90] Other factors cited included high worker productivity, high-quality transportation systems, and reliable legal system—factors that the U.S. had a clear advantage.[91] The proponents pointed to the rapid rise of Mexican wages in the years before the passage of NAFTA.[92] The further argument was that the passage of NAFTA would actually make job flight harder because it will boost Mexican wages.

It should be noted that during the debate over NAFTA, labour unions in the United States were very concerned about Mexican labour laws not being adequate enough to protect workers or not being adequately enforced. However, the situation on the ground in Mexico indicates otherwise. Befort and Cornett (1996) state:

> In reality, Mexican labor law provides the same basic rights and protections to Mexican workers that U.S. law provides to U.S. workers. Beyond those basics, and in contrast to the implications of much of the anti-NAFTA rhetoric, Mexican labor law is in many ways more protective of workers than U.S. law.[93]

The findings of Befort and Cornett are that even though Mexico has adequate labour laws, the problems that exist in Mexico have more to do with limited economic resources and that since the Mexican industrial base is limited in terms of employment opportunities, in most cases to be found in family-run businesses, it

---

[90] Hufbauer and Schott (1993), p. 11.

[91] Carney and Zagorin (1995), p. 58, quoted in Norton and Bloodworth (1995).

[92] Norton and Bloodworth (1995), p. 452.

[93] See Befort and Cornett (1996), p. 271.

makes it difficult to enforce labour laws. In their view, the Mexican situation is then not a neglect of the authorities in disregarding workers' interest.[94] With the objective of NAALC to improve working conditions by challenging each signatory to enforce its own labour laws, the increase in economic activity between the three countries with great benefits especially for Mexico, it could be reasonably expected that as the Mexican economy grows, so would wages and that adherence to labour standards would improve and become subject to better enforcement regimes.

The view of Murphy (1995) is that the critics of the Agreement tend to overlook the potential of the NAALC. In her opinion, each country has expressly agreed to "promote compliance with and effectively enforce its labor law", by hiring and training inspectors, monitoring compliance with domestic law, and inspecting suspected violations.[95] What the Agreement in effect does is the imposition of moral obligations on each Party to improve both the substance and enforcement of its domestic labour rights regime. This no doubt is a significant first step in protecting labour rights, and if built upon it could lead to improved labour standard adherence in the signatory countries. The monitoring system whereby each country's observance of its labour laws is carried out by the others ensures that workers do not only rely on the goodwill and promises of governments for adequate protection of their labour rights. This encourages compliance with each Party's obligations under the Agreement.

The focus on the NAALC has been more on the submissions filed, and under Article 11 of the Agreement, the parties are to engage in cooperative and research activities. The Secretariat of the Commission for Labor Cooperation has, under its mandate, been very active in organising meetings that are designed to assist in a better understanding of industrial relations in the three countries. The cooperative activities, according to the Commission, has contributed to two objectives: (i) "[e] ncouraging cooperation to promote innovation and rising levels of productivity and quality, and (ii) pursuing cooperative labor-related activities on the basis of mutual benefit".[96]

In its 2003 annual report, the Commission stated that the three countries have organised more than 60 cooperative activities. These activities have consisted of seminars, training sessions, working groups and conferences, joint research projects, and technical assistance projects. These cooperative activities have created the opportunities for government-to-government meetings on technical issues, leading to the establishment of working groups and trilateral conferences.[97] The conferences have also brought together participants of the three countries from nongovernmental organisations, trade unions, academicians, and corporations. Through these conferences, participants have been afforded the opportunity to

[94] Befort and Cornett (1996), p. 312.

[95] See NAALC, Article 3(1).

[96] NAALC Commission for Labor Cooperation, Annual Report 2003, see http://www.naalc.org/UserFiles/File/Microsoft_Word_-_A.Reprt03-Draft1En.pdf. Accessed 17 April 2014.

[97] NAALC Commission for Labor Cooperation, Annual Report 2003.

better understand the labour issues and practices in each of the three countries, "encouraging commonality in some measurements and practices, and inducing more transnational social networking which could contribute to a deepened regionalism in labour affairs".[98]

Further to the activities stated above, the NAALC also mandates the Commission to "encourage publication and exchange of information, data development and coordination, and joint studies to enhance mutually beneficial understanding of the laws and institutions governing labor in each Party's territory".[99] To fully meet this objective under the Agreement, the Secretariat of the Commission for Labor Cooperation has, in collaboration with the departments of labour in the three countries and the National Administrative Offices, conducted activities and published research papers; reports, for example, a guide to labour and employment laws for migrant workers in North America; briefs; and notes. The Secretariat in its research agenda has published studies and papers mainly in three areas: employment and labour law, labour markets, and employment relations. As at the end of 2007, the Secretariat had published over 14 research papers on topics such as anti-discrimination and equal pay, labour relations in North America, plant closing, and labour rights. The activities and research papers have enhanced mutual understanding among government officials, trade unions, and business executives and have fostered a greater degree of cross-border alliances.

Under Article 16(3) of the Agreement, "[e]ach NAO shall provide for the submission and receipt ... of public communications on labor law matters arising in the territory of another Party. Each NAO shall review such matter, as appropriate, in accordance with domestic procedures."[100] This provision in the submission process has led to unparalleled interaction, exchange, communication, and collaboration between the trade unions of the three countries. To use the NAALC effectively, trade unions and their supporters are compelled to collaborate across borders. This has led to solidarity among the labour unions, and the growth of this solidarity will, with time, allow the unions to gain political strength to effectively ensure that the enforcement mechanisms are improved and, in the future, allow organised labour to have a strong voice in the trade liberalisation process for the benefit of workers.

The NAALC has, in effect, brought the unions together in a way that would have been very difficult to achieve and, in so doing, created an environment in which labour will continue to interact. This environment is essential in their continued collaboration since organised labour recognises that they have much to gain by cooperating against violators of workers' rights. The three countries' trade unions have been active in the conferences and activities organised by each country's unions. Through such collaboration, the unions have been sharing information and

[98] See Finbow (2006), p. 195.
[99] NAALC Commission for Labor Cooperation, Annual Report 2003.
[100] NAALC, Article 16(3).

studies and finding novel ways of bringing their unions closer together for the common cause.

This has contributed to networking and deepening teamwork and understanding of each other's position. It has even been stated that the U.S. unions, in particular, have been moving towards what could be termed as a "social movement orientation".[101] This had led to opportunities for cross-border strategising. A case in point is that of the Echlin case, when the AFL-CIO worked together with their Mexican counterparts. A United Electrical Workers (a U.S. union) staff member is quoted as follows: "we cannot allow workers in our three countries to be pitted against one another in a race towards the lowest labor standard. Instead, we intend to use the strength of union solidarity across national borders to protect ourselves from corporate exploitation across those same national boundaries."[102]

Another way that the NAALC has contributed to the emerging social movement of the three-way collaboration is the efforts made by the U.S. unions. The U.S. unions, in order to combat the threat of wage decreases and the relocation of jobs to Mexico, have through their cooperation with Mexican unions provided support in organising campaigns for new unions pressing for higher wages and other benefits. In the view of the U.S. unions, strong and powerful unions in Mexico are a boon to U.S. workers since by winning increases in wages they make it less attractive for companies to relocate to Mexico.[103]

8.6.3 Overall Impact

In all, the impact of the NAALC should be assessed on the Agreement's two broad objectives: (1) to encourage the improvement of labour conditions in North America through cooperative activities in light of the 11 labour principles and (2) to provide a mechanism for mediating labour disputes.

With respect to the first objective, the activities of the Commission for Labor Cooperation have shown that the tripartite programmes have helped to increase awareness. Furthermore, the Commission's research agenda has publicised information on labour relations in the three countries and enhanced understanding of the labour issues in each of the three countries. In spite of the criticisms levelled against the NAALC, and the obvious limitations of the Agreement, it can be said that the NAALC has made it possible for a transparent discussion of labour issues in the

[101] Ian Robinson, cited in Finbow (2006), p. 222.

[102] Quote of Robert Kingsley, cited in Finbow (2006), p. 222.

[103] In a NAFTA fact sheet released by the Office of the US Trade Representative in March 2008, the Office stated that "Mexican wages grew steadily after the 1994 peso crisis, reached pre-crisis levels in 1997; and have increased each year since. Several studies note that Mexican industries that export or that are in regions with a higher concentration of foreign investment and trade also have higher wages" (at www.ustr.gov). The activities of the unions could have contributed in some measure to this increase in wages.

North American region and has, since its coming into force, highlighted the labour standards and international trade linkage through debates on regional trade agreements and trade liberalisation in general. With the increase in trade in the coming decades, and the importance of each country improving labour standards within its territory, especially in low-wage countries when they join a regional trade agreement, the debate started through the NAALC would work to the advantage of workers advancing their rights for the better.

Concerning the second objective of mediating disputes, the results have been not so clear-cut. Notwithstanding the division of the 11 labour principles into 3 tiers with only 3 of the 11 principles getting the full treatment (i.e., from NAO review to the possibility of monetary sanctions), and limited resolution procedures for industrial relations, the impact of the NAALC here should be as to whether the NAO review process has furthered the objectives of the Agreement—designed to be a cooperative process through consultation. Bazar (1995) concludes that "the NAO reviews show attempts at progress, especially in light of the limited power it possess. If nothing more, the NAO served the spirit of the NAALC in a diplomatic but positive manner."[104]

Can an agreement based on moral promises to enforce domestic labour laws provide a means of moral suasion to ensure compliance? Adams and Singh (1997) think:

> The NAALC through exerting social pressure on its members to comply with the principles embedded in the agreement, has the potential to increase respect for labour rights in employment relations. It has the potential to alter the malevolent convention under which employers disregard both the spirit and the letter of the law.[105]

Adam and Singh further concluded:

> Despite the scepticism of critics, the North American Agreement on Labour Cooperation and the institutions that is has spawned have had some modest successes in labour's favour. Although the agreement contains procedures that are far from ideal, they do have the capacity to advance the struggle for labour rights. Each of the three nations has formally committed itself to follow policies that will result in the effective attainment of a robust list of labour rights.[106]

What the NAALC has provided for organised labour and proponents of the labour standard–trade linkage is a tool to ensure compliance with the internationally agreed standards. This could, to some extent, be a blueprint for a multilateral approach by overcoming the shortcomings and building on the positive outcomes.

[104] Bazar (1995), pp. 457–458.
[105] Adams and Singh (1997), p. 178.
[106] Adams and Singh (1997), pp. 180–181.

8.7 Do FTAs Advance Workers' Basic Rights?

One of the major criticisms of the inclusion of labour standards in trade agreements is that they tend to be more "aspirational standards", which the Parties would want to achieve than real commitments that they have to enforce. The only exception of a trade agreement with labour provisions, which are considered to be the most rigorous provisions of any trade agreement, including national and international standards, is the U.S.–Jordan FTA. The agreements such as the NAALC, the U.S.–Chile FTA, and the U.S.–Singapore FTA are less rigorous in their enforcement provisions. And at the far end of the spectrum are the agreements with hortatory commitments, such as the U.S.–Peru and CAFTA-DR agreements, with no enforcement mechanism should a party fail to enforce its own labour laws. The different enforcement mechanisms have continued to fuel the debate that has been ranging on the proper role of labour standards in trade agreements since the signing of NAALC.

Although the FTAs with labour provisions have shortcomings in effectively enforcing labour standards, the observations made by the ILO Committee of Experts on the Application of Conventions and Recommendations (CEACR) indicate that a majority of countries that have entered into FTAs, especially with the United States, have made some progress with respect to compliance with and improvement of their labour laws. The comments of the CEACR on the application of labour standards in ILO member States is very important in gauging the extent to which States are complying with the international labour standards and especially with the CLS.

8.7.1 CAFTA-DR and Labour Standards Compliance

Has the trade agreement between the United States and the five Central American countries (Costa Rica, El Salvador, Guatemala, Honduras, and Nicaragua) and the Dominican Republic spurred progress in labour standard compliance?

During the negotiations on the FTA with the United States (the CAFTA-DR agreement), five countries (Costa Rica, El Salvador, Guatemala, Honduras, and Nicaragua) invited the ILO in 2003 to carry out an assessment by preparing an updated and objective study of the labour laws in all the countries. It is important to note that the importance of labour standards in U.S. FTAs most likely prompted the five Central American countries to request a study by the ILO to review the extent to which their individual labour laws conformed to the ILO Declaration on Fundamental Principles and Rights at Work and its Follow-up, adopted in 1998.

The ILO study stated that Costa Rica, Guatemala, Honduras, and Nicaragua have all ratified the eight fundamental Conventions referred to in the ILO Declaration. El Salvador was the only exception at the time of the signing of the FTA, having ratified six of the Conventions, except Conventions 87 (Freedom of

Association and Right to Organise) and 98 (Right to Organise and Collective Bargaining). In 2006, a year after the approval of the CAFTA-DR agreement, El Salvador ratified both Conventions.[107]

The ILO study, though not intended to provide a detailed analysis of the practice and enforcement of relevant country labour laws, did provide a good guide as to the state of CLS compliance in all the five Central American countries. The study did, however, confirm that the constitutions and the labour codes of all the countries incorporated the ILO CLS. The study indicated that the observations made by the CEACR with respect to compliance with Conventions 87 and 98 raised a number of issues. But it should be noted that issues on compliance with Conventions 87 and 98 are not only confined to the Central American countries but also extend to a great number of ILO Members.

The ILO study provided the six countries a good perspective of their level of compliance and prompted the countries to pay particular attention to responding to ILO recommendations and taking the necessary steps to improving enforcement of their respective labour laws. Due to the enforcement problems that the study highlighted, the governments of the six countries took an unprecedented step, by establishing a clear linkage between the effective implementation of the CLS and international trade, with the view to achieving a very high level of compliance.

A very important development in the run-up to the signing of CAFTA-DR was the *first ever* meeting of the Ministers of trade and labour of the six Central American countries on 13 July 2004. This is significant in the sense that the Ministers recognised that achieving compliance with the ILO CLS was critical to the successful functioning of the CAFTA-DR, stating that "[t]he obligations contained in the labor chapter of the agreement and the commitments to expand the capacity of the labor institutions represent both a significant challenge and an important opportunity for the countries".[108] The Ministers in a joint statement instructed their respective Vice Ministers to establish a working group, which should issue a report and provide recommendations on the efforts that should be made to enhance the implementation and enforcement of labour standards and how to strengthen the labour institutions in all six countries, and in so doing promote socio-economic development.

In addition to providing country-specific recommendations on strengthening compliance and enhancing capacity, the Labor Dimension also identified regional priorities under the five priority areas and proposed recommendations. For our purposes, we will only discuss the regional priorities. According to the Labor

[107] It is not clear if the signing of the agreement prompted El Salvador to ratify both Conventions. However, it cannot also be ruled out that El Salvador was influenced into signing as a result of being a signatory to the FTA.

[108] The Labor Dimension in Central America and the Dominican Republic, Building on Progress: Strengthening Compliance and Enhancing Capacity, A Report of the Working Group of the Vice Ministers Responsible for Trade and Labor in the Countries of Central America and the Dominican Republic, Submitted to the Ministers Responsible for Trade and Labor in the Countries of Central America and the Dominican Republic, April 2005 [hereinafter Labor Dimension].

Dimension, to improve implementation and application of labour standards in the region, technical assistance and capacity building were identified as critical. The report made reference to the many technical assistance and capacity-building projects related to labour but made the observation that due to the challenges and the priorities identified, what is even more important is a better and effective national and regional coordination effort.

We highlight below the priority areas and recommendations established by the working group since they are relevant to other developing countries and regional groupings (Table 8.2).

The emphasis on the regional coordination efforts is very essential since the ILO has stated that establishing an international legal framework on social standards ensures that a level playing field is achieved at the multilateral level. This, in the ILO's view, assists governments and employers not to lower labour standards to gain a competitive edge.[109] Further to this is the wording of Article 16.2(2) of the U.S.–CAFTA-DR FTA, which states: "The Parties recognize that it is inappropriate to encourage trade or investment by weakening or reducing the protections afforded in domestic labor laws."[110]

By coordinating implementation at the regional level through, for example, the establishment of a regional centre, the countries within this regional grouping not only avoid lowering labour standards but also are urged to achieve a greater degree of compliance. This is a major development in the labour-trade debate for which regional groupings can make a positive impact.

Following the Labor Dimension report, the Labour Ministers of the six countries drew up an Implementation Plan covering the period 2007–2010, with representatives from the judiciary and feedback from worker and employer organisations. Further to this, the countries requested the ILO to provide a report every 6 months to the Ministers as a means of verifying the progress made in line with the implementation plan at both the national and regional levels. As at July 2009, the ILO had prepared six reports highlighting the most important results that the countries had achieved under the implementation plan in the Labor Dimension report since the signing on April 2005 and provided suggestions on how to accelerate the implementation of the recommendations of the Ministers.

It is in the area of efforts to improve labour conditions in the Central American countries and the Dominican Republic that the Agreement, coupled with economic development in the region, could have a lasting impact. The Agreement in Article 16.5 (Labor Cooperation and Capacity Building Mechanism)[111] states that cooperating on labour matters could be important in making progress in the

[109] ILO (2009), p. 10.

[110] Article 16.2(2) of U.S.–CAFTA-DR FTA (see www.ustr.gov).

[111] Article 16.5 of CAFTA-DR is similar to the pending U.S.–Colombia FTA Article 17.6. It appears that the United States fully recognises the importance of capacity building in improving labour standards. This is also proving to be a trend in upcoming U.S. trade agreements with developing countries, that investment in capacity building programmes is a major step towards compliance with the ILO CLS.

Table 8.2 Regional Priorities and Recommendations of the Working Group

Priority Area	Recommendations
Labor Ministries	• Increase resources for key compliance functions, including inspectorates, and mediation and conciliation services. • Improve training of compliance personnel. • Improve infrastructure, information technology and case management capacity. • Reorganize operations of labor ministries to effectively focus on key priorities. • Enhance or establish where necessary offices focused on women's workplace issues and child labor. • Enhance or establish offices where necessary of special advocates for worker rights who can further assist workers and employers on effective compliance with labor laws. • Institutionalize improved enforcement procedures and initiatives focused on high priority concerns such as the dismissal of workers for legitimate trade union activities and gender discrimination, including any illegal pregnancy testing.
Administration of Labor Justice	• Make further investments in labor courts, judges and other personnel and equipment. • Enhance operation of the labor courts. • Establish comprehensive labor standards training initiative for judges, prosecutors, government officials and others involved in labor law administration. • Involve appropriate academic organizations in establishing a network of labor law training centers in each country. • Establish a regional labor law center to integrate best practices and assist in the harmonization of training capacity and other practices in the labor law administration area. • Establish additional alternative dispute resolution centers in countries that do not have one, and assure that the resources and training are available to make them successful.
Gender and Discrimination	• Establish a regional center for employment equality that would provide training, educational materials, a clearinghouse on best practices and other information, and support other programs focused on the elimination of employment discrimination concerns. • Undertake targeted training and enforcement support initiatives for the ministries of labor on effective compliance strategies for violations that might involve pregnancy testing or the exploitation of migrant or indigenous workers.
Worst Forms of Child Labor	• Establish a child labor free zone consistent with ILO Convention 182 by the end of the decade. • Develop viable timelines, needs assessments, and allocation of resources to accomplish the objective.
Promoting a Culture of Compliance	• Implement comprehensive training on labor rights for workers and employers. • Strengthen tripartite labor councils and make more effective use of their output.

Source: Labor Dimension (April 2005)

development of the economies of the Parties and for the improvement of labour standards. The Agreement further called upon all the signatories to advance common commitments regarding labour issues, including the principles embodied in the ILO Declaration and Convention 182 on the Worst Forms of Child Labour.

The United States government showed its commitment to the capacity-building initiatives of Article 16.5 when the then U.S. Trade Representative (Rob Portman) sent a letter on 28 June 2005 (2 days before the Senate's passage of the Agreement) to a member of the Senate Finance Committee indicating that the Bush administration intended to propose and earmark US$40 million for each of the years 2006–2009 as part of the government's labour and environmental enforcement capacity building in the six countries. The letter also indicated that out of the appropriated amount, the government would give the ILO US$3 million annually to fund an ILO "transparent public report" to be published every 6 months on the findings of progress in the six countries on their efforts to improve labour law enforcement and working conditions.[112]

The United States government made good on its promise to help improve labour conditions in the six countries by allocating US$60 (US$20 million each year between 2005 and 2007), for capacity building under CAFTA-DR, to assist in implementing the regional priorities and recommendations of the working group, namely (a) strengthening the labour ministries by improving the structure and function of inspectorates and also increasing the efficiency of the process of handling complaints; (b) strengthening the judicial systems in all six countries so as to improve the effectiveness in enforcing existing country labour laws; (c) working to reduce gender and other types of discrimination; (d) establishing benchmarking, verification, and monitoring procedures; and (e) promoting the development of a culture of compliance with labour laws.[113]

Under Article 16.5(b), one of the activities that the Agreement is to promote is the provision of opportunities for public participation, increasing the awareness of labour laws and institutions. This is important since it is only when workers know their rights that they can hold the government to account. Elliot (2004) reports on the progress that Costa Rican authorities claim to have made in increasing awareness among Costa Rican workers. The extent of the awareness programme is shown by workers regularly contacting the Ministry of Labour for information about their rights and to report problems. According to the official interviewed by Elliot, the government through the Ministry of Labour provides information for workers on its website; the Ministry also advertises how to get information on television and radio. The Ministry has, in addition, set up kiosks throughout the country distributing brochures and other information to workers.[114] The Costa Rican example shows how the efforts of a government ministry can be effective in public awareness and education, and this could be useful for the region under the regional centre initiative

[112] See Bolle (2005), p. 6.

[113] See http://www.state.gov/r/pa/prs/ps/2008/jan/99876.htm. Accessed 20 April 2014.

[114] Elliot (2004), p. 9.

in the effective promotion of a culture of compliance of labour laws. This is also an example worthy of replicating in other countries and regions.

8.7.1.1 Labour Enforcement Under CAFTA

As at the end of 2013, only one case had been brought under the CAFTA Agreement. This case was filed in April 2008 by AFL-CIO and six Guatemalan worker organisations for alleged violations by the Guatemalan government of its commitments under CAFTA-DR, for failing to enforce its labour laws. Upon initial review by the U.S. Department of Labor, the Department issued a report stating its findings. The report highlighted the significant weaknesses in Guatemala's failure to enforce its labour laws.

From the time of the issuance of the report, the U.S. Government, with input from the USTR and the Departments of Labor and State, conducted an extensive examination of Guatemala's compliance with its commitments under the agreement's labour chapter. The examination included three areas, namely (1) a thorough review of Guatemala's labour laws, (2) wide-range collection of factual evidence, and (3) an analysis of Guatemala's obligations under Article 16.2.1(a). As a result of this examination, the U.S. Government reached the conclusion that Guatemala seemed to be failing to meet its obligations in respect of labour law enforcement.[115]

On 30 July 2010, the U.S. Government pursuant to Article 16.6.1 of the CAFTA-DR requested consultations with the Government of Guatemala to discuss matters related to Guatemala's obligations under Article 16.2.1(a), as well as under the wider umbrella of Chapter 16. The issue was in respect of Guatemala's failure to respect its obligations under Article 16.2.1(a) concerning the effective enforcement of Guatemala's labour laws related to the right of association, the right to organise and bargain collectively, acceptable conditions of work, and in particular Guatemala's failure to provide adequate protection from violence for labour leaders. The U.S. claimed that Guatemala's failure to enforce its labour laws gave the country an unfair advantage that was detrimental to U.S. workers.[116]

The parties, as required under the CAFTA-DR rules, held consultations in September and December 2010, and on 16 May 2011 the U.S. Government requested a meeting of the Free Trade Commission (the ministerial body that supervises the implementation of the agreement) under Article 20.5. On 7 June 2011, the Commission met but failed to reach an agreement on an enforcement plan. When the issue was not resolved within a reasonable period of time (the 60-day consultation period), the U.S. Government then exercised its right under the

[115] See, http://www.ustr.gov/about-us/press-office/press-releases/2011/may/ustr-kirk-seeks-enforcement-labor-laws-guatemala. Accessed 20 April 2014.

[116] http://www.ustr.gov/about-us/press-office/press-releases/2011/may/ustr-kirk-seeks-enforcement-labor-laws-guatemala. Accessed 20 April 2014.

agreement in calling for the establishment of an arbitral panel under Chapter 20, which it did on 9 August 2011. The Panellists were appointed in 2012.

In April 2013, the United States and Guatemala agreed to a comprehensive enforcement plan that obliges the Guatemalan government to take concrete steps to implement the plan, and within specified time frames, so as to improve the enforcement of its labour laws. The enforcement plan consists of 18 points, such as strengthening of the ministry of labour to enforce labour laws and also strengthening of labour inspections, the need to expedite and streamline the process of sanctioning employers for labour law violations, a system to be put in place to ensure that workers are paid when factories are closed (receipt of severance pay), the government taking the necessary steps to improve labour law compliance by export companies, improvement in the monitoring and enforcement of labour court orders, and ensuring of transparency through the publication of labour law enforcement statistics and data.[117]

8.7.1.2 Impact of CAFTA-DR on Labour Standard Compliance

Guatemala has a history of lack of compliance with the CLS. Guatemala joined the ILO in 1945, and in recent years there have been a number of reported labour rights violations, and these have included violence, intimidation, and even murder of union leaders.[118] The International Trade Union Confederation (ITUC), for example, in 2009 concluded in its analyses of CLS in Guatemala that even though the country has ratified all eight core ILO Conventions, it has not taken the necessary steps to ensure compliance by putting in place effective enforcement mechanisms. The report highlighted these shortcomings and provided recommendations consisting of 18 points.[119]

Violations of freedom of association in Guatemala are well documented by the ILO. As at August 2013, there were 13 active cases, 7 follow-up cases, and 73 closed cases.[120] Concerns have been raised by the ILO CEACR for a number of years and as recently as 2013 at the ILO International Conference. The CEACR stated:

> The Committee notes the comments of the International Trade Union Confederation (ITUC), dated 31 July 2012, referring to matters already under examination by the Committee, and particularly the murder of seven trade union leaders and two trade union members between January and October 2011. The Committee also notes the comments on the application of the Convention made by the Trade Union Confederation of Guatemala

---

[117] http://www.ustr.gov/about-us/press-office/fact-sheets/2013/april/guatemala-labor-enforcement. Accessed 21 April 2014.

[118] CAWN Central America Women's Network Newsletter No. 20, Autumn 2005: http://www.cawn.org/publications/documentation/newsletter/CAWNautumn05.pdf. Accessed 21 April 2014.

[119] International Trade Union Confederation (ITUC) (2009).

[120] http://www.ilo.org/dyn/normlex/en/f?p=1000:11110:0::NO::P11110_COUNTRY_ID:102667. Accessed 22 April 2014.

(UNSITRAGUA), the General Confederation of Workers of Guatemala (CGTG) and the Trade Unions' Unity of Guatemala (CUSG), dated 30 August 2012, which refer in particular to numerous allegations of violations of trade union rights in practice, in both the private and public sectors, and to acts of violence against trade unionists, including the murder of a trade union leader in August 2012.[121]

The CEACR further stated:

The Committee recalls that for several years it has been noting in its observations serious acts of violence against trade unionists which have gone unpunished and has requested the Government to provide information on developments in this regard... The Committee observes that the Committee on Freedom of Association (in Cases Nos. 2445, 2540, 2609 and 2768) noted with concern that the allegations levelled in the context of its proceedings were extremely serious and included many murders and acts of violence against trade union leaders and members. The Committee recalls that the high-level mission which visited Guatemala from 9 to 14 May 2011 reported as follows:

The mission wishes to recall that the problems of violence referred to by the CEACR are the following:

- alleged murders of trade union leaders and members over the past 5 years: 2007: 12; 2008: 12; 2009: 16; 2010: 10; and 2011: two up to the month of May (a few days after the mission, a trade union leader of the SITRABI was murdered);
- death threats, abductions, raids, etc., alleged over the past four years.[122]

The observations made by the CEACR show the extent to which the government has been violating the CLS. Guatemala, compared to the other members of the CAFTA-DR, indicates that the level of impunity in dealing with trade unions is more widespread than in the other five countries.

This raises the question on how the CAFTA-DR would help ensure compliance in a country like Guatemala, given its long history of CLS violations. As discussed above, the 18-point enforcement plan mutually agreed upon by the United States and Guatemala is a promising sign of how to bring about the necessary changes by ensuring that the government meets its obligations in adhering to the CLS, both as an ILO Member and as a member of CAFTA-DR. Whilst it is too early to determine how the plan agreed upon would achieve the desired results, it is nevertheless a good first step in getting a country like Guatemala, with its history of CLS violations, to enforce its labour laws. This would also further entrench the respect for the CLS for the other five members of CAFTA-DR.

[121] Observation by CEACR—adopted 2012, published at the 102nd ILC session (2013), at http://www.ilo.org/dyn/normlex/en/f?p=1000:13100:0::NO:13100:P13100_COMMENT_ID:3084277. Accessed 26 April 2014.

[122] Observation by CEACR—adopted 2012.

8.7.2 Lessons from the U.S.–Cambodia Textile Agreement

Does the U.S. approach in the CAFTA-DR agreement and the pending Colombia FTA in providing resources for technical assistance and cooperation point a way to the future in bringing about compliance? The issue of adherence to CLS is a combination of increased trade, cooperation, and capacity building, leading to strong government institutions, trade incentives, and—equally important—political will. This shows how a multifaceted approach is vital in promoting compliance. The case of Cambodia is a positive example of how compliance can be achieved through a multifaceted approach. The U.S.–Cambodia Textile Agreement was signed in 1999 and expired in 2005. Under this agreement, the United States invested US$2 million over a 5-year period, leading to progress in promoting, verifying, and ensuring compliance with labour laws. The programme brought together public and private interests and, coupled with the promise of incentives, ensured that both government officials and the private sector bought into it.

The agreement set quotas for textile and apparel exports from Cambodia to the United States, which could be increased if Cambodia met all obligations to improve the enforcement of its own labour laws, and protect internationally recognised workers' rights in the textile and apparel sector. The United States increased the quotas by 9 % each year between 1999 and 2001, by 12 % between 2002 and 2003, and finally by 14 % for 2004.[123] The approach has been seen as successful by both the United States and Cambodian governments and also the firms and Cambodian workers in the apparel sector.

The success of the programme is seen in the significant improvements in wages and working conditions. Further to this is the report of the CEACR on Cambodia for both 2008 and 2009. In 2008, Cambodia was included in the list of countries for which the Committee noted with interest the measures taken by the government under Convention 87 (Freedom of Association and Protection of the Right to Organise Convention). And in 2009, the Committee also noted with interest the measures taken by the government under Conventions 138 and 182 (Minimum Wage and Worst Forms of Child Labour Conventions).

Three key reasons have been identified for the success of the approach in the U.S.–Cambodia agreement.[124] Firstly, the quota increase was determined on a yearly basis, as such, a linkage between the behaviour of firms, government, and the rewards for good deeds was established. Secondly, the incentives for the private sector were closely in line with those for the government. Since each firm stood to benefit under the quota increase arrangement, the firms saw the value of voluntary compliance with the labour laws and respect for workers' rights. In addition, the increase in quotas was dependent on improvement on a sector-wide performance so that non-compliance by any firm put the benefits for all at risk.

[123] Polaski (2004), pp. 21 and 25.

[124] Polaski (2004), p. 22.

Finally, a project that grew out of the textile agreement on the effective monitoring system of the garment factories provided information about the factories. The monitoring system run by the ILO monitors and reports on working conditions in the garment factories were based on Cambodia labour laws and international standards. The project called *Better Factories Cambodia*[125] makes unannounced factory visits to check on working conditions. The monitors have a checklist of about 480 items, which are checked through interviews with management, workers, factory shop stewards, and union leaders on a confidential basis.

The initial reports identifying problems of non-compliance with labour standards, including specific recommendations for improvement, are first communicated only to the factory manager. Allowing time for discussions and follow-up actions, a second visit carried out after about 6 months checks on progress made based on the earlier recommendations. A report is then made public on the project's website identifying the name and location of the factories visited and indicating what actions have been taken to improve conditions and the problems that still remain unresolved.

The Better Factories project is of great benefit as all exporting garment factories are included and the factories' common interest are represented. Due to the transparent nature of the monitoring process, foreign firms that are concerned about buying from factories with a bad reputation are able to source goods from the factories that have complied with national labour laws and international standards. In this way, the project has benefited consumers in countries where the products are sold and in Cambodia, helps workers to realise their decent work aspirations, and also contribute to poverty reduction.

The project would not have been possible without the cooperation of the Cambodian Ministry of Commerce. Since participation is a prerequisite for receiving export license, the Cambodian government has also benefited as the burden of enforcing the labour laws and ensuring compliance with the international standards, especially the CLS, is significantly reduced because the factories are forced to voluntarily comply. Although the Better Factories project is not intended to guarantee absolute compliance with national labour laws and labour standards as a whole, by focusing on continuous improvement it has contributed to great progress in labour relations. The tripartite nature of the project (comprising trade unions, employers' associations, and the government) has also contributed to both economic growth and social justice. It is relevant to note that the Cambodian garment industry, from its near insignificant beginning in 1994, has grown to represent about 80 % of Cambodia's export earnings. It is the largest industry in the country earning Cambodia about US$2.7 billion in 2007. The industry in 2007 employed about 350,000 workers, with a minimum wage of US$50 and average earnings per month of US$77.[126]

---

[125] For more information on this project, visit www.betterfactories.org. Accessed 23 April 2014.

[126] See www.betterfactories.org.

The positive experience of the Better Factories project in Cambodia, with its maximum transparency and efficient tripartite system, raises the question of how some of the features of that project could not be explored in other countries.

8.8 The Limits of Regional Efforts

8.8.1 Regional Efforts Versus Multilateralism

Regionalism and globalism have since the twentieth century been coexisting, but it is during the turn of the twenty-first century that the relationship has taken on great intensity. The assumption has been that regionalism is a shortcut to globalisation. For example, the ILO World Commission on the Social Dimension of Globalisation sees regional integration as a stepping stone and argues that through cooperation at the regional level an equitable pattern of globalisation could be promoted. The report of the Commission lists three ways of achieving an equitable globalisation.[127]

First, the Commission argues that through regional integration people can be empowered and countries would be better able to manage global economic forces. Regional integration by creating an economic bloc increases the size of their markets and thereby increases the capability of countries to withstand economic fluctuations so prevalent in a global economy. Through effective coordination of their policies, countries within a regional union would be able to reduce the spill-over effects of their neighbours. The creation of common frameworks in areas such as financial regulation, rights at work, coordination of taxes, and incentives for investment could help prevent a situation of a race to the bottom.

Second, the Commission believes that regional groupings would be able to build the needed capabilities for countries to take advantage of the opportunities created through globalisation. Third, through regional integration, countries can improve the conditions under which their citizens connect to the global economy. The example is given of the European Union, which has promoted human rights and democracy, and also Latin America and Africa, where human rights initiatives are high on the agenda. The Commission believes that a starting point for considering social issues on the global scale could be when these social issues are made part of the regional integration process and built into their institutions.

The views of the ILO Commission is in line with the aim of the recent wave of regional groupings, which are based on a much more comprehensive process to include both political and economic objectives, going beyond the trade, economic growth, and investment agendas.

As regionalism grows in importance and continues to become a vital element of global economic and political relations, much is being debated about its pros and

[127] ILO (2004), p. 71.

cons. It is not the aim of this section to discuss in depth the economic and political effects of regionalisation; however, a point of great interest in analysing the regional efforts vis-à-vis multilateral efforts in the area of labour standards is whether regionalisation could spur a move towards the economic development of developing countries so as to enhance their welfare for the betterment of their citizens.

In this respect, the European Union is an example of how deeper integration can be welfare enhancing. The EU has through integration established a common framework for an effective internal market economy, provided a supportive European-wide social protection system, and established minimum work standards. The Union has also through its legal system ensured that member states respect the rule of law, human rights, gender equality, and a thriving political climate for democracy to grow.[128] In addition, the economic success of deeper integration has led to phenomenal economic growth and compliance with international labour standards, as evidenced by the level of compliance of CLS among countries that have signed FTAs with the United States and some ACP countries.

Another case in point is that of the three signatories to the NAFTA Agreement. In their analysis of the trade benefits of NAFTA and for the purposes of this thesis on employment, impact on working conditions, and living standards in each of the three signatory countries, especially on Mexico, Hufbauer and Schott (2005) conclude that even though some work remains to be done, on the whole, NAFTA has been a "great building block".[129] And NAFTA has in great measure contributed to the tremendous expansion of regional trade since it went into force.[130]

Since the coming into force of NAFTA, trade between the three countries increased between 1993 and 2006 by 198 %, from US$297 to US$883 billion.[131] Hufbauer and Schott also state that the two-way merchandise trade between the U.S. and Mexico since 1993 has grown by 227 %, compared to U.S. trade with non-NAFTA countries at only 124 %.[132] For Mexico, in particular, the NAFTA agreement has brought benefits in such areas as agriculture (U.S. imports from Mexico has since the last 13 years increased by US$6.7 billion) and services (U.S. trade with Canada and Mexico grew by 78 and 59 %, respectively); U.S. foreign direct investment flows into Mexico increased from US$33 billion in 1994 to US$166 billion by 2003.[133]

---

[128] ILO (2004), p. 72.

[129] In this section, we will place more emphasis on the impact of NAFTA on Mexico, since it is the least developed among the three signatories, since any positive trade impact has also a positive influence on poverty reduction and thereby on labour standards.

[130] Hufbauer and Schott (2005), p. 18.

[131] See website of the Office of the United States Trade Representative.

[132] Hufbauer and Schott (2005), p. 18.

[133] For more information on the data quoted here, see the website of the Office of the United States Trade Representative and Hufbauer and Schott (2005), pp. 17–38.

However, it is in the area of employment and poverty reduction that the impact of NAFTA has been most encouraging. Hufbauer and Schott (2005) further state that the impact on employment in each of the three countries has been positive—though less than what the politicians promised and more than what the pundits predicted. The data indicate that there were net employment increases in all the three countries. The employment rate in the U.S. rose from 110 million in 1993 to 124 million in 2003, whereas Canada saw an increase of 12.9 million to 15.7 million during the same period. In the case of Mexico, jobs in the formal sector increased from 32.8 million to 40.6 million, some as a result of increase in trade and investment due to Mexico's membership in NAFTA.[134] In terms of the number of people living below the poverty line (below US$2 a day), Mexico witnessed a decline from 42.5 % in 1995 to 26.3 % in 2000. The OECD reported in 2008 that Mexico's poverty rate had fallen to 18 %.[135] The increase in trade since the coming into force of NAFTA could arguably have contributed to the fall in poverty rate.

Given the nature of global issues and the role of regional groupings, regionalism and multilateralism could function in a complementary way. However, in spite of the economic benefits and the evidence of adherence to the core labour standards by countries within regional groupings, and the fact that regionalism is in fashion, in the ultimate analysis, regionalism cannot be a substitute for a multilateral approach. The key to resolving such controversial issues as the labour standards and international trade linkage, it appears, lies with multilateralism.

There is no question as to the fact that regional standards could be useful in supplementing universal standards or addressing matters of specific interest to a region. Nonetheless, the regional standard setting cannot altogether replace the international standard setting.

Wolf (2005) shows how a world divided into small entities would not be able to achieve its full potential:

> Who imagines that the welfare of Americans would be improved if their economy was fragmented among its fifty states, each with prohibitive barriers to movement of goods, services, capital and people from the others? Who supposes that Americans would be better off if every state had its own capital market, or GE, Microsoft and IBM could operate in only one of these states? In such a Disunited States, without inter-state direct investment, capital markets or trade, the decline in standards of living would be precipitous. Some states would become prisons, with desperately unhappy populations locked inside. A similar disaster would befall Europe if policymakers once again fragmented the European economy into the isolated national economies of 1945.[136]

Wolf argues that the break-up of the world into smaller nation-states and each country expected to be economically self-sufficient is absurd. To achieve a high level of economic development would entail that there be greater economic integration, this would lead to the raising of the living standards of the less-developed

[134] See Hufbauer and Schott (2005), pp. 38 and 98.

[135] OECD (2008).

[136] Wolf (2005), p. 3.

countries. In working for the betterment of the poor, the role of the international community is very important. It is worth mentioning here the words of the former UN Secretary General Kofi Annan at the opening of the United Nations Economic and Social Council (ECOSOC) meeting in July 1998, when he stated:

> Multilateralism, let us not forget, has given us the international trading system. The international community has ample reason to be proud of this achievement. The open, rule-based trading system has generated an extraordinary surge in prosperity and dramatic reductions in poverty. It is also an outstanding example demonstrating that joint efforts and multilateral cooperation – where the strong respect the rights of the weak – are not a zero-sum game. The trade liberalisation process must continue.[137]

In the same way as multilateralism has given us the multilateral trading system, so it has given us the ILO. The creation of the ILO has three main roots, namely the defence of peace, the linkage to the promotion of social justice, and the response of the international community to global competition. The ILO process of standard setting and monitoring could lead to better labour standards globally. More than 90 years after its establishment, the role of the ILO is as relevant today as it was at its creation. Given the roles of the WTO and the ILO, the fact that the achievement of their objectives has a positive impact on adherence to the core labour standards, a coordination of their roles is very important to achieving a high level of compliance.

8.8.2 A Global Issue in a Regionalised World and Its Implications at the National Level

The reliance of countries on regional trade agreements to resolve the conflict between core labour standards and international trade, whilst it has achieved a measure of success, still falls short of addressing the fundamental problem of greater degree of compliance in all the five areas of the core labour standards. These gains give a glimpse of how gains could be made at the multilateral level, which raises the question as to whether a multilateral approach would achieve a greater degree of compliance. In a world in which regionalism is increasing with multiple memberships, gains made in a regional grouping could spill over into other regional groupings, thereby helping to achieve a higher level of compliance with the core labour standards. However, in a world in which the destinies of each country is intertwined with each other, regionalism can only act as a testing ground, but the ultimate solution lies with a multilateral approach. This raises the question of how regionalism could effectively resolve an issue that is global in nature.

The experience with multilateralism, for instance, in the area of trade negotiations has shown how countries working in concert can develop guidelines and come up with solutions that each country could benefit from. Whereas regionalism has

---

[137] Quoted in Lim (2014), p. 16.

acted as stimulus and laboratory for the multilateral system, it is eventually a multilateral approach built on the success of the RTAs that could provide the key to unlocking what could be termed a "closed door" in industrial and economic relations.

The analysis in Chap. 7 has no doubt shown how RTAs could have a positive influence on the multilateral trading system. And in Chap. 6 we discussed the positive influence of labour standard implementation and compliance, as shown by the example of countries that have entered into bilateral trade agreements with the United States. However, this influence and positive results at the global level can be fully achieved if RTAs operate in full openness and comply with the multilateral rules. Notwithstanding the important contributions that have been made by regional trading arrangements, they can never be a substitute for the multilateral trading system. This is a fact that the community of nations should realise and invest the necessary political capital in multilateralism.

The events in recent times, such as the global financial crisis, the changing landscape of trade relations, raise the issue of how an international social policy could be developed alongside the international economic order. Does the global nature of CLS demand the same approach as we have in the capital markets? Or as we pointed out in Chap. 2, economic development cannot be achieved in the absence of an effective social order. The social impact of the Asian financial crisis and the recent global financial crisis poses a challenge for social policy. With the increasing loss of jobs, foreclosures, the anticipated rise in poverty, with their attendant social distresses, the issue is whether it is enough to bail out Wall Street without also bailing out Main Street.[138]

The global crisis has also created an opportunity for a new world order—a world in which the concerns of the developing countries that account for the majority of countries, which find it increasingly difficult to comply with core labour standards, should be taken into consideration in the design of a new world architecture. Even as there are calls for more stimulus packages and the need to stabilise the financial institutions, there is little mention of also the need to develop and even strengthen social institutions.

In a world in which the only constant is change, there are new types of social relationships being created, as the economic and financial landscape alters, which in its wake also creates new areas of social and political conflicts. The world of labour standards has shown that in both developed and developing countries, the so-called traditional institutions for regulating labour relations are proving to be inadequate and ill adapted to the needs of an ever-changing global economy. The attempts to develop new institutions have, in many respects, failed to keep pace with the advances in economic and technological changes. Achieving a high level of adherence to core labour standards depends on many factors: such as the pace of economic growth, on investment policies, on the importance given to the

[138] http://fortune.com/2012/01/18/a-new-stimulus-have-wall-street-bail-out-main-street/. Accessed 1 May 2014.

development of industry and agriculture, on educational policies, social policies, and other factors.

As we explained in Chap. 2, the changing landscape of trade relations and the calls for a more concerted approach to global issues could create a unique opportunity for a multilateral approach to "killing two birds with one stone", in that the measures proposed, and if effectively implemented in addressing the economic challenges and well managed with economic benefits for the developing world, could create the right conditions for moving many people in the medium to long term from poverty to the middle class, thus effectively addressing issues such as the worst forms of child labour, discrimination in respect of employment and occupation, and forced or compulsory labour.

In Chap. 2 we also examined the views of the proponents and critics of a linkage between labour standards and international trade, which views tended to be more negative based basically on two outcomes: (1) the deterioration of labour standards, and (2) that even though labour is the most venerable of the two main factors of production, it is capital that is the most protected, thereby giving capital a strengthened bargaining power of capital vis-à-vis the power of labour. The prevailing view has been that globalisation has negative effects on labour standards and the bargaining power of labour.

References

Adams, R. J., & Singh, P. (1997). Early experience with NAFTA's labour side accord. *Comparative Labour Law Journal, 18*(2).

Bazar, J. S. (1995). Is the North American agreement on labor cooperation working for workers' rights? *California Western International Law Journal, 25*.

Befort, S. F., & Cornett, B. (1996). Beyond the rhetoric of the NAFTA treaty debate: A comparative analysis of labor and employment law in Mexico and the United States. *Comparative Labor Law Journal, 17*.

Bolle, M. J. (2005). *DR–CAFTA labor rights issues*. CRS Report for Congress, 8 July, Code RS22159.

Carney, J., & Zagorin, A. (1995). A tale of two jobs: One lost, one gained. *Time*, 27 September 1993.

Compa, L. (1995). The first NAFTA labor cases: A new International Labor Rights regime takes shape. *U.S.–Mexico Law Journal, 3*.

Demaret, P. (1997). The reciprocal influence of multilateral and regional trade rules: A framework of analysis. In P. Demaret, J. F. Bellis, & G. Jiménez (Eds.), *Regionalism and multilateralism after the Uruguay round, convergence, divergence and interaction*. Brussels: European Interuniversity Press.

Elliot, K. A. (2004). *Labor standards, development, and CAFTA (Number PB04-2)*. Washington, DC: International Economics Policy briefs.

Finbow, R. G. (2006). *The limits of regionalism: NAFTA's labour accord*. Aldershot: Ashgate.

Hufbauer, G. C., & Schott, J. J. (1993). *NAFTA: An assessment*. Canada: Peterson Institute.

Hufbauer, G. C., & Schott, J. J. (2005). *NAFTA revisited: Achievements and challenges*. Washington, DC: Institute for International Economics.

ILO. (2004). World Commission on the social dimension of globalization. A fair globalization: Creating opportunities for all.

ILO. (2009). *Rules of the game: A brief introduction to International Labour Standards*. Geneva: ILO.

International Trade Union Confederation (ITUC). (2009). *Internationally recognised core labour standards in Guatemala*. Report for the WTO General Council Review of Trade Policies of Guatemala, Geneva, 2–4 February 2009. http://www.ituc-csi.org/report-for-the-wto-general-council,5282. Accessed 21 Apr 2014.

LaSala, B. (2001). NAFTA and worker rights: An analysis of the labor side accord after five years of operation and suggested improvements. *Lab Law, 16*(3).

Lim, H. (2014). *Trade and human rights: What's at issue?*. Economic and Social Council, E/C.12/2001/WP.2 (www.ohchr.org). Accessed 26 Apr 2014.

Murphy, B. S. (1995). NAFTA's North American agreement on labor cooperation: The present and the future. *Connecticut Journal of International Law, 10*.

Nolan Garcia, K. A. (2011). Transnational advocates and labor rights enforcement in the North American free trade agreement. *Latin American Politics and Society, 53*(2).

Norton, J. J., & Bloodworth, T. L. (Eds.). (1995). *NAFTA and beyond: A new framework for doing business in the Americas*. Dordrecht: Martinus Nijhoff.

OECD. (2008). *Growing unequal? Income distribution and poverty in OECD countries*. Paris: OECD.

Polaski, S. (2004). Protecting labour rights through trade agreements: An analytical guide. *Journal of International Law and Policy, 10*(13) (University of California, Davis).

Robinson, I. (1995). The NAFTA labour accord in Canada: Experience, prospects, and alternatives. *Connecticut Journal of International Law, 10*(2).

Wolf, M. (2005). *Why globalization works*. New Haven: Yale University Press.

Chapter 9
Conclusion and Recommendations

9.1 Social Norms and Trade Liberalisation in a Globalised World

The discussion in this book has highlighted the conflict between the protection of social norms, on one hand, and globalisation and trade liberalisation, on the other. Globalisation of the world economy has revealed its impact on workers' rights, which in turn have brought to fore the linkage issue.

The reason for this conflict can be found in the following assertion: "There is hardly a walk of life untouched directly or indirectly by international trade regulation."[1] This statement indicates the extent to which trade agreements and disciplines pervade practically all spheres of economic, industrial, and trade activities in a country and its impact on social norms and development. What this also brings out is how trade liberalisation, as exemplified by the WTO Agreements, can restrict governments and labour organisations to protect workers in their respective economies.[2] Finding a midpoint that both the proponents and critics of the linkage issue can meet that would satisfactorily meet their demands is still an ongoing process.

The issue of the economic/social divide, which has resulted in narrowly looking at the inclusion of a social clause, has been examined. Are there separate economic and social spheres? The view that economic behaviour and social behaviour operate at different levels can lead to skewed economic analysis. And this is precisely what has happened with respect to the proponents of a social clause. Assuming that countries pushing for the linkage between trade and labour standards are motivated by altruistic concerns, then it would appear that it would be counterproductive to impose trade sanctions. Poverty appears to be the major reason why some families in the developing world permit their children to work. There is overwhelming evidence to the effect that as a country gets richer and living conditions improve,

[1] Cottier and Oesch (2005), p. 2.

[2] Burianski (2007), pp. 427–429.

K. Addo, *Core Labour Standards and International Trade*,
DOI 10.1007/978-3-662-44619-5_9

parents would like their children to obtain good education. It would therefore appear that instead of erecting barriers to trade, the prudent solution would be to encourage countries to adopt appropriate policies that would facilitate the greater participation of developing and especially least developing countries in the multilateral trading system.

Why would a social clause that would allow individual WTO Members to impose trade sanctions against other Members that violate the ILO CLS after the approval of the Dispute Settlement Body not achieve the objective of making Members comply with the CLS and even be detrimental to the very people for whom sanctions are administered? We provide here three main reasons why a WTO-administered social clause would be ineffective.

First, we have already argued above that the WTO dispute settlement system is not well suited for applying trade sanctions to issues with social connotations. The WTO dispute settlement system was created to provide security and predictability to the multilateral trading system, which is the flow of goods and services between Members. In this respect, the system could be said to ensure that the economic benefits that countries derive from the free flow of goods and services are not impaired or Members' expectations not nullified through other countries change in their trade regime or when countries fail to carry out their WTO obligations. Such a system, as discussed, is not well equipped to deal with social issues within the context of economic benefits.

Furthermore, the WTO dispute settlement system is based on the suspension of tariff concession and prohibits quantitative restrictions,[3] and also under Article 22 (4) of the DSU the suspension of concessions "shall be equivalent to the level of nullification or impairment". Put differently, the level of suspension must not exceed the damage caused by the other Member's failure to comply with the CLS, bearing in mind that a number of studies have shown that the lack of adherence to the CLS does not normally lead to much economic advantage for the country that violates the CLS, in which case the damage caused to the importing country is very minimal, making the suspension of concessions ineffective.[4]

Second, allowing WTO Members to apply trade sanctions based on a social clause in the MTS would not be as effective as when the sanction is applied based on an ILO recommendation. The reason is that when a WTO Member unilaterally

[3] Article 22(5) of the DSU, read in conjunction with GATT Article XI of GATT. Article 22.5 states: "The DSB shall not authorize suspension of concessions or other obligations if a covered agreement prohibits such suspension." Unless one of the many exceptions to the rule in GATT Article XI such as GATT Art. XIX (Safeguards: Emergency Action on Imports of Particular Products); GATT Art. XI:2(a) (Critical Shortage of Foodstuffs or Other Essential Products: Export prohibitions or restrictions temporarily applied); GATT Art. XI:2(b) (Removal of a Temporary Surplus of a Like Domestic Product for which the Imported Product can be Directly Substituted); GATT Art. XI:2(c) (Agricultural Products and Fish)—Agreement on Agriculture (Tariffication); GATT Art. XX (General Exception); GATT Art. XXIV:5 (Free-Trade Area and Customs Unions); GATT Art. XXI (Security Exception); Marrakesh Agreement Art. IX:3 (Waiver), applies.

[4] OECD (1996), p. 440.

applies the sanction against another Member, it would only affect the trade between the two Members, which would probably be a small percentage of the overall trade between the affected Member and the Member applying the sanction. Should that be the case, the affected Member could shift its exports from the sanctioning Member to other Members.[5]

In addition, problems relating to rules of origin could become prominent as a product cannot be discriminated against solely on the ground that a minor component has been manufactured with, for example, child labour. Another related problem is which countries would be entitled to impose the trade sanctions. Should it be the importing country or the entire membership of the WTO? The objective of trade sanctions would be easily defeated if countries are not mandated to impose them on products manufactured with prohibited labour. It is doubtful if all Members of the WTO will agree to impose sanctions on countries that fail to implement their obligations under the ILO Conventions.

Whilst the developed countries may be willing to implement the decision, most developing countries might shy away from it, especially when the culprit is a developing country. This may poison the atmosphere and lead to unnecessary confrontations between countries of the Southern (mostly against a linkage) and Northern (mostly for a linkage) Hemisphere. On the other hand, an ILO-recommended sanction could have the multilateral effect, i.e. applied by all Members against the violating Member, and could bring about the necessary changes.

Third, should the social clause be administered by the WTO, only the export sector of violating Members would be affected, leaving the domestic sector still with non-compliant offenders. In most cases, the compliance levels in the export sectors are much better than that in the domestic sectors. There would appear to be a disconnect in that instead of working towards compliance across all sectors, it is rather the sector with a better record of compliance that is targeted. In the case of an ILO-administered system, all sectors of the economy are covered.

What the three points raised above shows is that a WTO-administered social clause would be wholly ineffective in addressing the labour standard and international trade linkage. The other issue is the inadequacy of the ILO to enforce compliance with the CLS and especially with the 1998 Declaration. Would a joint ILO/WTO enforcement regime based on a combination of the ILO tripartite system (using the example of the recent IFAs, due to the fact even though the private sector does not take part in trade negotiations, the sector is the one that translates the trade agreements into benefits, both economically and socially), coupled with the RTA model, be a much effective regime in effecting compliance? A key factor in proposing the inclusion of the IFA model is that whereas the multilateral trading system and the recent wave of RTAs tend to be more geared towards a "producer-driven governance"[6] system, the IFA model would ensure that

[5] OECD (1996), p. 440.

[6] Abbott (2000), p. 63.

labour is protected in the new context of globalisation. Below, we suggest such a regime. But, first, we highlight the lessons learned from the regional experience.

9.2 Lessons from the Regional Context

Since the inclusion of labour standard clauses in the NAFTA side agreement and subsequently in any bilateral agreement between the United States and other countries and also in the agreements between the European Union and other developing countries, labour standard provisions in regional trade agreements have become the norm rather than the exception. However, these trade arrangements have both positive and negative impacts, making them what is termed as 'second-best enterprises'. This has come about because since the 'first best' choice (meaning multilateralism) is not attainable, the RTAs have become the alternative to meeting the trade policy demands of participants.[7]

The question is whether the labour provisions in these agreements led to some improvements in adherence to the core labour standards. And if so, could this inclusion be a benchmark for improving labour conditions through a multilateral approach? How could the lessons learned at the RTA and bilateral agreement level be applied at the multilateral level?

We have presented an evaluation of labour provisions in RTAs and the impact on labour standards in the countries that are signatories to these RTAs. Whilst it is still too early to conclude that the impact has led to effective compliance with the CLS, the evidence presented by the ILO CEACR indicates that countries that have signed bilateral agreements with the United States and the European Union have made some progress. The level of compliance achieved under the U.S.–Cambodia Textile Agreement through a multifaceted approach is an indication of how the approach in the RTAs could, when adapted to a multilateral setting, help achieve a level of compliance commensurate with the level of development of each country.

In spite of the shortcomings of the regional model, it appears to be the best tool available in reaching consensus on this vexing issue. The key is how the international community translates the lessons learned at the regional level onto the global scene and makes the regional approach a force for good.

The proliferation of regional trade agreements continue at a feverish pace, and in spite of the argument that these agreements could divert trade and be a stumbling block to a multilateral process, the other view is that the RTAs could even be complementary, acting as stimuli and laboratory for the multilateral system. In one important respect, the RTAs are tackling an issue that the multilateral system has failed to grapple with—the relationship between social issues and trade. Even though the link at present does not fully address the issue of workers' rights, it is

[7] Plummer et al. (2010), p. 1.

in great measure an improvement of the impasse in which the multilateral process presently finds itself in.

It is important to note that the inclusion of labour provisions in the regional trade agreements is to boost the ILO standards and confirm the important role of the international labour standards as administered by the ILO. Although the commitments and enforcement mechanisms in the regional and bilateral trade agreements do not appear strong and might also appear to provide political cover needed to ratify the trade agreements, the evidence indicates that whilst promoting freer trade, the labour provisions have had an important indirect impact by encouraging compliance with ILO CLS, at least to the extent that makes adopting an international framework based on the regional experience worth the effort.

As economies and societies become increasingly interconnected, the traditional conception that each country could develop economically and socially without regard to developments in other countries has become antiquated. The interconnectivity of the global economy demands building a much stronger international economic and social order based on a better international legal framework, which reflects the changing landscape of political and economic relations. This new international order must be based on the already established system, as for example the view that the core labour standards, as enshrined in the ILO Declaration, have reached the level too deeply embedded in international law that they bind all nations, irrespective of national consent. The core labour standards and even the international labour standards are such that the international community should consider them as part of fundamental human rights.

To make it more effective should entail reliance on a combination of hard and soft laws. As we have discussed, the ILO depends on moral suasion, which is the soft law approach and the hard law approach, as the advocates of the linkage propose is, for example, the WTO dispute settlement mechanism. We have indicated that the nature of the compliance with CLS is a combination of economic and social issues and political will, making it difficult to use either of the approaches. What is needed is a system that can combine the different approaches—ensuring compliance whilst bearing in mind that the level of development of a country should also be considered. This is not something that the WTO dispute settlement mechanism is capable of handling. This calls even more strongly for the new or improved international legal order, which is capable of effectively combining economic and social systems in enhancing economic growth and improving the welfare of workers. The inclusion of labour standards in regional and bilateral agreements point the direction in which the international community should take in achieving that.

The analyses above have shown the limitations of a regional approach to the labour standard and international trade linkage. However, the NAALC, in spite of the criticisms levelled against it, for example, contains a number of features that might be used in further developing a multilateral linkage. First, whereas the ILO lists five core labour standards, the NAALC has 11 labour principles, which go beyond the core labour standards. Second, the NAALC provides a model for ensuring access to the process and transparent discussion of labour matters within the North American region. Through NAALC, Labour Ministries and unions have been encouraged to meet and discuss issues and hold seminars and training programmes. Thus public awareness has been raised concerning the rights of workers. The NAALC system also allows ample opportunity for the involvement of trade unions and nongovernmental organisations in filing complaints and also in participating in public hearings. Third, through the procedures for review, evaluation, and arbitration, the governments of the three countries are forced to account for their domestic labour law enforcement in a public forum, both at the national level and at the international level.

The NAALC whilst preserving the domestic sovereignty of each country over labour matters has created the opportunity for a better process of collaboration between the trade unions of the signatory countries. This has led to better understanding of the position of each country on labour issues. Given the fact that at the time of the signing of NAALC American unions were concerned about the loss of jobs to Mexico, and had initially thought that Mexican labour laws were mediocre to that of the United States, the cross-border collaboration has helped put some of those fears to rest.

The EC, as shown in our discussions in Chap. 7, is using a different approach. The EC approach in the EC–Chile FTA is that both parties recognise the core labour standards, the first of its kind in EC trade relations with a developing country in linking social development with economic development.

Like the EC–Chile Agreement, the CARIFORUM–EU Economic Partnership Agreement only commits the Parties to respect the ILO CLS. It is relevant to note the linkage that the Agreement creates between the respect for the CLS and trade, with the objective of promoting the ILO decent work agenda at the regional level. The linkage that is established at both the national and regional levels between trade, respect for the CLS, and economic development is a clear indication of the EU approach towards sustainable development at both levels.

The EU–Korea FTA has also shown how the EU intends to resolve the linkage issue. Like the agreement with CARIFORUM, it only provides for a resolution of labour issues through consultations without sanctions; the EU–Korea FTA, through the introduction of civil society groups, made up of business, labour, and environment organisations, is a new development indicating that respect for the CLS is a combination of other issues going beyond the economic argument. Could this be a sign of achieving policy coherence as an example for a multilateral approach?

What is also worthy to note is that the EU–South Korea FTA contains an effective dispute settlement mechanism to ensure the enforceability of commitments taken, as well as a mediation mechanism to tackle non-tariff barriers. The procedures envisaged under the dispute settlement chapter foresee arbitration ruling within 120 days. This is much faster than in the WTO.

In all, what the inclusion of labour standards in RTAs has sparked off is the debate on the linkage between labour standards and trade policy. The RTAs have given increased attention to labour standards and how trade policy can be used to further compliance. This debate can provide the needed impetus for the efforts of the international community and especially the ILO into continuous, sustained, and effective promotion of the core labour standards.

We discussed in Chap. 6 how WTO Members saw the importance of the CRTA in determining the conformity of RTAs to Article XXIV of GATT 1994 and how the decisions of both the panel and the Appellate Body in the *Turkey Textiles* case appeared to some WTO Members as usurping their position. It appears that the views of some WTO Members and the analysis made support the view that RTAs' conformity is best determined by the CRTA rather than the WTO dispute settlement mechanism on the ground that RTAs not only have economic and legal connotations but also are created for political reasons. Should that be the case, how much more so the linkage between the CLS and trade that go beyond the reasons for RTAs' formation to also include the social connotation, something that a legal system such as the WTO dispute settlement mechanism is not in a position to deal with?

Just as WTO Members have raised concerns in light of the *Turkey Textiles* case that to avoid uncertainty and to create certainty and predictability, the decision as to determining overall consistency should be left solely to the CRTA, which may delegate its powers to a panel of experts, it is also recommended that the issue of the linkage between the CLS and trade should be left to a panel of experts from both the ILO and WTO with input from other international law, labour, and social science experts and also experts from the country where the issue is before the panel.

9.3 RTAs and an International Framework

What is recommended is the putting into place of a framework mechanism or blueprint that can be adapted to the needs of each regional arrangement, without sacrificing the objective of economic betterment for the members of the arrangement. In effect, what is proposed is a cooperative mechanism at the international level, through a combination of the WTO system of government to government and the ILO system of tripartite cooperation in promoting harmonious labour relations and in fostering social and economic progress.

It is important to state at this point that whilst governments enter into trade agreements, it is the private sector that is expected to translate the agreements into trade benefits. This raises the question as to the extent to which the private sector should be involved in the negotiations in arriving at the final agreement. The experience of many trade arrangements involving developing countries shows a lack of coordination with the private sector.

We discussed in the introduction the inextricable link between increased trade and development and how that development impacts positively on adherence to the CLS and how that link is not properly convened.

Multilateral trade negotiations have now become more complex with many issues being covered and also with 160 countries participating in the negotiations. Given the fact that it is now generally accepted that trade is an engine of economic growth and sustainable development, developing countries, especially when entering into trade agreements with developed partners, should aim to ensure that their interests are taken into account during bilateral/regional stage and that it reflects the situation on the multilateral stage.

A number of developing countries are entering into RTAs without undertaking impact assessments on how these arrangements would impact their economies and how they would assist in social development. In addition to the sometimes political motives for signing such agreements, there are also the economic reasons to integrate their economies into the global economy. They might know of the tremendous benefits that they could reap from the agreements, but sometimes they underestimate the challenges. They might also be unaware of the ramifications of the commitments that they assume in terms of their capacity to implement the onerous obligations and the effect that these would have on their economies.

The current nature of the global trade negotiations (and for our purposes the RTA negotiations) and policymaking require that there be intense consultation between the different stakeholders. However, mostly in many developing countries, there is a lack of an effective consultative mechanism between governments, the private sector, and civil society. Due to the complexity of such arrangements, the number of government agencies involved in trade-related issues has grown considerably. However, officials in these agencies may not always be aware of the implications of these issues for other government agencies, the private sector, and other stakeholders. This calls for greater co-ordination of activities and discussions in the formulation of trade policy and negotiating positions during bilateral/regional and multilateral trade agreements.

Economic development takes place in a politically secure environment, and it is especially in this area that RTAs play a major role in adding to the political stability of members in that arrangement. These arrangements, even if they are in most cases weak in terms of substance, especially for our purposes in seeking a high level of CLS compliance, nevertheless serve economic development in general and work toward the goal of policy reform in particular.

9.4 Development of a Global Labour and Trade Framework Agreement: Joint ILO/WTO Enforcement Mechanism

Our discussion has shown that the insertion of a social clause in the WTO Agreement that would trigger the use of the dispute settlement mechanism to impose sanctions against Member states that fail to implement the CLS is not an effective means of ensuring compliance. This section will outline the basic structure of a joint ILO/WTO enforcement mechanism to bridge the divide between adherence to the CLS and international trade.

The issue of the linkage cuts across economic, legal social, political, and even cultural factors. The WTO governance system traditionally reflects the interests of producers directed through government negotiators and is not suited effectively in a globalised world of diverse interests.[8] The ILO governance structure is a tripartite system that gives equal voice to governments, employers, and workers as means of ensuring that the views of all constituents are taken into account in the formulation of labour standards and the shaping of policies and programmes. Further to this are the demands of nongovernmental organisations and, in some cases, public demands for greater involvement in the global decision-making processes.[9]

Given the fact that each of these organisations on their own are not equipped to handle the linkage issue without encroaching on each other's area of expertise, and also taking into consideration the plethora of competing issues, there is the need for a multilateral enforcement mechanism built on a new governance structure to accommodate wider participation in, first, the formulation of policy at the national, regional, and multilateral levels, in a way that would allow balanced decisions to be made; second, an enforcement regime can be carried out with the participation of all Member states of both the ILO and the WTO and also the employers' and workers' groups.[10] This would help address the fear of protectionism since the participation of Member states in the establishment of the standards and enforcement procedures would ensure that no single state gains an unfair advantage by lowering its labour standards—also avoiding the so-called race to the bottom.[11]

9.4.1 Institutional Structure

It is recommended that the structure of the joint ILO/WTO, as we stated in the introduction, be based on the regional model through the development of a global labour and trade framework agreement (GLTFA) to ensure worldwide compliance, through international social dialogue, good practice, and the resolution of labour-management disputes. It is envisaged that the GLTFA would be adapted to suit regional trade agreements and thereby create a regional labour and trade framework agreement (RLTFA) as part of future RTAs. The proposal is based on the ILO tripartite system and, in particular, on the IFA model (the agreements signed between MNC and GUF to ensure that the CLS are respected across the global value chain). Such an agreement, it is envisaged, has the greater propensity to extend the protection afforded under the respect for the CLS beyond workers in the export sectors to also workers involved in domestic production.

---

[8] Abbott (2000), pp. 63 and 64.

[9] Abbott (2000), p. 64.

[10] Abbott (2000), p. 64.

[11] Ehrenberg (1995), p. 404.

The proposal is that ILO and WTO Members agree on a joint mechanism signed by governments, employers' associations, and global unions on behalf of all workers that links the respect for the CLS with international trade and in the operations of all MNCs involved across their operations worldwide. This it is envisaged not to create a new mechanism but rather to use the procedures of each: for the ILO, the Committee of Experts and their technical cooperation programmes and for the WTO, the trade policy review mechanism and panel procedures.

It is recommended that an ILO/WTO labour and trade commission be formed on an *ad hoc* basis to address the issues that arise from the linkage, depending on the particular core labour standard that is challenged. In this respect, the examples of the institutional structures under the RTAs (e.g., the NAO under NAALC, which has the responsibility to receive and process submissions) and the IFAs could provide a framework for further development. In the case of the IFAs, the MNCs and the GUFs engage in social dialogue to address issues that concern both sides leading to sound industrial relations and the creation of a framework for resolution of issues.

In the case of the RTAs, the experience of regional groupings shows how negotiations are sometimes more easily carried out among a smaller number of countries rather than a large number of countries. The history of RTAs also indicates how these regional and bilateral agreements have been used in testing out proposals before their application at the multilateral stage. By forging a much closer working relationship between these regional groupings and the ILO, WTO, and the employers and workers organisations, they could be able to exert a much stronger influence on the signatory countries and, in so doing, be furthering the linkage issue country by country and regional grouping by regional grouping.

9.4.2 Distribution of Governance Activities

Given the diverse areas that converge on the linkage issue, the distribution of governance duties to the organisation best situated to a particular subject area or achieving a particular goal is important but should be done within an integrated decision-making and enforcement structure.[12] This would help in accommodating the interests of developed countries, developing countries, the private sector, workers' organisations, and also civil society.

The work of the proposed ILO/WTO labour and trade commission should split the procedure for determination and remedy the alleged offense. Should there be a complaint filed against an ILO/WTO Member state, and activities of an MNC within a Member state, the commission would first need to determine whether the state or MNC has demonstrated a consistent pattern of gross and reliably attested

[12] Abbott (2000), p. 65.

violations of the CLS and also determine the extent of the practice. The second stage would be how to remedy the situation, the appropriate measures to apply, and the timeline for eventual resolution. It should be noted that irrespective of the split in the governance responsibilities, the role of each organisation should not be independent of the other. The expertise of each is relevant at each stage of the process.[13]

During the initial determination phase, the ILO should use similar procedures under its complaint procedure but in conjunction with the WTO. When a complaint is made, the ILO Governing Body and the WTO General Council should form an Inquiry Commission (the Commission), consisting of five independent members. Two members shall be selected by the ILO Governing Body and two by the WTO General Council and the fifth (Chairperson) chosen by both the Director Generals of the ILO and the WTO. The Commission should determine whether there has been a consistent violation of the CLS and how it impacts on trade relations. Should the Commission find that there have been violations and there has been an impact on trade relations, it would trigger the setting into motion of the second phase.

During the second stage, the two organisations should work to implement the recommendations of the Commission. The role of the ILO would be to ascertain whether the violations have ceased and what assistance to provide through their technical cooperation programmes. The WTO would also ascertain how the practices have impacted on trade flows and provide an evaluation. Both organisations would then oversee the compliance programme put in place and decide on the appropriate level of sanctions.[14]

9.4.3 Cooperation Between the ILO and WTO

Whilst the activities of both organisations in the area of cooperation should follow the ILO reporting procedures and the WTO Trade Policy Review Mechanism, the work of the Commission should be based on the GLTFA developed by both organisations. Although violations of CLS in the domestic sector would not fall within the trade-related standards as such violations would not impact on world trade, the joint reporting mechanism of both organisations would highlight these violations and bring public attention to the plight of such workers. In this respect, as we also mentioned above, like the NAALC, which allows the establishment of a Commission on Labour, the proposed *ad hoc* Commission could also coordinate the cooperative activities and joint studies on each of CLS and the linkage to trade.

The issue of labour standards, as we have discussed, is a means of achieving not only social justice in trade-related standards but also compliance with the CLS on the domestic front. This cannot be done through sanctions or strict rules alone, but it

---

[13] Ehrenberg (1995), p. 406.

[14] Ehrenberg (1995).

can be achieved through an efficient and effective set of social policies, in conjunction with the WTO and other organisations.

Bhagwati makes the point that non-trade measures tend to be more effective than using trade sanctions when advancing social agendas. He further argues that the notion that the ILO has no teeth is off the mark since God did not only give us teeth but also gave us a tongue, and a "good tongue-lashing" based on credible facts and evidence and also not biased has the potential to bring about changes in national policy for the better.[15] The impact of trade sanctions discussed above lends support to the argument that "tongue-lashing" could have greater impact in achieving compliance than the much talked-about sanctions.

The examples of the ILO's relationship with the CAFTA-DR countries and its role under the U.S.–Cambodia Textile Agreement are evidence of how the ILO can play a vital role in ensuring compliance. By providing recommendations to the CAFTA-DR countries on the implementation of their commitments, and its positive influence on the Cambodian textile industry, the ILO is having a direct impact on labour regulation in these countries. These two examples provide strong confirmation of how such a framework, including the WTO, could bring about changes for the better.

In Chap. 8, we discussed how the CAFTA-DR most likely prompted the Central American countries to request the ILO to conduct a study of their labour laws with respect to conformity with the ILO Declaration. This could form the basis of an ILO/WTO institutional structure in taking the lead in conducting studies of labour laws and how they impact on trade in countries that are members of RTAs and in the process of signing regional and bilateral agreements. Such report(s) could indicate how the countries might use the agreements to further compliance with both the principles in the Declaration and other conventions in line with world trade rules. This step, we believe, would help put the ILO and the WTO right in the middle of the linkage issue in such agreements and also help make the organisations play important roles under the agreements.

The CAFTA-DR also led to the first-ever meeting of the ministers of trade and labour. The CAFTA-DR countries have achieved what has eluded the international community since the start of the linkage debate a century and a half ago. The meeting and the joint declaration issued are a clear sign of how this regional agreement could be a catalyst to the bridging of the economic and social divide. A meeting of the ministers of trade and labour underscores the important role that increased trade can play in achieving the level of development that would allow countries to address the labour challenges related to bilateral trade agreements.

In this respect, the ILO and WTO, based on their respective expertise, could assist regional groupings to coordinate implementation at the regional level through the establishment of regional labour and trade law centres; provide training for labour, trade, and other related ministries; conduct research, integration of best practices; and use the centres to further social dialogue between the different actors.

[15] Bhagwati (2002), p. 79.

This is vital as it would discourage any one country within the grouping to lower labour standards to gain a competitive edge.

Should such similar meetings and discussions take place under the auspices of the regional centres, the ILO Governing Body, and the WTO General Council, it would be a major development in the labour standard and international trade debate, and it could in the future slowly lead from bilateral and regional groupings to the multilateral level.

9.4.4 Consultations

The parties to the agreement would have right to use the mechanism for enforcement by sending a written request to the Commission. These include Member states and employers' and workers' associations. The right of employers' and workers' organisations to access the regime should be governed by both the public communications system under NAALC and the ILO representation procedure. In the case of the NAALC public procedure, individuals or organisations can submit allegations to the NAO concerning specific violations of labour law in another member state that there has been a failure in that country to enforce its labour laws.

In this respect, the NAO is required to accept and, if appropriate, investigate allegations that another Party is not enforcing its domestic labour law as required by the Agreement. In the case of the ILO, the workers' and employers' organisations have the right to present to the ILO Governing Body a claim against any Member state that, in the view of the organisations, "has failed to secure in any respect the effective observance within its jurisdiction of any Convention to which it is a party".[16] The workers' and employers' organisations that make a representation should be certified by the ILO as authentic organisations within the definition of the ILO. As a departure from the NAALC experience, individuals would not be allowed to make representations to the Commission but can do so through their workers' or employer's organisations.

Upon review by the Commission as to admissibility, the claim would then move to the next phase of investigation by the *ad hoc* Commission. After completion of the investigation of the Commission, which may include hearings, and the Commission makes a determination that a Member state or an MNC has failed to comply with its obligations under the agreement, the Commission could recommend consultations under the auspices of the ILO Governing Body and the WTO General Council. The purpose of such a provision is to try and resolve as much as possible any dispute by engaging the parties in dialogue in a non-adversarial way through cooperation.[17] In this respect, the example of the EU–Korea FTA is followed,

[16] Article 24 of the ILO Constitution.

[17] This proposal is part of the functioning of the IFAs to engage in social dialogue as a means of building cooperative, collaborative relationships among the parties.

whereby resolution of labour issues is conducted through consultations by civil society groups, made up of business, labour, and environmental organisations and the Member states. Also under the auspices of the ILO's GB and WTO's GC, the Commission may recommend consultations at the Ministerial level. In this case, the Ministers of Labour and Trade of the parties would meet to try to resolve the matter. Should the Ministerial consultations fail to resolve the issue, either party shall have the right to convene a panel—a joint ILO/WTO Dispute Settlement Panel (Panel)—to review the claim and make recommendations.

9.4.5 Dispute Settlement

The Panel should consist of three members each from the ILO and WTO, with the chairperson jointly appointed by the Director Generals of both organisations. The panellists for the ILO would be selected from the members serving on the Committee of Experts or should that not be feasible from a roster of labour experts created by the ILO. The WTO panellists would be selected from the same pool of experts that have been created for the DSM, made up of governmental and nongovernmental panellists.

The Panel should review the complaint and produce a report of its findings on the issues that form the basis of the complaint. The parties would have the right to a hearing before the Panel and also have the right to make initial and rebuttal written submissions. The Panel will, in addition to the oral hearings, also seek information and advice from technical experts and review the reports of the ILO Committee of Experts and the WTO trade policy reviews.

Upon completion of the investigation stage, the Panel will produce its report, which should be divided into three sections. However, the Panel will use the agreed upon procedure in the GLTFA as the basis for its modus operandi: first, the descriptive part stating the complaint and the arguments of the complaints and respondents and also the Panel's findings of fact. The second part of the report would state the determination of the Panel as to whether there has been a persistent pattern of failure by the party complained against in adhering to the CLS. The third part will provide recommendations on how to redress the issues, reasonable period of time to comply with the Panel's recommendations, and technical assistance needed to achieve that.[18] The time period for the whole process, i.e., from the consultation phase; possible Ministerial consultations; and panel proceedings should not exceed 12 months. The implicated party would have 3 months within which to appeal the ruling of the panel. Should the implicated part appeal, the appeal panel would be constituted from the ILO and WTO roster of panellists. This process should not take more than 6 months.

---

[18] See Ehrenberg (1995), pp. 410 and 411.

The purpose of the panel process would first be not to punish parties that fail to comply with the CLS but to find a solution through the technical assistance that would be provided by both organisations. The technical assistance programmes should be jointly undertaken by the ILO and the WTO. The officials of both organisations should jointly undertake capacity-building missions to implicated countries. This would provide the opportunity to provide the needed assistance in implementing the Panel's recommendation and also on how to harmonise the policy directions the two organisations recommend to achieve the policy coherence lacking at the country level.

However, should there be persistent failure to comply after all the other options have been exhausted, the implicated party or parties should pay monetary compensation to be decided upon by an implementing committee constituted by the ILO GB and the WTO GC. Additionally, the particular goods produced as a result of lack of compliance in the dispute should be banned, or other Member states would be allowed to impose higher tariffs on them.

The implementing committee would review the implementation of the recommendations of the Panel and Appellate Panel and the technical assistance programmes and produce a quarterly report on their findings. Also, the ILO and the WTO could jointly provide a yearly report of the rankings of countries in respect of their adherence to the core labour standards and how these impact on trade and widely disseminate. Usually, in international relations, countries do not like to wash their dirty clothes outside, so the publication of such a report could be a factor in getting countries to adhere to the labour conventions and recommendations. This could be an effective tool in ensuring that each country makes the effort in complying with the conventions it has ratified.

9.5 Final Thoughts

The history of the linkage between the core labour standards and international trade is a long one. For about 150 years, the issue has remained unresolved and, in recent times, has become one of the most vexing issues that policymakers have to contend with. But the issue does not have to go another century before a solution has to be found. The issue is a mixture of political will, level of economic development, strength of national institutions, and willingness to find a global solution. The argument is that trade does not directly affect labour standards, but if a higher level of economic development is instrumental in achieving a high level of compliance, and trade is an engine of economic growth and poverty reduction, then trade, even if not directly affecting labour standards, does indirectly impact on countries adhering to the labour standards.

Regional trade agreements have become a testing ground for linking labour standards and international trade. The successes and failures of this model could hold the key in making trade work for development. The multilateral system could, in copying the successes and correcting the failures in a new global architecture, create a system that would ensure that the principles that have guided the ILO, and to which the international community subscribe to, are followed: "Whereas universal and lasting peace can be established only if it is based upon social justice; and whereas conditions of labour exist involving such injustice, hardship and privation to large numbers of people as to produce unrest so great that the peace and harmony of the world are imperiled" and also "poverty anywhere constitutes a danger to prosperity everywhere". Using trade and harnessing the forces of the market to achieve social justice is in the interest of all nations.

The recent financial crisis has shown the wide gap in the economic and social divide, making it essential for policymakers across the aisle to work together in finding common ground if the controversial issue of the CLS and international trade linkage is to be resolved in our time. At a time when the commitment of the international community has made multilaterism fashionable, and the views of many nations toward the United Nations is favourable,[19] it paves the way for garnering support for achieving the MDGs and improving the working relationship among the multilateral agencies.

With this increased support for multilaterism, the international community is being offered a unique opportunity to help create a system that would lead to the resolution of the age-old issue of the linkage between labour standards and international trade. Two factors lend support to this view. First, the private sector, irrespective of the recent wave of social responsibility programmes, cannot on its own ensure adherence to the CLS. Second, the social crisis due to the recent financial crisis is a clear sign that the markets alone cannot without government regulation work towards social justice and that policymakers would have to intervene.

Since their vehement opposition to the inclusion of labour standards in the WTO Agreement at the Singapore Ministerial meeting in 1996, and their signing of RTAs with labour provisions, the question that continues to come up is whether given the apparent progress at the regional level, it would be in the interest of developing countries to accept the inclusion of CLS in the multilateral trading system. We appreciate the views of developing countries that this inclusion could be used for protectionist purposes. However, finding a balance is very critical to the welfare of all. To find common ground in resolving this contentious issue would entail that each group (both proponents and critics) agree to a new set of rules, which are different from what the present system of international regulation offers—that is, to find a means of merging economic and social concerns.

This is a job that the WTO or the ILO alone cannot do. With the new found confidence in multilaterism, bringing the different multilateral agencies together in charting a "new way" is critical in addressing the age-old issue. And if the interest of the working people and the disadvantaged are the concern of the advocates of the

[19] In a Pew Global Attitudes survey conducted in 25 nations in mid-2009, the views of many were largely positive towards the United Nations. See http://pewresearch.org/pubs/1348/united-nations-global-opinion-more-popular. Accessed 5 May 2014.

linkage between labour standards and international trade and that the role of the RTAs could help reach that goal, the prudent thing is that an equitable multilateral system should be created, giving developing countries the needed support to live up to their commitments in complying with the core labour standards and turn the RTAs into a force for good.

The imposition of sanctions does not fit in very well within the framework of inducing social change since formulating social policy needs to be considered within a complex set of interrelated measures and must be carefully designed to achieve the lasting impact in realising the basic goals of society, social and economic progress, and equal opportunities for all. Realising these goals within a country setting cannot be isolated from the wider issues of poverty and underdevelopment for globalisation of the world economy has altered the rules of the game. This is what would make a joint ILO/WTO Commission play a critical role in assisting Member states to effectively bridge the economic and social divide.

If trade is good for development, as the evidence indicates, and development is good for employment creation, reduction in poverty, and improvement in the living standards of people, then there is the need to ensure that the dots between economic growth through a regional and a multilateral approach and social progress through adherence to the core labour standards built on a legal framework are connected to sustain growth. This will provide for the new governance architecture that would accommodate the diverse interests of Members states, employers' and workers' organisations, and the wider civil society in the policy formulation and implementation in the evolving changing economic and social climate. The legal framework and recommendations proposed provide a roadmap for such a connection.

The new architecture created would allow diverse viewpoints to be adequately channelled in decision-making structures,[20] giving each a voice. This would have a positive impact on economic growth and social justice. Should that happen, our time would be remembered as the time when the old gave way to the new. The time when the lessons learned from the RTAs were successfully implemented at the international level—our time would be an example for future generations in resolving contentious issues through a multilateral approach.

References

Abbott, F. M. (2000). Distributed governance at the WTO–WIPO: A evolving model for open-architecture integrated governance. *Journal of International Economic Law, 3*.

Bhagwati, J. (2002). *Free trade today*. Princeton: Princeton University Press.

Burianski, M. (2007). Is there a role for the WTO in the conflict between globalisation and the protection of social norms? In K. Byttebier & B. Van der Borght (Eds.), *WTO obligations and opportunities: Challenges of implementation*. London: Cameron May.

[20] Abbott (2000), p. 664.

Cottier, T., & Oesch, M. (2005). *International trade regulation: Law and policy in the WTO, the European Union and Switzerland: Cases, materials and comments*. Berne/London: Stempfli Publishers/Cameron.

Ehrenberg, D. S. (1995). The labor link: Applying the international trading system to enforce violations of forced and Child Labor. *Yale Journal of International Law, 20*.

OECD. (1996). *Regional integration and its place in the multilateral trading system*. Paris: OECD.

Plummer, M. G., Cheong, D., & Hamanaka, S. (2010). *Methodology for impact assessment of free trade agreements*. Manila: Asian Development Bank.

Lightning Source UK Ltd.
Milton Keynes UK
UKOW07n0232110215

246052UK00009B/107/P

9 783662 446188